Faith, Reason and the Existence of God

D1270277

The proposition that the existence of God is demonstrable by rational argument is doubted by nearly all philosophical opinion today and is thought by most Christian theologians to be incompatible with Christian faith. This book argues that, on the contrary, there are reasons of faith why in principle the existence of God should be thought rationally demonstrable and that it is worthwhile revisiting the theology of Thomas Aquinas to see why this is so. The book further suggests that philosophical objections to proofs of God's existence rely upon an attenuated and impoverished conception of reason which theologians of all monotheistic traditions might wish to reject. Denys Turner proposes that on broader and deeper conception of it, human rationality is open to the 'sacramental shape' of creation as such and in its exercise of rational proof of God it in some way participates in that sacramentality of all things.

DENYS TURNER is Norris-Hulse Professor of Divinity and Fellow of Peterhouse, University of Cambridge. He is the author of *Marxism and Christianity* (1983), *Eros and Allegory* (1995), *The Darkness of God* (1995) and *Faith Seeking* (2002).

Faith, Reason and the Existence of God

Denys Turner
University of Cambridge

CAMBRIDGE
UNIVERSITY PRESS

PUBLISHED BY THE PRESS SYNDICATE OF THE UNIVERSITY OF CAMBRIDGE
The Pitt Building, Trumpington Street, Cambridge, United Kingdom

CAMBRIDGE UNIVERSITY PRESS
The Edinburgh Building, Cambridge, CB2 2RU, UK
40 West 20th Street, New York, NY 10011–4211, USA
477 Williamstown Road, Port Melbourne, VIC 3207, Australia
Ruiz de Alarcón 13, 28014 Madrid, Spain
Dock House, The Waterfront, Cape Town 8001, South Africa

http://www.cambridge.org

First published 2004

Printed in the United Kingdom at the University Press, Cambridge

Typeface Plantin 10/12 pt.   *System* LaTeX 2ε   [TB]

A catalogue record for this book is available from the British Library

ISBN 0 521 84161 5 hardback
ISBN 0 521 60256 4 paperback

Deus vere [est] subiectum huius scientiae
Thomas Aquinas, *Summa Theologiae*
1a q1 a7 *corp.*

Contents

Preface

This monograph is intentionally narrow in focus: perhaps some will think perversely so. Beyond offering reasons of a philosophical kind for resisting some versions of the opinion, very commonly held, that the existence of God is incapable of rational demonstration, I do no more than to give further reasons of a theological nature why Christians should think, as a matter of faith, that the existence of God is rationally demonstrable, as a dogmatic decree of the first Vatican Council says. But nowhere in this essay do I offer any argument intended as proof of the existence of God, nor do I examine from the standpoint of validity any of the arguments which historically have been offered as proofs. This is because all the issues which appear to matter theologically speaking in connection with proofs of the existence of God arise in connection with the possibility in principle of a proof, and not with the validity of any supposed proof in particular. Hence, out of a desire to stick to the point, I have resisted a wider discussion which would have distracted from it. But some will find this restraint pedantic. At least they have been warned.

Also, since hardly any theologians nowadays think the existence of God is rationally provable, there will be those who wonder why I bother defending a cause quite so lost as this one. One reason for taking this trouble is that most theologians today do not so much think that the existence of God cannot be proved as seem altogether to have given up thinking about the issues involved, and simply assume – probably on unexamined arguments from Kant – the impossibility of it. Not to think a thing is not the same as thinking that it is not, and when once there is anything at all that theologians have stopped feeling the need to rethink, it is perhaps time to stop being a theologian in case it is the theology itself which has caused the thinking to stop, and to become a philosopher, or at least to ask some philosophical questions theologians should be asking for themselves. So it is in this matter more than in most. At any rate, one issue is plainly philosophical: theologians in the main seem to think the proposition to be beyond challenge that the existence of God cannot be proved, on any defensible account of rational proof. But that is a ground of logic

and epistemology, and the most ardent opponent of theological rationalism will have to concede that what counts for the validity of rational
proof cannot itself be a matter of faith. And if upon close examination the
purely philosophical issues at stake appear to intimidate the theologians
on account of their technical complexity, then it is that the theologians
seem happier to fall back into their own territory and rule out rational
proof on theological grounds, even on grounds of faith itself, which is
what they more commonly do today.

And when it comes to faith, here it is proclaimed by some as if it were
dogma that the existence of God is beyond rational demonstration in this
sense at least, that anything you could prove the existence of could not be
the true God of faith. Such theologians appear to be telling us that you
can have your proof and your 'God of reason' if you like, so long as you
keep the business of proving God off the territory of faith, thereby dis-
closing the underlying, and to me curious, belief that faith has a 'territory'
from which it is necessary to exclude at least some rational discourses. In
any case, it is hard to know how one is supposed to contest that sort of
claim, since, in the forms in which it is most frequently asserted, it is put
beyond all possibility of contestation. For it comes near to being claimed
analytically – as part of what it means to speak of God – that God's existence cannot be proved; or sometimes it seems as if, rather than a truth
being claimed, it is a stipulation being laid down: 'I am not going to allow
that you are talking about the same God I am talking about if your God's
existence is rationally provable, I don't care what you say.' But such an
attitude approximates to mere stubbornness, and to that extent may be
discounted.

If they are not analytic, or a mere stipulation, what are the grounds for
saying that the assertion of the rational provability of God's existence is
contrary to faith? After all, if it is claimed as a substantive truth of some
kind that the existence of the God of faith could not be demonstrable
by reason, as having to do with the nature of reason, or of faith, or of
both, then it must be possible to imagine the claim's being false, or its
being contested on some grounds. Here, at any rate, one is on territory
that once upon a time was in fact contested: for the bishops of the first
Vatican Council in 1870 declared it to be an article of faith that the existence of God can be known by reason alone. And if there were any at
all prepared to take the first Vatican Council seriously on this matter –
and nowadays Catholic theologians do in scarcely greater numbers or
degree of enthusiasm than your average Barthian Protestant – then a contestation with excellent prospects of theological progress in view could be
anticipated. Alas, hardly anyone I know of will join me in the exploration

of the possibility that the bishops of the first Vatican Council were right – and, after all, they might be. And if you say there is no need to argue about the matter, because they could not be right, then I say you are no theologian and I do not want to argue with you anyway – which comes to the same thing. For a person stops being a theologian just when he or she thinks there is nothing left to be argued about.

I have written this book, therefore, because I think that there is something to argue about, an issue can be stated with refreshing straightforwardness and clarity, between those for whom, on grounds of faith, the existence of God could not be rationally demonstrable, and those for whom, on grounds of faith, the existence of God must be rationally demonstrable. Also, the issue being refreshingly straightforward and clear, I can state my own position with, I hope, straightforwardness and clarity: I rather think that the bishops of the Vatican Council were right on a score of general principle in saying that to deny the rational demonstrability of the existence of God on grounds of faith is to get something importantly wrong not just about reason but also about the nature of faith.

But I have to confess that in what ensues I do not always argue the case with that directness that might be hoped for by some, for what at first was intended as a secondary and oblique approach to the issue took over as the primary one as I became increasingly interested to discover, particularly in Cambridge, where I had moved some four years ago, a fashion for enlisting Thomas Aquinas in support of the position to which I was opposed. And that puzzled me because I had always thought that it was from Thomas that I had acquired the conviction of the demonstrability of God's existence – and the bishops of the Vatican Council no doubt were of the same mind. Yet here were so many thinkers and scholars for whom I had acquired the greatest respect, some followers of the school of 'Radical Orthodoxy', others of a more mainstream Barthian persuasion, yet others influenced by Eastern and patristic traditions of theology, all telling me that, in accordance with a programme of 'revisionist' Thomism once popular among French Catholic theologians, I must read Thomas as more of an Augustinian and Platonist than would be consistent with the theological 'rationalism' I had attributed to him.

Just in principle, and in advance either of the scholarly evidence in the matter of interpretation of Thomas, or of arguments about the substantive issues, I was reluctant to abandon my Thomas of rational proof, for one reason that, as a Christian myself, I want to be able to talk and debate without prejudice with Jews and Muslims about God. And, for another, it seemed to me that, deprived of my 'rationalist' Thomas, not only I, but

the Western Christian tradition as a whole, would thereby be deprived of
its one significant representative of a theological alternative to its pervasive Augustinianism, an alternative which offers prospects, not otherwise
available to a mentality less confident of the theological claims of reason,
of being able to challenge on its own terms the atheological rationalism
of our modern times. There *is* an argument to be had with Dawkins and
Grayling about the existence of God; there is a potentiality for agreement
as to what the issue is about; and there is an equality of terms between
the Christian theist and the atheist as to how, in principle, the issue is
to be settled – that is to say, as to the standards of argument which are
to be met on either side. In short, if Christians cannot agree with atheists about the existence of God, at least there is a case for seeing the
disagreement as capable of being conducted on shared rational grounds,
even if it is also necessary to contest with most atheists on the nature
of reason itself, as in this essay I am much exercised to do. And Christians today need to restore lines of connection with theological traditions
unafraid to acknowledge the demands made on them by such standards
of rationality. Christians today need, therefore, my 'rational' Thomas: as
for Barthians, is not Karl Barth himself quite enough for them? They
do not need a Thomas Aquinas reconfigured by Catholics in Barth's
image.

But there were other reasons of a more personal sort for retrieving this
'rationalist' Thomas from the clutches of the Augustinian 'revisionists'.
Some years ago I devoted a monograph to the traditions of 'mystical
theology' in late-antique and medieval Western Christian thought. I
called that book *The Darkness of God* (Cambridge: Cambridge University
Press, 1995), and in it I studied some authorities central to the Western Christian traditions from Augustine to John of the Cross, for all
of whom the God of Christian faith is unknown and unknowable; traditions which are, however, notably lacking in that silence incumbent
upon them concerning that of which, as they themselves say, 'one cannot
speak'. Those traditions, in fact, embody complex and subtle accounts
of the relations between speech and silence, between what cannot be said
and the language in which that unsayability is gestured towards, a complexity whose embodiment within the articulation of the various theologies of those traditions constitutes their character, I argued, as 'mystical
theologies'.

Among the variety of responses which that monograph evoked two
struck me of such particular importance as to convince me that at some
point or other I would have to reply to them. The first came from my
predecessor in the Norris-Hulse Chair at Cambridge, Professor Nicholas
Lash, who in private correspondence wondered why, within the canon of

those included in my studies of 'mystical theologians', I had not included Thomas Aquinas, it being his view that Thomas met the condition I had imposed by way of excluding him, of being a 'Neoplatonist'. The second and much more pervasive comment was put in its most learned form by a theologian and historian no less respected, Professor Bernard McGinn of the University of Chicago. It was his opinion that I had in that work over-egged the apophatic pudding to the point of apparently denying that we can say anything true of God, and that I had to an anorexic degree restricted the diet of 'mystical experience', thus implausibly excluding from my canon of mystical theologians some who were self-evidently members of it, above all the manifestly 'experientialist' Bernard of Clairvaux.

Of course, it might seem very obvious that a tradition of thinking about theological language according to which 'all talk about God ultimately fails', as the 'mystical theologians' generally say, would have to be epistemologically at odds with a tradition according to which the existence of God is rationally demonstrable. For if 'the natural power of human reason' is capable 'with certainty' of knowing 'God, the source and end of all things', as the first Vatican Council declares, it would seem to follow, and with like certainty, that human language is after all capable of getting some sort of grip on the God thus known. It would seem, therefore, that an apophatic emphasis could not be happily wed with the 'rational', and for sure, historically, the inevitable divorce proceedings have preoccupied the attention of the theological judges since at least the fourteenth century, when the apparent incompatibilities between the 'mystical' and the academic or 'scholastic' theologians had seemed to have become irreconcilable, driving an oxymoronic wedge between the 'theological' and the 'mystical', the more the one, the less the other.

Theological offspring of this divorce, especially contemporary enthusiasts for the 'apophatic', might feel that they at least have good grounds in 'negative theology', and so in 'the mystical', for abandoning the case for a rationally demonstrable God, just as it has for much longer seemed to many, and on other grounds, that the distinctive gratuitousness of faith precludes such a God's being given to our native, unaided, rational powers. Therefore, I should make it clear from the outset, first, that I did not exclude the study of Thomas from *The Darkness of God* because I judged him not to be among the company of 'mystical theologians'; on the contrary, I regard Thomas Aquinas as a mystical theologian *par excellence*. Next, I excluded Thomas Aquinas from that study on the grounds that he offered a significant departure from the general run of 'Neoplatonist' forms of 'mystical theology' – and incidentally, though less controversially, I excluded Bernard of Clairvaux on the same grounds of non-Platonism, not because of his emphasis on 'the book of experience'. Further, I do not deny that Thomas is much influenced by some elements within the Neoplatonic traditions, and especially by Augustine, but I could see no good reasons for concluding that Thomas's differences with the 'Neoplatonists' were such as to diminish his credentials as a 'mystical theologian', on some standards represented by Augustine or Bonaventure or Eckhart; on the contrary, I thought I saw no problem of consistency between his 'rationalism' and his Christian 'mysticism'. Which brings me to the aim of this present work, which is, in short, to demonstrate – in full harmony with the 'apophatic' arguments I presented in the earlier essay – that for Thomas, to prove the existence of God is to prove the existence of a mystery, that to show God to exist is to show how, in the end, the human mind loses its grip on the meaning of 'exists'; such a demonstration is therefore designed to show that within creation itself, within our deepest human experience of the world, that mystery of unknowable existence is somehow always present within the world simply in its character of being created.

Hence, I should warn any Christian readers who might persevere to the end of this essay in the hope of finding it there, that they will be disappointed to discover nothing in my case for rational proof of God which derives from some easily dismissed 'Enlightenment' pretentiousness of reason, as if harbouring aggressive designs upon territory to which it has no right against the claims of faith. Neither will they find any defence of a unitarian 'God of reason' set in some terms of contrast and contest with a trinitarian 'God of faith'. Nor yet will they find in this essay, any more than they fairly could in *The Darkness of God*, that exaggerated 'apophaticism' which can barely distinguish itself from a sophisticated form of atheism. They will find that I do say – following Thomas – that 'we do not know what God is'. But they will not find me saying, any more than Thomas says, that we can know no truths about God, or that we have no way of removing falsehoods. They will not find me demoting faith from its priority over reason. But they will find me resisting such claims made for faith as would in turn deny reason its right to enter on its own terms into that mystery of creation which shows it to have been made, and so in a sense to be given – thus, also in a certain primitive sense, to be a grace, and a gift of love.

And they will find these things to be said and not said to a wider, and only partially stated, end, within which the narrower focus of the strict argument of this essay serves in but a limited degree. We are witness in our times and culture, particularly within the English context, to a failure of intellectual nerve. I refer to an intellectual timidity and not moral, or rather, I refer to that form of moral timidity which is primarily intellectual in character. But I refer to 'intellect' here in a rather special sense, which will be familiar to those who are students of the great patristic and medieval theological traditions but has otherwise been very nearly completely lost within our own. For us today, the word 'intellect' has become so narrowed in meaning – reduced to a capacity for those attenuated forms of ratiocination whose paradigms are those of mathematical argument, or else of empirical justification – that we are scarcely able to read about intellect or reason in our own earlier traditions of theology without grossly misreading them. My colleague Dr Anna Williams is in the course of completing what I know will be a major and influential study – much needed – of those broader and deeper conceptions of 'intellect' and of 'reason' which are to be found in the Greek and Latin theological traditions of East and West, and I offer but a few preliminary reflections on the same. But this much can safely be said, that, for Thomas, as for the long tradition which he inherits, you begin to occupy the place of intellect when reason asks the sorts of question the answers to which you know are beyond the power of reason to comprehend. They are questions, therefore, which have a double character: for they arise, as questions, out of our human experience of the world; but the answers, we know, must lie beyond our comprehension, and therefore beyond the experience out of which they arise. And that sense that reason, at the end of its tether, becomes an *intellectus*, and that just where it does, it meets with the God who is beyond its grasp, is, I argue, the structuring principle of the 'five ways' of the *Summa Theologiae*.

It is a depressing thought that much theology today serves in effect to reinforce ideologically the cultural pressures to deny a place to reason and intellect in that expanded ancient sense, and so to the asking of those questions which could not be answered, preferring, it would seem, to offer answers on grounds which, being merely the 'choices' of faith, can be rejected if one happens to choose otherwise. If faith is merely a matter of choice, then the most natural choice is to reject it as banal. There is something to be said, therefore, for attempting to remind Christians, if no one else, of an older conception of 'intellect', according to which faith can be genuinely present only within a mind compelled by its immanent energies to engage with the mysterious 'givenness' of creation, whether or not it does so in the manner of academic theology – which, as Thomas sensibly comments, hardly anyone will be able, or need, to do. This is not to say, of course, that there is within our human power some immanent demand for faith, as if reason could know in advance what is needed to supplement it. But it is to say that a faith is impoverished and denatured which is so understood as to entail resistance to, or denial of, the natural dynamism of intellect, of which it is in some way the perfection. It is in the nature of faith that it is *quaerens intellectum*; but an *intellectus* which is not allowed to press its own *quaestio* to that limit which is in fact the unlimited mystery of creation can be partner only to an impoverished and much diminished faith. And that is why the first Vatican Council declares it to be a matter of *faith* that reason can know God. And I think Thomas agrees.

Acknowledgements

My first, and principal, debt of gratitude is to my wife, Marie, who not only has helped me with advice about some details of the text of this work, but has throughout the long and painfully slow process of its composition selflessly provided me with the kind of support and encouragement without which that process could not have been easily endured. Nor can I imagine ever having completed this book without her having created the sort of personal and domestic circumstances in which alone academic writers can work. Hidden as such support is, none but its recipient can fully appreciate the magnitude of the debt owed.

Other kinds of indebtedness are with similar infrequency acknowledged. All academics know how very great theirs is in the production of a monograph such as this to the daily converse they have enjoyed with colleagues and students. It is normally somewhat more difficult to identify precisely where within those conversations one's own voice is to be distinguished from those of such partners in intellectual enquiry. But in the case of this present work I have been able to identify explicitly the contributions of several scholar colleagues, both senior and junior members of my Faculty of Divinity at Cambridge and elsewhere, who have offered comments on earlier drafts which in some cases caused me to adopt significantly different argument strategies than those I had at first envisaged, and in all cases required of me some important response. I have, in consequence, been able to incorporate some of these comments into the text itself and to acknowledge their authorship *in situ*, so that in places within the text it has become as palpable as it is invariably true that the final result is the outcome of long-running and many-sided conversations between academics and friends.

If, first, I acknowledge my indebtedness to my colleague Dr Catherine Pickstock, this is because I feel myself singularly privileged to have worked alongside her since I came to Cambridge some four years ago, and to find myself almost continually in a quandary as to whether, and if so how far, we disagree as to many of the issues canvassed in this book – and just as much as to the issues canvassed in her own many writings. For

I have found that quandary to be altogether a matter of creative stimulus. I have had a similar experience in a more recent teaching collaboration with my colleague Dr Anna Williams, and with both colleagues the one thing of which I am certain is that if we do disagree with one another, it is on intellectual ground occupied in common by all three of us in different ways, for, as the reader will find me often asseverating in this book, *eadem est scientia oppositorum*, or, roughly, worthwhile disagreements are on common terms of dispute. It has been a pleasure and a privilege both to occupy that common ground and to dispute with them.

That said, it is to a cohort of outstanding PhD students at Cambridge that much of the eventual shape of this book can be attributed. Susannah Ticciati had much to do with how I constructed the argument in relation to a 'Barthian' perspective in chapter 1, indeed an almost endless series of emails between us contributed so much to this chapter that in the end I found myself engaging almost more with her views than I do with Barth's own. In that same first chapter, the intervention of Dr Karen Kilby, my former colleague at the University of Birmingham, now of the University of Nottingham, prevented my making at least two foolish errors of interpretation. Fr Christopher Hilton offered a number of helpful and clarifying comments on my exposition of Bonaventure in chapter 3. Without my acquaintance with Férdia Stone-Davis's research on theology and music I should not even have thought of writing as I have, however naively I may have responded to her views, about music in chapter 6, nor, without Vittorio Montemaggi's work on Dante, poetry and theology, should I have understood the importance and relevance to my case of the 'rhetorical' dimension of human rationality discussed in chapter 5 – though here the earlier influence of a former PhD student in the University of Birmingham, Dr Rebecca Stephens, was also of decisive importance to me. It was Rebecca's work on Marguerite Porete which caused me to understand what Eckhart's vernacular sermons 'do' by means of their 'saying'. Mary-Jane Rubenstein, formerly of the Cambridge Divinity Faculty, now a PhD student in Columbia University, offered invaluable assistance with an extensive revision of chapter 8, and Hannah Pauly, then a final-year undergraduate in Cambridge, contributed an important point of clarification in the interpretation of Nietzsche. With Kevin Loughton I engaged in a long-running debate, by no means yet concluded, concerning the argument of chapter 10: his persistence in pressing me to be clear has left us still in disagreement, but little in an academic career can equal the pleasures of such constructive discussions and debates as I have enjoyed with Kevin, as with Susannah, Karen, Chris, Férdia,

Vittorio, Rebecca, Mary-Jane and Hannah over the time of this book's gestation.

It goes without saying that none of these scholar friends and colleagues may be held responsible for the use I have made of their contributions. Even as I thank them they will observe how often I have stubbornly persisted in views with which I know they disagree. Moreover, since some of their contributions, as I have incorporated them into the text, had their origin in comments made *ad hominem* on earlier drafts – and often orally or in the transitory medium of electronic mail – they should not necessarily or always be taken to be the final, formed opinions of their authors, even where they are attributed to them by name. I stand by what I have said, but I cannot in the same way expect them to be held to comments made on my text out of views of their own which were and are, obviously, still in the process of formation.

Finally, the person with whom I have most intimately engaged in the conversations out of which this book has emerged, and my longest-standing academic friend and conversation-partner, has been Professor Oliver Davies, of King's College, London. My intellectual and theological debts to Oliver over several decades are more pervasive than apparent, but are in any case profound.

It is, therefore, to this group of friends, and many others not mentioned by name, who have in various ways helped to make this work at least a good deal better than it would otherwise have been, that I dedicate this book, as an expression of my gratitude for the truly exhilarating experience of having worked with them.

Part I

The 'shape' of reason

1   Clarifications and issues

Faith and proof: Vatican I

Within theological circles in our times there can scarcely be a proposition less likely to meet with approval than that which, on 24 April 1870, the first Vatican Council decreed to be a matter of faith, to be upheld by all Christians, namely:

that God, the source and end of all things, can be known with certainty from the consideration of created things, by the natural power of human reason: *ever since the creation of the world, his invisible nature has been clearly perceived in the things which have been made* [Rm 1, 20]. It was, however, pleasing to his wisdom and goodness to reveal himself and the eternal laws of his will to the human race by another, and that a supernatural, way. This is how the Apostle puts it: *In many and various ways God spoke of old to our fathers by the prophets; but in these last days he has spoken to us by a Son* [Heb 1, 1–2].[1]

Hence,

The perpetual agreement of the catholic church has maintained and maintains this too: that there is a twofold order of knowledge, distinct not only as regards its source, but also as regards its object. With regard to the source, we know at the one level by natural reason, at the other level by divine faith. With regard to the object, besides those things to which natural reason can attain, there are proposed for our belief mysteries hidden in God which, unless they are divinely revealed, are incapable of being known. (Ibid., p. 808)

Nonetheless,

Since human beings are totally dependent on God as their creator and lord, and created reason is completely subject to uncreated truth, we are obliged to yield to God the revealer full submission of intellect and will by faith. This faith, which is the beginning of human salvation, the catholic church professes to be a supernatural virtue . . . (Ibid., p. 807)

---

[1] *Dogmatic Constitution on the Catholic Faith*, in Norman P. Tanner, *Decrees of the Ecumenical Councils* II, *Trent to Vatican II*, London: Sheed & Ward, p. 806.

Moreover,

> Even though faith is above reason, there can never be any real disagreement between faith and reason, since it is the same God who reveals the mysteries and infuses faith, and who has endowed the human mind with the light of reason. God cannot deny himself, nor can truth ever be in opposition to truth . . . Therefore, we define that every assertion contrary to the truth of enlightened faith is totally false. (Ibid., pp. 808–9)

On the strength of these considerations, therefore, the first Vatican Council issued the following canons:

> 2.1 If anyone says that the one, true God, our creator and lord, cannot be known with certainty from the things that have been made, by the natural light of human reason: let him be anathema. (Ibid., p. 810)

And,

> 3.2 If anyone says that divine faith is not to be distinguished from natural knowledge about God and moral matters, and consequently that for divine faith it is not required that revealed truth should be believed because of the authority of God who reveals it: let him be anathema. (Ibid., p. 810)

Faith and proof: clarifications

Since the purpose of this essay is to provide a theological and philosophical defence of these propositions of the Vatican Council, some preliminary comments by way of clarification seem appropriate. We should first note that these statements are decrees of a council of a Christian church taking responsibility for its own proper concerns, which are with the accurate statement of the nature of Christian faith and belief. As such none of them, not even canon 2.1 above – which is *about* what the natural light of reason can know of God – are intended to be philosophical statements, whose truth is proposed as known by 'the natural light of reason'. That canon is intended as a statement of faith, concerning what a true understanding of faith entails about the capacity of human reason to know God, namely that it *is* possible for human reason to know God and that the God of faith is one and the same God as the God who can be known by reason. But as such, it is not, as it were, some pretentious, cross-disciplinary claim to a merely arbitrary epistemic hegemony of faith as if, say, equivalently, a microbiologist were on grounds of some need of microbiological theory absurdly to require the mathematician to come up with a particular mathematical result regardless of whether it could be defended on mathematical grounds. For, as we shall see (though only towards the end of this essay), if, on grounds of faith, it seems necessary to conclude that the existence of God is rationally demonstrable, then it must also be the case that that demonstrability of God's existence is knowable rationally – or, at the very least, it must be possible rationally to rebut counter-claims. For, as the Vatican Council says, even though faith is 'above reason', there can never be any real disagreement between faith and reason, for God has created both, and 'God cannot deny himself'. Faith cannot invent rational truths for itself of which reason could not know on its own terms.

However, the proposition that faith can know of a purely rational possibility might, at first blush, seem to contain a logical oddity if one notes further that the council offers no support for any particular way of knowing the existence of God by the light of reason, except to say that it can be known thus 'with certainty from the things that have been made'. And since I take the expression 'known with certainty' to mean that the existence of God can be formally and validly proved by rational argument, the logical oddity would seem to be that of declaring *a priori* that a proposition is rationally demonstrable in the absence of any commitment to how and by what means that proposition might be demonstrated. But it is not clear that there is any real logical oddity there, since, as mathematicians say is the case, there are mathematical procedures for proving the provability of a theorem which are not themselves proofs of the theorem; and, in another sort of case, there is no problem knowing that whether there is or is not a cat on the mat is an issue which can be settled empirically even if you have no idea where the cat or the mat actually is or of how to find either of them. That the council knows of the provability of the existence of God by faith without commitment to any particular proof is not, on that same account at least, logically incoherent.

Conversely, the council's claim for a hegemony of faith in respect of reason's capacity is not merely a matter, as it were, of faith's external relations with an alternative source of knowledge of God. Lying within the claim for an autonomous rational theological capacity is a concern with the necessary condition of faith's own self-articulation through the exercise of reason *within* faith, that is to say, with what reason must be capable of in its own terms if it is to serve its purpose within faith's self-exploration as *quaerens intellectum*. The council's decree is as if to say: if human reason is to serve faith, and so theology, within that strategy of 'seeking understanding', then it must be equipped so to do. And the view of Vatican I seems to be that that capacity of reason must be such that the certain knowledge of God from creatures lies within its own reach strictly as reason. Hence, it is not so much that having to hand some rational proof of the existence of God is required by faith, still less that faith can dictate which arguments validly prove it. The council's decree is negative:

to deny reason that capacity in principle is so to attenuate its scope as to limit excessively its service to faith.

But even as thus moderately interpreted (and nowhere in this essay do I defend a stronger interpretation than that), the Vatican Council's doctrinal decree would seem to stand in more than one form of conflict with most philosophical and theological opinion of recent times. To consider just three such opinions, it stands in conflict in one way with the critical philosophy of Immanuel Kant, in another with the Protestant theology of Karl Barth, and in yet a third way with certain schools of thought within Roman Catholic theology in the twentieth century.

The 'Kantian' objection

As to Kant, the Vatican decree that the demonstrability of the existence of God by reason alone must be conceded on grounds of faith is *prima facie* exactly to reverse the priorities argued for in the *Critique of Pure Reason*, that it is on grounds of faith that such rational demonstrability must be denied. But the conflict is more complex and less direct than any such simple opposition of terms might suggest, if only because Kant argues at length and on purely philosophical grounds not only that all actual arguments for the existence of God fail of validity,[2] but also that all possible arguments of speculative reason for the existence of God must in principle so fail.[3] Moreover, when Kant says that he has 'found it necessary to deny *knowledge* in order to make room for faith',[4] what he means by 'faith' is not the faith the council refers to, Christian faith as such, the divine gift of participation in God's own self-knowledge, but rather a rational moral faith, what he calls a 'postulate of practical reason'. In fact, what is at stake for Kant is the fundamental principle of his 'critical' philosophy, for which all forms of transcendent rational speculation must be denied in so far as to do so is required for the possibility of morality's proper freedom and rationality.

In summary, Kant's argument rests on the proposition that moral agents are free agents. But we cannot know, Kant argues, that we are free agents on the strength of any experience of freedom, for as natural beings our knowledge is limited by the constraints of 'experience' to appearances, and within the limits of appearance our actions are entirely subject to the necessities of causal law. Hence, within the limits of human experience freedom is excluded. Nonetheless, if we cannot 'experience'

---

[2] Immanuel Kant, *Critique of Pure Reason*, B599–642, trans. Norman Kemp Smith, London: Macmillan, 1965, pp. 487–514.
[3] Ibid., B659–70, pp. 525–531.   [4] Ibid., Bxxx, Preface to 2nd edn, p. 29.

freedom, or establish it on the strength of any inference directly from sensory experience, we can 'think' – postulate – it, because we know that were we not free, then moral obligation would be impossible: for 'ought' implies 'can'. But moral obligation is possible, for the experience of it is a fact. Therefore, we are compelled to 'think' freedom as the condition of the possibility of moral experience, even if it can in no sense be an object of that, or any other, direct experience, for, as Kant says, 'we do not understand [freedom]; but we know it as the condition of the moral law which we do know'.[5]

If in one way freedom is thus a 'postulate of practical reason', so in another way are God and personal immortality. For practical reason can be sure of its hold on our minds and wills as categorical moral obligation only on condition that a moral order as such can be guaranteed. And that there is a moral order requires that virtue in its connection with human happiness is secured untroubled by the arbitrary vicissitudes of our secular condition (in which, *de facto*, they are frequently sundered). But an essential, and not merely contingent, connection between virtue and happiness can be guaranteed only by God and only if we survive beyond the arbitrary circumstances of our *pre-mortem* existence.[6] However, none of these three, God, freedom or immortality, is given to us in any possible experience. All are postulates of practical reason and are in that sense 'faith' (*Glaube*) in that they are known not by any demonstrations of speculative reason from the world of appearance –'nature' – but only as the conditions of the possibility of morality.

Moreover, it is not just that, as 'postulates', they *are not* 'given in experience'. In that morality is possible, they *could not be* knowable within the limits of experience; and therefore the possibility of a demonstration of the existence of God *must be* ruled out for speculative reason in the name of practical reason. For if it were possible speculatively to demonstrate God's existence, or our freedom and immortality, 'from the consideration of created things' (as Vatican I puts it), then that freedom on which the possibility of morality depends would be cancelled thereby. For if causality *in* the world of appearances could be demonstrated to apply transcendently *of* the world – and that is what such a demonstration of God's existence would have to show – then, just as natural causality within

---

[5] Immanuel Kant, *Critique of Practical Reason*, trans. and introd. Lewis W. Beck, New York: Liberal Arts Press, 1956, Preface, p. 4.

[6] Kant is, of course, quite clear that happiness cannot be a proper *motive* of virtue, or of moral obligation generally. The connectedness of virtue with happiness must, however, be secured if moral obligation is to be construed as properly rational, that is to say, as having the character of an *order*. On all this see *Critique of Practical Reason*, II.II.v., pp. 128–36.

the world of 'appearances' rules out freedom as an object of experience, so a causality supposed to have application in the transcendent realm beyond appearances would have to rule out freedom there too, and with it the possibility of morality. In order, therefore, to make room for 'faith', that is for human freedom, immortality and God, and so for morality, the pretentious claim of speculative reason to a transcendent reach has to be denied it. And so Kant tells us that 'all attempts to employ reason in any merely speculative manner are altogether fruitless and by their very nature null and void, and . . . the principles of its employment in the study of nature do not lead to any theology whatever. Consequently, the only theology of reason which is possible is that which is based on moral laws'.[7] Hence, the teaching of the Vatican Council that Christian faith entails the possibility of speculative rational proof of God stands in more or less straightforward conflict with Kant's view that moral faith, if not Christian faith as such, excludes just that possibility. At any rate, what the Vatican Council affirms is just that which Kant denies.

The 'Barthian' objection

One different kind of ground for contesting the propositions of the Vatican Council – I shall characterise it in terms which are broadly 'Barthian' – is distinguishable from Kant's in that on this account an authentically Christian faith rules out the standpoint of natural theology as rivalling Christian faith as if with an alternative 'standpoint of unbelief', as Alvin Plantinga puts it.[8] On this account of Barth's position, natural theology is a form of betrayal of the divine purposes of creation, for it would seem that, for a natural theology (these are Plantinga's words again), 'belief in God is rationally acceptable only if it is more likely than not with respect to the deliverances of reason', from which it would seem to follow that a natural theologian's 'ultimate commitment is to the deliverances of reason rather than to God'.[9] This is, perhaps, rather to overstate the case, and the 'Barthian' point can be more sensitively put[10] as consisting less in a hostility to rational proof on the sort of general epistemological grounds on which Kant opposed it than in a subtler and more complex objection

---

[7] Kant, *Critique of Pure Reason*, B664, p. 528.
[8] This is the reading of Barth's position as expounded by Alvin Plantinga in his 'Reason and Belief in God', in Alvin Plantinga and Nicholas Wolterstorff, eds., *Faith and Rationality: Reason and Belief in God*, Notre Dame: University of Notre Dame Press, 1983.
[9] Ibid., p. 70.
[10] I am much obliged to Susannah Ticciati, PhD student in the Faculty of Divinity at the University of Cambridge, and to Dr Karen Kilby of the Department of Theology at the University of Nottingham, for advice which saved me from some egregious errors of interpretation in this chapter.

to the 'standpoint' occupied subjectively by the would-be natural theologian. What seems most to trouble Barth about the project of 'natural theology' in principle is the sort of theological mentality, the intellectual and moral disposition, which motivates it, attaching value to it as to some sort of theological starting point preliminary to, and so 'outside', faith. And it might just about be fair to say that, for Barth, such a mentality amounts in effect to a 'standpoint of unbelief' because the standpoint of faith – understood as the *act* of faith itself in response to our gratuitous *election* – is such as completely to relativise any purely 'natural' standpoint, or standpoint of creation. A 'natural standpoint' can have no true purchase on God precisely in so far as any epistemologically autonomous claims are made for it. For the Christian knows that there *is* nothing 'on the outside' of election, and so neither 'outside' of Christ, not even creation itself. As Barth himself says, 'it is impossible to separate the knowledge of God the Creator and of his work from the knowledge of God's dealings with *man*. Only when we keep before us what the triune God has done for us men in Jesus Christ can we realise what is involved in God the Creator and His work.'[11] Nor has there ever been a condition of 'pure creation', as if to say: there was, chronologically first, the *ex nihilo* of creation, and then, afterwards, the *ex nihilo* of election. On the contrary, for Karl Barth, the creation of the world *ex nihilo* is already and always has been itself within our election *ex nihilo* for, as Susannah Ticciati puts it, 'election is God's gratuitous decision to create in the first place: a decision made in (and also by and for) Jesus Christ. Christ is thus the "space" in which creation comes into being, and exists.'[12] The *ex nihilo* gratuitousness of creation is properly understood only as occurring within and for the gratuitousness of election in Christ.

It follows from this that any attempt to occupy a 'standpoint of creation' *independently* of our election in Jesus Christ will succeed only at the unacceptably high cost of rupturing the nexus between election and creation, thus to set them in *opposition* to each other, the outcome being inevitable: 'always, when man has tried to read the truth from sun, moon and stars or from himself, the result has been an idol'.[13] Since creation *ex nihilo* is, on Barth's account, *already* our election in Christ, a standpoint of 'pure' creation such as appears to be presupposed to the project of natural theology is a standpoint which amounts to the *rejection* of Christ, in whom creation and election are one. In short, the standpoint for which creation is, as Barth puts it, 'a vestibule in which natural theology might

[11] Karl Barth, *Dogmatics in Outline*, trans. G. T. Thomson, London: SCM Press, 1949, p. 43.
[12] In a written comment on an earlier draft of this chapter.
[13] Barth, *Dogmatics in Outline*, p. 43.

find a place'[14] is a symptom of that dislocation and disruption of creation and of our epistemic relation with it which is sin, the improper desire and design of a human reaching out to God by some route other than that which God himself has given us. The natural theologian's distinction between creation and election therefore inevitably becomes a disjunction.

Within that 'fallen' perspective, then, a natural theology appears possible, but only so as to reconfigure the relationship of radical dependence of creature on Creator, and so of the radical asymmetry between them which is implied by the *ex nihilo* of election, misrepresenting it as one of reciprocity and symmetry between the creaturely knowing subject and God as object known. That standpoint of creation, in so far as it is construed as accessible to rational powers alone, would therefore appear, on this 'Barthian' view, to tie God and creation into a relationship which, being governed by reason and bound by its logic, obliterates the freedom of both by obliterating the gratuitousness of their *ex nihilo*. Faith, by contrast, the response to election, is our re-entry into that creation which is at once 'new' and at the same time 'originary', a relationship which continually questions the 'natural' relationship of creature to Creator; it disrupts the seeming epistemic security of a fallen rationality and calls into question the stabilising reciprocities and symmetries between knowing subject and object known which a purely rational standpoint would seem to imply as obtaining between creature and Creator. And so it is our election, our 'new creation' by faith and grace, which is the true *creatio ex nihilo*, relativising every natural standpoint, for our election is given by God in absolute freedom, and is embraced in the absolute freedom of faith by the believer.

Susannah Ticciati therefore puts the case against 'natural theology' succinctly and somewhat more subtly than does Plantinga. She writes,[15] in Barthian spirit, that

election is to be understood as more fundamental than creation. This gives rise to a historical ontology in which there is no point of stability other than God's faithful activity of questioning, which calls everything else into question. A rational proof of the existence of God would be such a stable point outside this activity of God. But in so far as God brings the questioning and reasoning self itself into question, such a 'proof', being a function of the rationality of this self, is also called into question and uprooted. It is possible [consistently with this] to concede that the human's purpose exists in asking questions about that which lies beyond human comprehension, but such questioning results in a historical transformation in which the human being probes deeper and deeper into God and self [and] there is nothing outside this historical transformation that assures the existence of God at the end of the questioning . . . Only God's faithful interrogation can constitute this assurance and continuity. All else is continually uprooted in its being transformed.

---

[14] Ibid.   [15] In a written comment on an earlier draft of this chapter.

It is not, therefore, Karl Barth himself who sees the natural standpoint of creation and that of election as polarised. Rather, it is Barth's
view that creation and election *become* polarised within any theological
project which allows for an independent natural theology. Consequently,
the position of Vatican I does on this account stand condemned – in principle – in so far as it allows room for the possibility of a purely rational
and certain knowledge of God. I shall examine in the next chapter one,
neo-Barthian, revival of an aspect of this critique of natural theology, that
of Colin Gunton, who supposes that any 'natural' doctrine of creation,
such as is found (as both he and I believe) in Thomas Aquinas, must
work against the freedom of God to create and the freedom of the creature's response. Such a reading of what is implied by Thomas's theology
of creation cannot, I shall argue, be defended. In the meantime, however,
some provisional comment is required on the general proposition that the
standpoint of faith precludes the possibility of any standpoint of 'pure'
creation 'external' to it, and so external to faith's historical specificity as
the divine 'election' – as any such standpoint as that of a natural theology
would seem to make claim to.

Powerfully as Ticciati's case is made, it seems to share with Barth's
the likelihood of its being truer in what it affirms than in what it denies,
for while the 'Barthian' and the Vatican Council are at one in affirming the epistemic authority of faith over reason, and the primacy of the
historical events of salvation over the non-historical, timeless, standpoint
of 'nature', all that would seem obviously to follow from that priority is
the tautology that faith must exclude as false any standpoint which is
defined or posited as 'natural' in some sense of 'natural' which *a priori*
rivals faith as a 'standpoint'. At any rate we should at least note – if at this
stage of the argument we do no more than note it – that when Barth says
that 'what God does as the Creator can in the Christian sense only be
seen and understood as a reflection, as a shadowing forth of [the] inner
relationship between God the Father and the Son',[16] Thomas Aquinas
agrees[17] with the reservation that in thus far agreeing with Barth he
appears to observe no inconsistency with saying also that the Creator God
can be known by reason. For Thomas, Barth is right except for his 'only'.
Indeed, otherwise than on the assumptions of a Kantian agnostic rational

---

[16] Barth, *Dogmatics in Outline*, p. 43.
[17] The 'Father has caused the creature through his Word, which is the Son; and through
his Love, which is the Holy Spirit. On this account it is the processions of the Persons
which are the source-principles of the production of creatures in so far as they include
the essential attributes of knowledge and will.' – 'Et Deus Pater operatus est creaturam
per suum Verbum, quod est Filius; et per suum Amorem, qui est Spiritus Sanctus.
Et secundum hoc processiones Personarum sunt rationes productionis creaturarum,
inquantum includant essentialia attributa, quae sunt scientia et voluntas.' *ST* 1a q45 a6
corp.

epistemology – ever present in the background to Barth's theology – there seem to be no *a priori* grounds for supposing that a standpoint of faith must be so understood as to rule out a natural standpoint *however* defined. For that would amount to the proposition that there can be no theological standpoint 'external' to Christian faith *simpliciter*, however consistent with faith that standpoint may be construed to be – it would be the externality to faith as such which would be excluded, or 'abrogated'. And such an account of faith would seem to be prescriptive in a manner too *a priori*, since it would rule out in advance and simply by *fiat* what might upon investigation turn out to be a real possibility, namely that reason possesses some theological potential in its own right. It is not clear why, as against that possibility, a dichotomy between 'history', even 'salvation history', and the timelessness of 'ahistorical reason' should be so polarised *a priori* as it appears to be in Barth.

Secondly, 'questioning', even the divine 'questioning', can always yield more than one answer, and for sure there will be those strategies of theistic proof which are – and perhaps those strategies of theistic proof which are not – radically subverted by God's interrogation of them through and in faith: and Barth is right that a philosophical form of idolatry is always a possibility. But it ought not to be supposed *a priori* that 'reason' cannot, by its own powers, ever achieve a truly radical *ex nihilo*, that it cannot itself challenge any merely rationalist 'normalisation' of the relation between creature and Creator. On the contrary, it is my case that Thomas's proofs of God's existence have precisely that character of challenge to any such 'normalisation': they too question any epistemic 'symmetry' between the knowing subject and the God known. As we shall see, the proofs prove a radically *unknowable* God, and so just as radically 'question' the cognitive subject as such: the apophaticism of the proofs already radically destabilises the epistemic subject; they throw down any form of idolatrous and pretentious rationalism. And by contrast with any *fiat* of faith which would rule out that apophatic possibility in advance, it seems that the Vatican Council's decree insists only upon leaving it open, as a condition required by faith's epistemic superiority to reason. The difference between Ticciati's 'Barthian' case and that of the Vatican Council would therefore appear to be direct in this degree that, for the 'Barthian', a natural theology in principle and however defined would, whereas for the Vatican Council it would not, necessarily offer such a rival standpoint, the council leaving entirely open the question of how a natural standpoint not in conflict with faith might be construed.

The 'open-ended' character of the Vatican decrees seems therefore to have been intentionally self-limiting: those decrees are designed simply to exclude an exclusiveness of faith, disallowing any account of the relation between a standpoint of natural theology and a standpoint of faith as being mutually exclusive, whether construed 'objectively' as alternative sources of truth about God, or 'subjectively' as regards the acts of response respectively of reason to creation and of faith to the divine election. They are not mutually exclusive 'objectively', for 'it is the same God who reveals the mysteries and infuses faith, and who has endowed the human mind with the light of reason. God cannot deny himself nor can truth ever be in opposition to truth.' Not 'subjectively', for the charge of 'unfaithfulness' would seem relevant only to a case made for a natural theology according to which faith needs it as supplying a cause, motive, or object of personal faith. And no such case is made by Vatican I.

And so some clarifications at least as to what the Vatican Council does not say or imply seem at this stage to be possible. To maintain that the existence of God is in principle rationally provable is not to hand over one's 'ultimate commitment to the deliverances of reason rather than to God' or to 'make reason a judge over Christ';[18] nor is to say, as the Vatican Council says, that the possibility of rational knowledge of God is *entailed* by faith, to place faith's authority in thrall to a merely theoretical rational possibility; nor yet is it to place a rational condition upon the possibility of personal faith in Jesus Christ: none of these consequences follows from the Vatican Council's decrees if, as I hope to show,[19] it is precisely on account of Christ that this confidence in reason is justified. In any case, nothing is said by the Vatican Council to suggest that the act of faith presupposes an *actual* proof of God; nor is anything affirmed about the credibility of what faith assents to being dependent upon anyone's actually knowing even the *possibility* of rational proof, for you can truly believe and not know that God can be known with certainty by reason: obviously nearly every Christian in fact does, and there is nothing inconsistent with the Vatican Council's decrees in that fact. What is claimed is only that the God who is revealed in Jesus Christ is a God who is so related to the world known by our rational natures that his existence is capable of being known from that world, as Paul says; that the mind which believes, the intellect to which the gift of faith is given, is a mind and intellect created with some capacity of its own to *recognise* what is given to it in that revelation, a capacity which could, at least theoretically, be expanded out into a formal proof of the existence of God. It may be that no actual valid proof is ever discovered; the Vatican Council does not imagine that faith would thereby be weakened for want of rational support. But *suppose*

---

[18] As Plantinga describes Barth as concluding, see Plantinga, 'Reason and Belief in God', p. 71.
[19] See chapter 10 below.

the thing could be done: then on the Vatican's view neither is faith thereby threatened. Hence, there is something misguided in the account of faith for which even the attempt to prove, never mind successfully proving, the existence of God would entail faith's downfall as a personal act of complete trust in God. And by no means is this to say, as Plantinga's 'Barth' appears to think, that 'belief in God is [thereby deemed to be] rationally acceptable only if it is more likely than not with respect to the deliverances of reason'.[20] No such proposition is maintained or implied by the decrees of the Vatican Council.

The objection of the 'nouvelle théologie'

A third sort of grounds for contesting the propositions of Vatican I – on my account of them – draws the issues closer in with the sources in Thomas Aquinas on which my defence of them partly relies, and causes me to anticipate here a distinction which, by the end of this essay, will turn out to be all-important. Put in its plainest form, my case is that there are reasons of faith for maintaining that the existence of God must be demonstrable by reason alone, and that by 'demonstrable' is meant that the existence of God is a true conclusion validly drawn by inference from premises known to be true about the world. Moreover, it is my belief that Thomas Aquinas maintains just this proposition about the relation between reason and faith. This first proposition, however, needs to be carefully distinguished from a second, which is that the existence of God is knowable with certainty by reason *but only* within and as presupposing the context of faith, and that it is only in such terms that Thomas's proofs of the existence of God are to be understood, for that, it is said, is how he views them.

It would be misleading to align with any one theological school all those who reject the first proposition in favour of the second, whether either is taken absolutely and in itself or as a reading of Thomas Aquinas' mind on the matter. Nonetheless, there is no doubt that the influence in the first half of the twentieth century of the so-called 'nouvelle théologie' of revisionist Thomism, especially in the version of it promoted by the French Jesuit theologian Henri de Lubac, has decisively shifted contemporary readings of Thomas in favour of the second proposition. As a result there is by now very largely a consensus among Catholic theologians in a series of general propositions which, if not exclusively to be attributed to de Lubac's influence, certainly characterise it. First, it is said[21] – here

---

[20] Plantinga, 'Reason and Belief in God', p. 71.
[21] What follows is not meant as a formal paraphrase of de Lubac, but is rather a set of propositions which, under the powerful influence of de Lubac's thought, would seem

occupying some common ground with the 'broadly Barthian' position just described – that to suppose that reason can, by virtue of its own native powers, 'know God with certainty' is to suppose the existence of a pure abstraction – 'reason alone' – which has no historical actuality. For there is not, and never has been, any actual human condition of 'pure nature' in which 'pure reason' could operate. Nature, and so reason, has always historically been graced, and any proposition about 'nature' or 'reason' which neglects this fact of history's *always* having lain under the divine providential and salvific action is bound to presuppose, or entail, an unacceptable dichotomy between creation and redemption, or between 'secular' and 'salvation' history, or, most likely, both. Thomas, it is said, made no such presupposition, and permitted no such entailment.

Consequently, whatever reason may attain to by way of knowledge of God – and on this account 'reason' can know God with certainty – it can attain only in so far as reason at least implicitly presupposes something that it cannot by its own powers know, even if, at the same time, it *needs* to know it. For secondly, there is in all human beings a natural desire for beatitude, for a happiness so complete that the desire for it could not be satisfied by the contemplation of any God which reason alone could know, but only by the vision of God of a directness and immediacy which reason is absolutely powerless to achieve and of which it cannot even know the possibility. Therefore, what human beings naturally desire cannot be satisfied by what human beings can naturally know. It follows from this, thirdly, that even that natural *desire* for God, which must be frustrated by the incompleteness of the contemplation of any naturally known God, cannot be known in its full character of frustration, except from the standpoint of faith. For it is only by faith that we can know of the possibility of that complete vision of God to which human reason fails to attain. Hence, the 'noble genius' of the pagan philosophers – of Plato, Aristotle, Plotinus and Proclus – who *did* know God by reason, and who, as Thomas says, could experience only a 'great anguish' of frustration at reason's limitedness, did not know the true nature even of their anguish, for they did not, and could not, know that goal of human desire and knowledge by the standard of which theirs fell short. It follows from this, as Kerr puts it, that if the pagan philosophers did know God, nonetheless 'Thomas clearly thinks that the proposition "God exists", held as true by a non-Christian on the basis of theistic proofs, does not

to represent a minimum consensus among contemporary interpreters of Thomas, especially, but no longer exclusively, on the European continent. For de Lubac himself see *Surnaturel: Etudes historiques*, Paris: Aubier, 1946; 2nd edn, Paris: Desclée de Brouwer, 1991. This work has no English translation, but see his *The Mystery of the Supernatural*, London: Geoffrey Chapman, 1967.

mean the same as the proposition "God exists" held by a believer'. He adds by way of emphasis that the distinction here is not that between two ways, the pagan and the Christian, of knowing the same truth of God's existence, meaning the same by it, but that 'even the proposition [itself] "God exists" means something radically different when held on the basis of philosophy and "under the conditions that faith determines"',[22] thereby seeming to imply, if not exactly affirming, a conclusion not easy to distinguish from that of Karl Barth, namely that a 'God of reason' is a *false* God. As Barth says: 'God is always the One who has made Himself known to man in His own revelation, and not the one man thinks out for himself and describes as God. There is a perfectly clear division there already, epistemologically, between the true God and the false gods.'[23] In short, on this account it is false to say what I propose to argue in this essay, that we know by faith that the existence of God is knowable by reason alone, for what can be known by reason – operating as no doubt it can, in purely philosophical mode – could not be one and the same God as he who is known by faith. Moreover, on this account, it is false to say that Thomas maintains any such proposition.

In clarification, therefore, of how I propose to conduct the argument of this essay, I should say, first, that I do not propose to contest with those who defend these propositions of the 'nouvelle théologie', step by step, text by text, over the exegesis of Thomas's position – for such would require a very different sort of book from this, and in any case it has already been written by Fergus Kerr, albeit from a standpoint of Thomistic interpretation opposed to mine. I shall rather more simply make out the best case I can manage in support of my reading of Thomas. Moreover, I do not propose to respond directly to the challenge thrown down to my defence of the first, substantive, proposition by those of the 'nouvelle théologie' tendency who defend the second proposition, if only because, as in the case of Barthian neo-orthodoxies, it seems to me that they are broadly right in what they affirm, wrong only in what they deny. For in general I think it true that Thomas's proofs of the existence of God, the 'five ways' of *Summa Theologiae* la q2 a3, are in fact arguments set out by a Christian theologian attending to Christian theological purposes, not by a theologian masquerading for some purpose or other as a pagan philosopher. I fully accept that the 'five ways' are therefore proposed as proofs within a context of faith and of Christian practice, and so of theological instruction, of personal and sacramental worship and of a prayer whose

[22] See Thomas, *Summa contra Gentiles* 3.48; Fergus Kerr, *After Aquinas: Versions of Thomism*, Oxford: Blackwell, 2002, p. 67.
[23] Barth, *Dogmatics in Outline*, p. 15.

consummation lies only in the supernatural vision of God in himself. But I deny that it follows from these undoubted truths about the context in which Thomas sets these 'proofs', that their character *as proofs* depends logically upon that context's being presupposed to them; I deny, in short, that they could stand as proofs only in so far as they presuppose the truths of faith within which they are set. At any rate, it does not *follow* from the fact that, for Thomas, these proofs form part of a wider and explicitly theological argument-strategy, that they lack the formal features of a valid rational argument in their own right. Nor do I think that Thomas believes this conclusion to follow: indeed, I shall argue that he thinks it false.

The 'formal' and 'material' objects of faith and reason

As a first step in setting out how this argument will proceed, let us note a crucial ambiguity in Kerr's conclusion from the propositions of the 'nouvelle théologie' that the 'God exists' of the philosopher's reason 'means something radically different' from the 'God exists' affirmed by the Christian 'under the conditions of faith'. This is partly, but only partly, true, and to see in what sense it is true and in what sense false, we can ask: why does the Vatican Council, in distinguishing what it calls 'two orders of knowledge', distinguish them not only in respect of their source – the one being the product of reason, the other of divine faith and revelation – but also in respect of their 'object'? The question matters, for long before the 'nouvelle théologie' – at least since Pascal – there has been a quite generalised scepticism abroad whether, even supposing you could demonstrate a 'God of reason', that God of reason could be demonstrated to be the same God as the 'God of faith'.[24] The answer to that question lies in the council's implicit reliance upon an ancient scholastic distinction between the 'material' and the 'formal' objects of knowledge: we can be acquainted with the same material object by sight and by touch; but sight acquaints us with it in respect of its colour, touch in respect of its sensitivity to temperature; so what they acquaint us with is the same thing materially – I see what is warm, I feel what is red – but differing formally: it is not *as* warm that I see it, not *as* red that I feel it. Hence, the knowledge they yield is in either case determined by its formal object, the material object being the same for both.

---

[24] 'Le Dieu des Chrestiens ne consiste pas en un Dieu simplement autheur des veritéz géométriques et de l'ordre des élements; c'est la part des Payens et des Epicuriens . . . Mais le Dieu de l'Abraham, le Dieu d'Isaac, le Dieu de Jacob, le Dieu des Chrestiens, est un Dieu d'amour et de consolation.' Blaise Pascal, *Pensées*, ed. H. F. Stewart, London: Routledge & Kegan Paul, 1950, pp. 6–8.

This is not a wholly implausible way of construing the relationship between the God of the philosophers and the God of faith – the same God can be known under different descriptions, as 'warm' and 'red' are, and within different relations of knowing, as touching and seeing stand in differing relations of immediacy to their objects. And in fact the analogy with the different formal objects of the senses has, within the history of the subject, been employed directly, especially in the late Middle Ages. Giles of Rome, who (rather unconvincingly) thought of himself as a disciple of Thomas Aquinas, explained that the God of the philosophers is known as it were 'by sight', and the God of the theologians by 'touch' and 'taste'; for the philosophers know God 'at a distance' and intellectually across a gap crossed not by means of direct experience but by means of evidence and inference, and so through a medium, as sight sees; whereas, through grace and revelation, the theologian is in an immediate and direct experiential contact with God, as touch and taste are with their objects – touch and taste being analogies for the immediacy of love's knowledge.[25] There is something to be said for this way of construing the relationship between the 'God of the philosophers' and the 'God of faith', for to do so is at least to acknowledge that the manner in which an object is perceived – the cognitive relation to it in which one stands – is determined by the descriptions under which it is perceived, while allowing that *what* is perceived in either case is one and the same object. As the philosophers say, the descriptions under which an object is perceived may be 'intentionally' distinct but 'extensionally' equivalent: the Morning Star is the same star as the Evening Star, though 'Morning Star' does not mean the same as 'Evening Star'. So it is, on Giles's analogy, with the natural and revealed knowledge of God.

Not every theologian, however, could have welcomed Giles's polarisation of philosophical detachment – 'seeing' – in opposition to theological experientialism – 'touching' and 'tasting' – and Thomas Aquinas nowhere does, providing us with a probably more helpful, because less polarised, account of sameness and difference of 'object'. What I see at a distance is a dark patch I can distinguish as a human being moving towards me. When it is close enough to me, I can see that it is Peter. When the object was at a distance what I saw *was* Peter, but it was not *as* Peter that I

---

[25] 'If we wish to speak of the contemplative life in terms drawn from the senses, we could, in a manner of speaking . . . say that the contemplation of the philosophers gives delight to hearing and sight; whereas the spiritual contemplation of the theologians gives delight to taste, smell and touch.' See my *Eros and Allegory: Medieval Exegesis of the Song of Songs*, Kalamazoo: Cistercian Publications, 1995, p. 364. I have translated this passage from Giles's text, misattributed to Thomas Aquinas, in the Venice edition (1745) of Thomas's *Opera Omnia* I.

saw him. Thus the God of reason in relation to the God of faith.[26] The
God the philosopher knows *is* the God of Abraham, Isaac and Jacob
and of Jesus Christ; but the philosopher cannot, otherwise than by the
reports of faith, know her God *as* the God of faith.[27] This is the meaning
of that famous, and famously derided, formula which Thomas Aquinas
appends at the end of each of his 'five ways': *et hoc omnes dicunt Deum*.[28]
As Thomas concedes, the proofs of God prove very little indeed, but
just enough: as 'proofs' they fall into that class of 'demonstrations' which
merely show *that* something exists by way of explanation (*demonstratio
quia*), from which, no doubt some properties are derivable which must
hold true of whatever thus far explains. But they are not explanations
of 'effects' by way of what we demonstrate about them from the nature
of their cause (*demonstratio propter quid*)[29] because in any case (as we
shall see[30]) we do not and cannot know the nature of God, we do not
know what God is. Haldane explains:[31] we can know from the fact that
the water pressure to my shower is lower than in the rest of the system
that there is a blockage in the inflow pipe to my shower-head. But just
because I do not thus far know that what is obstructing the water supply
is a small piece of masonry, as the plumber later discovers, it does not
follow that what I know as 'blockage' is not what the plumber discovers
to be a small piece of masonry, even though 'blockage' and 'small piece
of masonry' do not mean the same. In parallel it should not be supposed
that, having demonstrated the existence of a 'prime mover' or of a 'necessary being', Thomas imagines that 'all people' know God under such
descriptions, still less that they worship God under such descriptions,
even less still that they could love God under such descriptions. For this
reason it is undoubtedly true that, as Kerr says, the 'God exists' of the
philosopher does not *mean the same as* the 'God exists' known under the
conditions of faith. And of course, in affirming that the God of his 'five
ways' is what all people call by that name, he is by no means affirming
that they do mean the same. The Latin *et hoc omnes dicunt Deum* should
be translated not as 'this is how all people speak of God' or even that
'this is what all people *mean* when they speak of God', for manifestly they
do not, and Thomas knows this: it should rather be translated as 'and
this is the God all people speak of'. The descriptions of the philosopher
and of the ordinary believer are, as I have put it, extensionally equivalent; but of course they do not mean the same thing. How, then, do
we know that these 'Gods' are extensionally equivalent, are one and the

---

[26] *ST* Ia q2 a1 ad1.   [27] *ST* Ia q2 a1 ad 1.   [28] *ST* Ia q2 a3 *corp.*
[29] *ST* Ia q2 a2 *corp.*   [30] See pp. 40–3 below.
[31] J. J. C. Smart and John J. Haldane, *Atheism and Theism*, Oxford: Blackwell, 1996, p. 143.

same God? Only by faith: reason alone could not know that – it is the plumber, after all, not I, who knows that the blockage is a small piece of masonry.

Therefore, all the decrees of the first Vatican Council quoted above are statements of, or articulations of statements of, faith alone, for 'human beings are totally dependent on God as their creator and lord, and created reason is completely subject to uncreated truth'. So much by way of initial clarification.

Issues

What, then, are the issues, and how will the argument proceed? As to the issues, two very broad questions are the subject of this essay: first, is a natural theology – the claim that the existence of the one true God can be known by human reason alone – possible? And this is a philosophical question. For even if the Vatican decrees are statements intended as articulations of faith, and are not proposed on philosophical grounds, nonetheless what they make a claim for is a rational, philosophical, possibility. That being so, it is a claim in principle vulnerable to philosophical counter-argument, namely to the demonstration that the existence of God could not in principle be proved, as many philosophers other than Kant have in fact argued. Moreover, if the possibility of proving the existence of God is said to be entailed by the nature of faith, as the Vatican Council says it is, then it would after all seem to follow as the 'Barthians' would have it that, in accordance with its account of faith, faith itself is logically, if not in fact, vulnerable to philosophical refutation, that is to say, it is refutable via its philosophically refutable entailment. And this much I concede to be true, that faith *is* logically vulnerable to philosophical, as also to empirical, refutation. For there are possibly true, if in fact false, states of affairs such that, if they were actually true, then Christian faith would be false: manifestly the claim to the existence of the historical person of Jesus is an empirical claim, and so it logically *could be* false, and if it were, then all Christian faith must fail. But note that even this does not place faith in thrall to the 'deliverances of reason' or of 'history', as the 'Barthians' would say, for the Vatican Council is emphatic: there cannot be any conflict between faith and reason, and such is the epistemic superiority of faith over reason that 'every assertion contrary to the truth of enlightened faith is totally false'.

At this point, then, it is necessary to enter one further point of clarification. The Vatican Council declares that it is 'contrary to faith', and therefore false, to say that the existence of God cannot be known with certainty by reason. It follows, on this account, that philosophical arguments, such as those of Kant, which purport to show the impossibility for speculative reason of the demonstrability of God, must fail on their own terms of philosophy. The case here seems to be in most ways epistemologically parallel to that of belief in the resurrection of Jesus. For if, in faith, you maintain that the body of Jesus, which was his in his *pre-mortem* natural life, is one and the same with that body of Jesus which is now raised by the Father to immortality, then your faith would appear to be in principle vulnerable to empirical refutation. And so indeed it is – in principle and as to its epistemic standing. For if, as is logically possible, the archaeological discovery were to be made of the bones of Jesus' natural body preserved somewhere in the deserts of Palestine, then it could not be true that that identical body was raised by the Father to immortality, and belief in the resurrection – in those terms – would turn out to be false and indefensible. And this, of course, is the reason why many theologians today, wishing to preserve the epistemic autonomy of faith, deny that the resurrection of Jesus requires belief in the numerical identity of Jesus' *pre-mortem* and raised bodies. For if that numerical identity obtained, then it would have to follow that the tomb in which Jesus was buried must have been empty on the third day after his death, and that, some say, would appear to make an object of faith out of a merely empirical fact. But such a ploy, fraught as it is with conceptual difficulties about personal identity,[32] is not needed in the defence of faith's epistemic precedence over reason, for to maintain on grounds of faith that the tomb was empty is not to entail that its being empty or not ceases to be a matter of plain empirical fact; neither, conversely, is the empirical standing of the claim that it was empty such as to place faith in thrall to empirically factual refutation.

For if it is true that the dead body of Jesus is that identical body which was raised by the Father, then it is true that no such archaeological remains will be discovered, for they could not exist – and you will know that in faith. For any true proposition, just in so far as it is true (and however known to be true), rules out the possibility of there being any facts conclusively to falsify it. And this entailment holds even for empirical

---

[32] Quite how such theologians propose to guarantee the continuing identity of the *pre-mortem* person Jesus with him who is raised, without appeal to some non-bodily, and so potentially 'dualist', criterion of personal identity (which they seem equally inclined to reject) is not often made clear. Could one also be permitted to note here that just because belief in the resurrection of Jesus is logically defeasible by evidence that the tomb was not empty, it does not follow that the resurrection of Jesus can be believed on the evidence that it was empty, or that resurrection faith is reduced to some empirical, quasi-historical, fact? 'If resurrection-belief is true, then the tomb was empty' is not reducible to 'Belief in the resurrection is belief that the tomb was empty', even on the condition that, were the tomb not empty, resurrection belief would be false.

truths. It is a common fallacy (having its origin in Plato) to infer from the *de dicto* necessity of the proposition, 'What is known is true', the *de re* conclusion, 'Only the necessarily true is known.' Just because if it is true that Jesus' body was raised from the dead then necessarily there are no bodily remains resting in Palestine, it does not follow that there being no remains of Jesus' dead body in Palestine is a necessary and not an empirical truth. As Thomas Aquinas says, so long as the proposition 'Socrates is sitting' is true, then necessarily Socrates is sitting. But it does not follow from this that Socrates' sitting is necessary, for 'Socrates is sitting' is plainly a contingent truth. He just has to stand up and walk away, and the proposition 'Socrates is sitting' becomes false.[33] In the same way, even if we know for certain that, Jesus having been raised from the dead, there cannot be such bodily remains awaiting archaeological discovery, it remains an empirical truth that there are none such and an empirical falsehood that there are such.

The case is thus far analogous to the relationship between faith and reason generally, on the Vatican Council's account. If, in faith, you maintain that the existence of God is rationally demonstrable, then it follows that there cannot be any philosophical arguments which succeed in demonstrating the impossibility of such a proof. Of course, the force of the 'cannot' here is such that the proposition 'Rational proof of God is impossible' is false; but it is not nonsense to think it true, the proposition being quite plainly intelligible. For which reason, it does not follow from the falsity of that proposition, that there are no philosophical arguments to be had with those philosophers who, contrary to what faith entails, maintain it. Hence, on the Vatican Council's account of the relationship between faith and rational proof, while it would seem worthwhile for apologetic reasons to show if you can that Kant is wrong philosophically, it will not matter from the point of view of your personal faith if Kant's philosophical arguments are too much for you and you are not intellectually up to pulling off a refutation. No more does it matter from the point of view of your personal faith if you cannot get a satisfactory rational demonstration of the existence of God off the ground, or even if no one ever does. But theologians ought to view it as a role of theirs, as far as they are able, to rebut any philosophical argument to the effect that a proof of the existence of God is a rational impossibility. Even then, though any such rebuttal will have to be philosophical in kind, from the fact that there is a genuine philosophical argument to be had about the possibility of proof of God it does not follow that faith is thereby placed in thrall to the debatable outcome of a rational argument. And much of the argument of this book

[33] *ST* 1a q14 a13 ad3.

is concerned with such philosophical rebuttals: for in this matter, the truth lies in whatever survives the *elenchus*, that is, in whatever survives the refutation of the counter-arguments.

Defending the rational possibility of proof of God against philosophical objections is therefore one main purpose of this essay; that purpose is connected intimately, however, with a second question: is the Vatican Council right about what Christian faith entails by way of rational proof? Is it perhaps true, after all, that the case for the possibility of a natural theology – even if it can be defended in philosophical argument – is inconsistent with what Christians claim for the God of faith? Are the 'God of reason' and the 'God of faith' the same God? The answer which is most common among Christian theologians today is that a correct understanding of faith excludes in principle the possibility that the God believed in by Christian faith can be known to exist without faith. For a theologically pretentious 'reason', it is said, is a reason which seeks to occupy the territory proper to faith's knowledge of God with that to which it can attain from within its own resources; and such could offer nothing theologically but the displacement of the God of faith, truly revealed in Jesus Christ, by means of an idolatrously diminished godlet of reason's own devising. A god known through creatures is, it seems to be thought, a god limited by the scale of creatures, for, it will be said, however extrapolated from creatures and projected upon an infinite object, such a god could be no more, logically, than an infinitely inflated creature. A god whom creatures can know *by* reason is a god all too knowable because all too creaturely, being inevitably contained *within the bounds* of reason: hence, a God known by reason is not the true God but an idolatrous displacement. Much of the argument of this essay is designed as a rebuttal of just that inference.

The argument

The decrees of the Vatican Council maintain, then, that we know by faith that it is possible to know God by human reason with certainty. In what follows I propose to defend this proposition in three distinct but interlocking stages, which relate, respectively, to 'reason', to 'the knowledge of God', and to 'certainty'. First, then, I will consider on what account of 'reason' it can be said that rational knowledge of God can be had, here showing that in a certain general character human reason replicates, as it were 'by anticipation' and in an inchoate way, the 'shape' of faith itself, first because the shape of reason in its deployment in proof of God 'anticipates' that interactivity of 'affirmative' and 'negative', of the 'cataphatic' and 'apophatic' moments, which are inherent to the epistemic structure and dynamic of faith itself. Reason, in this respect, therefore has the same 'shape' as faith, for, at any rate according to Thomas, while we may and must speak of God, and while we can show by reason the necessity of doing so, we know that we do not know what God is, whether by reason or by faith. And showing this will occupy us in chapters 2 and 3.

As a second stage of argument in chapters 4, 5 and 6 I shall attempt to clarify more fully what Thomas means by 'reason'. I argue for a much expanded conception of what reason is by comparison with our contemporary conceptions of it, here showing that in its complex character on the one hand of being inherently self-transcendent, and on the other hand of being firmly rooted in our nature as animals, reason possesses, now by a more particular 'anticipation' of faith, the 'shape' of the sacramental, an openness of embodied existence to that which altogether lies beyond its grasp. And that will conclude the argument of Part One.

Part Two will, then, be concerned with the nature of the divine unknowability, for what reason could know about God is principally that if it is indeed God that it knows, then what it knows is unutterable mystery. But within the inevitable discussion of some medieval, as also of some recent, accounts of the apophatic – essentially the business of determining the nature of God's unknowability – the central problem for my argument begins to press with ever greater urgency. If the 'gulf' of unknowability must be fixed so unfathomably deep between the human mind and God as it must – on pain otherwise of an idolatrous theological reductivism – then how could reason in principle be said to bridge it by means of its own native resources of 'proof'? And the solution to that problem forms the agenda for Part Three.

Part Three, then, is concerned with the nature of that 'certainty' with which reason may be said to know God and so with the nature of 'proof' – for I take it that reason's characteristic certainty lies in proof in a strict sense, such that 'proof' is obtained when a conclusion is validly drawn by inference from true premises. Specifically, I argue that reason can demonstrate the intelligibility of a *question* – a question which therefore lies within its own reach – but one of such ultimacy that its *answer* must be unknowable, and that the name of that unknowable answer must be 'God'. Here, though, the argument becomes increasingly complex and impossible to paraphrase in advance, for, in the course of seeking to clarify the 'argument-strategy' of Thomas's proofs of God the link needs to be established between that narrower expression of reason which consists in 'ratiocination' from premises to conclusion in the course of proof, and that broader sense of 'reason' which, in chapter 6, was said to possess the 'shape' of the sacramental. For only through that link may the central proposition of this essay be secured, namely that not only does reason as deployed in proof of God have the *shape* of the sacramental, but also that this is so because creation as such – the world's being created – is itself quasi-sacramental and that reason is a sort of human participation in that 'sacramentality' of the world. It is, that is to say, in its grasp of the world as brought to be 'out of nothing' that reason knows God: indeed, it is just that knowledge of the world in its character as created – and so in its form of the sacramental – which *is* our rational knowledge of God. And here my argument ends, leaving unsaid and merely gestured towards, perhaps for another occasion, much that needs to be added of a Christological character by way of securing it fully in place: for, as everyone knows, any account of sacramentality gets its form and character from a Christology, the human nature of Christ being the form and character of every sacrament. Hence it is precisely because of what is revealed to us in Christ that we know that reason too, as the Vatican Council says, can 'know the one true God, our creator and lord, with certainty from the things which have been made'.

2   Negative theology and natural theology

Natural theology and 'onto-theology'

As a first step in response to what seems to be a widespread and general hostility to 'natural theology' we must next begin a long process of consideration of two particular forms that the criticism takes, sometimes linked, sometimes not, as directed at some key high and late medieval theologians, including, some say, Thomas Aquinas, while others find them in Duns Scotus but not in Thomas. The first accusation is that of the theological error which, since Martin Heidegger, is described as 'onto-theology', an egregious offence committed by those, if indeed there are any who commit it, who suppose that there is some 'common conception of being' – or at least, some excessive degree of 'continuity of being' – of which common conception, duly differentiated by the distinction between infinite and finite being, God and created things are instances, or 'beings'. That, at any rate, is one opinion of what the error consists in, for Philip Blond says that an onto-theologian 'elevate[s] a neutral account of being above the distinction between the Creator and his creatures, allowing both God and finite beings to share in this being in due proportion'.[1] But in recent times the accusation seems to have been levelled with little discrimination as to its exact nature, for, on the contrary, Lawrence Hemming in the same collection of essays tells us that 'onto-theology' is the error of asserting that 'God as univocal *primum ens* is the same as being' and that 'God is not subsumed under being where being is a separate (and so higher) category from God, but that God as highest (infinite) being subsumes all created things as univocally dependent on him'.[2] There might be error in either opinion, or in both. But they are not the same error.

[1] Philip Blond, 'Perception', in *Radical Orthodoxy: Suspending the Material*, ed. John Milbank, Catherine Pickstock and Graham Ward, London: Routledge, 1998, pp. 232–3.
[2] Lawrence Paul Hemming, 'Nihilism', in ibid., p. 94.

In view of this uncertainty among theologians concerning what 'onto-theology' is, perhaps the matter is best left in Heidegger's own terms, upon whom Western philosophies have commonly relied for a form of enquiry called 'metaphysics' which confines itself to the study of *beings*, neglecting that which is 'hidden', as it were, 'behind' beings, namely 'Being'. Heidegger appears to have Aristotle's *Metaphysics* in mind as a model for this degenerate enquiry, and for Heidegger Aristotle's is a 'metaphysics of substance', that is to say, an account of ultimate reality in terms of what there is, of what things there are, and in terms of what accounts for what there is; or, to put it in other terms, 'metaphysics' is a philosophy of 'existents' rather than of 'existence'. For Heidegger, more-over, this metaphysical failure of ultimacy is not merely Aristotle's, for it pervades the Western philosophical and theological traditions; though it is easy to show at least that there are exceptions, Meister Eckhart being but one, though Bonaventure will do just as well.

For Bonaventure, the proper study of being is God.[3] But though 'being' is properly speaking the name of God, this 'Being' is not an object of our knowledge, which it eludes. For 'Being', God, is not *a* being; it is beings which are the natural objects of knowledge. However, Being is the light in which we see beings. But the light in which we see beings cannot itself be seen, for if it could be, then it could be represented only as another object to be seen – and God cannot be in that sense an object of thought, since God is not *a* being. That much, at any rate cannot fairly be con-strued as an 'onto-theology' in Heidegger's sense. Indeed, Bonaventure's emphatic declaration both that God is 'Being' and that God cannot be known as *a* being constitutes a neat reversal of Heidegger's description of the 'onto-theological' logic, according to which, he says, 'metaphysics thinks about beings as being . . . Metaphysical representation owes this sight to the light of Being. The light itself, i.e., that which such think-ing experiences as light, does not come within the range of metaphysical thinking; *for metaphysics always represents beings only as beings*'[4] – which Bonaventure clearly does not do. Nor, as I have shown elsewhere, does Eckhart, his similar declarations that *esse est Deus*[5] notwithstanding. Nor again, as we will see, can Thomas.[6] But, driven by the inertia of a historical

---

[3] See *Itinerarium Mentis in Deum* 5.3, in *The Works of St Bonaventure* II, ed. Philotheus Boehner OFM, and Sr M. Frances Laughlin SMIC, New York: The Franciscan Institute, 1990.

[4] Martin Heidegger, 'The Way back into the Ground of Metaphysics', in Walter Kaufmann, ed., *Existentialism: From Dostoevsky to Sartre*, New York: Meridian Books, 1969, p. 207 (emphasis added).

[5] See my *The Darkness of God: Negativity in Christian Mysticism*, Cambridge: Cambridge University Press, 1995, pp. 142–8.

[6] See pp. 187–90 below.

generalisation, hard to warrant,[7] Heidegger insists that what he calls 'metaphysics' can represent to itself only beings; and it follows that any attempt 'metaphysically' to represent Being can result only in the misrepresentation of Being as *a* being. The onto-theologian, therefore, in making Being into God, makes Being, and so God, into *a* being, hence into the supreme object of metaphysics, and so, on the 'Aristotelian' conception of metaphysics, into a sort of all-embracing quasi-substance. And this is aptly named 'onto-theology' because it both makes 'Being' into God and, thereby, reduces God to *a* being. Now one obvious and easy way into this error, it is said, is to set out from the start on to a metaphysics of God, in short upon a 'natural theology'.

This second offence of 'natural theology', briefly stated, would appear to consist in maintaining that it is possible to establish by purely rational means and, at least logically, if not in fact, in advance of anything we might come to know about God by revelation and faith, some account of the divine existence and nature, and of God's creation of the world out of nothing. In short, this second offence is conveniently summarised by the decrees of the first Vatican Council reported above. 'Offence' it may or may not be, but it is, I argue, the view of Thomas. It is also mine.

In recent theological literatures these supposed errors are variously thought to be linked in a number of historical and systematic forms, not all such accounts being consistent with one another. Some so connect logically the (as it is thought) erroneous case for natural theology with the onto-theological error that any defence of the first must, logically, depend on the second. You cannot, some think, be a 'natural theologian' without being an 'onto-theologian', since for the natural theologian the existence of God is demonstrable by reason alone; and a philosophical demonstration of the existence of God would be logically valid only on condition that the predicate '. . . exists' can legitimately be predicated in the same sense, or 'univocally', of God and of creatures, which is, or at least entails, the 'onto-theological' error. Some such, most particularly those belonging to the self-named school of 'Radical Orthodoxy', are so convinced of the logical force of this dependence that, believing, rightly in the matter of historical interpretation, that Thomas is no 'onto-theologian', they are constrained to conclude that he could not consistently have maintained any such propositions about the natural knowledge of God as those professed by the Vatican Council. For Thomas decisively rejected the proposition,

---

[7] For an excellent 'deconstruction' of Heidegger's critique of 'onto-theology', see Mary-Jane Rubenstein, 'Unknow Thyself: Apophaticism, Deconstruction and Theology after Ontotheology', in *Modern Theology* 19.3, July 2003, pp. 387–417.

some decades later advocated by Duns Scotus, that existence is univocally predicated of God and creatures. Consequently, Radical Orthodox thinkers, but especially John Milbank, expend much exegetical ingenuity and energy in the persuasion that Thomas did not in fact propose his 'five ways' as formally valid, philosophically independent, proofs of the existence of God. In later chapters I shall test for genuineness the Radical Orthodox reading of Thomas in relation to the thought of Duns Scotus. For the time being I venture some rather more preliminary remarks about another, closely related, position.

Thomas on creation: a skirmish with Gunton

Colin Gunton, in an extensive and influential theological output, has consistently offered a reading of Thomas on creation, exemplary of a very common and hostile theological evaluation, which it is an important purpose of this essay to contest. It therefore seems not to be in a merely *ad hominem* spirit to examine this reading in some detail. For example, in one of his last works,[8] Gunton maintains that Thomas's account of creation is in error theologically, or is at least dangerously ambiguous, since it contains elements which others identify as onto-theological, though Gunton himself makes no use of this term. Moreover, he argues, here agreeing in principle with the Radical Orthodox view of the logical connections of thoughts (though not of course as a reading of Thomas), that this is demonstrated by his partiality for a natural theology.

Gunton writes of the 'Babylonian captivity' in which the doctrine of creation was confined by medieval theologians, but especially by Thomas (Gunton, p. 99); by which he appears to mean that Thomas fell into the error of 'natural theology'. This he is said to have done by offering a purely philosophical account of creation *ex nihilo* which owed nothing, or at least too little, to the explicitly trinitarian creationism of the great Greek patristic theological traditions as found, for example, in Athanasius and Basil. They at least, Gunton says, understood the act of creating as an act of the free personal agency of the second person of the Trinity and, on that account, they could deflect the tendencies inherent in so many of the pagan Greek Neoplatonic sources, on which much early Christian theology depended, of an 'emanationist', 'monist' and 'necessitarian' doctrine of creation. Even so, he says, this unambiguously trinitarian creationism of the East 'was never secure enough in the West

---

[8] Colin Gunton, *The Triune Creator: A Historical and Systematic Study*, Edinburgh: Edinburgh University Press, 1998. References hereafter to 'Gunton' in the text. Sadly, Colin Gunton has died since the completion of this discussion of his critique of Thomas.

to prevent outbreaks of virtual pantheism, so that some commentators [including, he adds, himself] have even noticed pantheist logic in the thought of Thomas Aquinas'. He explains in a remarkably expansive gesture of historical generalisation that 'the doctrine of the Creator God has always contained seeds of a kind of continuity between God and the world, with the result that a mind divided between Greek and Hebrew remains to this day' (ibid.).

Those 'seeds of continuity' between God and the world, Gunton thinks, flourish in the soil of the doctrines of the hierarchy of being and of analogy, because in those residual elements of a Platonist ontology of scales of 'reality', which remained unexpelled by his Aristotelianism from Thomas's thought, there remains necessarily connected with them the notion that there is some common scale extending from matter to God. Hence, he sees the doctrine of analogy in Thomas as a device of logic and metaphysics governing the stretch of language along the extent of that scale, thus permitting the description of God 'by analogy' from the things of creation. Although, as Gunton concedes, Thomas has an account of creation *ex nihilo* – a doctrine of radical *dis*continuity between God and creation which ought, of course, to subvert any Platonist tendencies to 'emanationism' – the Platonist and emanationist elements in Thomas's thought countervail with force sufficient to override those of discontinuity.

Gunton finds it therefore unsurprising that there are detectable in numerous structural features of Thomas's account of creation the 'symptoms' of this Platonist thinking, though some of these supposititious symptoms may very well surprise the reader familiar with Thomas's writings.[9] Such will not have anticipated being told that a symptom of this Platonist emanationism consists in Thomas's *rejection* of Peter Lombard's opinion that the act of creation can be 'delegated' to creatures (Gunton, p. 100). For in his famous *Sentences* Peter had considered the case against God's having communicated to human ministers the power of inner regeneration which is baptism, that, if God were able to communicate that power to creatures, then it would follow that God could communicate to creatures the power to create *ex nihilo*. But that is impossible,

---

[9] Quite apart from the fact that Thomas explicitly affirms the theological opinions about creation and the Trinity which Gunton denies him: see, for example, *ST* 1a q45 a6 *corp.*, where, having explained that creation belongs to God 'in respect of his *esse*' (*secundum suum esse*), which is common to all three Persons, he adds, 'and the Father has caused the creature through his Word, which is the Son; and through his Love, which is the Holy Spirit. On this account, it is the processions of the Persons which are the source-principles of the production of creatures in so far as they include the essential attributes of knowledge and will' – 'et Deus Pater operatus est creaturam per suum Verbum, quod est Filius; et per suum Amorem, qui est Spiritus Sanctus. Et secundum hoc processiones Personarum sunt rationes productionis creaturarum, inquantum includant essentialia attributa, quae sunt scientia et voluntas'.

the argument goes, for God can give to no one the power to be what he is, and since he cannot share his power of creation *ex nihilo* he cannot share his power of baptismal re-creation. Peter's response is to retain the objection's connection between the delegation of baptismal re-creation and creation *ex nihilo*, but to turn the argument on its head: as *instrumental* causes, humans can baptise. But if they can baptise as instrumental causes, then they can create as instrumental causes. For 'God can create things through another, not through another as their author, but by a ministry, with which and in which he works; just as in our good deeds both he and we act, not he alone, nor we alone, but he with us and in us'.[10] And vice versa: if God can give creatures the instrumental power to create, then God can on the same ground communicate the power to baptise.

One might have supposed that Peter's view that creation can be thus ministerially 'delegated' is precisely what one would have expected of a Christian theologian who is *over*impressed by Neoplatonist emanationism, and that the *rejection* of Peter's view, such as is found in Thomas, would indicate something less than enthusiasm for that 'emanationism'. At any rate it is Thomas's explicitly stated view that, contrary to Gunton's expectations of him, to allow the possibility of creation's being 'delegated' is necessarily 'emanationist'. The reason, Thomas says, that creation *ex nihilo* cannot be effected even instrumentally by any mediate cause is that mediations are processes enacted upon pre-existing matter, and, *ex hypothesi*, nothing is presupposed to creation *ex nihilo*. It could hardly be clearer from the texts of Thomas's case against Peter's view of 'delegated' or 'instrumental' creation that the primary purpose of Thomas's discussion is precisely to resist Peter's 'emanationist' tendencies – and this is clear enough even in his own *Scriptum* on Peter's *Sentences*, where Thomas is willing to concede what he can to Peter's view,[11] never mind in the much later *Summa Theologiae*, where he takes no hostages at all on

---

[10] 'Posset Deus per aliquem creare aliqua, non per eum tamquam auctorem, sed per ministrum cum quo et in quo operaretur: sicut in bonis operibus nostris ipse operatur et nos, non ipse tantum, nec nos tantum, sed ipse nobiscum et in nobis.' *Petri Lombardi IV Libri Sententiarum* IV d1.

[11] 'Since it pertains to the meaning of creation that there be nothing pre-existing, at least in the order of nature . . . taken on the part of the Creator, that action is called creation which is not founded on the action of some preceding cause. In this way it is the action of the primary cause alone, because all action of the secondary cause is founded on the action of the primary cause. Hence, just as it cannot be given to any creature that it should be the primary cause, so it cannot be given to it that it should be the Creator.' *Super Libros Sententiarum Petri Lombardi Scriptum* 2 d1 q1 a3 *corp.*, ed. P. Mandonnet and M. F. Voos, Paris: Lethielleux, 1929–47. Translation by Steven E. Baldner and William E. Carroll, in *Aquinas on Creation*, Toronto: Pontifical Institute of Medieval Studies, 1997, p. 80.

the matter.[12] So it is difficult to know how Gunton can have understood a 'delegated' conception of creation otherwise than as entailing the very emanationism which he accuses Thomas of failing to avoid by rejecting it. For Thomas's part, it is crucial to resist the influence of that Platonising tendency of 'hierarchicalist continuities' which could not be squared with an adequate understanding of the radical discontinuities between God and creation implied by creation *ex nihilo*. As Thomas says, the relation of creating can only be unmediated; to fail to see this is to fail to understand the meaning of the expression 'out of nothing'.

Next, Gunton notes Thomas's denial that, in creating the universe, God acts to achieve a purpose, and suggests that this amounts to the denial that God's creative act is free (Gunton, p. 101). It would seem to be Gunton's view that only acts calculated as means to achieve some end can be said to be free acts, though he nowhere tells us why we should be expected to accept this inference, since it is clearly not true even of human beings that only such calculative acts are free acts – unless one wished for some reason to rule out as unfree all acts of simple enjoyment or of aesthetic delight, and all acts of simple, uncalculating love – and one is at a loss to know what reason there could possibly be for doing so. On the contrary, it is just such acts which, for Thomas, are maximally free and nearest in character to the freedom of the divine creativity. It would be absurd, he says, to envisage the Creator God entertaining goals and purposes of maximum advantage to himself (acting *propter suam utilitatem*), and then calculating how best to achieve his ends. God, he says, in all he does acts out of pure goodness, by an act of will unconstrained by the necessities imposed either by nature[13] or by given ends upon the

---

[12] 'The Master (of the *Sentences*) says that God can communicate the power of creating to a creature so as to create instrumentally, not on its own account. But this cannot be so . . . nothing can act in a dispositive and instrumental manner to this effect (of creating), for there is nothing presupposed to the creating to be "disposed" by the action of an instrumental cause.' – 'Magister [Sententiarum] dicit quod Deus potest creaturae communicare potentiam creandi ut creet per ministerium, non propria auctoritate. Sed hoc esse non potest . . . non potest aliquid operari dispositive et instrumentaliter ad hunc effectum, cum creatio non sit ex aliquo praesupposito, quod possit disponi per actionem instrumentalis agentis.' *ST* 1a q45 a5 *corp.*

[13] 'God must love his own goodness, but from this it does not follow necessarily that creatures must exist to express it, since God's goodness is perfect without that. So the coming to be of creatures, though it finds its first reason in God's goodness, nevertheless depends upon a simple act of God's will.' – 'Sic igitur quod Deus suam bonitatem amet, hoc necessarium est: sed hoc non necessario sequitur, quod per creaturas repraesentatur, cum sine hoc divina bonitas sit perfecta. Unde quod creaturae in esse producantur, etsi ex ratione divinae bonitatis originem habeat, tamen ex simplici Dei voluntate dependet.' *Summa contra Gentiles* 3.97, *Opera Omnia* XIV, Leonine edn, Rome, 1926. *Aquinas: Selected Philosophical Writings*, trans. Timothy McDermott, Oxford: Oxford University Press, 1993, p. 274 (hereafter cited as 'McDermott').

availability of the means.[14] In any case and in principle, God cannot be construed as having to deliberate about whether or what to create. For deliberation is a kind of change or process which cannot be envisaged in God, because a process takes time, and time is itself a creature. There cannot be, he says, here echoing Augustine's famous discussion in *Confessions* book 11, any time 'before' creation, but only after: hence there can be no deliberation, which, in the nature of the case, has to *precede* action.[15]

It follows that the only way we have of characterising the divine creative act is as the utterly free act of an unconstrained will; hence, Thomas says, *et ille est maxime liberalis*, which we might translate as: '[God's] generosity is absolutely free-handed.'[16] And once again, for Thomas, this *absolute* freedom of the divine creative causality follows directly and only from the conception of creation as being *out of nothing*. For, since it is 'out of nothing', absolutely nothing is presupposed to the act of creating which could constrain the choice to create. Which is why one can say that it is out of pure goodness that God creates; and the only other way of saying the same that I, or Thomas, can think of, is to say that God creates out of the pure love and joy of doing so – that is to say, in a paradigmatically free way, *maxime liberalis*.

Next, Gunton says that symptoms of hierarchical emanationism are exhibited by the fact that, for Thomas, creation is a relation of causality, conceived of not as a temporal relation between cause and effect, but as a vertical one of dependence (Gunton, p. 99). Ignoring as we may the much vexed philosophical question of whether causal relations have to be relations of temporal sequence, we cannot ignore the fact that even had Thomas supposed that they ordinarily are temporally bound,[17] he would

---

[14] 'For all those agents which act for an end beyond their will, their will is guided by that end. Hence [such a will] wills to act at some times and not at others, according to those things that help or impede attaining the end. The will of God, however, did not give being to the universe for the sake of some end existing beyond his own will, just as He does not cause motion for some other end . . . because the more noble thing does not act for the sake of something less than itself. Therefore, the fact that God does not always cause an effect is not due to something persuading Him to act or preventing Him, but to the determination of His own will, which acts from a wisdom which is beyond our understanding.' *Scriptum* 2 d1 q1 a5 ad12 (Baldner and Carroll, *Aquinas on Creation*, p. 101).

[15] *Expositio in Octos Libros Physicorum Aristotelis* 8.2, 990, ed. P. M. Maggiolo, Turin: Marietti, 1965.

[16] 'He alone is absolutely free-handed, because he does not act on consideration of some usefulness to himself, but out of his very goodness alone.' – 'Ipse solus est maxime liberalis: quia non agit propter suam utilitatem, sed solum propter suam bonitatem.' *ST* 1a q44 a4 ad1.

[17] Thomas thinks that in most cases created causal sequences are temporarily bound, but not in all: 'as soon as there is light there is illumination', as Baldner and Carroll put it.

even then have been forced to conclude as he anyway does, namely that the sense in which God can be said to be the 'cause' of the universe cannot be any ordinary one: for causes ordinarily are processes whereby one thing acts on something else so as to produce an effect in it. Now creation, he says again, cannot be a 'process'; for processes take place in time. And since there is no time before creation, nothing can be said to 'happen' by way of a process of creative causality. In any case, thinking as he does of divine creative causality on an analogy with efficient causal dependence, the same conclusion follows. For created causality is effected in something given, out of which an effect is produced. 'Nothing', however, is given to the creative activity. Nor again should we be misled by the 'out of nothing' into supposing that 'nothing' is a sort of given, as if the 'nothing' in 'nothing is presupposed' named a curious sort of negative '*something* presupposed'. The negation in *ex nihilo* does not function to designate a soupy undifferentiated blob of 'nothingness' out of which the universe is created; as Thomas observes, the negation in *ex nihilo* qualifies the '*ex*', so as to mean: 'there is no "out of" here'.[18] Hence, if there are reasons for describing the divine creative activity as 'causal' – and it is quite another matter why Thomas thinks that there are[19] – there are equal reasons for denying that this causality can be construed in any ordinary sense.[20] But then, Gunton appears to know nothing of the strictures Thomas imposed

---

So there are created analogies for the divine creative act. Thomas says: 'No cause that instantaneously produces its effect precedes its effect necessarily in duration. But God is a cause that produces His effect, not through motion, but instantaneously. Therefore, it is not necessary that he precede his effect in duration.' *De aeternitate mundi contra murmurantes, Opera Omnia, Opuscula* I, Rome: 1882, (Baldner and Carroll, *Aquinas on Creation*, p. 116).

[18] 'If the negation includes the preposition *ex*, then succession is denied, and the meaning is "made out of nothing", that is "not made out of anything" – just as to say, "he spoke of nothing" is to say that he did not speak of anything.' – 'Si . . . negatio includat praepositionem [ex], tunc ordo negatur, et est sensus, *fit ex nihilo*, id est, *non fit ex aliquo*; sicut si dicatur, *iste loquitur de nihilo*, quia non loquitur de aliquo.' *ST* 1a q45 a1 ad3. See also *De Potentia*, q3 a1 ad7 (McDermott, pp. 255–6).

[19] See pp. 248–54 below.

[20] Part of the problem here is in any case with *our* notions of cause 'in any ordinary sense'. For since Hume it has become common to think of causes simply as events preceding other events ('effects') and linked by some statement of regularity. There is, in Thomas, a quite different conception of causality 'in the ordinary sense' as modelled on 'agent causation', roughly, as Kerr explains, 'on an analogy with a person's own experience of bringing things about' (Kerr, *After Aquinas*, p. 46). I do not know of my actions of bringing something about by observing the regularity connecting my action with the event it causes; I know of my causality 'without observation', just as (normally) I know where my head is 'without observation'. For sure, any reading of Thomas on the divine causality which construes God's actions as antecedent events linked to divine effects on some statement of regular succession is bound to construe God's creative causality in an entirely idolatrous fashion.

on theology by the *via negativa* – or, on the evidence of this account, of how Thomas thought the logic of analogy works.

Next, Gunton traces out, as one of the conclusions he expects to be able to draw from an excessively Platonist philosophical doctrine of creation, a corresponding underrating of the autonomy of the creature (Gunton, pp. 101–2). Of course, from the misreadings of Thomas already described, it is easy to see why Gunton would conclude that Thomas's account 'fails . . . to give the creature space to be' *as a creature*. Suppose you maintain, as 'Proclan' forms of Neoplatonism do, that creation issues by necessity out of the divine nature; suppose you think that this creation issues forth, not *ex nihilo*, but, as it were, *ex Deo*, like a sort of laval flow progressively hardening into colder and more massy solidities as it descends further down the hierarchy of beings from the pure liquid fire of the divine source; suppose, then, that on such account, the energy and drive of your theology is all in the direction of continuities between God and creation, these continuities justifying a return direction of flow by which language, ascending upon the back of these continuities, can by analogy reach up to God; then, on these suppositions you might very well conclude that creation has not been given 'space to be' created. For creatures, on this account, will look much more like bits of degraded divinity than independently existing creatures which stand on their own account in their own relation to 'nothing'. What is more, if somehow you have managed to persuade yourself that Thomas's doctrine of creation is, in spite of some contraindications (as Gunton concedes), distorted by the influence of such thoughts and inferences, you might expect to find in Thomas some depreciation of 'the creature's value as creature'; for, as Gunton thinks, his residual Platonism entails 'a denial that creation puts a reality into a creature except as a relation', and this 'detract[s] from the proper substantiality of the creature'.[21]

This, however, is to miss the point of what Thomas means and wholly ignores the proper subtlety of his thought. For Thomas, it is precisely our freedom and autonomy as creatures which are 'given' to us by that relation of dependence; we are most self-subsistent in that dependence, and the more self-subsistent the more that relationship is one of dependence. Nor

---

[21] Gunton, *Triune Creator*, p. 101. Thomas does indeed say, in *Summa Theologiae* 1a q45 a3 ad1, that 'the relation of God to creatures is not real in God, but only a relation of reason. But the relation of creatures to God is a real relation' – 'relatio in Deo ad creaturam non est realis, sed secundum rationem tantum. Relatio vero creaturae ad Deum est relatio realis.' And in *De Potentia* q3 a3 *corp.* he says: 'creation is really nothing other than a relatedness to God consequent upon starting to be'. *Quaestiones Disputatae de Potentia*, q3 a3 *corp.*, Turin: Marietti, 1953 (McDermott, p. 261).

is there any unresolvable paradox in this: by our participation in God's own being, we participate in, and come to possess for ourselves, that which belongs to the divine nature. For Thomas, we are, in a created way, all that God is as uncreated. Hence, even if, as Thomas says, our goodness as creatures is possessed by us only in virtue of the divine uncreated goodness, still, that created goodness is something inherent in us, and is properly ours, and we can name it so.[22] Even if our created causality depends on the divine causality for its effectiveness, still we are causes in our own right, for creatures truly cause.[23] And this is, above all, true of that which is *most* characteristic of the divine nature, which is *self-subsistence*. Precisely because we participate as creatures in all that the Creator is, we possess for ourselves all that we possess in our own measure of subsistence. As Thomas says, 'God's goodness . . . in sharing itself out causes things not only to resemble him in existing but also to resemble him in being active.'[24] Therefore, we are most ourselves – given the 'space to be' – precisely in that relation of created dependence.

Now if it were not for the fact that these misreadings of Thomas were driven by a more serious, more general and more plausible critique of Thomas's theology, it would not be to our purpose – easy as it is – to rebut them. But there is something more plausible in Gunton's critique, and it is a suspicion of Thomas's general theological strategy, of offering what appears to be a purely philosophical doctrine of God and of creation as some sort of prolegomenon to a more properly theological reflection on the faith of Christians.

Proof and 'foundationalism'

Which brings us back to the offence of onto-theology. Though Gunton does not accuse Thomas in just that term of 'onto-theological' error, he clearly links the supposed deficiencies of his doctrine of creation with what he perceives in Thomas to be an excessive degree of indebtedness to Neoplatonic hierarchical continuities across some common scale of

---

[22] 'Thus it is, therefore, that each thing is said to be good by virtue of the divine goodness, as the first exemplary, effecting and final origin of all goodness. Nonetheless, each thing is said to be good on account of a likeness to the divine goodness *inherent to it*, which is *formally its own goodness* by which it is named.' (my italics) – 'Sic ergo unumquodque dicitur bonum bonitate divina, sicut primo principio exemplari, effectivo et finali totius bonitatis. Nihilominus tamen unumquodque dicitur bonum similitudine divinae bonitatis sibi inhaerente, quae est formaliter sua bonitas denominans ipsum.' *ST* 1a q6 a4 *corp.*

[23] 'One must not understand the statement that God is at work in everything in nature as if it meant that the thing itself did nothing; rather it means that God is at work in the very activity of nature and free will.' *De Potentia* q3 a7 *corp.* (McDermott, p. 302).

[24] *De Potentia*, q3 a7 *corp.* (McDermott, p. 300).

being, on which God is situated, albeit as top doh, but still situated on it. And of course to situate God on *any* common conceptual ground with creatures such that God and creatures are represented as instances of that same conception, however otherwise distinct, is onto-theological error. Hence, even if it is all too easy to show that Thomas is no 'emanation-ist' of the sort Gunton thinks he is, it may not be so easy to defend him against accusations of onto-theology when we observe how convinced he is – perhaps I ought to say at this stage of the argument, 'appears to be' – of the possibility, indeed of the necessity, of a natural theology: the pos-sibility and the necessity, that is to say, of rational, non-faith-dependent, demonstrations of the existence and nature of God. For, leaving on one side the particularities of Gunton's reading of Thomas on creation, the suspicion of onto-theological error seems to be aroused in principle by Thomas's broader theological strategies.

For it would seem that in principle any conception of faith – hence of theology – which requires the rational demonstrability of the existence of God must be committed to a form of rationalist 'foundationalism', which appears to be the proposition that in some way (and there will, no doubt be a variety of ways) Christian theological truth is *logically dependent upon* rationally established truths about God. And since I do not here propose to consider this particular objection to natural theology – since I know of no defence of so strong a form of foundationalism – let me say in passing that there does appear to be a form of weak 'foundationalism' implicit in the Vatican decrees. For sure, we have seen that those decrees offer no 'strong' foundationalism, for, as we have seen, they say nothing at all about having to prove the existence of God by the natural light of reason before any Christian theology can get off the ground; or that in any way at all you would have to know the existence of God to be demonstrable by reason in order to do any Christian theology. They say merely that if you have not mistakenly articulated your Christian theology, then it will follow from what, within it, you can say about the trinitarian God, first, that the existence of the one Creator and Lord God is demonstrable by the natural light of reason, and, secondly, that the God thus known by reason is one and the same God, not formally but materially, as the trinitarian God of Christian faith. In short, a test of whether your Christian theology has truly grasped its own object in faith is whether, on that account, reason has been permitted a place for the possibility of knowledge of its object in its own 'natural light', whether or not that place has been explicitly acknowledged.

It would seem that Gunton's principal objection to Thomas's theolog-ical procedure concerns the second of these two propositions, for in the fact that – if fact it be – in his most mature theological exposition, the incomplete *Summa Theologiae*, he prefaces his theology of the Trinity with what has seemed to some to be a 'purely philosophical' treatise *de Deo uno*, it would seem to Gunton that 'monist', 'necessitarian' and 'emanationist' tendencies have been allowed to disorientate and distort the authentically Christian and trinitarian doctrine of creation.[25] The distinctively Christian theology, Gunton thinks, must begin with the trinitarian Godhead, for it is not Christian theology until it does. No Christian theology which begins, as Thomas's appears to him to begin, with a divinity whose credentials as God have to be established first rationally, can ever proceed thereafter in Christian authenticity. And the evidence for that, if not provided on grounds of logic, is to be found at least in the facts of the matter: it is for this reason, he thinks, that Thomas's doctrine of creation is ridden with monist infection, and so entails a marginalisation of trinitarian faith. And the virus is natural theology.

The *ratio Dei*

It is possible that a certain rather aprioristic cast of mind might offer a quasi-foundationalist defence against Gunton, thinking it reasonable to suppose that a Christian theology, whether of the incarnation, or of the Trinity, or of creation, or of any other Christian doctrine, would have to set out first some account of what God is, some conceptual presuppositions, concerning at least minimal criteria (or perhaps 'heuristic' anticipations) governing what would count as talking about God when you are talking about the incarnation, or the Trinity, or creation.[26] You might particularly suppose this to be necessary if you reflect upon the naivety of the assumption which appears to underlie Gunton's polemic against Thomas, who, Gunton supposes, cannot be talking about the Christian God when in the *Summa Theologiae* he prefaces his discussion of the Trinity and creation with a philosophically derived account of the existence and nature of God as 'one'; whereas he, Gunton, can be guaranteed to be talking about the Christian God just because he explains creation

---

[25] Gunton, *Triune Creator*, p. 99.

[26] And Thomas does say that in the context of a demonstration of God's existence you would at least need to know something about what you are attempting to prove the existence of. But even then Thomas explicitly denies that we can know in advance of proof what God is, for it is what we show the existence of which shows what God is. What we need by way of equipment for the purposes of proof is knowledge of the divine effects and some knowledge of the grammar of the noun 'God': 'ad probandum aliquid esse, necesse est pro medio *quid significet nomen*, non autem *quod quid est*: quia quaestio *quid est*, sequitur ad quaestionem *an est*. Nomina autem Deum imponitur ab effectibus . . . unde, demonstrando Deum esse per effectum, accipere possumus pro medio quid significet hoc nomen *Deus*.' *ST* 1a q2 a3 ad1.

in trinitarian terms. In this theological naivety, Gunton appears not to be alone. Christians commonly tell us, rightly, that the God of Christian faith is the triune God; from which they appear to derive the complacent conclusion that just because they talk of the Trinity they could not be talking about anything other than God. But no such consequence follows, and Feuerbach's *Essence of Christianity* ought to serve as a warning against such complacent assumptions, for there he demonstrates quite plausibly that it is possible to extend your 'theology' over the whole range of Christian doctrines and practices – the Trinity, the incarnation, the church, the sacraments, even devotion to the Virgin Mary – and to preserve every manner of Christian theological jot and tittle in the exposition of them, but entirely as translated out in terms of the human, by the simple device of inverting, as he puts it, subject and predicate.[27] Thereby he demonstrates, to put it in Christian terms, the possibility of a purely idolatrous theological exposition of the entire resource of Christian belief and practice, in which, in the guise of the soundest doctrinal orthodoxies, the Christian theologian but worships his own nature, in the reified form of 'God'. One is reminded of the idolatrous schizophrenic who, when asked how he knew he was Jesus Christ, replied that it was really quite simple, for when he prayed he found he was talking to himself. And if Feuerbach fails to convince, Jesus might: not everyone, he once said, who cries, 'Lord, Lord', is worthy of the kingdom of heaven (Matt. 7:21).

It might therefore be thought that it is in view of such considerations that Thomas, when asking what is the formal object of *sacra doctrina*, dismisses the obvious answer that it is the study of central Christian doctrines, such as the sacraments, or redemption, or Christ as person and as church, since those and other such doctrines give you the material object of *sacra doctrina* but not its formal object: that answer, he says, would be like trying to define sight in terms of the things that you can see – human beings, stones or whatever – instead of things *qua* visible, that is, as coloured. The formal object of *sacra doctrina* is rather, he says, all those things revealed to us through Jesus Christ, but specifically *sub ratione Dei*: either because they are about God, or because they have a relation to God as their origin and end: *unde sequitur quod Deus vere sit subiectum huius scientiae*.[28]

If that is so, then we need to know what would count as the consideration of the Christian revelation *sub ratione Dei* – as distinct, therefore, from a consideration of the same content of that revelation in the manner

---

[27] Ludwig Feuerbach, *The Essence of Christianity*, trans. George Eliot, New York: Harper Torchbooks, 1957, pp. 17ff.
[28] *ST* 1a q1 a7 *corp.*

of a Feuerbach, *sub ratione hominis*. In view of this a certain kind of aprioristic mentality might suppose that this is a conceptual matter which needs to be settled by a pre-theological definition, and, if pre-theological, then necessarily by a philosophical definition; and by a philosophical argument which establishes that the definition is instantiated – and thus proves the existence of the God so defined. This, if we could take it to be Thomas's opinion, would explain and lend credence to that account of his theological procedure which so worries the theological Guntons and causes in them such suspicions of onto-theology, whereby after a preliminary discussion of theological method in the first question, Thomas engages in the *Summa Theologiae* in no fewer than twenty-five questions – some 149 articles – in 'natural theology' before he gets round to even preliminary discussions of the Trinity. It is as if the necessity of establishing what would count as the *ratio Dei* before doing properly Christian theology, and as a regulative criterion of when we are doing it, requires proofs 'by the natural light of reason' of the existence of God, and then of his attributes. Moreover, once you have supposed that that is Thomas's procedure, it would come naturally to mind that it is that 'necessity of faith' which the first Vatican Council had in mind when it decreed it to be a dogma that such proofs are available to us.

On what God is not

But any readers of Thomas's *Summa Theologiae* who supposed that that was his procedure would be much puzzled by what they find in the course of the argument of those twenty-five questions: first, because Thomas sets about demonstrating the existence of God without giving even preliminary thought even to a 'heuristic' definition of God. In fact, the reader will be at a loss to find *any* 'definition' of God anywhere at all, even were he to read right through to the end of the *Summa*. All Thomas appears to say on this matter, at any point, is immediately at the end of each of the five ways, when he says, with that demotic optimism which we have already noted (and to the dissatisfaction of most readers today who misunderstand the point), that the prime mover, the first efficient cause and the necessary being and the rest, are 'what all people call God'[29] – exactly the proposition which Gunton is pleased to contest in the name of his trinitarian priorities. Secondly, when, immediately after his discussion of whether God exists, Thomas does appear to set about the more formal discussion of what it is of which he might have proved the existence, he tells us flatly that there is no definition to be had, for there can be no

---

[29] *ST* 1a q2 a3, *corp.*, and see p. 19 above.

answer to the question of what God is, but only of what God is not. 'Once you know whether something exists', he says,

> it remains to consider how it exists, so that we may know of it what it is. But since we cannot know of God what he is, but [only] what he is not, we cannot enquire into the how of God ['s existence], but only into how he is not. So, first we must consider this 'how God is not', secondly, how he is known by us, thirdly, how he is spoken of.[30]

That said, the reader will be further puzzled by the fact that, nonetheless, Thomas then proceeds for a further nine questions to discuss what, on most accounts, will be considered classical attributes of God – his simplicity, perfection, goodness, infinity, ubiquity, immutability and unity – as if thereby ignoring what he has just said and supplying us with what to many will appear to be a quite unproblematised account of God's multiple 'whatnesses'. And as if that were not bad enough, after first telling us that we can know only what God is not, he then says that, once he has shown that to be so, he will go on to tell us how God is, after all, known and spoken of – a case, we might imagine, of knowing the unknowable, of describing the indescribable, or perhaps of self-defeatingly throwing your cake away in order to eat it. Something is badly wrong here: either, on this way of understanding Thomas's theological method, he is plainly muddled and inconsistent, or, if consistent, then some other way of reading his method will have to be found.

It is charitable at least to try for a consistent Thomas. Nor is it difficult. Nothing is easier, to begin with, than to see that, in his discussion of the divine simplicity in question 3, what is demonstrated is not some comprehensible divine attribute, some affirmation which marks out God from everything else, but some marker of what constitutes the divine *in*comprehensibility, as distinct from the incomprehensibility of everything else. It is helpful, in this connection, to take note of David Burrell's distinction between those names of God which denote substantive 'attributes', such as 'goodness', 'beauty', 'justice' and 'mercy' and so forth, and those names of God which denote what he calls 'formal features' – among which he numbers 'simplicity' and 'eternity'. Whereas the 'attributes' predicate of God, on whatever logical grounds justify such predications, terms predicable of creatures, the 'formal features' 'concern our manner of locating the subject for characterisation, and hence belong to a stage prior to considering attributes as such'.[31] In this sense, Burrell's

---

[30] *ST* 1a q3 *prol.*
[31] David Burrell, 'Distinguishing God from the World', in Brian Davies OP, ed., *Language, Meaning and God: Essays in Honour of Herbert McCabe OP*, London: Geoffrey Chapman, 1987, p. 77.

'formal features' are markers of what Thomas calls the *ratio Dei*, for it is, Burrell says, 'the formal features which secure the proper distinction of God from the world, thus determining the kind of being (so to speak) said to be just and merciful, and hence establishing critical modifications in those attributes'.[32] It is in this same sense, moreover, that Thomas's exploration of the *ratio Dei* through the 'formal feature' of 'simplicity' is designed to establish a first line of defence against idolatry. For what Thomas recognises to be in need of determination about the *ratio Dei* – that which in some way is criterial for speaking of God's otherness as distinct from all secondary, created othernesses – is the precise nature of *God's* incomprehensibility, lest it be mistaken for that more diffused and general sense of the mysteriousness with which we are in any case confronted within and by our own created universe – for there is puzzlement enough in creatures. You do not know the nature of God, he says. You know only that you do not know what God is. But all the same, there is a job to be done of determining whether the 'unknowability' you may have got to in your contemplation of the world is in truth the divine unknowability, the divine 'otherness' – as distinct, for example, from simply giving up on seeking to know at some lesser point of ultimacy. For the penultimate unknowability of creatures is always less than God's ultimate incomprehensibility.

Therefore the argument for the divine simplicity in *Prima Pars*, question 3, is designed to demonstrate that the 'how' of that ultimate divine 'otherness' is incomprehensible to us so that we could not confuse that divine otherness with any lesser, created form of otherness. Not only can we not know the 'how' of God's existence, so other is it; *so* 'other' is God, that that otherness has itself lost its threads of straightforward continuity with any conception of 'otherness' of which we do know the how. We do not know, therefore, how 'other' God is: which is why Thomas is at one with the pseudo-Denys's saying that, at the climax of ascending scales of God's differences from all else, God must be thought of as off every scale of sameness and difference as such and thus to be beyond 'every assertion . . . beyond every denial'.[33] Therefore, if the theologian is to know what the *ratio Dei* is, that standpoint from which speech about God is marked out as properly theological, then the answer is: he knows he is talking about God when all theological talk – whether it is materially about the Trinity, or the incarnation, or the presence of Christ within church or sacrament, or about grace, or the Spirit in history, or the manner of our redemption – is demonstrably ultimate, when,

[32] Ibid.
[33] Pseudo-Denys, *Mystical Theology* 5, 1048A, in *The Pseudo-Dionysius: The Complete Works*, trans. Colm Luibheid and Paul Rorem, New Jersey: Paulist Press, 1987.

through the grace of revelation, we are led deeper than we otherwise might be into the unknowability of the Godhead. For Thomas, faith deepens everything that reason knows, including the 'darkness' of its knowing. The believer has a stronger sense of mystery than the philosopher, not a weaker. For even if in truth Christians do know by grace and revelation what the philosopher can never know – and they do – such knowledge as faith teaches us can serve only to draw us into a darkness of God which is deeper than it could possibly be for the pagan; it is deepened, not relieved, by the Trinity, intensified by the incarnation, not dispelled. For which reason, Thomas says: 'in this life we do not know what God is [*even*] *through the revelation of grace*, and so [by grace] we are made one with him as to something unknown'.[34]

A 'metaphysics of Exodus'

At this point it is necessary to dispel a myth which may have been thus far reinforced by my own lax terminology. Thomas's 'simple' God is not, in the first instance at least, a 'God of the philosophers', as I, in a dubiously helpful concession to Pascal, may appear to have been saying. Thomas's God, whose simplicity is ultimately guaranteed by the divine identity of *esse* and *essentia*, is, at least so far as he is concerned, the God of 'Abraham, Isaac, and Jacob', that is to say, the God of the Hebrew scriptures. Here, as in other places too, Thomas is providing what Kerr calls a 'metaphysics of Exodus',[35] specifically a metaphysics of Exodus 3:14, where, having been asked by Moses for his name, Yahweh replies: 'I am who am. This . . . is what you must say to the sons of Israel'. It was, of course, the contention of Etienne Gilson that it is to this scriptural authority that Thomas appeals when he concludes that the proper name of God is *ipsum esse subsistens*, he who is so utterly simple and one, in whom there is no distinction of *esse* and *essentia*, that that name is utterly incommunicable, not capable of being shared with anything else.[36] As a grammatically common noun, Thomas adds, the name 'God' is the most appropriate, for it signifies the divine nature which is, of course, shareable, since all creation in one way or another can and does share in the divine nature.[37] But if you want a proper name with which to name

---

[34] 'Per revelationem gratiae in hac vita non cognoscamus de Deo quid est, et sic ei quasi ignoto coniungamur.' *ST* 1a q12 a13 ad1.

[35] Kerr, *After Aquinas*, pp. 80–2.

[36] *ST* 1a q13 a11 *corp.* See Etienne Gilson, *L'Esprit de la philosophie médiéval*, Paris: de Vrin, 1944.

[37] It is important not to be misled here. Grammatically *Qui est* is a proper name, on all fours therefore logically with 'Peter' and 'Mary'. Hence it is logically absurd to suppose that

God as absolutely 'distinct' – such that the people of Israel can be told of their God, without ambiguity or confusion with any other 'God', which is what Moses was asking for – then this is it, Thomas says: 'I am who am' – *ipsum esse subsistens*.

It is, of course, disputable and disputed how far Thomas's 'metaphysics of Exodus' can be permitted to stand as an exegesis of Exodus 3:14,[38] and in any case Gilson made no claim to there being any sort of Thomist metaphysics *in* Exodus, only that Thomas's metaphysics of the divine *esse* corresponds with the God of Exodus.[39] Be that as it may, undoubtedly Thomas thought it a defensible interpretation. That being so, it would seem to follow that if we are with any degree of textual and historical sensitivity to assess Thomas's account of what he is doing, methodologically and theologically, in questions 2–25 of the *Summa Theologiae*, we should see those discussions as an elucidation of the *ratio Dei* in and through an attempt to develop the implications of what the Hebrew scriptures reveal to us about God – precisely, therefore, as the God revealed to Abraham, Isaac and Jacob, and to the prophets of Israel. If, therefore, there are problems in Thomas's account concerning the relationship in which that God stands to the trinitarian God of Christian faith, these will not be best understood as problems of how a philosophical 'God of oneness' stands in relation to that 'God of faith', but as problems, if indeed there are any, which will have to be faced in one way or another by any Christian theologian whatever, of the relation between the God revealed to the people of Israel paradigmatically in the great Exodus theophanies, and the God revealed to the people of Israel, and preached to all nations, in Jesus Christ. After all, it is Israel's God, the God of Exodus, whom Christians believe to be incarnate in the human person, Jesus Christ.[40] To that extent, at least, Thomas has no problems to face of general theological method which have not to be faced by a Gunton or Barth or any other Christian theologian whatever.

---

there could be more than one *Qui est*. That is not to say that we can identify God as the individual named in the same way that we can identify Peter and Mary as the individuals named. Grammatically, 'Deus' is a common noun, on all fours therefore logically with 'man' or 'giraffe', denoting the divine nature. Hence, though undoubtedly false, it is not logically absurd to suppose that there is more than one God. That is not to say that we are able to comprehend the divine nature that the noun denotes, in the way we can tell the difference between a man and a giraffe because of their different natures. On all this, see pp. 172–3 below.

[38] For example by André-Marie Dubarle, 'La signification du nom de Yahweh', *Revue des sciences philosophiques et théologiques* 34, 1951, pp. 3–21.

[39] Gilson, *Esprit*, p. 50. See Kerr, *After Thomas*, pp. 94ff.

[40] I have heard it suggested that Jesus' own self-proclamation, 'Before Abraham ever was, I am' (John 8:58), was a self-consciously explicit appropriation to himself of the Exodus epiphany.

And if Thomas incurs further problems of theological method not incurred by a Gunton, this will be because Thomas thinks that the Exodus theophanies can be thought through in philosophical terms which Gunton cannot accept, as if supposing that, in doing so, Thomas were setting up a 'philosophical' God of 'oneness' incapable of reconciliation with the trinitarian God of faith. But, as we have seen, this also seems *prima facie* untrue. Thomas's God of the Hebrew scriptures is a God utterly beyond comprehension, a God whose name is indeed given to us (Exod. 3:14), but one whose 'face no one may see and live' (Exod. 33:20–23); and the root of that unknowability of God lies in exactly that which licenses us to call God by the name 'I am': to know the name of God *is* to know in what lies the divine incomprehensibility. And that God, the God of Abraham, Isaac and Jacob, is none other than the God of trinitarian faith, to whom, as Thomas says, we are by grace 'made one, as to something unknown to us'.

On what Thomas does not do

What, then, are we to say in a preliminary manner are the methodological principles underlying questions 2–25 of the *Summa*? First of all, even if we are to read Thomas's 'five ways' as being offered as a rational demonstration of the existence of God, he is not to be represented as setting out on a venture of such proofs from a definition of 'God' in some neutral terms of 'natural theology'. This is at least for the reason that if Thomas has a 'natural theology' the first thing it knows is that the nature of God is unknown, and unknowable, to us. Of course, just how this 'unknowability' of God is to be reconciled with the reading of the 'five ways' as formal proofs remains to be seen, and in any case as much needs to be settled as to whether Thomas does indeed think of the 'five ways' as proofs at all. Secondly, it is not the case that, for Thomas, you need some philosophical definitions and proofs of God, a natural theology, before you enter the domain of revealed theology, as if the latter were in some way built up only on the strength of its philosophical foundations; that, in view of his scepticism about the attainment of philosophical certainties, would in any case be, for Thomas, to build houses on foundations of sand.[41] Nor is it that, for Thomas, the formal object of revealed theology, what is to count as the *ratio Dei*, had somehow to be authoritatively refereed by some *pre*-theological and purely philosophical demonstration, as the condition on which theology was to be guaranteed its own authenticity.

---

[41] *ST* 1a q1 a1 *corp.*

Nor yet is it that those first twenty-five questions are to be construed as a philosophical treatise *de Deo uno*, as if philosophical theology and revealed theology were to be distinguished by their subject-matters, the one confined to the divine unity, the other adding something further, on the trinitarian nature of God. Nor, again, when Thomas says, in the prologue to question 2, that he will deal first with the 'divine essence' and then with the distinction of persons, does he propose to embark upon some preliminary work of definition of an 'abstract philosophical' God with which the trinitarian God will have to be made to fit. Nor yet again is Thomas's quite startlingly 'negative' account of our knowledge of God confined to reason's potential, as if to say, as some do: by reason we know God's essence to be unknowable, but by faith that ignorance is made good by the revelation of the Trinity of Persons. Finally, neither does the reverse hold, as some might think: that the God who can be known by reason is a 'knowable' God – indeed, perhaps, all too knowably placed within our human grasp to be 'God' – by contrast with the mysteriously unknowable trinitarian Godhead given to us by faith.

My account concerning what Thomas is proposing in these early questions of the *Summa* carries us thus far. First, you cannot be guaranteed to be doing Christian theology just because you quote Scripture and use a lot of Christian theological terms unavailable to non-believers: there are plenty of Christian idolaters. Second, you are doing theology when you enquire into what has been revealed to us *sub ratione Dei*. Third, if we are to do our theology with any assurances at all that it meets with its distinctive responsibilities, we need some account of what it is to think within that revealed truth *sub ratione Dei*, to do which is to be drawn participatively into the divine unknowability. Fourth, then, what Thomas is engaged with in these preliminary questions is an essentially theological task, even if it is also a *meta*-theological[42] one of cutting down the odds on doing theology idolatrously; he is conducting a properly theological enquiry into the nature of theology's own formal object, into that which determines its character as theological. And if doing that requires engaging also with what others than Christians would recognise as doing

---

[42] Note that, for Thomas, a *meta*-theological task is also, and necessarily, a *theological* task. A meta-mathematical discussion is not a mathematical discussion; a meta-scientific discussion is not a scientific discussion. But a meta-theological discussion has nothing higher than theology to appeal to: not even the divine self-knowledge itself (*scientia*), in which, by faith, it participates. Theology just *is* that participation: there are other participations in that divine science, but none higher which can function as a court of appeal to settle theological disputes or uncertainties, not even the church's *magisterium*. For the *magisterium* may have greater *authority* than the theologian has, but it has access to no repository of *higher knowledge*.

philosophy, and even if we can make the case for the view that within that philosophical enquiry room is made for the possibility and necessity of proofs of God, then that philosophical enquiry is engaged in simply as the necessity of faith's own theological self-clarification: *fides quaerens intellectum sui*. In short, Thomas is doing as theologian what the first Vatican Council was doing as *magisterium*.

3 The darkness of God and the light of Christ

The apophatic and the cataphatic

That Thomas's theological starting point lies in the defeat of the human mind by the unknowability of God, whether in the mind's own nature as rational or as transformed by grace, will perhaps seem hard to reconcile with any case for the demonstration of the existence of God unaided by faith – for such a case, if any does, would seem to lay claim to 'know God', indeed to know God all too well. But this unknowability will seem, on the other side, just as hard to reconcile with the nature of that faith itself. Perhaps it will be conceded for the one part that it is right to say, as I shall argue shortly, that the apparent conflict between Thomas's severe apophaticism and his equally apparent confidence in the theological capacity of reason to know God is reconciled in his view of rational proof as demonstrating, precisely, the existence of an unknowable mystery of creation. But even if it were thus conceded, for the other part a problem would still remain: should we not say that even if reason shows us the darkness of God, the revelation of faith sheds upon that darkness the light of Christ? What reason can demonstrate that it cannot know, in a sort of self-subverting act of its own, it might be thought in Christ is made good, so that an apophaticism of reason might be thought defensible, but only if it is held in conjunction with a cataphaticism of faith.

On neither side of the 'reason/faith' distinction may such a proposition be defended as a reading of Thomas Aquinas. For the distinction and relation between the 'cataphatic' and the 'apophatic', between the necessity of speech about God and its equal deficiency, are, as we shall see more fully later, already given in reason's claim to know God, for the 'five ways' are intended to show both that we can speak truly of God and that all such talk falls radically short of him. In this chapter, however, our concerns are to take one step further, though along a subsidiary route, our claim that it is in faith itself that the demand is made for the possibility of rational proof, that subsidiary route leading us to see that the same complex interrelation between the cataphatic and the apophatic which structures a 'natural theology' (as Thomas conceives of it) is given in the very structure of faith itself.

That this is so should not be in the least surprising: after all, what is being examined, in seeking to determine that complexity of relation between the cataphatic and the apophatic, is the very nature of the theological act of knowing as such, so that any intellectual enquiry deserving of the name 'theology' is so structured, whether it is 'natural' or 'revealed'. Moreover, as I have argued elsewhere, that relationship is definitive in just such terms of an enquiry's epistemological character as 'mystical'.[1] In short, on any grounds on which an enquiry deserves the name 'theology', whether in terms of reason alone or in terms of revelation, on just those same grounds does it require that articulation of the affirmative and the negative, and to deserve the name 'mystical'. At any rate, these things were thought to be so within a mainstream tradition extending from the Fathers to the late medieval period.

Therefore in this chapter I propose to examine briefly, and through two medieval test cases, just how a complex dialectic of 'affirmative' and 'negative' weaves its way through the distinctively Christian theological enterprise; through, that is to say, the articulation of faith's doctrinal formulation. This examination, however, meets with a preliminary problem of terminological and conceptual clarification. At various points in this essay I shall want to be able to say that Thomas's theology is a 'mystical theology' – or rather, though it is not characteristic of Thomas's style or vocabulary so to describe what he does, that his theology is thus well named. But without some clarification of how I intend that expression, together with a cluster of cognate terms, to be understood, there is great risk of the argument's being obscured.

For if today within the revival of interest in medieval theological models the acknowledgement of a theological apophaticism is once again fashionable, it is open to question whether our contemporary retrievals of medieval apophaticism have not sometimes missed the point. For though there are many who will acknowledge the claims of negative theology in what, it is thought, is its own sphere – located safely in the territory of the 'mystical' – there appears to be less evidence that this passion for 'unknowing' and 'deconstruction' has much tendency to realise its potential across the whole theological field. No more than at any time previously within the period of modern theology is there much acknowledgement of the need to do *all* theology under the constraint of these tensions between

---

[1] See my *The Darkness of God: Negativity in Christian Mysticism*, Cambridge: Cambridge University Press, 1995, especially chapter eleven. Of course, the notion of the 'mystical' is not exhausted by its epistemological conditions. There is more to the 'mystical' than the account of theological language to which it is tied.

an apophatic parsimony and the superfluousness of the cataphatic, of this self-subversive excess of speech and of knowledge. Much in recent theology, as also in comparativist and historiographical scholarship, serves to reinforce a notion of a distinct territory marked out by the name 'mysticism', which is the proper homeland of some free-standing apophaticism, where disruption of speech can go its subversive way uninhibited, on condition that, thus confined, its capacity for generalised theological mayhem is thereby contained.

Many who will appear to concede the centrality of a negative theology for a 'mystical' purpose will have reservations about conceding its structural centrality to the whole theological project. We have already observed one reason why. The Christian scruple will make its presence felt in reaction to any case made for an ultimacy of the apophatic, especially if the apophatic is sheared off from its moorings in an equally ultimate cataphaticism. And to that extent the scruple is justified. For in so far as a 'mysticism' is tied into the 'apophatic' in isolation from its inner dynamic of tension with the cataphatic, it may with justice be asked how, within all this negativity and unknowing of God, due weight can be placed upon the positive revelation of God in Jesus Christ. It is no better to postulate, in reaction to so exaggerated an apophaticism, some ultimacy of the cataphatic, as if free of the restraints of the apophatic, and as if to say that though God in himself is dark, Christ is light, the visibility of the Godhead, the source of all theological affirmativeness; hence, whatever licence may be given to the apophatic in the meantime, in the end is the Word as it was in the beginning, therefore in the end there is speech, not silence. For in this way to postulate an absolutism of the cataphatic is the same error of theological epistemology as that of an absolutism of the apophatic, just the reverse side of the same counterfeit coin. Worst of all is to indulge the connected thought – it is an ancient doubt which is drawn on here, stretching back at least to the high Middle Ages, and further into the earliest years of Christian intellectual history – that negative theology, indeed, 'mysticism' itself, is really but an alien import into Christian theology, a concession made to pagan and especially Neoplatonic sources, mainly to Plotinus and Proclus.[2] For then a whole cluster of thoughts falls into a familiar pattern of complex and historically misleading linkages: that 'negative theology' equals 'mysticism', that 'mysticism' equals Platonism, and that theologies which mix Christian revelation with

---

[2] Typically, Jean Gerson (1363–1429) thought that the 'unknowing' of the philosophers was 'Socratic', the simple recognition that after all its efforts an exhausted reason hits upon a boundary, a theological *ne plus ultra*. This is no apophatic entry into a mystery, but is rather the denial that the reason of the philosophers can make any headway with God at all, and at best acknowledges this. See below, pp. 77–8, for more on Gerson.

Platonic mysticism produce an unacceptable, distorting theological hybrid, unrecognisable in the thoroughbred purity of a gospel Christianity – perhaps above all that such 'mysticisms' reveal their pagan provenance in preferring God to Christ, the one God to the Trinity.[3] It is perhaps from some such concatenation of scruples that the doubts of a Gunton proceed concerning the intrusions of philosophy in general, and so of 'natural theology' in particular, within the project of an authentically Christian theology.

In the last chapter I did no more than initiate a case for rejecting any such interpretation of Thomas. It became clear that the articulation of Thomas's natural theology forces into open prominence a complex interplay, or dialectic, of affirmative and negative tensions, which are the architectonic principles at once of his natural as of his revealed Christian theology proper. Now because in the last chapter the manner of my presentation may have suggested otherwise, the purpose of this chapter is to demonstrate that within some key representative theological sources of the high Middle Ages – in Bonaventure in one way, in Thomas in another – it is far from the case that this architectonic dialectic finds its justification principally in any philosophical doctrine of 'God', Platonic or otherwise, but that it arises first and foremost out of strictly Christian theological, above all Christological, necessities. That is to say, even if it is the case – and without any doubt it is – that there are Greek philosophical sources on which the apophaticisms of Bonaventure and Thomas directly or indirectly draw, that they do so derives not from some willingness to superimpose an alien conceptual framework distortingly upon a pure source of authentic Christian faith in Christ. Rather, these two authorities inherit conceptual opportunities already embedded in the patristic articulations of Christian teaching which bear witness to tensions of knowing and unknowing inherent within the structure and dynamic of that faith itself. In the case of Thomas Aquinas, therefore, it is not his natural theology which presses this dialectic upon *sacra doctrina*; rather, that natural theology reflects and replicates within reason the tensions between affirmative and negative moments which structure the inner nature of belief itself. For Thomas, then, reason already, and in its own nature, as it were 'anticipates' the structurally 'mystical' character of faith itself. Nor are Thomas's priorities unique among medieval theologians; for, though in so many other ways differing from Thomas in respects which place him with majority theological opinion in his times, Thomas's Franciscan contemporary and friend, Bonaventure, shares this much with Thomas that for him too,

---

[3] See, typically, Anders Nygren, *Agape and Eros: A Study of the Christian Idea of Love*, Part I, trans. A.G. Herbert, London: SPCK, 1932, especially pp. 23–27.

this Neoplatonic, 'mystical' dialectic of affirmative and negative derives from, just as it structures the articulation of, his most central theological teachings. For Bonaventure, the dialectic of affirmative and negative derives, as the structuring principle of *all* revealed theology, from its ultimate, Christological, source. In a later chapter[4] we shall see that a 'Christocentric apophaticism' is crucially determinative of theological method also for Thomas, while here we pause to note that for Thomas, that same dialectic of affirmative and negative is shown to derive as much from his eschatological account of the relations of the 'presence' and 'absence' of Christ in the Eucharist. The reason for the emphasis in this chapter on Thomas's Eucharistic teaching will become clear in chapter six.

Bonaventure and the centrality of Christ

In Bonaventure's *Itinerarium Mentis in Deum*[5] we find a complex interweaving of at least three strands of theological tradition. First, there is his own Franciscan piety and devotion, which place at the centre of Christian thought and practice the human nature of Christ, but very particularly the passion of Christ. Secondly, there is a rampantly affirmative theology of 'exemplarism', in which, in classically medieval style, he constructs a hierarchy of 'contemplations' of God, beginning from the lowest *vestigia* in material objects, upwards and inwards to our perception of them, through the *imagines* of God in the human soul, especially in its highest powers, further 'upwards' and beyond them to 'contemplations' through the highest concepts of God, 'existence' and 'goodness'. In just such an ascending hierarchy, constructed in the first six chapters of the *Itinerarium*, does Bonaventure construe the whole universe as the 'Book of Creation' in which its author is spoken and revealed; all of which theological affirmativeness is resumed in the human nature of Christ, only there no longer is it merely the passive 'book of creation' in which the Godhead can be read, but now the 'Book of Life', who actively works our redemption and salvation.

But in the transition from the first six chapters of the *Itinerarium* to the seventh, Bonaventure effects, thirdly, a powerfully subversive theological *transitus*, from all the affirmativeness with which creation in its own terms, and with which Christ as the résumé of all creation, speak God, to a thoroughgoing negative theology. For beyond the knowing of God is the unknowing of God; nor is this 'unknowing' merely 'beyond': through the

---

[4] See below, pp. 216–25.
[5] In Philotheus Boehner OFM and Sr M. Frances Loughlin SMIC (eds.), *The Works of St Bonaventure* II, New York: The Franciscan Institute, 1956. See my fuller discussion of Bonaventure's Christocentric apophaticism in *Darkness of God*, pp. 102–34.

increasing intensity and complexity of its internal contradictoriness this knowing *leads to* the unknowing. As one might say, the very superfluity of the affirmativeness sustained by the Books of Creation and of Life collapses into the silence of the apophatic: and chapter seven consists in little but a string of quotations from the more apophatic sayings of the *Mystical Theology* of the pseudo-Denys. But the organising symbolism of that theological *transitus* from the visibility of the Godhead in Christ to the unknowability of the Godhead brings Bonaventure back to his Franciscan starting point; for that *transitus* is also effected through Christ – more to the point, through the passion and death of Christ. For in that catastrophe of destruction, in which the humanity of Christ is brought low, is all the affirmative capacity of speech subverted. Thus it is that, through the drama of Christ's life on the one hand and death on the other, through the recapitulation of the symbolic weight and density of creation in his human nature on the one hand and its destruction on the cross on the other, the complex interplay of affirmative and negative is fused and concretely realised. In Christ, therefore, is there not only the visibility of the Godhead, but also the invisibility: if Christ is the Way, Christ is, in short, our way into the *un*knowability of God, not so as ultimately to comprehend it, but so as to be brought into participation with the *Deus absconditus* precisely as unknown.

The structure of Bonaventure's *Itinerarium* is, however, in one respect misleading if not properly understood, and can seem to work an effect opposed to his manifest intentions. It is perhaps a consequence of the medieval passion for hierarchical structures of thought – the obsession with theological construction modelled on the metaphor of ladders of ascent – that, as Bonaventure sets out his argument in the *Itinerarium*, you would have the impression that affirmation and negation are successive theological moments, that, as it were, you have first to climb the ladder of affirmation only to throw it away into the gulf of unknowing after you have reached the top. First, we unproblematically affirm; then, as if in a distinct theological act, differently and separately motivated, we deny. The consequence is not as such to suggest – though one has the impression that many a modern takes this view anyway – that affirmative and negative theologies are distinct theological strategies, even optional strategies, but that at the very least they are successive strategies. In any case, Bonaventure's metaphorically generated scalar structure of exposition would certainly appear to imply that affirmation and negation are theologically linked, not so as to interpenetrate at every level of theological discourse, but as hierarchically ranked. It is as if there were an ascending scale of affirmativeness which is rounded off with a top doh of negativity – even, one fears to be told, of 'mysticism'.

But then, there is an equally marked tendency in late medieval thought to construe the hierarchy to the opposite effect as far as ranking order goes, even if with the same outcome of successiveness. In the fifteenth century, an enthusiastic follower of the pseudo-Denys, Denys the Carthusian, is as 'apophatic' a theologian as might be wished, but he is quite sure that you could not let the silence of negation have the last word. For, when all our denials of God are said and done, he comments, 'there is still a remainder of affirmation and positive meaning which is implied by and presupposed to [those denials]'.[6] There is, of course, a real problem which leads Denys to say such a thing. How, if there is no theological discourse at least ultimately untroubled by the destabilisations of the negative, will it be possible to distinguish the negative theologian from the atheist? For sure, there must be some way, he seems to think, of distinguishing between the atheist, who will not climb the ladder at all because he says no such ladder exists, and the theist, who insists that it must be climbed if only to throw it away. Both will conclude with Denys that 'it is better to say that God does not exist',[7] but they will mean the opposite; and for Denys, the only ground on which his conviction of this negativity will be distinguishable from the atheist's is if, in the end, the ladder props up on a stable residue of affirmation, standing clear and invulnerable to any negative qualification.

But whichever you think this ascending scale ends in, affirmation or negation, the common mistake – as Bonaventure is more properly understood to say – is in the shared misconstrual of the relationship between the moments of affirmation and the moments of negation; for that relationship structures theological utterance at every stage. Indeed, it is this interplay of negativity and affirmation which structures all theological discourse precisely as theological. In more general terms, this point can be made in all sorts of ways, of which this is just one: many students of the medieval 'mysticisms' broadly categorise them into 'apophatic' and 'cataphatic' forms. Eschewing altogether the question of how they come to be called 'mysticisms' in the first place, Bernard of Clairvaux more obviously than most will fall into the class of 'cataphatic' mystics on the strength of the floridly erotic affirmativeness of his *Sermons on the Song of Songs*; so too will Julian of Norwich, whose exuberance of affirmative metaphor is unrivalled in the medieval period even by Bernard. But

---

[6] Denys the Carthusian, *Difficultatum Praecipuarum Absolutiones* a2 (Appendix attached to his *Commentary on the Mystical Theology* of the pseudo-Dionysius), in *Doctoris Ecstatici D. Dionysii Cartusiani Opera Omnia* XVI, Tournai: Typis Cartusiae S.M. de Pratis, 1902, p. 484C.

[7] Denys the Carthusian, *De contemplatione*, 3.5, *Opera Omnia* XVI, p. 259A–B.

then by contrast, the *Cloud of Unknowing* will have to be deemed typically 'apophatic', characterised as that text is by 'unknowings' and 'nothings', 'nowheres' and 'darknesses'; so too Meister Eckhart, on account of his 'deserts, abysses and no why's, no whatnesses and no things'. This may be well and good as serving as a preliminary distinction of metaphorical habits, but it hardly gets to the core of the matter. For of course a negative metaphor is still a metaphor. The preference for negative metaphors as 'more true' of God than affirmative[8] is thus far no less or more a vote of confidence in speech than is the preference for affirmative. The fact is that Julian's riotous prolixity of affirmative metaphor is no less apophatic than the *Cloud*'s astringency; nor is the language of the *Cloud* any the less dense of metaphor than is Julian's. Though the metaphors differ and the apophatic strategies approach from different directions, they converge in a common perception that all language of God fails all the way along the line (or up the ladder); and in fact, this sense of the simultaneous necessity and deficiency of language is in some ways exhibited more sharply in Julian's habit of constructing metaphors which subvert themselves in the act of their very utterance; as when she shatters the imageries of gender precisely in the exploitation of their full potential: 'In our *Mother* Christ', she says, 'we grow and develop; in *his* mercy *he* reforms and restores us.'[9]

The theologically non-technical Julian of Norwich may seem an unlikely source for the exploration of formal theological epistemologies. Yet her whole text, and nearly every part of it, is governed by that principle explicitly formulated in Bonaventure and Thomas, that theological language as theological is caught within the tensions between saying and unsaying, between the necessity and equal deficiency of all speech, and so reveals the symptoms of the pressures those tensions exert upon it. In fact, to return to Bonaventure, the impression which could be gained from his *Itinerarium*, that he conceives of these affirmative and negative moments of theological utterance as successive phases, first, of pure unproblematical affirmation followed by a second phase of unqualified negation, is

---

[8] The pseudo-Denys does indeed say that 'negations' are more appropriately said of God than are affirmations (*Mystical Theology* 1, 1000B; *Complete Works*, p. 136), but this statement needs to be understood in relation to what he describes as the 'true' apophatic negations, which consist in the negation of the negation between both affirmations and their corresponding negations: the 'Cause of all', he says, is 'considerably prior' to the 'negations . . . beyond every denial, beyond every assertion'; ibid.

[9] *Revelations of Divine Love*, c.58. Though, as Christopher Hilton has pointed out to me, Julian's apophaticism is more formally and systematically expressed in her trinitarian eschatology, in her resolute refusals to 'solve' the problem of sin, and so in her insistence that we cannot know how it is that 'all manner of thing shall be well'.

a disastrous misimpression, visiting catastrophe upon a carefully articulated theological structure.

Affirmative and negative in Bonaventure's Christology: 'statics'

For there are two general principles which organise the structure of the
Itinerarium, embodying, as it were, the theological statics and the theological dynamics. They are of equal theological importance. As to the
'statics', these are most visible in the purely formal elements of exposition
and chapter division of the work, though they are by no means merely
formal in their significance. The work is set out on the model of a 'ladder
of ascent' and so on conventional principles of medieval hierarchy. The
metaphors of 'lower' and 'higher', of 'outer' and 'inner' predominate.
There is no doubt that the *vestigia* of God, which can be read in the 'Book
of Nature', are more 'outer' and 'lower' in their theological significance
than are the *imagines* of God which are read within our inward powers of
the perception of creation. For the contemplation of these *vestigia* in the
book of nature yields knowledge of its author only indirectly. We know the
author thus only from the book, only, that is to say, as what we must say
about God on the evidence with which nature provides us. Thus, from the
Book of Nature we know God only as Creator, and that only by inference
from evidence. But in the book of our inner powers of self-reflection,
that is, of understanding, memory and love – and here Bonaventure does
little more than paraphrase Augustine[10] – we find an image of the inner
life of God himself, a trinitarian life, which those inner powers not only
perceive through that image, but also, through grace, participate in, so
as in a manner to live by that very trinitarian life which they perceive.
Through grace, our remembering and knowing and loving participate in
the relations of Father, Son and Holy Spirit, and so in the inner life by
which they live in the Godhead itself.

Higher yet are those contemplations by which we know God no longer
indirectly through *vestigium* and *imago*, but in some way directly through
concepts proper to God, 'being' and 'goodness'. For to know God as
'existence' is to know God in his own light, for being is God. But our
minds are not naturally habituated to know 'being'; 'being' as such is not
that which we see, for it is particular 'beings' which are the proper objects
of our minds. Rather 'being' is the light in which we see 'beings'. Hence,
when the mind turns its gaze away from particular beings towards the
light of 'being' in which it sees them, it appears to see nothing at all. For

[10] In *De Trinitate* VIII.

just as the eye, intent on the various differences of colour, does not see the light through which it sees other things, or if it does see, does not notice it, so our mind's eye, intent on particular and universal beings, does not notice that being which is beyond all categories, even though it comes first to the mind, and through it all other things. (*Itin.*, 5.4, p. 83)

Thus turned away from 'beings' they are turned towards 'that Being which is called pure being and simple being, and absolute being is the first being, the eternal, the most simple, the most actual, the most perfect, and the supremely one' (*Itin.*, 5.5, p. 85).

Consequently, this knowledge of God, gained from our human grasp of 'being' as supremely One, surpasses our comprehension. For

our mind, accustomed as it is to the opaqueness in beings and the phantasms of visible things, appears to see nothing when it gazes upon the light of the highest being. It does not understand that this very darkness is the supreme illumination of our mind, just as when the eye sees pure light, it seems to see nothing. (*Itin.*, 5.4, p. 83)

Therefore, for Bonaventure, as for Thomas, this incomprehensibility of God derives from the divine simplicity: not that this simplicity of God is such as to remove the possibility of multiple names of God. On the contrary, Bonaventure piles up, as a series of entailments from this very simplicity, predicate after predicate, name after name. God, understood as 'being', is supremely 'one'; but this oneness of God is such that of it every variety of name may be predicated that can be truly predicated of a creature (God is *omnimodum*; *Itin.*, 5.7, p. 87), because God is the supreme cause of everything (ibid.). There is here in Bonaventure, however, a distinctive emphasis not found in Thomas. For as these names pile up in Bonaventure's exposition, one name leading to another – because it is 'being' it is ' simple'; because 'simple', 'first'; because 'first', 'eternal'; because 'eternal', most 'actual'; because 'actual', most 'perfect', and so supremely 'one' (*Itin.*, 5.6, p. 85) – they are increasingly represented in pairs of contraries. For 'being' is *both* 'first' *and* 'last', 'eternal' and 'most present', 'simple' and 'the greatest', 'supremely one' and 'containing every mode' (*omnimodum*); moreover, in each case it is the one *because of* being the other, it is 'precisely the last *because* it is the first', 'entirely present' *because* 'eternal', and so through all the other names which derive from the divine simplicity (*Itin.*, 5.7, pp. 85–7). The result is a complex 'dialectic', and in the very strictest sense of the word: for each name entails, and is entailed by, its contrary.

Therefore, that which is in itself supremely one and simple is known to us only through that dialectical complexity: in God there is a coincidence of opposites, but there is no one name in which they all coincide so that in it their oppositions are reconciled, for each name both entails another and is at the same time opposed by what it entails. If there is a 'dialectic' here it is an unresolved, ultimately 'open' dialectic, by which is defined the ultimate incomprehensibility of the Godhead. If, therefore, the manner of reaching this conclusion differs, the apophatic conclusion is exactly the same as that of Thomas. What we can know of the God of metaphysics, the 'God of reason', is that we cannot know the meaning of that which we must say of him.

Moreover, as in Thomas, the light of Christian faith proper, through which is revealed to us the inner nature of God as a Trinity of persons, does nothing to remedy this apophatic deficiency; rather the emphasis on the divine unknowability is intensified by this revelation. 'When you contemplate these things [of the Trinity], take care that you do not believe you can understand the incomprehensible' (*Itin.*, 6.3, p. 91), Bonaventure says, proceeding to list the names and relations of the Trinity of persons. Each considered singly will lead to the Truth, but compared with one another will 'lift you up to the heights of admiration', such is their irreconcilable complexity (*Itin.*, 6.3, p. 93). But that complexity is brought to its final degree of intensity, and our awe the more provoked, by that most ultimate of all mysteries, which is the hypostatic union of all possible predicates, all the names of all that is, all the names of all creation, the *vestigia* of the external world and the *imagines* of the inner, the names of the highest metaphysical concepts of 'being' and 'goodness', the names of God as One and as Three, united in the two natures in one person, which is Jesus Christ. In Christ is

the first Principle joined with the last. God is joined with man . . . the eternal is joined with time-bound man . . . the most simple is joined with the most composite; the most actual is joined with Him who suffered supremely and died; the most perfect and immense is joined with the insignificant; He who is both supremely one and supremely omnifarious is joined to an individual that is composite and distinct from others, that is to say, to the man Jesus Christ . . . (*Itin.*, 6.5, p. 93)

. . . [who unites] the first and the last, the highest and the lowest, the circumference and the center, the *Alpha* and the *Omega*, the caused and the cause, the Creator and the creature. (*Itin.*, 6.7, p. 95)

It is precisely at this Christological juncture of his exposition that it is possible to see the point of the open-ended apophaticism of Bonaventure's account of the 'being' and 'goodness' of God, his doctrine of the divine oneness and Trinity. For were Bonaventure to have allowed, as any form of possibility to the human mind, whether through its own naturally acquired knowledge or through divine revelation, that that dialectic should close in on a conceptual resolution, on some definition of God, some finally resolved description of the divine nature, then that 'co-incidence of opposites' which so characterises his Christology would have collapsed into the simple incoherence of straightforward contradictori-ness. It is one thing to say that we have to name Christ by so many names that we have no way of knowing how they can thus coexist as true of one and the same person; for that is but to say that the hypostatic union of natures in Christ is an incomprehensible mystery. It is quite another to say that two or more names which we know *could not* coexist, which are contradictories, are true of one and the same subject, for that is quite comprehensibly to say nothing at all about anything, as to say of one and the same shape that it is both a square and a circle is not to say anything, nor is it anything said *about* anything.

Now it is precisely because we know that we cannot know the *quid est* of God – that we cannot know the divine nature – that it follows that to say of one and the same person that he is both human and divine cannot be a contradiction. For the Creator and the creature could stand in relations of exclusion one of the other, as circles and squares do, only if the Creator stood on the same ground as the creature such that the one could exclude the other from it.[11] Bonaventure's elaborate – indeed sometimes baroquely rhetorical – rehearsal of the 'coincidence of opposites' within the divine oneness and Trinity is designed not to show that contradictory predicates are true of God, but that those things must be affirmed of the divine being in such a degree of complexity that there could not be any proper concept of God at all: we simply could not know what it is to be God. If it follows from this that the union of the Creator in the creature must be utterly incomprehensible to us, this is also to show that that union is not impossible with the impossibility of an incoherent self-contradictoriness. Because, and only if, God is unknowable to us is the Chalcedonian doctrine of Christ possible.

Therefore, if Christ is truly 'the *image* of the invisible God' (*Itin.*, 6.7, p. 95), then equally this same Christ is our access precisely to that invisi-bility itself; if Christ is, in some sort, a résumé of all the created order, that book in which some knowledge of the author can be read, then equally it is in Christ that the unknowable mystery of that author is most deeply inten-sified. In Christ, therefore, are united and intensified to their maximal degree both all that can be said about God and the incomprehensibil-ity of that speech, its failure. In Christ we learn how to speak of God; but in Christ we discover that speech to be broken open into brilliant failure – a knowing-unknowing, a 'brilliant darkness'. It is impossible, in

---

[11] For further discussion of this point, see pp. 216–20 below.

Bonaventure, to construe the darkness of God and the light of Christ in opposition to each other.

Affirmative and negative in the Christology of Bonaventure: 'dynamics'

Which brings us to the 'dynamics' of the structure of the *Itinerarium*. We have noted that the hierarchical principles of Bonaventure's exposition could lead us to read the movement from *vestigia* through *imagines* to the highest concepts of God, from 'outer' to 'inner' thence 'above', as successive phases of affirmativeness into an ultimate negativity. But such a reading is defensible only on neglect of a contrary movement of 'centring', a movement which clearly predominates in Bonaventure's thought. In any case, as I have explained elsewhere,[12] within the classical medieval accounts, even hierarchical structures are not properly understood in terms of a simple successiveness; for each level in a hierarchical order 'contains' and 'resumes' the levels below it. From 'above', as it were, hierarchy has to be understood inclusively; it is only from 'below' that there is any 'exclusion'. From 'below', therefore, what we know of God from *vestigia* provides no access to what we know of God from *imagines*. From 'above', however, what we can know of God from *imagines* includes all that we can know from *vestigia*. If, therefore, the static structure of the *Itinerarium* would suggest a rising scale of 'knowing-unknowing', from our imperfect and indirect knowledge of God in inanimate nature, to the perfect image of God in Christ, we shall have to remember that in Christ is resumed, as in a *minor mundus* (*Itin.*, 2.3, p. 53), all that can be known of God from all creation and all revelation.[13]

It is in Christ, therefore, that the structuring hierarchical principle of 'ascent' converges upon a centripetal Christological dynamic: all creation and all divinity centre upon the hypostatic union in Christ, there to be dissolved in the dramatic destruction of Christ's death on the cross. Just as we might have thought that some higher synthesis had been achieved, some resolution which held together within a comprehensive and comprehensible grasp the apparent opposition between the human and the

---

[12] See my *Darkness of God*, pp. 113–14.

[13] Christopher Hilton puts it neatly (in a draft of his Cambridge PhD dissertation on *The Theology of Contemplative Prayer: The Shewings of Julian of Norwich and its Later Appropriations*): 'The *scala* [of Bonaventure's *Itinerarium*] should be seen not as a linear ladder, but as a circular stairway where with each turn of the stairway the climber comes again to the same place on the circumference of the circle, but on a higher, richer, more complex level. With each level the climber is able to see the inclusive relation of the steps . . . The circular stairway has joined earth with heaven, with the Crucified as the central core around which the stair turns necessarily at all levels.'

divine, between the temporal and the eternal, between the divine simplicity and unity and the diverse complexity of creation, that resolution
is dashed from our hands by the *transitus*, the 'passing over' into death,
which is Christ's passion; 'in this passing over', Bonaventure tells us,
'Christ is the way and the door' (*Itin.*, 7.1, p. 97).

> Let us, then, die and enter into this darkness. Let us silence all our care, our
> desires, and our imaginings. With Christ crucified, let us pass *out of this world to
> the Father*, so that, when the Father is shown to us, we may say with Philip: *It is
> enough for us* [Jn, 13:1]. (*Itin.*, 7.6, p. 101)

In Christ, therefore, is resumed all our knowledge of God, indirect and
inferential through the external created order of nature, 'inner' through
the graced image of the Trinity in the soul, 'above', through our understanding of the highest names of God; and in Christ is resumed also the
'passing over' of all that knowing into the darkness of unknowing, both
the affirmativity and the negativity and the interactions of the one with
the other, their simultaneous necessity and deficiency: all are in Christ,
and are demanded, as necessities of Christological theology. Therefore,
if we do our natural theology, our metaphysics of God, if our epistemology must be formulated in terms of complex articulations of the relations
between the apophatic and the cataphatic, it is because of, not in spite of,
what a properly Christian theology demands of the human mind. Indeed
it is *in* Christ, especially in the cross of Christ, that those articulations are
most concretely realised.

It is in some such terms that we can speak of Bonaventure's 'mystical theology'. For if, speaking now quite generally, the 'mystical' is in
some way tied up with the moment of theological negation, of a 'passing
beyond', and if, on an adequate account of the apophatic dimension of
theological discourse, it has to be understood as determinative of that
discourse as mystical in principle and as such; then this can be so only
in so far as we have abandoned a whole raft of accounts of the relations
between the 'apophatic' and the 'cataphatic'. For we are diverted from
this account in so far as we suppose that there is some such discourse
as 'apophatic discourse'. The apophatic is not given in some negative
vocabulary which takes over from the affirmative when we get a mystical urge; it is not engaged in by means of some negative chasing game
with the affirmative up the ladder of speech about God, thus at the top
either to win or to lose out to the affirmative. Rather it is that the tensions between affirmation and negation within all theological speech are,
precisely, what determine it to be theological speech, and to be, in the
only worthwhile sense of the term, 'mystical'. In Bonaventure's terms,
therefore, the 'mystical' is essentially incarnational and Christological.

Moreover, those tensions which characterise theological language at once as theological and as mystical are finally unresolvable: the necessity of our linguistic resources of theology can never supply their deficiency; nor can the perception of their deficiency ever reduce the necessity of them. We know both the need for, and the failure of, theological talk simultaneously in the one act of its utterance; we both say and unsay in the same theological word. And if these constraints of thought and speech hold for Bonaventure's Christocentric theology, demanding of him a philosophical epistemology equal to the theological claims made upon it, they will be seen to hold for Thomas's account of Eucharistic presence: as in Bonaventure, for Thomas, these dynamic interactions of the affirmative and negative are demanded by theological exigencies and by the nature of faith itself in its doctrinal articulations.

Presence and absence in Thomas's Eucharistic theology

Our merely illustrative examination of Thomas's Eucharistic theology may begin in an iconographical setting. In the once medieval Catholic, now Calvinist-maintained, cathedral at Bern in Switzerland, one is confronted by a visibly Calvinist architectural revision. Altars once richly ornamented are stripped; niches once containing images of saints are now empty; walls, once brilliantly hued, whitewashed; the glass now plain; the orientation reversed, the stalls facing north, not east. The effect is dramatic, not merely because of the powerful but relative impact of the stripped-out decorative condition of the cathedral – relative, that is to expectations which derive from our historical knowledge of what is missing, its former ornateness of iconography, its lurid colour schemes, its architectural orientation towards a high altar in the east. For the overwhelming sense of 'absence' is reinforced by the more absolute and architecturally organic effect of the Gothic style itself, which could be said to give priority to the engineering and organisation of space rather than to the articulation of solid mass. Bern Cathedral is now, one might say, a place of absence, indeed a holy 'place of absence' or a place which 'sacralises' absence, a place fit for a community witnessing to absence. It 'speaks' absence as a theological – and still to some degree as a theological-polemical – and liturgical statement.

But if we were to turn history back to the year 1500 we should have to reconstruct the former condition of the cathedral, to fill its niches with statues of saints, the Virgin Mary and Christ, and the windows with glass representing Moses and the prophets in the north transept, the apostles in the south, the ascension in the west end and the resurrection in the east; we should need to daub the walls with colour and picture, and above all to refocus the building upon an elaborate triptych before which stands an ornate and elevated altar at the east end – in short, to re-equip the cathedral with all that, one may reasonably imagine, was stripped from it forty years later. What will then be the theological-liturgical statement which in that condition the appointments of the cathedral make? The answer would seem to be obvious. Here you have a statement of 'holy presence', a fullness of theological affirmation, a space filled with presence and with a community in that presence.

And it might seem obvious in what the contrast between the present condition of the church and its former state consists. Now its architecture is rhetorically apophatic, then it was cataphatic; now it witnesses to a Zwinglian theology of Eucharistic absence, then to a Catholic theology of Eucharistic presence. Superficially these things are obvious, and since they are even, in a way, true, let us spell them out a little more fully.

Return then to the cathedral in 1500. It is full. But what it is full of is sign. Therefore, it might be said – but on a certain account of signs with which, I shall argue, it is not possible to be entirely happy – that it is 'full of absence'. I once facetiously explained to a student that you could account for the difference between the Catholic and the Protestant view of the presence of Christ in the Eucharist by analogy with a conference meal-ticket which he had been showing me. The Protestant thinks that the meal-ticket represents the meal you can purchase by means of it; the Catholic eats the meal-ticket, thinking that that is what you are getting for lunch. Of course, this is a travesty of the difference; indeed, a common sixteenth-century Protestant travesty of it, for this version of what Catholics believe entirely ignores what Catholic theology had always been fully aware of, namely the distinction between the material reality of the signifier and the formal character of the sign precisely as signifying. And of course in that formal character the sign signifies the body and blood of Christ precisely in so far as they are 'absent', where 'absence' is defined by contrast with the material presence of the sign itself; and so, in so far as by signifying the body and blood of Christ the appearances of bread and wine make them present in one way, they do so only in so far as in another, that is, in the manner in which the sign itself is present, they are absent.

It is for this reason that Zwingli is, of course, right, and in agreement with Thomas at this single point of convergence, when he says that Christ cannot be present *in* the Eucharist in the way in which the sign itself is present in its material reality, that is to say, as in this place. And Thomas and Zwingli agree on this notwithstanding the difference that for Thomas the bread and wine *become* the body and blood of Christ which they signify, whereas for Zwingli they only *signify* the body and blood of Christ. For both, however, the material sign – the bread and wine – are present in a time and place, here in Bern in 1500. And if Christ is anywhere locally in 1500 it is not, as Thomas agrees, where the bread and wine are in Bern in 1500. For Christ has risen, is ascended into heaven, and is seated at the right hand of the Father.[14]

But, for Zwingli, a theology of the Eucharist need say no more than this about its character as a 'sign': all you need to say about the presence of Christ in the Eucharist is that he is there 'in the sign' only; and all you need to say about the absence of Christ is that Christ's not being there is in the Eucharist's character as a sign, for on this account signs displace the reality of what they signify, it being the sign which is really present, and so not the signified. For Thomas the position appears to be quite different and fraught with much tougher problems, and for reasons which show that his agreement with Zwingli about the meaning of 'absence' is at best superficial. Thomas wants to say that Christ is really present, and *also* absent. But, whereas Zwingli thinks this absence simply follows from the nature of a sign as such, so that the sign's 'real presence' excludes the real presence of what it signifies, it is not clear that Thomas maintained that view of signs at all. In any case, for him sacramental signs constitute a set of special cases, in which the conditions of absence follow not as such from the nature of signs but from the nature of a sacrament, and in the very special case of the Eucharist the necessity of Christ's absence does not exclude the real presence of Christ, but rather lays down conditions for the description of that real presence. For Thomas, therefore, if you are going to say that Christ is 'really present' in the Eucharist, your account of the word 'real' is going to have to begin from the fact that he cannot be there as in that place (*localiter*), because he is raised and ascended to the Father in heaven. And that starting point lays down three conditions for the meaning of the word 'real' as said of the Eucharistic presence: first, Christ is not there as he was in his historical *pre-mortem* existence; second, that though it is the risen Christ, ascended into heaven, who is present in the Eucharist, Christ is not there as, in the kingdom, he will be seen by us at the right hand of the Father; yet, third, any meaning of the word 'real' requires that the Christ who is present in the Eucharist is numerically one and the same Christ as he who once walked the shores of Lake Galilee and is now at the right hand of the Father.

---

[14] *ST* 3a q75, a2, *corp.* where Thomas argues, exactly as Zwingli, that Christ could not be present *locally* in the Eucharist, else he would have left heaven: 'corpus Christi non incipit esse in hoc sacramento per motum localem . . . quia sequeretur quod desineret esse in coelo'. Christ 'is not present in the Eucharist simply as in a sign, however, even if every sacrament is a kind of sign, [but rather] in the manner appropriate to this sacrament' – 'non intelligimus quod Christi sit ibi solum sicut in signo, licet sacramentum sit in genere signi . . . secundum modum proprium huic sacramento'. *ST* 3a q75 a1 ad3.

From this it follows that if Christ is really present in the Eucharist then he will have to be present in the Eucharist in his body. For no sense of Christ's presence which evacuates it of bodiliness will have the force of being 'real', since numerical identity of persons requires sameness of body. Hence, to capture the force of the word 'real' as said of Christ's presence in the Eucharist, we shall have to say that he is present in his body, but neither in the natural condition as known to Peter and James and John two thousand years ago, nor as they now know him in his and their condition as raised in the beatific vision of heaven. So the question for Thomas is not whether Christ is present in the Eucharist as in a sign *as opposed* to his being present there 'really'; it is rather, given that Christ is present in the Eucharist as in a sign, how we can find a sense for the word 'real' which is consistent with the Eucharist's eschatological temporality. In short, the core problem for Thomas's account of the Eucharist is the problem of how the future – the kingdom of our communication with the risen Christ, the resurrection – can be bodily present now to us, given our fallen and failing, as yet unraised, powers of bodily communication and given his raised and totally communicating body. And that problem of how the raised person of Jesus is present in the body to us in our as yet unraised bodies just is the problem of how to do a 'negative theology' of the Eucharist. The need for a negative theology arises out of Eucharistic exigencies.

Zwingli, by contrast, thinks that he has no such problem, and that no Christian ought to have it. But in this he appears to be mistaken. For turn again to our metaphor of the stripped-down cathedral of 1535. Here the relations of 'presence' and 'absence' are worked out along altogether different lines. Whereas in 1500 the repleteness of signs works its power of signifying only in the medium, as it were, of the absence of what is signified, in 1535 it is absence which is the very sign itself. In 1535 it is emptiness of sign which *is* the sign, its emptiness in no way diminishing the cathedral's character of being a sign, for just as negative metaphors are still metaphors, negative signs, for all their negativity, are still signs. Note that the 1535 cathedral can effect its negative signification only if it contains no signs at all. It could not do its work of signifying absence if there were a single sign in the cathedral, for the incomplete emptiness would simply have the effect of focussing attention upon the signifying power of that one sign; the cathedral would then be full of that single sign. As a matter of fact, the cathedral is possessed of one sign which draws attention to itself in that way, but that sign only reinforces the sense of absence, for it is itself empty, being a vacant cross. So here too the cathedral, its emptiness, is 'full of sign', for the signs of absence are not the absence of signs.

Hence, if the 1535 condition of the cathedral signifies by means of its absence of sign, if, to repeat, it is absence which is the sign, that absence can possess no less the materiality of a sign than does the fullness of sign in 1500. It may be a mistake to eat the meal-ticket thinking it is the meal; but if that is the case it is exactly the same mistake to identify the physical, material absences of Zwingli's cathedral with the absence of Christ which they signify. For if our analogy between the two conditions of the cathedral and the relations between affirmative and negative theology holds in general, it holds very particularly here. Just as affirmative and negative metaphors are equally metaphors; just as affirmation and negation are equally linguistic acts; just as the 'mystical' is therefore characterised by its transcendence of both affirmation and negation, so too are the signs of presence and the signs of absence equally signs, are equally material conditions which signify. Hence, if it is possible materialistically to displace the signified by the reification of the sign in the one case, so it is possible in the other. In short, 'absence' as a sign is but a material state of affairs – specifically, an architectural and decorative state of affairs – which signifies only on condition of the absence of what it signifies. So Zwingli's empty cathedral is not itself the absence of Christ which it signifies, but is only the sign of it, making that absence present only on the condition that it is not the thing itself.

And this seems to be important. Zwingli seems to think that he can overthrow the arguments of the papists simply by appeal to the bodily absence of Christ since the ascension. It is enough to overthrow those arguments that Christ is not 'there' *localiter*. Constantly in his polemic *On the Lord's Supper*[15] he appeals to John 16:5–11, where Jesus tells his disciples that it is to their advantage that he go away, 'for if I do not go away the Counsellor will not come to you' (John 16:7). So, Zwingli comments,

> if he has gone away, if he has left the world, then either the Creed is unfaithful to the word of Christ, which is impossible (for it affirms that he will be with us always) or else the body and blood of Christ cannot be present in the sacrament. (Ibid., p. 214)

Hence Zwingli, maintaining, as Thomas does, that Christ is not present in the sign *localiter*, draws the conclusion, which Thomas rejects, that what is present is the sign of absence, a presence of Christ in the sign, on condition that Christ is not really present in body and blood. Given, then,

---

[15] Ulrich Zwingli, *On the Lord's Supper*, in *Zwingli and Bullinger*, ed. and trans. G. W. Bromiley, Library of Christian Classics XXIV, London: SCM Press, 1953, pp. 195–238.

that Zwingli's starting point is an account of sign such that the presence of a thing in a sign *excludes* its being present as 'real' – a word the force of which Zwingli, like the Catholics, takes to mean 'in his body' – he naturally concludes that

[a] sacrament is the sign of a holy thing. When I say: 'the sacrament of the Lord's body', I am simply referring to that bread which is the symbol of the body of Christ who was put to death for our sakes . . . But the very body of Christ is the body which is seated at the right hand of God, and the sacrament of his body is the bread and the sacrament of his blood is the wine . . . Now the sign and the thing signified cannot be one and the same. Therefore the sacrament of the body of Christ cannot be the body itself. (Ibid., p. 188)

And so the root difference between Zwingli and Thomas becomes clear: Zwingli's 'Eucharistic' absence is the simple *material* absence of Christ's body *localiter*, an absence which Thomas can concede. For Zwingli, however, this 'absence' is such as to exclude 'real presence'. For Thomas, on the contrary, the presence of Christ in the Eucharist is the real presence of Christ's body. But the force of the word 'real' is such as to require an absence which is *eschatological*. For what the Eucharist 'realises' is a bodily presence which is not yet, a *real* absence, a body making really present that of which, as yet, we cannot take possession. For Christ's body is raised, and our bodies are not. Hence, if we cannot, in the fallen condition of our bodiliness, enter fully into communication with the presence of the absent, because raised, person of Jesus, then neither can we enter fully into communication with that absence. For just as we cannot yet know that kingdom which one day we shall see and fully enjoy, so neither can we have any grasp of how far we fall short of communicating with it. We fail even in our calculation of the degree to which our Eucharistic communication fails. Hence, if there is a problem about how Christ is present in the Eucharistic sign there must equally be a problem of accounting for how that absence is present within it; and that problem is not to be resolved on any account of the nature of signs, but only on some account of the relationship between the apophatic and the cataphatic, that relationship being itself defined only under the constraint of the eschatological. If, therefore, we ask: 'How is Christ present in the Eucharist?' Thomas's answer is: 'Really, as bodies are present to one another.' And if you ask: 'How is Christ's body present?' Thomas's answer is: 'Sacramentally', that is, 'eschatologically', as the raised body of Jesus can be present to us in our *pre-mortem* condition as unraised. And that is a mode of 'real absence' as much as it is a mode of 'real presence'. For such is the nature of a sacrament.

'Effecting what is signified'

Which brings us to the issue of sacramental efficacy. Since the twelfth century it has commonly been said to be in the nature of a sacrament to 'effect what it signifies'. And while there is no call to quibble with this formula as such, it needs to be said that, largely because of post-medieval and distinctly empiricist notions of causality, it is now a highly misleading formula. For these reasons.

I have suggested that we ought to distinguish between the formal character of a sign in virtue of which it signifies and its material existence as an event or thing in the world. Now I propose to misuse a famous distinction of J. L. Austin's between 'illocutionary' and 'perlocutionary' performative speech-acts, so as to distinguish, in analogous fashion, within types of performative, between what one might call the formal and material efficacy of a performative utterance, and so between what you are doing *in* saying something – for example, promising in uttering the words 'I promise' – and what you are doing *by means of* saying it – for example, misleading the promisee when you have no intention of carrying out the promise.[16] We might, even more generally, distinguish between what it is that your words effect in virtue of what they mean and what it is that your act of saying those words effects in virtue of their being uttered. This distinction is easiest to see in the case of what we might call 'performative contradictions', where the two fall apart: arguing at tedious length in favour of maximum participation at the seminar means one thing, which the prolixity of your saying it inhibits; reading the Riot Act, as in 1922 the British army officer did to a peaceful assembly of striking Welsh miners, means: 'Behave in an orderly fashion, or else I shall use military force to disperse you', but the intended (and actual) effect was so to anger the miners as to provoke the riotous behaviour it prohibits, thus to justify employing the force the Act then permits; or, more recently, creating racial conflict in the manner of the late British member of Parliament, Enoch Powell, by means of lurid warnings against its dangers; these are all cases in which people subvert what they are saying by the act of saying it. They say one thing, but what their saying of it does says the opposite.

Now this last formula may need a little explanation. It is possible to balk at the notion of an utterance being 'contradicted by' its being uttered, since only meanings can be in relations of contradiction with one another, not actions with meanings. But the notion is not after all so problematic. We are, since Austin, accustomed to the notion of a performative

---

[16] J. L. Austin, *How to Do Things with Words* (Oxford: Oxford University Press, 1962), pp. 7–11.

utterance. We ought to be as used, since Wittgenstein, to the notion of an uttering performance, that is to say, of an action's bearing meaning. We all know that actions 'speak', and, that being so, we should note that utterings too are actions. There ought therefore to be little difficulty with the notion that utterances not only utter what the words spoken say, but also, being actions, can speak *qua performances*. For this reason, there ought to be no greater difficulty in principle with the analysis of the recursively contradictory behaviour, say, of the parent who smacks the child in order to teach her not to solve problems by means of violence.

Now rituals and liturgies are, *par excellence*, complex behaviours constituted by their interactions of performative utterances and uttering performances. Every liturgical action gets its rationale from what it means, which is to say, every liturgical action is a sign; and the central utterances of a Eucharistic liturgy are performative utterances: they are signs 'which effect what they signify', they *do* what they *say*. The utterance 'I baptise you' *baptises*; the priest's saying 'This is my body' over what appears to be bread makes 'this' *to be* the body of Christ.[17]

These distinctions are, at least theoretically, fairly clear. All the same, there lies in them a source of very common confusion. I have suggested that Austin's distinction between an 'illocutionary' and a 'perlocutionary' speech-act roughly corresponds with my distinction between what an utterance effects by virtue of its meaning and what the action of uttering effects by virtue of that action's meaning. There is, of course, a distinction between my uttering the words 'I promise', which, by virtue of the meaning of the utterance, enacts a promise, and the effect which flows from my uttering it; for example, your being persuaded that I mean what I say. An illocutionary act performs what it says by virtue of what the words mean;[18] the words of a promise do not *cause* a promise to be made, they *are*, appropriate conditions being met, a promise made. By contrast, a perlocutionary effect is caused by an utterance; by promising I have caused you to have confidence in my word. Now there are many

---

[17] Thomas contemplates a conundrum at *ST* 3a q78 a5 *corp.*: are the words of institution true? He replies that they are, notwithstanding the objection that the 'this' in 'this is my body' cannot refer at the time of utterance to anything but the bread, since it is not until the utterance of the whole formula that the bread is changed into the body of Christ. The problem does not arise, he says, because the utterance is not a mere *description* of what is the case, but is one which *makes* 'this bread' to be the body of Christ: the utterance realises its own truth in practice, or, as he agrees, *efficit quod figurat*, 'makes to be what it discloses'.

[18] Of course, generally speaking it will do so only under 'due conditions', as Austin says (*How to Do Things with Words*, pp. 8–9). A 'practice Mass' is not a Mass; the Queen's rehearsing the words of naming the ship do not name the ship; telling someone what 'I promise to pay you five pounds' means is not to promise that person five pounds. Performatives are not magic incantations.

who confuse the two, and I suspect that Zwingli is one such. But then perhaps he is no more confused than some contemporary theologians of the Eucharist.

For the effects of a liturgy's system of signs being enacted are not to be confused with what those signs realise as sacramental signs. For Thomas, the efficacy of a sacrament is guaranteed by God and is brought about, in the sign, by God alone. But God does not guarantee, for any ritual whatever, that the empirical effects it gives rise to as perlocution are just those which, as sacramental sign, the ritual act signifies and effects.

A somewhat stereotyped if not entirely fanciful example may serve to illustrate, by analogy, some of the complexity with which illocutionary and perlocutionary forces interact with one another. Let us suppose a celibate male preacher delivering his sermon, as it were, from the height of his authoritarian pulpit, on the equality of all the people of God, priests and laypeople, women and men. Now we should not, on the strength of the distinction I have made between the formal message of a speech-act and the perlocutionary message of its being uttered, analyse these elements into separate, unrelated factors, the egalitarian communication and the fact that, as it happens, it is delivered from an authoritarian pulpit by a member of an exclusively male priesthood. For the point about the authoritarian pulpit and the exclusive maleness of the priest is that they are in themselves already sermons: as I said, actions also speak, as do this pulpit and the maleness of this priest, which communicate quite effectively enough within the words of the egalitarian sermon. We might suppose it is adequate to say that the pulpit or the maleness is but part of the *materiality* of the preacher's act of saying, as if thereby to suggest that it can play no part in the total communicative act. But this would be to misdescribe the distinction. The pulpit communicates too, as does the exclusivity of the priest's gender, for they both internalise and exhibit the character of the preacher's relationship with the congregation, and the significance of that materiality – its possessing its own meaning – practises its own hermeneutic upon the explicit formal meanings of the preacher's words. This is why the performance of an utterance can 'contradict' the utterance it performs, as in this case. For here those words of the preacher become the bearer of a condensation of conflicting meanings which, precisely in so far as that complex semantic whole lies outside the intended communication of the preacher, exists independently of those intentions, while at the same time subverting them. The total result is a social reality constructed upon a contradictoriness which is internal to the communicative act.

For it is in the facts of this contradiction that the members of the worshipping community are socialised. They perceive their relationship to the act of worship via the condensation of contradictory meanings, for at one level they attend, perhaps with approval, to the egalitarian message of the preacher and *in so doing* they reciprocate the authoritarianism of his act of saying it. Consequently, the preacher and the congregation enact a relationship constituted by the contradiction in which they are jointly socialised. Thus as they live out their relationship with the egalitarianism of the preacher's message through the authoritarian structures of its communication, so they live out their relationships with the authoritarianism of those structures through mystified categories of egalitarianism. In short, what such rituals effect is a rupture between what the ritual signifies as illocution and what it effects as perlocution. And when a ritual effects this rupture as a routine – when, in other words, it socialises the participants in this rupturing – then we can say that such rituals have the character of a certain kind of 'false consciousness', as Marxists used to say. In more theological terms we can also say that they parodise the sacramental character which they are supposed to exhibit. For they are rituals whose effects *contradict* what they signify: thus do the participants, as Paul says, 'eat and drink judgement on themselves' (1 Cor. 11:29).

Now these phenomena of bastard liturgies all have to do with the *perlocutionary* effects of the enactment of liturgical signs, in other words with what, as perlocutions, the signs effect under certain empirical conditions of their reception. The issues which arise here are altogether different from (if not entirely unrelated to) the issue of the *sacramental* efficacy of a sign, which is not in the same way causal. For if the Eucharistic 'presence' is to be seen, as I have suggested it must, as an act of radical communication – the 'Word' – spoken to us by the Father in Jesus, then the signs which sacramentally 'effect' that communication must be seen as more like Austin's illocutions than like his perlocutions, and the causal language of the traditional formula as in some way obscuring that distinction. For the way in which the Father communicates with us in Jesus through the eating of bread and wine is efficacious of that communication rather more in the way in which to say the words 'I promise' *is* to promise, *is* to communicate in that way, not, as Austin says, as being the *cause* of some mysterious 'promising event' over and above that communication. Thus too, the uttering of the words 'This is my body' and the subsequent eating and drinking of what appears to be bread and wine is not in a quasi-perlocutionary fashion the *cause of* something miraculous *by means of* a communication: it *is* the communication, or, as we say, the communion, in the body and blood of Christ. That is how Christ is present, not the less 'really' because it is a communication through signs, as if by saying it is a 'communication' one had denied that it was 'real'. For that is pure Zwinglianism.

And so we return to the central point of Thomas's Eucharistic theology. The Eucharist is the presence of Jesus' raised body – the resurrection – in so far as it can be present as communication to our unraised bodies. At the heart of Thomas's theology of the Eucharist is the conviction that the resurrection of Jesus does not diminish his bodiliness. It fulfils it: we might say that it radicalises it. In his natural life, Jesus' presence was limited by time and space and contingency, for his body was thus limited. We should not say: Jesus' presence, his availability, his power to communicate, was limited by his body. We should say rather: his power to communicate was limited by his body's mortality, by its being a 'body of death'. Therefore, by overcoming death Jesus' body was released from its limitations; and so, raised by his Father to immortality, he was more 'present' – signified more – to his disciples in the room when, after his resurrection, he ate a fish with them, than he had been when on the hillside he multiplied loaves and fishes – not less. He is more present to us now, in the Eucharist, than he could have been had we walked with him on the shores of Lake Galilee – not less. And so he is more bodily now, precisely as signifying more fully now when raised, not less, than before his death:[19] this presence of mine, he said to his disciples, is not that of a ghost (Luke 24:39).

But if that is how Christ is present to us – in an act of radical communication – it is also how Christ is absent. For until we too are raised, that communication with the risen Jesus can only fail of ultimacy. The Eucharist is not yet the kingdom of the future as it will be in the future. It points to it as absent, not because, as a sign, it is in the nature of signs to signify in the absence of the signified, but because by means of the Father's action this human, bodily, sign of eating and drinking acquires a depth, an 'inwardness' of meaning, which realises the whole nature of our historical condition: what, in its essential brokenness, the Eucharist haltingly and provisionally signifies, can be fully realised only by the sacrament's abolition in the kingdom itself. The Eucharistic sign, the bodily acts of eating and drinking, thus caught up in this eschatological two-sidedness, becomes thereby and necessarily a two-sided sign:[20] it is affirmation interpenetrated by negation, presence interpenetrated by absence; and it is *that* complexity of utterance, of 'sign', which is made 'real' in the Eucharist, inscribed within a *body's* presence.

In this perspective it is now possible to see just what is wrong with Zwingli's 'absence'. It is a one-sided absence which gets its meaning by

---

[19] For further discussion of this relationship between bodiliness and significance, see pp. 89–94 below.
[20] Cf. *ST* 3a q73 a4 *corp.*

reaction against a rather mechanistically causalist account of Eucharistic efficacy: as if the doctrine of real presence he denies maintained that the sign 'effects what it signifies' in a perlocutionary manner, such that the uttering of the words pulls off the effect of Christ's presence in the way in which a provocative remark pulls off a provocation; so that, if you are to deny that account, the only thing you are left with is sign, with no 'reality' effected, a sort of one-sided negativity. As we have seen, this is not in any case what the formula means, even if there are indeed Catholic theologians who, unlike Thomas, appear to have thought it. But then Zwingli does not reject that position in the name of any less mechanistic an account of sacramental efficacy, since for him no account of Christ's presence as 'real' is possible other than in such mechanistically causal terms. As a consequence, for him, what the sign effects is merely the negative significance of absence in the minds of the Eucharistic community.

And this, in the end, is what, in Zwingli's account, 'overthroweth the nature of the sacrament', namely that he supposes the efficacy of the sacrament to lie in what it causes to occur 'in the mind' *by contrast with* what occurs 'in reality'. Zwingli's theological opponents, of course, will only reinforce the error of Zwingli's ways if they affirm, as Zwingli thought they did, that what the sacrament effects is something 'in reality' by contrast with its occurring 'in the mind', or 'in the sign'. And those opponents might be all the more tempted to say such things when they hear it said, as I have explained Thomas to be saying, that what the sacrament effects is an act of 'radical communication'; at any rate, they will be so tempted in so far as they suppose, as many nowadays seem to suppose, that communication itself is something which occurs 'in the mind' rather than 'in reality'. But Thomas, at any rate, will have nothing to do with such epistemologies, which split off from one another the 'significant' from the 'real' and the 'real' from the body – if only for the sake of a coherent theology of Eucharistic presence. For Thomas, it is within such a theology that the dialectic of affirmation and negation, of the darkness of God and the light of Christ, is first, that is to say, primordially, located and sourced. It is located, for Thomas, in the body, in a bodily action so caught up in the eschatological temporality of faith that body and communication, matter and significance, become entirely transparent to one another, all significance and all body and the one because of the other. This, for Thomas, is the general significance of the Eucharist as sacrament: it is the body as language, our language of communion with one another made into the Father's language of communion with us through Christ, who is at once present and absent. And it is that dialectic of presence and absence which is made real, 'realised', in the Eucharist. For Thomas, then, this doctrine of the Eucharistic presence is not formed by that dialectic – as if those relations of affirmativity and negativity stood preformed in some Platonic or pagan philosophy of language about God thus to determine the shape of Eucharistic theology *a priori*. Rather it is the reverse: for Thomas it is in the eschatological dynamic of the Eucharist, and so in the more general character of sacramentality as such, that the complexities of presence and absence, of realisation and failure, of its multi-faceted temporalities, are forced upon us as quite universal and constitutive features of theological language as such. And for that matter it is in the equally oxymoronic dialectic of visibility and invisibility in Bonaventure's Chalcedonian Christology, and of oneness and threeness in Nicaean trinitarian orthodoxy, that those Platonic dialectics of affirmation and negation are forced upon us as theological necessities of thought. Giving a coherent conceptual construction on those dialectics requires much philosophy, one which is no doubt in Thomas's case, as in Bonaventure's, indebted to their Neoplatonic forebears. But it is the philosophy which yields to, and does not impose, the radicalness of faith's claims upon it.

4   Intellect

If we may fairly say that in the general character of an argument for the existence of God (as Thomas conceives of it) there converge the twin pressures of the knowability and the unknowability of God – of the cataphatic and the apophatic; and if, as we saw in the last chapter, those pressures converging in a rational proof but replicate the structural exigencies of faith itself; and if, more specifically, they replicate a certain sacramentally 'mystical' structure of faith, we must next, in this and the next two chapters, begin a more explicit exploration of *how* reason, in the exercise of its own native powers, in some way 'replicates' or 'anticipates' this shape of faith. But it will be clear from the outset that any such conception of reason will, in principle, run counter to those current within our own contemporary culture, whether formally philosophical, or more casually prevailing. For it is, it seems, a characteristic of many of our contemporary theological epistemologies that this delicately constructed tension between the apophatic and the cataphatic *within* both reason and faith has been readjusted into a polarity between the negative possibilities of reason and the positive possibilities of faith. Among theologians the view which predominates therefore tends, by comparison with that of Thomas, to a generalised sceptical negativity concerning reason, combined with a theological positivism concerning faith.

That being so, it may come as something of a surprise that Thomas insists so resolutely upon an apophaticism across the whole range occupied by both reason and faith. For as to reason, Thomas's optimistic insistence that, as I hope to show, a rational proof of God is possible, combines with the pessimistic insistence that such proof proves the existence only of an unknowable God. Hence, his position contrasts sharply in two ways with the mainstream tendencies within modern theology: first, with that pessimistic rational scepticism which denies proof on the grounds that to permit it would concede too much to a rationally knowable God; and secondly, as to faith, Thomas's pessimistically apophatic account of it will perhaps all the more surprise, since the theological positivists will ask: 'Do we not, then, know more about God through the revelation of Jesus Christ than we can know by reason?' After all, is not Christ the 'image of the invisible God'?

As we have seen, Thomas's articulation of the relations between the 'cataphatic' and 'apophatic' cuts across both reason and faith. It does not in any way cut *between* them. And Milbank is therefore right to insist upon the most fundamental principle of that articulation, which is that you cannot construe Thomas as having opposed a simple apophaticism of reason to a simple cataphaticism of faith. For whatever Thomas's view of the distinction may be between a philosophical and a revealed theology, it cannot consist in philosophy's being capable of an answer to the question whether God exists (*an est*), but incapable of an answer to the question what God is (*quid est*), of which revealed theology is capable: for 'both can do the former', he says, and 'neither can do the latter'.[1] This is clearly Thomas's view, though Thomas's apophaticism is from one point of view even more radical than Milbank's formula might suggest: unaided reason's is the less powerful theological capacity, for it knows only the half even of our ignorance. For through revelation we know that there is more to the unknowability of God than reason could ever have suspected: after all, reason does not know that it knows nothing of the inner trinitarian life of God, or of the incarnation of the Word in Jesus. Even more, reason only half-knows even what it does know that it cannot know. For through faith that unknowability is deepened experientially, and not merely extended; for faith is the manner of our participation in the unknowability of God, so that that unknowable mystery grounds not merely our thought – as philosophy does, knowing the divine darkness only, as it were, from within its own incapacity for it and from the outside – but also our personhood and identity and agency and our community. As Thomas says, through grace '*we are made one with* [*God*] as to something unknown'.

The retreat from intellect: medieval 'affectivism'

If such is the widespread modern orthodoxy, a more common late medieval revision of Thomas's position shares with the modern its scepticism of the rational, while in at least one respect sharing with Thomas his apophaticism about faith. For even in Thomas's own time, and before, we encounter a rising tide of late medieval anti-intellectualism which became a flood in the fourteenth and fifteenth centuries, a tendency – it is not a

---

[1] See Milbank's extended article, 'Intensities', in *Modern Theology* 15.4, October 1999, pp. 445–97. Much, though not all, of this article was republished in the monograph *Truth in Aquinas*, jointly authored by Milbank and Catherine Pickstock, London: Routledge, 2001. For the most part I refer to Milbank's article rather than to the later monograph.

movement, for it characterises a wide diversity of theologies – involving a drastic revision of what may fairly be called a 'classical' conception of 'intellect', and a drastic curtailment of its scope. It is in the fourteenth century at least, if not earlier, that *intellectus* (in the sense of the power of 'understanding') comes close to being identified with *ratio* (in the sense of the power of 'ratiocination'), that is to say, of philosophical argument.

It is safe to say that this conceptual revision of an 'intellect' cut back to 'reasoning power' is driven by wider institutional forces, which it is not our place to consider here, except perhaps to say that in consort with the conceptual revision there is a tendency to identify 'intellect' with the sort of reasoning which was thought to go on within the universities, whether in the faculties of Arts or of Divinity, and so to associate both 'intellect' and 'reason' with the dry impotence of the 'academic'. At any rate, in late medieval polemic against the intellectuals unfavourable contrasts are made with ever greater frequency between the sterile theological practices of 'school' theology and those of practical piety; between what is known theologically by the academics exercising their 'intellects' and what is known by the 'knowledge' of love – unfavourably, that is to say, of course, to the former. Even so resolute an 'intellectualist' as the fifteenth-century Denys the Carthusian (1402–70) has bitterly to admit to the deficits of holiness among Masters within the university faculties: 'How few of them are saints,' he notes, 'Thomas and but few others.'[2]

Moreover, just as it is a characteristic of some thirteenth- and fourteenth-century 'affectivists' to force a deep wedge between the 'intellectual' and the 'affective', so it is a characteristic of the same tendency to realign the dimensions of the 'cataphatic' and the 'apophatic' theologies along parallel lines. Thomas Gallus Vercellensis (d. 1246), Hugh of Balma (fl. 1300), Giles of Rome (1243–1316) and Jean Gerson (1363–1429), differing as they do from one another in much else, all agree that the true 'mystical darkness' of the theologian requires the incapacitation of intellect – and for them this means the natural cognitive power of the philosopher – which can attain to no more than a mediated, distanced, abstract and detached knowledge of God. It is not denied by any of these that the God whom the philosophers know by intellect is the same God as he who is known to the theologian by faith. But it is said by all of them that if we are to enter into the true 'mystical' darkness of the divine, then the intellectual knowledge of the philosopher has to be set aside in order to leave room for the God of faith, known, it is said, not by intellect, but

---

[2] Denys the Carthusian, *Difficultatum Praecipuarum Absolutiones*, a5, *in Doctor Ecstatici D. Dionysii Cartusiani Opera Omnia* XVI, Tournai: Typis Cartusiae S. M. de Pratis, 1902, p. 494D.

by love. For *amor ipse notitia est*,[3] love is itself a kind of knowing, of which intellect can know nothing.

Now it is part of this 'affectivist' mentality that the characterisation of the unknowability of God, though couched in the same metaphoric vocabularies as those of Thomas Aquinas, as also drawing on their common source in the *Mystical Theology* of the pseudo-Denys, differs sharply from that of both. By contrast, for these late medieval affectivists what accounts for the 'darkness' of God is but the simple dismissal of intellect, no knowledge which intellect possesses having any place in the divine encounter, at any rate in its highest degree or level. Therefore, in order finally to enter into that darkness, the soul must be led by love alone, having left intellect behind, its companion thus far in the ascent to God. As Gallus puts it, at every stage of the soul's ascent to God, up to and including the penultimate, intellect and love walk 'hand in hand'; but the breakthrough into the true 'darkness of God' can be achieved only at the price of love's breaking with intellect so as to step out on its own; here, in the divine unknowability, are found

the highest aspirations for God, the excesses and inflowings which go beyond understanding, burning brilliance and brilliant burnings; understanding cannot be drawn into the sublime ecstasies and excesses of these lights, but only the supreme love which unites.[4]

Hugh of Balma is even more emphatic: 'in the mystical upsurge of love', he explains,

it is necessary to abandon all activity of intellect or thought, and to rise up under the impulse to union by means of a longing love which transcends all understanding and knowledge; therefore the true lover rises up without any prior knowledge and on the impulse of longing love.[5]

Here we encounter, as if by anticipation, that later, Kantian, reduction of the dynamic apophaticism of reason and intellect to a mere passive agnosticism. Within this 'affectivist' mentality, the 'darkness' upon which love enters in its encounter with God is a darkness consequent upon intellect's having to be abandoned, since it possesses no inherent capacity to be drawn into the divine unknowability itself. Intellect's unknowing,

---

[3] Gregory the Great, *Homelia in Evangelia* 27.4, Migne, *Patrologia Latina* LXXIV, p. 1207.
[4] Thomas Gallus, *Super canticum Canticorum Hierarchice Exposita*, in *Thomas Gualterius, Abbas Vercellensis: Commentaires du Cantique des Cantiques*, ed. Jeanne Barbet, Textes Philosophiques du Moyen Age 14, Paris: de Vrin, 1967, p. 67. For a partial translation of this text see my *Eros and Allegory: Medieval Exegesis of the Song of Songs*, Kalamazoo: Cistercian Publications, 1995, p. 323.
[5] Hugh of Balma, *Viae Sion Lugent*, Quaestio Unica 11. The critical edition of this text is by Francis Ruello in *Sources Chrétiennes*, Paris: Editions du Cerf, 1995, from which I have translated this passage.

therefore, is a mere passive ignorance. As Jean Gerson says, the pagan philosophers knew not the true apophatic unknowing of the Christian; they espoused 'Socratic ignorance' – the knowledge that they do not know – out of the mere frustrations of an exhausted natural intellect straining against the inadequacy of its own powers:

> I am much mistaken if it is not an obvious truth about the greatest philosophers, that, after all their enquiries, they declared in weariness of spirit, their labours having done nothing to refresh them, that the one thing they knew was that they did not know.[6]

Fraught as this medieval affectivism is with many polarisations – between knowledge and love, between intellect and will, between the affirmative and the negative ways, and between natural and revealed knowledge – it is the last of these polarisations which concerns us most directly. For all four medieval authorities, what intellect can know of God it knows by natural means, a knowledge ultimately having no place within the construction of Christian theology – at any rate, at that point at which theology is properly described as 'mystical'. Hence, for all the obvious differences in so many other respects, the late medieval affectivists share with the majority of post-Kantian modern theologians that common scepticism of reason combined with a positivism of faith. What in the end unites the medieval and the modern is a common fear – in today's terms of a 'rationalist foundationalism' – which leads in both cases to a recasting, by comparison with Thomas, of the relations between the affirmative and negative 'moments' within the construction of the theological enterprise. For in the hands of both the post-Kantian and the late medieval affectivists, the 'apophatic' is recast as lying in the simple deficiency of reason – no longer, as in Thomas, its *apotheosis*; and as an *ignorantia indocta* – no longer, as in Thomas (and as in the pseudo-Denys) a *knowing* unknowing.

By contrast, for Thomas, the affirmative and the negative, the cataphatic and the apophatic, are held poised in the tensions of simultaneity, even within reason's capacity; indeed, for Thomas, these tensions between knowing and unknowing reveal the very structure and dynamic of reason itself. What shows the existence of God shows that we *can* speak of God – theology is possible. But precisely that which shows the existence of God shows also and at the same time, and in the same determination of proof, that we cannot have any final hold on what we mean

---

[6] 'Fallor si non apparuit in maximis philosophis, qui post omnes inquisitiones suos tedio affecti, quia non refecti, dixerunt hoc unum se scire quod nichil scirent.' Jean Gerson, *De mystica theologia: Tractatus Speculativus*, in *Jean Gerson, Oeuvres Complètes* III, ed. Palémon Glorieux, Paris: Desclée et Cie., 1960–73, 1.34, 15–17.

when we do so – so theology is inherently uncompletable, open-ended, a 'broken language', as Nicholas Lash says.[7] Consequently, for Thomas, the cataphatic (we can speak of God by many names) and the apophatic (what these names mean is beyond our comprehension) have one and the same root and source in the possibility of proof of God's existence, just as we have also seen them to do in the Exodus theophany. Or we could say that that interrelation of the cataphatic and the apophatic structures the very nature of reason itself, and that it is precisely in and through its deployment in the demonstration of God's existence that that complex nature of reason is shown forth. That these things are so at this point I merely asseverate. The case for saying them awaits a fuller discussion in later chapters.[8]

'Augustinian intellectualism'

In the meantime, it is safe to say that as fourteenth- and fifteenth-century theologians read him, Thomas was a radical 'intellectualist'. This 'intellectualism', however, does not entail anything much which could be derived from any understanding of the word 'intellect' current today, and certainly has little to do with what is exclusively confined to academics. For us, as for the medieval 'affectivist', 'intellect' is a *discursive* power. It is what we use in calculations, whether of a theoretical kind, such as in numerical, logical or empirical reasoning, or of a practical kind, such as in the devising of the means to the ends of action. By contrast, for Thomas, *intellectus* has a twofold meaning, one of which is general, and is inclusive of all human rational powers together with all that those rational powers depend upon for their exercise; but the other is more narrowly and specifically conceived, as that 'higher' than rational power itself on which our rational powers depend. In this narrower sense, *intellectus* is a mental activity distinct from our 'ratiocination'; it is precisely not the discursive activity of arguing on what grounds something might be true, or of calculating how something might be got, but is rather the non-discursive act of *seeing* a truth as such or the desirability of some good. 'Reasoning' is an activity of step-by-step argument to a truth; 'intellectual' seeing is a form of contemplative rest in a truth, and is a higher form of knowing than any achieved by reasoning, for it is typically exercised in the knowledge of those truths on which any power of reasoning itself depends, whether theoretical or practical.

---

[7] Nicholas Lash, *A Matter of Hope: A Theologian's Reflections on the Thought of Karl Marx*, London: Darton, Longman and Todd, 1981, p. 144.
[8] See chapters 9, 10 and 11 below.

Of course, if it would be misleading to translate Thomas's *intellectus* by our 'intellect', it would be equally wrong to assume a uniformity of terminology from one time to another within the Middle Ages, and between one author and another even within the same period. This is not the place to account for all the variations and nuances of meaning of the Latin *intellectus* across times and authorities, but it is worthwhile offering some elements of clarification in a very confused matter of technical vocabulary. A starting point for such discussion is inevitably found in Augustine, who, in a famous passage in *Confessions*, argued that the power of the mind by which it exercises its native capacity to judge of mutable and contingent things as to good, better and best, cannot itself share that character of mutability and contingency; that the senses of our bodies, the inner power of 'imagination' and paradoxically even 'reason' itself, 'to which whatever is received from the bodily senses is referred for judgment', are themselves too fraught with changeability to ground that capacity to judge of changeable things – so to say, you cannot measure length with an elastic tape. 'Wondering therefore what was the source of my judgment when I did thus judge', Augustine concluded that though 'reason' is what we judge with, it does and can do so not by means of its own autonomous light but by means of the 'unchangeable and true eternity of truth above my changing mind'. Thus the mind (reason) judges by means of a light which is both *in* it and not *of* it.[9] Now clearly, that appropriation of the divine light of truth by which changeable, contingent reason judges of the changeable, contingent world cannot itself be the work of reason; and one of the terms which Augustine used to describe that *locus* of the mind in which the 'eternal light of truth' is situated is *intellectus*. But only one of them. For Augustine sometimes casts this distinction between *intellectus* and *ratio* in the different terms of the distinction between 'higher' and 'lower' *reason*.[10] And in this terminological laxity he is followed by many another medieval authority: typically, for example, by William of St Thierry[11] in the twelfth century, but also by Denys the Carthusian in the fifteenth, who, in his polemical reaction against the predominant affectivisms of his contemporaries, advocates a return to that classical tradition of 'intellectualism' of the twelfth-century Victorines on whom Thomas himself draws. Denys clarifies his own terminology in terms which succinctly paraphrase also that broad twelfth-century consensus to which he is so indebted:

[9] Augustine, *Confessiones* 7.17.23, ed. L. Verheijen, *CCSL* 50, Turnout: Brepols, 1981.
[10] Augustine, *De Trinitate* XII, 1, 2.
[11] See, for example, *Meditations* 3.10.10, in *The Works of William of St Thierry: On Contemplating God, Prayer, Meditations*, trans. Sr Penelope CSMV, Kalamazoo: Cistercian Publications, 1977, p. 107.

one and the same power is called *reason* in so far as it is discursive; *intellect* in so far as it knows intuitively by a simple glance; *intelligence* in so far as it contemplates things divine and the supremely exalted Godhead.[12]

But if Denys's terminology is thus identifiably Augustinian, his source for his conception of 'intellect' is distinctly that of the pseudo-Denys. The human mind is characterised principally by its middle-ranking place within the hierarchy of beings, extending from the very highest form of angelic life, that of the seraphim, down to the very lowest forms of matter. Each level of hierarchy is at once differentiated from every other but also related by complex relations of inclusion and overlap. The angelic mind is both higher than and differentiated from the human in that whereas the angelic mind is purely intellectual and intuitive, the human mind is characteristically rational and discursive. Conversely, the human mind, in its highest part, overlaps with the angelic mind and thus possesses some purely intellectual potential: 'according to the divine Denys, the lowest level of a higher order has a certain measure of "fit" with the highest level of the [next] lower order'.[13]

And so, in the outflow of beings from the first principle there is a certain 'linkage', as of a chain, and an order. Since, therefore, the human soul is made 'in the shadow of intelligence', as Isaac says in his book of *Definitions*, that is, in the order of things immediately after the angels, it follows that some element remains in the [human] soul of the perfection and manner of understanding proper to the angelic mind.[14]

And concerning this ground which the human mind shares in common with the angelic, Denys is prepared to say just what Augustine says about it, namely that it is in that highest part that the human mind knows, non-discursively, the eternal truths the knowledge of which is the necessary precondition of its rational activities. This 'spark of the soul', he says, 'is signified by the eagle, for it is the highest [part of the] soul . . . and soars above the rational power, at any rate in so far as by 'rational power' is meant that which functions by discursive reasoning'.[15]

---

[12] 'Nempe eadem vis dicitur ratio, in quantum est discursiva; intellectus, in quantum est simplici apprehensione intuitiva; intelligentia quoque in quantum est divinorum ac superaltissimae Deitatis contemplativa.' *De contemplatione* 1.5. 140B.

[13] Pseudo-Denys, *Divine Names* 7, 868C (*Complete Works*, p. 107).

[14] 'Secundum divinum Dionysium, infimum superioris ordinis cum supremo ordinis inferioris aliquam habet convenientiam. In processu equidem entium a primo principio est concatenatio quaedam et ordo. Quoniam ergo anima rationalis in umbra intelligentiae facta est, secundum Isaac in libro Definitionum, utpote in ordine rerum immediate post angelum; constat quod aliquid de perfectione et modo intelligendi mentis angelicae in anima perseveret.' *De contemplatione* 1.6, *Opera Omnia* XVI, p. 141B–C.

[15] 'Unde . . . haec scintilla . . . significatur per aquilam, quoniam est supremum in anima . . . et rationalem virtutem transcendit, videlicet ipsam rationem secundum quod ratio dicitur a ratiocinationis discursu.' *De contemplatione* 1.6, *Opera Omnia* XVI, p. 141A′–B′.

However great the differences of source or of vocabulary may be, there is common ground identifiable in high medieval thought in a series of metaphors and in a general distinction. The metaphors serve to describe that place in the soul where, as one might put it, the human mind 'lives beyond its own powers' – for that is the essential notion shared by Augustinian and Dionysian theologies, that even to be the human thing that it is, the human mind must be more than human. Augustine himself spoke of the *acies mentis*, the soul's 'cutting edge',[16] and in other places of the *scintilla rationis*,[17] the 'spark of reason', and medieval authors generally took up the Augustinian metaphors, speaking variously of the *acies intellectus* or of the *apex intellectus* or *mentis* and sometimes of the *scintilla synderesis*;[18] and what all these metaphors denote is the presence within the human mind of a source of its knowing which exceeds the human, the point in the soul where it overlaps with that which is above it. In short, the common opinion sustained by all these metaphors is that to be a human and to know as a human require our being *more than* human, both as to being and as to knowledge.

That said, it remains the case that to 'know' in the way human beings distinctively do is to exercise 'reason' – and by that word is meant the specifically human discursive power of stage-by-stage progression from evidence to conclusion, from ends to the means required to achieve them, a power which places us above the sensate animal world and below the purely 'intellectual' world of the angels. We could say, somewhat epigrammatically (and in any case as capturing best the thought rather of Thomas than of the generality of medieval authorities), that 'intellect' plus a body equals reason: for discursive rationality is what intellect is when *embodied*; rationality is the sort of intellectual power which can be exercised by a being whose knowledge is dispersed around and organised in the multitudinousness of the body's sensory inputs. Nonetheless, though the human mind is essentially rational, it could not be rational if it were not also, in part, functionally intellectual.[19] And that, the intellectual power, where the divine light of truth resides, is the highest part of the soul, the *apex mentis* where, in some sort, the soul meets with God in its – and in God's – deepest intimacy.

---

[16] See e.g. Augustine, *Enarrationes in Psalmis* 134.6, *Patrologia Latina* XXXVII, p. 1742.
[17] Augustine, *De Civitate Dei* 22.24.2, *PL* XLI, p. 789.
[18] The term *synderesis* is of obscure origin: it seems to have been invented by Jerome (*Homelia in Hezechielem* 1.6, *Patrologia Latina* XXV, p. 22) out of a corruption of the Greek *suneidesis* ('conscience') and was taken by Thomas to refer to the mind's immediate apprehension of fundamental moral truths; see *ST* 1a q79 a12 *corp.*
[19] Thomas denies, however, that 'intellect' and 'reason' are distinct powers; they denote different and complementary exercises of the same power, named *intellectus* by synechdoche.

Thomas on 'intellect'

In this broad, undifferentiated, sense Thomas Aquinas is undoubtedly an 'Augustinian', but what is distinctive about how Thomas places himself within this tradition is the precise point at which he departs from it in one crucial respect. In *Confessions* 7.17 Augustine recounts his discovery of the presence within his mind of the 'divine light of truth' as having been the outcome of an *upward* surge of the mind from its lowest sensory perceptions, through imagination, to reason in its discursive capacities, into the awe-inspired encounter with that 'eternity of truth' on which reason, in that discursive capacity, must depend. And for sure what Augustine is here recalling is a pre-conversion experience, one which, at face value, he was able to encounter before his baptism; and so it might appear as if he represents that experience rather as one which led him to accept a broadly Platonist epistemology – moreover, rather on broadly Platonist and philosophical grounds than on any which depended upon the insights of his Christian faith to which he later came to adhere. But I think it wrong to read even this passage recounting a pre-conversion event as being told in pre-conversion terms, thinking it on the whole better to read the entire narrative of Augustine's intellectual autobiography as having been written, of course chronologically after his conversion, but also hermeneutically in the light of the Christian understanding of faith to which that narrative led as outcome. Put more simply, I do not think that it follows from the fact that in *Confessions* 7.17 Augustine tells of his discovery of *intellectus* as having occurred before his conversion, that he was supposing this discovery to be the outcome of an unaided, pre-baptismal, ungraced reason. On the contrary, it is Augustine's opinion, persistent throughout his theological writings from the first to the last, that the presence of the divine light of truth in the soul is a discovery made only through the downward irruption of grace in the soul, which illuminates human reason in its upward striving towards it. For Augustine, therefore, we could not know by reason alone that 'true eternity of truth' on which the exercise of our rational powers depends, without the irruption of grace into the mind – at any rate 'unaided' reason could have no experience of its own source of truth without that grace. What Augustine is describing in *Confessions* 7.17, is, therefore, already a graced experience; what is 'pre-conversion' about it is simply that he was not, at that stage, in possession of the explicit faith by which he could recognise it as such.

One way of situating Thomas's account of reason in its relation to this Augustinian tradition is by placing it at a point of differentiation between the 'radical Augustinianism' of Henry of Ghent (1217–93) and

the 'minimalist Augustinianism' of Duns Scotus (1265–1308). The rad-
icalism of Henry's 'Augustinianism' pushes the doctrine of divine illumination to a point at which, in Scotus' view, no natural cognitive activity
productive of universal, scientifically necessary truths is left to the human
mind itself. Scotus' criticism of Henry's extreme Augustinianism is that it
leaves the human mind with no strictly intellectual capacities of its own,
since, on Henry's account, Augustine's emphasis on the 'mutability' and
'contingency' of our rational power of judgement is so stressed as to
remove any possibility of a universal and necessary truth being present in
the mind, except as produced in it by the divine light itself. As Scotus puts
it, for Henry, the mind possesses no created 'exemplar' – or, as we might
say, no universal concept – of its own making by which contingent, mutable objects may be known, but only the uncreated 'exemplar' in the mind
of God by which our human minds are illuminated. Hence, the universals
in the human mind are not the product of our created rationality as such,
being received in them from their source in the divine light itself. In that
case, Scotus reasonably asks, in what sense can the human mind itself be
said to know anything at all, if it has no properly intellectual activity of
its own capable of appropriating the divine light by means of its native
capacity for universal and necessary truth?[20] He adds (just as reasonably) that there is no justification for any appeal to Augustine's authority
in support of a view which entailed so extreme a conclusion. The sense
in which we do 'properly speaking' see and judge of the mutable world of
objects 'in the Light [of eternal truth]' is that in which 'it could be said
that . . . the Light is the cause of the object[s]'[21] which move the intellect
to its knowledge of universal and necessary truths. But that transaction
itself between the mutable thing known and the necessary character of the
certain judgement concerning it is one which falls within our own human
natural capacities. Were this not so, were Henry's reading of Augustine
to be permitted, this 'would imply the impossibility of any certain natural
knowledge'.[22]

---

[20] Duns Scotus, *Ordinatio* 1, d3 q4 a4, *Opera Omnia* III, pp. 164–5. Otherwise known
as the *Opus Oxoniense*, this work is Scotus' first commentary on the *Sentences* of Peter
Lombard, begun at Oxford in the last years of the thirteenth century and completed,
perhaps by 1304, in Paris. The edition of the text used for translations is found in
Doctoris Subtilis et Mariani: Joannis Duns Scoti Ordinis Fratrum Minorum Opera Omnia,
Civitas Vaticana: Typis Polyglottis Vaticanis, 1950 – . Except where noted as being mine,
the translations are taken from William A. Frank and Allan B. Wolter, *Duns Scotus:
Metaphysician*, Indiana: Purdue University Press, 1995.
[21] 'Proprie posset dici intellectum nostrum videre in luce, quia lux est causa obiecti.' *Ordinatio* 1, d3 q4 a5, *Opera Omnia* III, pp. 162–3, my translation.
[22] 'Istae rationes [Henrici] videntur concludere impossibilitatem certae cognitionis natu-
ralis.' *Ordinatio* 1, d3 q4 a1, *Opera Omnia* III, p. 133.

For Scotus himself, however, the natural knowledge of God by inference from creatures is possible, but only (as we shall see in chapter 7)
on the basis that the understanding of God thus obtained is obtained
through at least some concepts univocally related to our understanding
of creatures themselves. In that sense at least, what reason can achieve by
way of an understanding of God remains closed within a circle circum-
scribed by reason's natural inferential capacity, where that capacity is itself
limited by the necessarily univocal character of the relationship between
the creaturely conditions which serve as premises and the divine nature
which is the conclusion inferred. Intellect, therefore, demonstrates nothing to exist which transcends its own natural powers – we can perhaps say
that Scotus' 'reason' is never, within its own discursive nature, 'stretched
beyond itself' and can demonstrate the existence only of a God whose
'transcendence' is contained within the ambit of its univocally discursive
reach. In short, in Scotus, the Augustinian *intellectus* has been effectively
excised.

Speaking in general terms, therefore, Thomas's account of *ratio* and
intellectus seems to lie somewhere between the position of Henry of Ghent
and that of Scotus. On the one hand, like Scotus and unlike Henry, for
Thomas human reason is able to construct for itself, through its own
natural powers, its own access to universal and necessary truths,[23] even
if, of course, such access is itself a form of participation in the divine
light of truth,[24] here also sharing common ground with Scotus, who,
like Thomas, is quite happy to concede to the moderate 'Augustinian'
view of the matter, that 'the active intellect . . . [is] a participation of the
Uncreated Light'.[25] For reason could not attain to any universal truths
by its own means of reasoning if it did not know *without* those means
the fundamental principles which govern speculative reasoning as such–
the principle of contradiction and 'other like principles' – and, as governing its practical reasoning, the principle that 'the good is to be done
and evil avoided'.[26] Though governing discursive reasoning, whether theoretical or practical, these principles cannot be known discursively, for
of course you could not demonstrate to be true the principles on which
the validity of all demonstration itself depends. Hence, as to the *source* of
reason's power of judgement, this lies in intellect's grasp of truths beyond
the power of reason as such to know. But even if that intellectual grasp

---

[23] 'Oportet virtutem quae est principium huius actionis esse aliquid in anima.' *ST* 1a q79
a4 *corp.*
[24] *ST* 1a q79 a4 *corp.*
[25] '[Intellectus agens] qui est participatio lucis increatae'. *Ordinatio* 1, d3 q4 a5, *Opera
Omnia* III, p. 61, my translation.
[26] *ST* 1-2ae q94 a2 *corp.*

of reason's fundamental governing principles may fairly be described as a form of participation in 'the divine light of truth', this, for Thomas, is little more than to say that their truth is in some way a reflection in the human mind of the divine self-knowledge: to say which is not to say, and nowhere does Thomas say it, that it is in some human knowledge of the divine mind itself in which they participate that you know their participation. For we can know that the principles of reasoning hold without knowing even *that* they so participate in the divine mind, still less knowing them *in* the divine mind. And thus far, Thomas and Scotus would be in broad agreement: as to the *source* of its reasoning power, human reasoning outreaches itself in its intellectual grasp of first principles and thus far participates in the 'divine light of truth'.

Nonetheless, Thomas and Scotus part company in that they cannot be said to have the same view of what the participation of the human mind in the divine mind entails for reason's natural capacity in respect of its *destination*. For Thomas, reason so participates in the divine self-knowledge that it can, by the exercise of its distinctively natural capacity of reasoning – that is to say, of properly constructed inference – attain to a conclusion the meaning of which lies beyond any which could stand in a relation of univocity with the created order, which, of itself, is the ambit of reason's own, natural, objects. For Thomas, that is to say, reason's powers, pushed to their limit, open up into the territory of *intellectus*: and they do so, as I shall argue, precisely in the proofs of the existence of God. In those proofs, we could say, reason *self*-transcends, and by its self-transcendence, becomes 'intellect'.

Now although we must concede that Scotus in no way intends any scaling down of the divine transcendence as such – which, as we shall see, he thinks is sufficiently secured by his careful distinctions between 'finite' and 'infinite' being – and although, like Thomas, he wishes to place the demonstration of the existence of God within the scope of natural reason, there is little doubt that the implications of Scotus' having diminished the scope of reason to a 'closed' circle of univocity are, in the terms of Heidegger, 'onto-theological' in effect, and in medieval terms, amount to a severing of reason from *intellectus*. In Thomas, rational demonstration of the existence of God is reason stretched to the end of its tether; and though reason reaches the end of its tether by its own means of discursive inference and argument, what it reaches there, where its tether ends, is the territory of 'intellect', a territory altogether beyond reason's scope – which is another way of stating the paradox, oft-repeated in this essay, that what the 'proofs' prove is at one and the same time the existence of God and that, as said of God, we have finally lost our hold on the meaning of 'exists'. Reason, to adapt a phrase of Hegel's, realises itself as 'intellect' in its abolition as 'reason', and abolishes itself as knowledge in its realisation as unknowing.

If, for Thomas, as for Scotus, there are some truths which reason alone cannot know – indeed, all the truths, strictly, of faith – such limitations of reason's scope are, for Thomas, wrongly conceived as a determinate boundary-line prescribing reason's scope, as if consisting in some final truth-claim to which reason attains and at which it must stop. To suppose that there could be some such way of determining a fixed perimeter to reason's power would be rather like supposing that there is some boundary-line at the limit of space, a *ne plus ultra*, as if you could stand there at the limit, but could not put a foot across it into the beyond: such is a conceptually incoherent, merely imagined, possibility. For Thomas, what lies at the end of reason's tether is a demonstrated unknowability, an opening up of possibilities of knowing, not a closing down of those possibilities, not a final truth – for how could a truth be known to be 'final' except from a standpoint which is already on the other side of it? On this side of its limits reason knows only the existence of a mystery whose depths it knows – demonstrates – it cannot know, for its character as mystery consists in its lying beyond reason's reach. In that 'unknowing' lies reason's self-transcendence as intellect. And the act by which it thus self-transcends is proof of the existence of God.

By the end of this essay I hope to have shown that on Thomas's account, what drives reason to the limit of its powers is a certain kind of questioning, a strategy of rational exploration and explanation, a strategy whose 'end-point' is not an answer, but, on the contrary, is an unanswerable question – a question, moreover, which it knows to be unanswerable: there, where it knows that it does not know, 'reason' becomes 'intellect' and depletes itself in its fulfilment. To understand the nature of that questioning is to understand the 'argument strategy' of Thomas's proofs of the existence of God, as eventually we shall see in chapter 12.

5   Reason and rhetoric

In just one respect, therefore – we could say in a loose metaphor, 'from above' – Thomas's 'Augustinian' understanding of 'reason' is much expanded by comparison with any which is common in everyday current speech – and for that matter, with any of its technical, philosophical senses today. For within that ancient tradition, human reason sits in a hinterland between the 'rational' in its narrowest sense, in which 'discursiveness' predominates, and the 'intellectual', in which a certain kind of pure 'seeing' predominates; and I used formulas expressive of the relationship between reason in this narrower sense, and intellect, which relationship properly characterises 'rationality' in that broader sense. We could not be rational if we were not also more than rational; human beings are not rational beings unless they are also intellectual.[1] And I even went so far as to say in the last chapter, correctly in itself, but misleadingly if nothing else were said to qualify it, that for Thomas, 'rationality' is what intellect is when embodied – which is misleading only in so far as the formula may perhaps suggest a certain 'dualism', of that kind according to which human beings are strictly angels thrust into bodies, as if being of their nature more happy in an unembodied condition.

As we shall see, necessary as it is to correct such misimpressions of Thomas's 'Augustinianism', it is as essential not to neglect the truth which Thomas saw in it. Nothing that Thomas has to say about our being rational animals should cause us to neglect his 'Augustinian' insight that we are also incarnate angels, an insight which for Thomas had no implications of a 'dualist' kind – as it did for some other contemporary Augustinians. The question Thomas faced was how these two emphases can be held together coherently; and, if there were many intellectual battles which Thomas was caused to wage, more or less willingly and under pressure of opposition, the fight which he deliberately set about picking was

---

[1] 'Intelligere enim est simpliciter veritatem intelligibilem apprehendere. Ratiocinari autem est procedere de uno intellecto ad aliud, ad veritatem intelligibilem cognoscendam.' *ST* 1a q79 a8 *corp*. Intellect and reason are, he goes on to say (ibid.) related as rest is to movement, and so are not distinct powers, just different activities of the same power.

with two sets of opponents who, for quite opposed reasons, were uncomfortable with his conviction that in being 'embodied intellects' we are essentially rational animals. Radical Augustinians – for whom it seemed almost a matter of regret, and an offence to our intellectual natures, that humans are animals – were for Thomas curiously at one with radical Averroists (otherwise the natural opponents of Augustinians), who, for equal though opposite reasons, displaced the human intellectual centre of gravity from its location within our animality and on to a single, 'separate possible intellect' common to all humans. Neither extreme Augustinians nor Averroists could seem to get the picture of human nature focussed where Thomas felt it should be, upon the individuated unities of intellect with reason in human animality.[2]

Hence, if Thomas's conception of rationality is much expanded 'from above' by comparison with any conception of rationality which we possess today, it is equally expanded by the same comparison with our contemporary meanings for it 'from below'. We are essentially rational animals, and I use the word 'essentially' not as a word of common emphasis, but technically. Our essence, for Thomas, is to be 'rational', and if rational, then we are essentially a certain kind of animal; to be 'rational' *is* to be an animal. Hence, all we humans do, we do as animals do it. If we think, this is how we humans come to understand, namely as animals can understand; indeed, for Thomas, only animals can think; angels understand but do not think; God understands but does not think. And if cats do not think, this has to be put down to the kind of animals they are, not to their being animals *tout court*. If we desire, we desire as only an animal can, and if my cat cannot reciprocate love as another human being can, this is not because she is an animal, but because she is not a rational animal; so I love as rational animals do. If I feel pain in my finger, it is because I am an animal; angels have no fingers in which to feel pain and, if God can be described, as the Psalmist describes him, as behaving like a soldier with a hangover (Ps. 78:65), we know that this has to be a metaphor: it has to be literally false to say this, otherwise we can make no sense of the metaphor. But if the pain in my finger plays a different role in my life from that which her injured paw plays in my cat's life, this is not because I am rational and my cat is an animal, but because my animality is a rational animality, and my cat's is not. We can even say, faithfully to what Thomas has in mind, that human beings have rational fingers to feel with, as anyone who has observed the sheer intelligence and grace of a musician's fingers will know, and it is those musically informed fingers which feel

---

[2] See Thomas's *De unitate intellectus contra Averroistas*, in *Aquinas against the Averroists*, ed. and trans. Ralph McInerney, West Lafayette: Purdue University Press, 1993.

the pain; whereas a cat's paw is a merely sensate, mechanically complex, leg-ending which cats do not know of as 'paws'; and so its pain has but a feline, sensate, significance, quite unlike that of a musician. For this reason, whether I think, or love or feel pain, whether I feel depressed or elated, whether I work or I play, whether I am exercised in understanding the meaning of the square of minus one or simply enjoying the sunset or sex, these are all done as it is in my nature to do them; which means that, my nature being that of a rational animal, feeling pain and all the rest are expressions of, ways of being, a rational animal. Such, at any rate, is how Thomas Aquinas thinks of the matter. We human beings do nothing at all except as rational animals do it.

Therefore, to be a rational being is, for Thomas, one particular way of being an animal. It is clear that while 'thinking' in its narrowest meaning as argument, inference, conclusions derived from evidence, and calculation of means to ends, is a distinctively human activity in the sense that no other kind of being does these things at all, 'thinking' is a synecdoche for our rational nature, as 'deckhand' is a synecdoche for a low-ranking sailor on a ship. The fact that human beings 'think' is determined by the kind of bodies human beings have, and just those characteristics of our bodies which have to do with the fact that human beings 'think' also have to do with the distinctive ways in which human beings love and have sex, contemplate sunsets, make music, work, play and rest, none of which are discursive activities in that narrowest sense of 'thinking'. In short, for Thomas, it is because of the kind of bodies we have that we are the sort of rational animals that we are.[3]

Central to how our bodies determine our rationality is the fact that all our mental activity has its origin in the senses, and that the senses are five mutually exclusive, organ-dependent, ways of apprehending any object of perception. Our senses are 'organ-dependent' in that without nerve-endings on the surface of the skin we cannot feel anything, without the retina's sensitivity to light we cannot see anything, without vibrations on the ear-drum we cannot hear anything, and so forth – and without any of those we cannot come to think anything. And they are 'mutually exclusive' in that, though of course we can see what we can also hear, or taste what we see – for we can hear the crunch of a smooth, juicy, red, musky-smelling apple, all five sensations in one go as we eat it – we cannot see the taste or smell the colour or taste the redness or hear the smoothness of its skin.[4] For Thomas, much of what characterises the 'rational'

---

[3] This is because, as Thomas says, any soul (including the human soul) is the 'substantial form of a physically organised body' – 'forma substantialis corporis physici organici', *De unitate* I, 3 (p. 21).

[4] *De unitate* I, 19 (p. 39) – 'visus coloris tantum, auditus sonorum et sic de aliis'.

starts here in our knowledge's rootedness in the physical dispersal of the senses, which divide, by way of what he calls their 'formal objects', any material object of knowledge into five, discrete, sensory 'inputs'. Indeed, in what is for once a helpful appeal to etymology, Thomas notes that the 'discursiveness' which so characterises the rational gets its meaning from the Latin *discurrere*,[5] calling to mind the fact that 'reason' has to 'run about' from one dimension of what it knows to another, pulling together into the unity of judgement that which our bodies diversify fivefold. Reason divides in order to unite, diversifies in order to relate.

Another way of putting this is to say that for Thomas we are linguistic animals: which will be true enough on condition that no more here with 'language' than correspondingly with 'reason' should we permit that narrowness for which 'language' is understood exclusively in terms of formal, verbal, speech and writing, or, as we may put it compendiously, in terms of naming.[6] For, as we have seen, action also 'speaks'. Indeed, we could not make sense of how it is that structured vibrations in the air, or structured shapes on a page, can possess the significance they do as spoken or written words, unless it were the case that language in that narrower sense were a special case of a general possibility, namely that of matter being capable of bearing significance. We may or may not be in possession of some adequate account of how these squiggly shapes on the page in front of you, <'I love you'>, say what we read them to mean, or how it is that the 'scare-quotes' which surround those shapes say that I have quoted the words, not told you, dear reader, that I love you;[7] but we possess such an account only if it thereby explains how also a kiss says, 'I love you', and is sufficient to explain how a kiss can even be the bearer of irony, as was Judas' kiss of betrayal, cynically quoting, not sincerely saying, what kisses say. For the explanation, in either case, must be the same: on whatever account you give of how words mean, there can be

---

[5] *ST* 1a q29 a3 ad4.

[6] There should otherwise be no problem with this equivalence. Some have difficulty with it, supposing that concepts, being what we understand, may or may not be expressible in language, and so that thought – experience generally – is contingently connected with the language in which it is expressed. Thomas at least will not allow that problem. For him 'concepts' are not what we understand about something else, so that there might be some general problem about how concepts connect with what they are concepts of. Of course, particular concepts may or may not be good ones, and so our understanding of such-and-such may misconstrue it. But 'the concept of such-and-such', good or bad, is not *what* we understand, it *just is* our understanding of such and such: 'species . . . do not relate to possible intellect as what is understood, but as species by means of which the intellect understands, just as the species that are in sight are not the things seen, but that whereby sight sees' – 'species . . . non se habent ad intellectum possibilem ut intellecta, sed sicut species quibus intellectus intelligit, sicut et species quae sunt in visu non sunt ipsa visa sed ea quibus visus videt'. *De unitate* V, 110 (p. 131).

[7] Much, of course, as I do.

no greater mystery in how the words and scare-quotes say what they say than there is with how kisses say the same. Both are bits of matter bearing meaning. Explain the one if you can, but only on such terms as explain both.

Language, in this broader sense, is simply how bodies are significant, how they possess and exchange meanings. It is more strictly in accordance with the mind of Thomas Aquinas to say, however, that a human being is not a body plus meaning: for Thomas, a human being is matter plus meaning, *that is*, a body, just as language is not words plus their meanings, but bits of matter organised into meanings, *that is*, words. As Thomas puts it in his own terms, a human being is not a body plus a soul; a human being is matter informed by a soul, *that is*, a body, matter alive with a certain kind of life. For, as Aristotle says, a dead body is not a 'body' except equivocally.[8]

For Thomas, then, to say that human beings are 'rational animals' is to say, in this broader sense of the word, that we are linguistic animals, speaking organisms, animals which are the bearers, originators and transactors of meanings, animals which make signs. Our being 'rational', therefore, consists in anything which these organisms can do which bears, or is capable of bearing, a significance. It follows that to ask what is the place within this broader sense of 'rationality' of that narrower and distinctive sense of the word which consists in 'ratiocination' – the construction of inference and argument, the collating of evidence with explanation, the construction of theory – is parallel to asking what is the place of verbal speech and writing within language in this broader sense. I shall turn to this question at a later stage.[9] In the meantime it seems prudent to anticipate this much of that later clarification, lest I should be misunderstood to have argued for more than I intend: I should not be taken, in what I have argued so far, to have made a case for eliminating all distinctions between how an action can 'speak' and how human beings speak in words. For while I have argued that, in general, it is important to understand verbal communication as a specific case of the wider human activity of transacting meanings, and while I have argued, in parallel, that it is important

---

[8] *Metaphysics* VII, 10, 1035b 20–25. For the human soul is that by which the composite body-and-soul exists. What exists when a person is dead is what was that person's body and now is not. But such a soul can survive death, for the human soul, which is the form of the body and makes it *to be* a body, 'does not exist simply in virtue of the composite . . . but rather the composite exists in virtue of its existence . . . a form through whose existence the composite exists . . . need not be destroyed when the composite is destroyed' – 'nec est per esse compositi tantum . . . sed magis compositum est per esse eius . . . non autem oportet quod destruatur ad destructionem compositi illa forma per cuius esse compositum est'. *De unitate* I, 37 (p. 57).

[9] See pp. 116–17 below.

to understand 'rationality' in its narrower sense of 'ratiocination' against the background of our human rational animality, this is not to say that in either case the narrower sense is simply reducible to the broader.

Why is it 'important' not to effect a reductivism of this kind? It is important at least for the central purpose of this essay, which in general terms is to explore the role of reason in its deployment as argument within the context of Christian faith: and it is true that for the most part my discussion will be limited to the exploration of the role of reason in that narrower ratiocinative sense. It has seemed to me, however, that the case I make out for so robust a role for reason in that narrower sense – and no robuster role can be made out than that defended by the first Vatican Council – is vulnerable from two sides. On the one side the threat is posed by that 'closed' conception of reason which we have come to identify rightly or wrongly with the Enlightenment, according to which the 'space' in which reason functions is (of course) unlimited, infinite, but it is infinite with the infinity of the 'curved' space of the contemporary cosmologist, so that reason must ultimately return upon itself; hence, however endless its questioning may be, its endlessness and unlimitedness, its 'discursiveness', are those of a comet unceasingly chasing its own tail. On this account, reason can never, in the manner in which I have argued it can, pose to itself that unanswerable question which leads it beyond itself into the unknowable darkness of God.

Consequently, it is possible to welcome the Radical Orthodox critique of this 'Enlightenment' conception of reason, at least in so far as it calls for an extension of reason from 'above', as it were. Without doubt, the reconnecting of reason, in its discursive, ratiocinative, role with its foundation in the intuitiveness of 'intellect', the reconnecting of reasoning therefore with 'vision', restores to reason its capacity for an encounter with a 'transcendent otherness'; but in the hands of the Radical Orthodox it does so at a price, which is an excessive 'subalternation' of reason to faith – indeed, to a degree to which it becomes tempting to say that 'reason' as conceived of within certain writings of the Radical Orthodox school comes closer to the conception of Henry of Ghent than to that of Thomas.[10] The 'space' which intellect opens up for reason is opened for it only by an 'Augustinian' illumination, by what Milbank calls 'a certain pre-ontological insistence of the ideal', an 'Augustinian a priori', without which 'reason' is 'innate[ly] deficient'.[11] For Milbank and Pickstock, it is not merely that, were there not some participation of the human mind

---

[10] See pp. 194–7 below.

[11] There is a huge literature of controversy concerning the meaning of reason's 'innate deficiency' in respect of its own object. I do not propose to engage with these literatures. Suffice it to say that concerning reason's 'innate deficiency' one has to ask by what

in the divine self-understanding, then the human mind could not know its own proper, created, objects. Thomas indeed thought that, as we have seen. It is not enough for Milbank that, as Bonaventure thought, the human mind sees in a light which cannot itself be seen. The 'Augustinianism' favoured by Milbank and Pickstock is more emphatic than that, and its emphases begin to reveal their sources in the 'nouvelle théologie' discussed in chapter one: the illumination which is in the human intellect is not just a necessary condition of human knowing, in that logical sense 'prior' to any act of reasoning in which the necessary condition of a thing must be satisfied if what it conditions is to obtain. This illumination is also, in an inchoate form at least, an object of our knowing, known prior to anything known by reason; our 'pre-ontological' experience of the 'ideal' is presupposed to any exercise of reason. Hence, as Milbank puts it, 'the only thing that authenticates perfection (and indeed, the only thing that defines it), must be some sort of experience of its actuality'.[12] And that 'Augustinianism' goes far beyond any defended by Thomas, who says nothing at all, anywhere at all, about the human intellect's participation in the divine self-understanding involving any kind of *experience* of its actuality,[13] not even of a 'pre-ontological' kind.[14]

This, in connection with the assessment of Thomas's 'five ways', must inevitably lead to a scepticism of their standing as proofs. For, as construed against the background of this Augustinianism, they would fail as

---

standard is reason being said to be 'deficient'. If by the standard of what only faith can know, it is true but trivial to say that reason is deficient 'innately', just as it is true but trivial to say that sight is 'innately deficient' in respect of sound. But to say that reason is deficient by the standard of its *own* object is quite another thing, and is ambiguous. It might mean that reason's knowledge of God must end in apophatic darkness, which I not merely concede but argue for. If it means that reason cannot by its own power reach out to that apophatic darkness, cannot by its own powers know that it cannot comprehend God, but can know this only through the illumination of faith and grace, this I deny: indeed, it is the main purpose of this essay to show why it is false to say this.

[12] Milbank and Pickstock, *Truth in Aquinas*, p. 29.

[13] It would be extraordinarily odd if Thomas had made any such assertion without commenting on the very great difficulty which would be involved in determining in what sense the divine perfection could be the object of 'experience'. Of course, just because Thomas does not ever use the substantive '*experientia*', or the adjectival form '*experimentativus*', or any other Latin word which would normally be translated by the modern English 'experience' in any connection which has to do with our knowledge of God *in via*, it does not follow that Milbank could not be justified in using the modern English term 'experience' by way of exposition of Thomas's position. One would, however, expect a good deal of textual evidence in support of such an account. What is odd, therefore, is that Milbank gives us no explanation at all of the epistemology of his English 'experience', or any of what family of Latin terms in Thomas would be well served by such a translation into English. There is a startling deficiency of direct evidence that such translation does any sort of justice to Thomas's theological epistemology.

[14] Whatever that can mean. Milbank does not explain.

proofs by a vicious circularity. Of course, there is no problem of circularity in that a person who on some grounds or other knows God to exist should also seek a rational proof of the existence of God – Thomas, after all, *knows* God exists before ever setting out to prove it, just as mathematicians who *know* that $2 + 2 = 4$ can still see a reason for proving the theorem. A problem of circularity arises if a person should suppose that she is in possession of a proof of the existence of God some premise of which could be true only if the existence of God is in some way presupposed to it. But such would appear to be the position to which Milbank and Pickstock have reduced rational proof in Thomas. For if it is the case that some experience of the 'ideal' is presupposed to any exercise of reason, then at least implicitly the existence of God is 'given' in that experience of the ideal prior to reason's exercise. It would follow, therefore, that any supposedly *a posteriori* proof of the sort commonly ascribed to Aquinas would logically depend upon a prior experience of just that which it is supposed to prove. Thomas's 'five ways' would then turn out to be not proofs which are in any apodeictic sense constructed upon the experience of created imperfection entailing the conclusion that an ideal perfection exists, but theological extrapolations of a primary 'experience' of perfection, leaving room neither for the need for, nor for the possibility of, rational proof in any strict, formal, inferential, sense.

Moreover, as Milbank and Pickstock conceive of it, 'faith' in the proper, fully articulated, Christian sense is but an intensification of this intellectual vision 'along the same extension'.[15] If one wants to understand Thomas's account of the relationship between faith and reason, then, as Milbank and Pickstock envisage it, it is on the territory of *intellectus*, where faith and reason meet, that that relationship is to be understood. For on their account 'reason', in the narrow sense of 'ratiocination', depends for its functioning on that intellectual vision which is a participation in the divine self-understanding not other than, but experienced only in a lower degree of intensity than, faith itself. In turn, that faith 'deploys' reason, whose role as exercised by its own powers is reduced to the instrumental, however 'enhanced' that rational capacity is said to become through its subordination to faith. 'Reason alone', therefore, remains for Radical Orthodoxy a supposititious thing, an impossibility. Were 'reason alone' to be a possibility, it would be what 'reason alone' was for Kant: and a 'religion within the bounds of reason alone' would for Radical Orthodoxy therefore be nothing more than the contemptibly diminished Kantian concoction of bourgeois moral praxes supposedly deduced from the moral teachings of Jesus.

---

[15] Milbank and Pickstock, *Truth in Aquinas*, p. 21.

Of course, powerful as this 'Augustinian' influence is upon its theological epistemology, it is far from true that, in reaction to Enlightenment rationalism, Radical Orthodoxy has neglected human 'animality', or that it is driven by its 'Augustinian' and 'Platonist' impulses into a 'dualistic' spiritualisation of the human. On the contrary, one of the major contributions which Radical Orthodoxy has made to recent Christian theological debate is to exactly the opposite effect, namely to the re-carnalisation of theology and to important, if contentious, re-readings of both Plato and Augustine in anti-dualist terms – most effectively perhaps by Catherine Pickstock.[16] On the other hand, Radical Orthodoxy does, it seems to me, depart from a fundamental principle of Thomas's anthropology in its restriction of the capacity of ratiocination to reach above itself – in so far as it allows reason no access of its own to the transcendent precisely as reason, as ratiocination; and so in its way it disallows, as much as Kant does, the possibility the defence of which is the main purpose of this essay: the possibility, that is, of a transcendent ratiocination, a proof which proves more than we can know and proves that we could not know it. But it also narrows the range of reason from 'below', in so far as, though like Thomas it allows full scope to human animality, unlike Thomas it cannot concede to this 'animality' any power to self-transcend in its own terms. If to be rational is, for Thomas, in all things to act as animals do, then should we not also say that human beings know God as animals may, that is to say, 'rationally'? But if so, from either point of view, whether from 'above' or from 'below', the Radical Orthodox appear to have cut the range of reason back in so far as reason's distinctively ratiocinative powers as such are confined within the narrow scope of a univocal ratiocination and to have lost touch with Thomas's central conception of the human, that to be human is to be a rational animal. It is little wonder, therefore, that Radical Orthodoxy remains as firmly set against any possibility of an *a posteriori* proof of the existence of God standing on rational ground alone as any Enlightenment atheist ever was, since Radical Orthodoxy shares with such atheists the same, attenuated, conception of reason, at any rate in its strictly ratiocinative capacity.

That being so, it seems central to my case for the rational demonstrability of God that, both in principle and as a matter of the interpretation of Thomas Aquinas, a clear account can be given of how 'reason', in that narrow sense in which it is exercised in demonstrative argument, stands in relation to 'reason' in that wider sense in which human beings are said to exercise their rationality in all that they do as animals. For we

---

[16] See Catherine Pickstock, *After Writing: On the Liturgical Consummation of Philosophy*, Oxford: Blackwell, 1998, pp. 27–32.

cannot understand what it is to be rational in either sense unless we can understand what it is to be rational in the other. But before setting about the task of more formally defining that relationship between the narrower and broader senses of rationality, we need to give closer attention to some of the ways in which rationality in that wider sense is deployed; and to do this we need to return to the matter, touched on in chapter three, of the 'uttering performance'.

'Uttering performances' revisited

In revisiting the subject of 'uttering performances' we may be brief. Actions 'speak', as gestures do. Verbal utterances are actions too, and so 'utter' as all actions speak, and not just as words uttered. Therefore, within verbal utterances we may distinguish between what is said *in* saying the words, and *the meaning which the action of saying them* bears. Judas greets Jesus with a kiss. But there is irony in the kiss because what the kiss says is subverted by what Judas' action of betraying Jesus by means of it says. One and the same act has a double meaning, therefore, only because there are to be distinguished what is said by an utterance, and what its being uttered says. And these two ways in which a communicative act can 'mean' may stand in many different kinds of relationship with one another. They may ironically contradict each other, as with Judas' kiss; or they may complement each other, as when a beautiful poem is complemented by the beauty of its typography, or when its beauty is doubly enacted by the beauty of its being uttered. In that case, the shapes of the squiggles on the page, or the musicality of the speech, are from one point of view that which we read or hear, the words; from another point of view, those same shapes or sounds seduce by their typographical or tonal beauty, so the same shapes or sounds speak twice and do not twice 'say' the same. Sometimes the relationship is 'hermeneutical'; for the thing said is interpreted in a particular way by the material qualities of its being said, as when, in a poem, rhythmic speech-patterns read a layer of significance into what the words themselves say. 'Thou mastering me / God' are the opening words of Hopkins's *The Wreck of the Deutschland*, and the combined effect of alliteration and of natural inflection, which is to pile the first three words up upon one another and to cause a caesura before the fourth, alerts us to the fact that the poem opens with a vocative address, and that the first three words form a single compound hyphenated adjective qualifying the fourth: 'Thou-mastering-me//God!': and so the rhythm reads the sense.

To say that human beings are 'rational' is to say that human beings cannot help but that their grossest actions should speak, they cannot do anything meaninglessly. Hence, they cannot speak but that their action of speaking also says something. We may be able to choose to say something, or not. But even the avoidance of speech, being an action, can say something, as when we grasp the significance of a silence, or as when someone noticeably fails to say 'thank you'. And if we speak, we may be able to choose what we say, but we cannot choose what our utterance means, and often enough it does not mean what we intended to say. And all this is what is meant when we say that human animality is rational; all human action is speech, including the speech-acts themselves. All human 'performances' utter.[17]

I shall say, simply to stipulate a terminology, that everything to do with how the actions of human communication themselves speak is the domain of 'rhetoric'. The 'rhetorical', therefore, refers to those features of human speech-performance which are themselves meaningful *qua* performed, as distinct from what the speech itself means, however enacted; and, as a next step in the exploration of human rationality, we must consider two ways in which rhetorical features of language interact with semantic features, in, in turn, the poetic and the musical. And the purpose is to explore in what way human language as such, and therefore human rationality in its broadest conception, lays itself open inherently to the transcendent.

Theological rhetoric

Anyone who has had the least acquaintance with the writings of Thomas Aquinas and of Meister Eckhart will be struck by how it is that the writings of these two Dominicans, educated as both were (albeit some forty years apart) in the same priory at Cologne, and possibly taught by the same Albert the Great, could differ so starkly in rhetorical 'feel'. It would be easy to put these differences down to a relatively superficial matter of style and imagery, dictated by differences of intellectual temperament, if it were not for the fact that those differences of style and imagery derive from a difference of another kind, more fundamental than the first, which indicates what would appear to be a difference of theological strategy of a wider significance, which is historical and more than merely personal. For what is distinctive in Eckhart exhibits an important development in late thirteenth- and early fourteenth-century theology, a marked shift towards a more conscious cultivation of a distinctive theological rhetoric.

---

[17] Thomas distinguished between an *actus hominis* – an act performed by a human being but without human significance – and an *actus humanus*, which is an act performed by a human *qua* human; *ST* 1a q1 a1 *corp*. Human beings are no different from any other material object if, having jumped off a bridge, they fall to the ground. Only a human being, however, can commit suicide.

It is possible that this explicit cultivation of new rhetorical techniques at the service of theology is connected, in turn, with the emergence of vernacularity as a major theological medium; what is certain is that from the late thirteenth century onwards there emerges a volume of theological writings whose vernacularity enabled the emergence of that sort of new theological strategy of which Eckhart's *Sermons* are so strikingly representative.[18]

At any rate, the superficial differences between Thomas and Eckhart in style and imagery are obvious: Oliver Davies has pointed to the significance of rhetorical features of Eckhart's theology, features which are, of course, more prominent in the vernacular sermons – naturally enough, since they are sermons – but by no means absent from his more technical, Latin treatises. As Davies says, Eckhart's theology is a sort of 'poetic metaphysics', in which, as in all poetry, there is a certain 'foregrounding' of the language itself, of the signifier;[19] and, one might add, this 'poeticisation' of theological discourse goes along with a certain rhetorical 'performativeness', or, as one might say, a quasi-sacramental character. For it is a characteristic of Eckhart's language that it does not merely say something: it is intended to do something by means of saying, and, as we have seen, on the classical medieval account that is the nature of a sacrament: it is 'a sacred sign which effects what it signifies'.

When, therefore, we note the obvious, but otherwise incidental, fact of the extreme negativity of Eckhart's theological language – saturated as it is with images of 'nothingnesses' and 'abysses', by the featurelessness of 'deserts' and 'ground', and by 'nakedness' and 'emptiness' – we can begin to see that the rhetorical devices have a centrally theological point. Listen to Eckhart's homiletic rhetoric (it is essential to listen, even in modern English translation):

Then how should I love God? You should love God unspiritually, that is, your soul should be unspiritual and stripped of all spirituality, for so long as your soul has a spirit's form, it has images, and so long as it has images, it has a medium, and so long as it has a medium, it is not unity or simplicity. Therefore your soul

---

[18] And not alone in Meister Eckhart. I am much obliged to several years of discussion with Dr Rebecca Stephens, who brought to my attention the theological significance of parallel rhetorical features in the *Mirouer des ames Simples* of Marguerite Porete, the 'sometime Beguine' burned at the stake for her theological pains in Paris in 1310. It may be that Eckhart knew this text, and there are those who claim a direct influence of the *Mirouer* on Eckhart's subsequent preaching, though Dr Stephens thinks the claims some have made for this influence to be exaggerated. In most of what is contained in this section I am much indebted to those many discussions I had with her, and to the PhD thesis which she completed at the University of Birmingham, *Orthodoxy and Liminality in Marguerite Porete's Mirror of Simple Souls*, 1999.

[19] Oliver Davies, *Meister Eckhart: Mystical Theologian*, London: SPCK, 1991, p. 180.

must be unspiritual, free of all spirit, and must remain spiritless; for if you love God as he is God, as he is spirit, as he is person and as he is image – all this must go! 'Then how should I love him?' You should love him as he is nonGod, a nonspirit, a nonperson, a nonimage, but as he is pure, unmixed, bright 'One', separated from all duality; and in that One we should eternally sink down, out of 'something' into 'nothing'.[20]

It is true that, looked at from a literary standpoint, the negativity of Eckhart's imagery is very striking. But it is also true that, looked at from the standpoint of the formal articulation of his negative theology, this negative imagery is 'incidental', and this is important, because so often it is that negativity of metaphor which is taken to be in itself indicative of Eckhart's apophaticism. It cannot be emphasised enough that, as I argued in chapter 3, negative imagery is, for all its negativity, still imagery; negative language is still language; and if the 'apophatic' is to be understood as that which surpasses all language, then, as the pseudo-Denys says, it lies beyond both 'affirmation' and 'denial': for *eadem est scientia oppositorum*, as Aristotle had said,[21] what is sauce for the affirmative goose is sauce for the negative gander. Not incidentally, there are connected with this fundamental failure to understand medieval forms of apophaticism all sorts of nonsense, still unfortunately to be heard and read these days, about 'apophatic language', and worse, of an apophatic language which 'transcends Aristotelian logic': in so far as it is language which is in question, theology cannot transcend Aristotelian logic; in so far as the 'apophatic' is in question, it is not language, but the failure of language, to which we refer. Eckhart's explosive theological rhetoric is far from being, or even encouraging of, an irrationalism.

All this is clear to Meister Eckhart. And it is clear from this typical passage that the negativity of Eckhart's theology is not just something said by means of emphatically negative vocabularies, for it consists in his sense of the failure of all language as such, even of negative language. Nonetheless, Eckhart the preacher wants theological language in some way to participate, as one might put it, in the event of its own failure. Negativity, therefore, is not just a stylistic or decoratively metaphoric emphasis of Eckhart's theology; it is a living, organising, feature of the language itself and is intrinsic to its compositional style as theological writing. It is as if Eckhart were trying to get the paradoxical nature of his theology (it is at once a language, but, as Michael Sells has so aptly put it, 'a language

---

[20] Sermon 83, *Renovamini Spiritu*, in Meister Eckhart, *The Essential Sermons, Commentaries, Treatises and Defense*, trans. and ed. Edmund Colledge and Bernard McGinn, London: SPCK, 1981, p. 208.

[21] Aristotle, *De interpretatione* 6, 17a 33–35; see also Aquinas, *ST* 1a q58 a4 ad2.

of unsaying'[22]) into the materiality of the language itself, so that it both directly says and as directly unsays in the one act of saying; he 'fore-grounds' the signifier only immediately to disrupt its signification, block it, divert it, postpone it. Thereby the language performs rhetorically what it says technically: the performance utters what the utterance performs. And this rhetorical device, as it were of forcing into the sensuous, material sign the character of its own self-subversion as signifier, is what accounts for that most characteristic feature of Eckhart's language: its rhetorical self-consciousness, its strained and strenuous, hyperactively paradoxical extravagance – its apophasis by excess. The language, naturally, bursts at the seams under the pressure of the excessive forces it is being made to contain, the language *as body* bursts open under the pressure of its overloaded weight of significance.

The superficial stylistic contrast with the deliberate sobriety of Aquinas' theological discourse could not be more marked. If Thomas can under-state the case, he will seize the opportunity to do so. If a thought can be got to speak for itself he will do as little as necessary to supplement it. Thomas is famous for his lucidity; as it were, the materiality of his the-ological signifiers disappears entirely into what is signified by them, and there is, in Thomas, an almost ruthless literary self-abnegation, a refusal of eloquence: the language is made to absent itself in any role other than that of signifying. Hence, for the most part, Thomas's theology aims for a language of pure transparency; it has the transparency of the language of physics, or of any strictly technical discourse, in which terms are as far as possible got to do no work of any kind except to mean the one thing that is stipulated by the language-game to which they belong. On a con-tinuum occupied by the purely technical, stipulative lucidity of physics at one end, and the material densities of poetry at the other, Thomas's the-ological language is closer to the former, Eckhart's closer to the rhetorical densities of poetic diction.

And it would be easy to suppose that there is a more fundamentally theological reason for this difference on the score of theological rhetoric. Thomas's economy of speech accompanies, and probably derives from, a fundamental confidence in theological language, a trust that our ordi-nary ways of talking about creation are fundamentally in order as ways of talking about God, needing only to be subordinated to a governing apophaticism, expressed as a second-order epistemological principle: that all theological affirmation is both necessary and deficient. We must say of God anything true of what he has created, because that is all there

---

[22] Michael A. Sells, *Mystical Languages of Unsaying*, Chicago: University of Chicago Press, 1994.

is to hand with which to say anything about God, because there is no special 'hyperessential' meaning available to the theologian, and because we therefore know that whatever we say is in any case inadequate. Once we know that everything we say about God fails anyway, we can freely indulge the materiality of those metaphors, the carnality of that imagery, and calmly exploit all those possibilities of formal inference and logic, which appear so to unnerve the anxious Eckhart.

It is for this reason not difficult to see why there are those for whom Eckhart shares something spiritually with a post-modern mentality here not found in Thomas, a commonality which has led some post-modern writers to take an interest in his work, as we shall see. And there is indeed something to be said for the view that with both Eckhart and the post-modern the rhetoric appears fraught with anxiety, with a fear of the sign, a horror of the constative. Eckhart seems perpetually afflicted with a theological neurosis lest he get God idolatrously wrong, so he watches his theological language with a vigilance so anxious – violent even – as to arouse a suspicion: that he writes as if striving for that which he also knows to be impossible, as if there were some superior ideal theological syntax reserved for addressing God in correctly, to which his rhetoric strains, deficiently, to attain; or, as Derrida puts it, Eckhart's language strains for an impossible hyperessentiality – a 'hyperessentiality' which, for all its impossibility, nonetheless figures as a spurious measure of our apophatic failure. I once heard a theologian say that it was a mark of our philosophical sinfulness that we make the pattern of our existence to be the pattern of the divine – and he said it as if supposing that there were some, even notional, alternative state of affairs, some other, pre-lapsarian possibilities of language about God from which, through sin, we have fallen away. There is a dangerously Origenistic sound to this view, and in any case, it is to be wondered what this theologian could possibly have been imagining, which made him so worried about our fallen speech. What else could speech be but that which, before God, fails? That failure is down to language, not to sin; to our being human, not to our failure to be human. Thomas, knowing that you will never get God finally right anyway, seems less anxious, and that applies to anything you say: hence, an unstrained, technical, but demotic ordinariness of speech is all as right, one way or another, as it will ever be, for there is no other, higher, language by which its deficiency can be measured. Why this difference in theological temperament and style?

One reason appears to be that Eckhart, as I have said, wants to constrain all the paradoxical tensions of the theological project into each and every theological speech-act. It is the language itself which is the bearer of these contrary forces of saying and unsaying, of affirmativeness and negativity, and so his discourse must be got endlessly to destabilise itself. And Eckhart must in this way compel the material rhetorical dimension of his discourse into a constant interplay with its formal significance, he must bend and twist and stretch theological language, because he wants theology as language 'poetically' to do what it says, and so, as it were, to speak its own failure as speech. Eckhart does not simply preach the unknowability of God. He wants to transact that unknowing in the very discourse itself with the congregation to which he preaches. Eckhart wants his act of preaching to draw his listeners into the unknowing he preaches about, into a community in that unknowing.[23]

And on account of these things, undoubtedly true of Eckhart's distinctive theological style, I confess that I used to think that perhaps in the end Eckhart differs from Thomas on a point of very fundamental theological principle: that Eckhart cannot trust creatures to proclaim God and so mistrusts the ordinariness, the demotic character, of theological speech as Thomas conceives of it. In that linguistic ordinariness, from which there is no escape, no impossible and distorting alternative envisaged, we can, for Thomas, speak confidently of God, because that same theological act by which our carnal speech is shown to be justified as theology also shows that the God thus demonstrated lies, in unutterable otherness, beyond the reach of anything we can say. Hence, unlike Eckhart, there is for Thomas no need to try especially hard to say it. We have not, and could not have, and should not anxiously seek to have, any measure of the deficiency of our speech about God; we could not know and should not try to know how far all our language falls short of God. In fact one could well imagine Thomas's offering to Eckhart the advice the angel gave to Gerontius in Newman's *Dream*: 'it is thy very energy of thought which keeps thee from thy God'.[24]

There is something to be said for reading the rhetorical contrasts between Thomas and Eckhart as deriving from some such differences of theological temperament, though to deduce from these differences

[23] Vittorio Montemaggi, research student in the Faculty of Divinity at the University of Cambridge, has pointed out to me that much the same can be said of that greatest of all theological poets, Dante. The *Commedia*, he says, not only speaks *of* the communities in which God may truly be known (and notoriously of the communities in which God is denied), but is itself a theological transaction with its readership, transacting through poetry an incorporation into that community. And that poetic transaction is central to Dante's conception of the theological act itself. As poetry, the *Commedia* is therefore itself quasi-sacramental in character: the poetic act and the theological act coincide as one and the same act. See Montemaggi's article '"La rosa in che il verbo divino carne se fece": Human Bodies and Truth in the Poetic Narrative of the *Commedia*', forthcoming in *Dante and the Human Body*, Dublin: University College Dublin Foundation for Italian Studies, 2004.

[24] Cardinal J. H. Newman, *The Dream of Gerontius* III, London: Mowbray, 1986, p. 21.

any picture of Eckhart's theology in the thoroughgoing anti-metaphysical, post-modern and anti-foundationalist terms that some have seems to lack serious justification. It is of course not difficult to see why, on such a reading, theologians of a post-modern mentality should be tempted in this way to enlist Meister Eckhart in support of a project of theological deconstruction, of an apparent displacement of rational argument by an apophatic rhetoric, and should experience no such temptation to enlist the support of Thomas Aquinas to that end. But such a reading does Eckhart no justice: Eckhart himself could have had little sympathy with the anti-metaphysical implications of such a post-modern reading. Indeed, Oliver Davies has argued persuasively that post-modern attempts to skim Eckhart's rhetorical 'apophaticism' off from the medieval cosmology and metaphysics on which it is for him firmly based inevitably result in a failed attempt to repeat, by means of an uprooted rhetoric alone, that which is possible only on a metaphysical ground. Thereby Eckhart's dialectical theology would suffer reduction to a *mere* rhetoric, to a rhetoric, one might say, *as* 'mere'. As Davies puts it: 'if we jettison the medieval cosmology which underlies Eckhart's system of participation, then we appear to want the fruits of a medieval world view without buying into the fourteenth century physics which supported it'.[25] It is only on an unjustifiably selective account of Eckhart that it is possible to be misled about his purposes, as not only some of his contemporaries were, into suspecting a certain, paradoxical, 'hypostatisation' of the negative, a certain reduction of theology to a rhetoric of postponement, indeed into suspecting a sort of post-modern spirituality or 'mysticism'. But in fact Eckhart's rhetorical devices have a strictly theological purpose, and one which, after all, is not at odds with any purpose Thomas envisaged for theology, howsoever obvious may be the differences of rhetoric.

For after all, if with Eckhart as with Thomas, all theology must begin in, be mediated by, and end in the darkness of unknowing; and if, that being so, all creation in some way speaks God as irreducibly 'other' than it, why should not our language itself, being the natural expression of human rationality in its created materiality, speak God as unutterably other, not only in what we say in it, but also in the manner in which we say it, in its rhetorical forms themselves? That Thomas rarely exploits these rhetorical possibilities himself is neither here nor there, for Eckhart's enthusiastic exploitation of them is perfectly consistent with Thomas's theology. Thomas *says*: all theological language fails. Eckhart's rhetoric

---

[25] Oliver Davies, 'Revelation and the Politics of Culture', in *Radical Orthodoxy? A Catholic Enquiry*, ed. Laurence Paul Hemming, Aldershot: Ashgate, 2000, p. 121.

gets theological language itself to fail, so that its *failure* says the same. Thomas *says*: all talk about God breaks down. Eckhart gets the *breakdown of language* to say the same: the rhetoric says what he and Thomas both say in it. The material voice of the rhetoric speaks theologically at one with the formal significance which it utters.

There is therefore something almost frighteningly 'materialistic' about Eckhart's theology which, when looked at in this way, could with good reason be cause to revise some assumptions about Eckhart's dauntingly high-minded, and supposedly elitist, 'mysticism'. Eckhart's theology is in principle a demotic theology, and in his sermons it has taken on the character almost of a drama; at any rate, theology has become an act, for it enacts in its performance what it is about as word. For when Eckhart looks for God, he looks for him in what is most 'material', even 'animal', within our rational nature: in the materiality of the 'fore-grounded signifier'. And if in this respect Eckhart's theology has, as Davies says, something of the character of the 'poetic', we can also say that it has something of the character of the sacramental: its enactment says what it signifies. It is as true, therefore, of Eckhart as it is of Thomas that he wants to find God in the created order; but he differs from Thomas in that he discovers and 'makes' the divine transcendence as much in our created language itself as in the creation that language describes. But then it is not in language's theologically expressive ability that he finds God, except in so far as that expressive ability is supremely exercised in its being pushed to the point of its failure, in the sustaining of quasi-poetic tensions between signifier and signified, each in turn subverting and transcending the other. In so far, then, as God is found in human language, within its characteristic rationality, God is found not, as Nietzsche thought, in the good order of 'grammar',[26] but in the disordered collapse of speech into paradox, oxymoron, and the negation of the negation. And it is within this disordered and theologically contrived dislocation of language, a dis-location which must be endlessly repeated and renewed, that our created discourses open up towards a space which they can, as it were, gesture towards, but cannot occupy: through the cracks in the fissured surface of theological language there is glimpsed the 'space' of the transcendent. For Eckhart, therefore, reason, language, 'at the end of its tether' has the same shape as it has for Thomas, the form of an openness to an unknowable otherness. Thus does Eckhart's rhetoric say for itself that which cannot be said in it.

---

[26] See below, pp. 150–3.

And as an account of how human reason – our animality – can in some sort speak God, this is also pure Thomas, just as, when Eckhart preached in Strasbourg that we 'should love God as he is nonGod', he said nothing that Thomas had not already written in his study in Paris when he tells us that 'by grace . . . we are made one [with God] as to something unknown to us'.

6   The 'shape' of reason

Music as the 'limit' of reason

If within Eckhart's 'poetic metaphysics' there is, as Davies says, a certain 'foregrounding of the signifier' which enables him to set up a subtle interplay between the formal and material significance of his theological speech, a strategy of deconstruction, then this suggests the intriguing possibility that one theoretical 'limit' case of human rationality is to be found in music.[1] For we could say that in music the signifier is 'foregrounded' so absolutely that all is reduced to it, with nothing left to it in the character of verbal language at all. If speech may enact 'rhetorically' what it says semantically, music is nothing if not enacted: it is pure performance. We may say with some qualifications that music 'speaks' in the same way that a kiss, or a smile, may speak.[2] In consequence, music can have no 'constative' character; there is nothing it is 'about' in the way in which there is something which verbal utterance can be 'about'. If, within poetry, there is a sort of 'dialectic' between the meaning carried by material features of the language and that uttered as the formal significance of its words – between, therefore, what is 'said' by the features of assonance, rhythm and inflection on the one hand, and what is said formally by the words on the other – in 'pure' music there is nothing 'said' other than that 'meaning' which is achieved by the structuring of its material features alone: the rhythms; the sequence of pitches, of tempi and of volume; the melodic, harmonic and tonal organisation. In the terminology which

[1] In the few remarks which follow about music, I am much indebted to a long-running conversation with Férdia Stone-Davis, research student in the Faculty of Divinity at Cambridge, whose comments on an earlier draft have enabled me to avoid some otherwise serious errors. This is not to say that she would agree with all that I say here, but everything I do say reflects in some way those conversations in which we have engaged in consequence of her research.
[2] Though, as Vittorio Montemaggi has pointed out to me, there are important differences: see note 11 below.

I stipulated above, we could say that music is rhetoric in its purest form, for it is nothing else but a rhetoric.[3]

I should not wish to take such a proposition any further than by means of it to entertain a theoretical possibility, one which might help with the clarification of what is definitive of human reason. For in one sense of the word 'defined', a territory is defined by its extremes, as a nation's territory is defined by its borders. And in this way, it might be possible to describe music as a 'definitively' rational human pursuit, because on the one hand it is the most 'formal' of the human means of expression – there is nothing it is 'about', its 'significance' is internal to its own structures, and there is nothing for the signifier to interact with by way of formal signification: the 'meaning', whole and entire, is in the sound itself and in its 'form' – while, on the other hand, it is also the most 'material' – indeed 'animal' – mode of human expression, for there is nothing else to music except what it achieves by the structuring of patterns of sound;[4] it is in that sense pure body. On this account, therefore, music is sound and fury, signifying nothing that the sound and the fury do not themselves signify. So it is that, in saying that music is rhetoric in its purest form, this is the same as to say that music is the body in its purest form as language.

Herbert McCabe once said that 'poetry is language trying to be bodily experience, as music is bodily experience trying to be language',[5] and there is some truth in the epigram, except for the 'trying to be'. For although music is well understood as 'language' – and it would seem that there is nothing intrinsically misleading with understanding it in those terms – it is not as if it aspires to the condition of verbal speech, and fails, for music is not in that sense 'trying to' say anything.[6] Rather the

[3] Stone-Davis points out that since Plato, through Augustine to Kant, the word 'rhetoric' has acquired almost entirely negative connotations, which might appear to entail some form of depreciation of music as a form of human communication. It will be clear, however, from my argument so far that by 'rhetoric' I refer not to some degenerate form of communication – 'degenerate', that is to say, by the standards of formal verbal communication – but to all forms of human transaction of meaning in their 'performative' character as such, as distinct from what is transacted by the meaning of words themselves.

[4] This is carefully put. Gordon Graham argues that music is *nothing more than* the structuring of patterns of sound as the exploration of purely *aural* experience. This is too limited an account of music in my view. Music is indeed the exploration of aural experience; but more is *achieved by* this exploration than an exploration of the aural alone, for, as I shall argue shortly, by means of that exploration is achieved an understanding of how the body itself is capable of significance, specifically through the articulation and expression of emotion. See Gordon Graham, *The Philosophy of the Arts: An Introduction to Aesthetics*, 2nd edn, London: Routledge, 2002, pp. 70–3.

[5] Herbert McCabe OP, 'The Eucharist as Language', in *Modern Theology* 15.2, April 1999, p. 138.

[6] Here I am much reliant upon Férdia Stone-Davis's unpublished paper 'Plato, Kant and the Reduction of Music' presented to the Conference of the Music Research Group on 'The Intellectual Frontiers of Music' at the University of Aberdeen, June 2002.

matter is better put the other way round: music is, in a certain sense, closer to those sources in the body of all meaningful human behaviour on which the possibility of verbal speech depends than is verbal speech itself. Hence, as against what is implied by McCabe's epigram, it seems better to say with Stone-Davis that verbal language is the wrong model for how music 'signifies', for there is no sense in which music signifies by way of 'representation' in the way verbal language does. Moreover, it is thus far possible to agree with Nietzsche that 'music itself . . . has no need at all of images and concepts, but merely tolerates them as an accompaniment . . . which is why language, as the organ and symbol of phenomena, can never, under any circumstances, externalise the innermost depths of music'.[7] But while it is possible to agree that music is not to be understood as a failed form of verbal speech, that denial does not entail that music does not in any way signify – if not in the same way as, still every bit as much as, verbal language does. Music is the body in its most elemental form as language, because it is language in its most embodied form; but it is also the body in its most transparently significant form. Music is therefore the most fundamental and elemental form of human rationality, and so of 'language', in that wider sense in which I have been trying to explain them. We could say that verbal speech is possible only because the human body meets those conditions of significance on account of which music is possible. If human beings could not be musical, then they could not be verbal.[8]

For this reason it is important to correct a possibly misleading impression. As Stone-Davis has commented, to say that music is 'pure rhetoric' and that, in music, 'there is nothing for the signifier to interact with' by way of verbal communication – as there is in poetry – could appear to have the consequence that, as she rightly says, 'the partnership of words and music', such as is found in opera or more generally in song, 'is undermined'. For if the 'formal' character of music were so to be emphasised as to remove from it all capacity to signify what verbal communication signifies, then there could be no possibility in song of an interplay of significances between the words set to music and the music it is set to. And this consequence, Stone-Davis argues, is clearly counter-intuitive, as indeed it is.

---

[7] Friedrich Nietzsche, *The Birth of Tragedy*, ed. Raymond Geuss and Ronald Speirs, trans. Ronald Speirs, Cambridge: Cambridge University Press, 2000, p. 36.

[8] To the extent that, on this account, music is envisaged as in some way more 'elemental' than verbal speech, it is in accord with Nietzsche's proposition that in even that most musical of the literary arts, lyric poetry, 'we see language straining to its limits *to imitate music*. . .With this observation we have defined the only possible relationship between music, word, and sound: the word, the image, the concept seeks expression in a manner analogous to music and thereby is subjected to the power of music' *Birth of Tragedy*, p. 34.

And so it is necessary to clarify the statement that music is 'pure rhetoric'. Far from its being the case that the interplay, such as I have identified in poetry, between what is signified verbally and what is signified by the materiality of the sign, is absent from song, it is, on the contrary, intensified in song. In fact it is possible to construe the relationship between the words and the music to which it is set as an *intensified* poetics; for what takes place in, for example, a Mozart opera, is an intensification of the interplay, characteristic of the 'poetic', between the two levels of signification, that of the words and that of their 'rhetorical' (that is, in the case of opera, their musical) setting. Of course, the word 'setting' is too weak to do justice to the role of music within opera, most especially in the greatest operatic composers, Monteverdi, Mozart, as also in Wagner. What is composed is the conjunction, in all its complexity of interplay, between words and music, and therefore between the ways in which they both 'signify'. For this reason there is something to be said for the view that, on the contrary, poetry is a weakened form of song, for in poetry the 'rhetoric' consists simply in the material, aural, character of the words themselves, and the 'interplay' consists in the structuring of the aural qualities of the words in their relationships with their formal significations, as we saw in the last chapter.

But since this is so, then it follows that the character of music as 'pure rhetoric', whether as setting words or as purely instrumental, cannot be so understood as to preclude its bearing a meaning in *some* way analogous to that in which words do. And of course music does so bear meanings, in its own terms. When in *The Marriage of Figaro* Mozart sets to music the Countess's aria 'Porgi amor', he sets sad words sung sadly, indeed to one of the saddest melodies in music. We would be at least much puzzled if Mozart had set the Countess's expressions of grief at the Count's betrayals to a melody of Haydnesque jolliness, and we would be forced to suspect an irony of some sort, just because we recognise the emotional qualities of music directly from the music itself. In just the same way as a man 'may smile and smile and be a villain', so verbal text and music can transact meanings in all manner of interactions, which could be the case only if music had its own capacity to 'mean' independently of the verbal meanings.

But how are we to square this obvious fact of such interactions between verbal and musical significance with the statement that music does not signify anything 'other than itself' and is 'pure rhetoric'? What, and how, *does* music 'signify'? Is there anything it is 'about' and how? Put in more abstract terms, how do the 'formal' and the 'material' coincide in music's distinctive capacity for significance? A first step towards an answer must be that music stands in some kind of relation with emotion. If it is an error which, as Nietzsche says, 'strikes our aesthetics as offensive'[9] that individual listeners are constrained 'to speak in images' upon hearing a symphony of Beethoven, it cannot be in the same way arbitrary to describe a piece of music as 'sad', or 'elated', or 'tormented', as it would be to describe it as 'pastoral'. Indeed, it cannot be an error at all to describe music in terms of emotions, unless, once again, it is said on a representational model of how it may so be described. Sad music does not *represent* sadness. The hearer experiences the sadness upon hearing the music. But the musical experience of sadness is not itself a sad experience. On the contrary, the experienced *Sturm und Drang* of Schubert's string quintet is sublimely elevating. How so?

In his *Confessions* Augustine notes with puzzlement how it is that he can attend a tragedy in the theatre in Milan with such intense pleasure.[10] Bitter distress is so artfully represented in the drama that Augustine cannot but be drawn into the experience of it in a manner which directly engages his emotions. Augustine feels the pain enacted as his own, to a degree of intensity which perhaps outstrips any that he has ever felt *in propria persona* – but he does not experience it *as* pain. It will not do, therefore, to say, as Plato might have, in explanation of the pleasure Augustine takes in the tragedy, that the emotion Augustine experiences is felt only in an indirect, 'detached' way, or that Augustine is drawn passionately into what is but a pale imitation, an illusory representation, of a sadness and pain which stand at one remove from the experience as it would have felt had it been some personal experience of tragedy of Augustine's own. Nor will it do justice to the experience to say that it is a matter of sympathy for another's real distress, for there is no pleasure in that. Nor yet is it enough, by way of explanation of this complex experience, to say that what we take pleasure in is the 'art' with which the emotion is evinced in the audience or hearer – that what we enjoy is the skill, what is 'sad' is the experience into which that skill draws us. For both the directness of our experience of the sadness, and the pleasure of the experiencing it, are part of one and the same, single, emotional response to the music or to the tragic drama. There is, somehow, pleasure *in* the enacted experience of sadness, so that, although directly experienced, it is not itself a sad experience.

What appears to permit this same complexity of emotional response in the case of music – and at the same time permits our descriptions of music in the vocabulary of emotion in a stronger than metaphorical sense – is precisely that complexity of the 'material' and the 'formal' which we have seen to characterise human rationality as such. For when we are drawn

---

[9] Nietzsche, *Birth of Tragedy*, p. 34.   [10] Augustine, *Confessions* 3.2.

into the 'sadness' of the second movement of Schubert's 'Death and the Maiden' quartet we do indeed experience that sadness directly, but not as being a sadness about anything, nor as being anybody's sadness – not yours, not mine, not even Schubert's. Of course, you may, as you experience it, contingently be caused to recollect the tragedy of Schubert's predicament as he wrote that movement, or you may, as it happens, be caused to recollect some sadness of your own. But such personal experiences of sadness are strictly irrelevant to the music's own character as sad. For what you experience is sadness *as such*, the pure form of the emotion, but as subjectless and as objectless.[11] Hence, on the one hand, you do experience the sadness in its inner character as sadness – and not merely the skill of its expression – but on the other, you experience it not as yours nor yet as originating in any actual cause or as directed at any object in particular. This is not to say that the experience of music's sadness or joy is not a personal experience, for of course it is. But it is the personal experience of an emotion in its pure character as that emotion, so that just as the musical expression of that emotion is without subject and without object, so is 'my' experience of it.[12] Through my experience of the music I enter a 'space' in which I can experience a transcendence of the opposition between subjectivity and objectivity within the experience itself – which is also the reason why music has no 'constative' character as such; for language to 'state' something there has to be a subject stating and an object stated. And music prescinds from both subjectivity and objectivity. As Nietzsche puts it, 'the whole opposition between the subjective and the objective . . . is absolutely inappropriate in aesthetics since the subject, the willing individual in pursuit of his own, egotistical goals, can only be considered the opponent of art, not its origin'. [13] And this self-transcendence of one's own subjectivity, its being stripped away by music's refusal equally of subjectivity as of objectivity, and entering a space 'beyond' it, is itself the object of pleasure: the desire thus

---

[11] In this respect music differs from a smile, as Montemaggi says. Beatrice's famous smile directed to Dante (in *Paradiso*, cant. XVIII, 4–20) gets its power to communicate precisely as Beatrice's act of drawing Dante into community with her and with the blessed in paradise. The specificities of Beatrice and Dante are intrinsic to the communicative act itself.

[12] 'Therefore music does not express this or that particular and definite pleasure, this or that affliction, pain, sorrow, horror, gaiety, merriment, or peace of mind, but joy, pain, sorrow, horror, gaiety, merriment, peace of mind *themselves*, to a certain extent in the abstract, their essential nature, without any accessories, and so also without the motives for them.' Artur Schopenhauer, *The World as Will and Representation* I, book 3, 51, trans. E. F. J. Payne, New York: Dover Publications, 1969, p. 261. I am grateful to Férdia Stone-Davis for alerting me to this passage.

[13] Nietzsche, *Birth of Tragedy*, p. 32.

satisfied is, as Plato says, the sort of desire which can be satisfied only by the beautiful.

But if in this way music creates the space for a kind of self-trans-cendence, it creates it in the most purely *bodily* form. Music is body as pure meaning, it is body as *trans*formed. For as emotion is rooted in our carnality, so the space created by music for this emotional self-transcendence is also the space in which that carnality achieves a trans-parency to meaning, a transparency which bestows upon music in its own right, and on no particular analogy with verbal speech, the name of 'language', a language which is all 'foregrounded signifier', properly called by the name 'language', even if, as Stone-Davis rightly says, it is about nothing but itself. Music, *par excellence*, is our animality as rational. It is also our rationality as 'self-transcendent'. It is the body in its purest form *as language*, as communicative.

In this way, then, what is to be said about the 'meanings' which music communicates is neither more nor less, and neither more nor less puz-zling, than what is to be said about how a kiss or a smile signifies meaning. Whether of music or of any bodily gesture, we should say that they are absolutely bodily and absolutely significant, at one and the same time wholly material and wholly formal, saying what they say not in distinc-tion from, and certainly not in contrast with, their bodily character. What is materially done is what does the saying. 'Form' and 'matter' are the one 'speech'.

That music should be in this way at once the most material and the most formal of kinds of human expression is no unresolvable paradox. For the paradox of music is in its way but a 'limit' case of the more general connectedness between 'rationality' and 'animality', between the formal and the material, between the achievement of significance and the performance of the signifier; and music is a 'limit' case of that connect-edness, because music collapses the signified whole and entire into the signifier. It therefore stands at one extreme of the continuum of forms of 'rationality', a continuum occupied at the opposite extreme by a purely stipulative technical discourse, such as mathematics, which collapses the signifier whole and entire into the signified: a mathematical symbol per-forms nothing but to signify; music signifies nothing but what it performs.

It is perhaps for this reason that, in its character of a purely natural self-transcendence, music serves the end more spontaneously than do most other forms of human activity of a 'natural theology', even if, as we shall see, it can only half serve it. And if this is so, it is because of those paradoxical conjunctions of music's being closest to us in its intense phys-icality and yet wholly open as to its significance, in its being indeterminate and lacking in particular *reference*, in its being purely *formal*: and being so, it opens up spaces of experience beyond our particularity, beyond our confined individuality. Ancients did not think, as we do now, of some music as sacred and some secular. They thought music was sacred as such, and, whatever the reasons of the ancients, perhaps it is still possible for us moderns intuitively to know what they mean. At any rate we may share with the ancients the feeling that music has a natural capacity for the transcendent, that it is the most 'natural' of natural theologies, and it may be that this common perception has to do with the fact that music's very impersonality and 'otherness' are what allows for such a free, spontaneous, and utterly personal, but at the same time self-transcendent, response. Perhaps that is why music is still the most commonly experienced form of what the medievals called an *excessus*, or in Greek, *ekstasis*, or in English, taking leave of your senses; but in music, by the most sensual, most bodily, of means. If we can say that music is the body inserted into language, we must also say that music is the body inserted into unknowing. Music is, as it were, the body in the condition of ecstasy.

Moreover, it is just because in music the most sensual is conjoined with the most transparently meaningful that we can say, linking back to the argument of chapter 3, that music is, in a certain way, proto-typically 'Eucharistic'. For though there is much to the Eucharist beyond this, still, in the Eucharist is brought to the absolute limit of possibility – that is to say, to the limit possible before our resurrection – that conjunction of absolute bodiliness and absolute transparency of meaning; for the Eucharist is a communication which is all body, and a body which is all communication: or, and this is just another way of putting it, in the Eucharist we have a 'real presence' which pushes to the very limits any force we can lay hold of for the word 'real' and for every meaning we can have for the word 'present'. And then we have to add, 'and beyond'; that is to say, beyond any such force we can lay hold on for those words 'real' and 'presence'. For the doctrine of the 'real presence' of Christ in the Eucharist is, in Thomas, also a doctrine of the 'real absence'. What the Eucharist makes 'real' is both the 'now' and the 'not yet', and it is just that *conjunction* of presence and absence which is made 'real', for the Eucharistic presence is caught up into an 'eschatological', not a merely 'linear', temporality. In that lies its character as a sacrament, inscribing in the body in its present condition an openness to a future which is not yet: the Eucharist is the resurrection of the body as only it can be within and for our unraised, historical, contingency. The Eucharist is, then, eschatology as body: the bread and wine *become* that body of the resurrection, a body which is all communication, the flesh made most perfectly to be Word, *futurae pignus gloriae*, as Thomas says in one of his Eucharistic prayers, 'a pledge of future glory'.

It is in all these respects that music is both central to what we mean by 'reason' and 'proto-typically Eucharistic' – at any rate, we could mean that much by 'reason' if we did not simply abase ourselves before the altar of some recent intellectual history which has reduced 'reason' to 'ratiocination'. And music is proto-typically Eucharistic in one more sense besides: for it is the common experience of *all* great music, it does not matter whether it is happy or sad, that it is in a certain way sad, for music is the *lachrymae rerum* – at any rate, whether it is that weird and terrible Trio of the Schubert string quintet, or the hushed moment of reconciliation of the finale of *The Marriage of Figaro* – at whichever end of the emotional spectrum it is to be found, or wherever it is placed between, *all* music is the cause of tears, whether tears of sadness or of joy. And I venture the speculation that if there is a certain ultimate melancholy to music, it is because music is in a way a shadow cast on to human sensibility of that eschatological temporality of the Eucharist; the sadness of music is a sort of sensual nostalgia for what one has caught some glimpse of but cannot yet possess; it is, as it were, a premonition of a premonition; it is a kind of pre-*anamnesis*, a depth dug into memory, scoring it with a sort of hope made real, but as loss and as absent, made present, but as yet to be real. Music is proto-sacramental in that it is proto-eschatological. It occupies the same human, bodily, space that is occupied by the Eucharist.

At this point, in their bearing on my argument generally, I shall say only this much about the relevance of these considerations, for it will be possible to make the full point of them clear only at the end; and it is that a 'speaking animal' in this, now the widest, sense of 'speaking' is the 'raw material' of the sacramental, and that an animal which speaks God is already in some way in the form of the sacramental, so that reason as such has, as it were by anticipation, a quasi-sacramental 'shape', the *form* of the Eucharist. Here, in music, it is reason in its broadest sense which is shown to have this shape of a maximum 'embodiment' bearing a maximum significance, of a materiality which is most perfectly formal. Later,[14] it is reason in its narrower sense of 'ratiocination' which is shown also to have this 'Christological' shape.

Reason, the 'central' case

If music may be said to be 'definitively rational' in the sense of being a 'limit' case, defining a boundary, there is another sense of the word

---

[14] See chapter 10, pp. 216–25 below.

'definitive' in which the 'definitive' is that which constitutes the central case; and in that latter sense I should say – and it is one of the principal purposes of this essay to defend the proposition – that the 'central' case of human reason is that which is exhibited in a formally valid proof of the existence of God. But to be clear in what sense this 'transcendent ratiocination' (as I should call it) is 'central' to human reason, it is necessary to be clear in what sense of the word 'central' this is being argued.

I have said that for Thomas Aquinas, to be rational is a way of being animal; there are, for him, no non-animal rational beings. Moreover, everything a human being does as an animal – feed, feel pain, have sex – a human being does as a rational kind of animal does it. And conversely, even though only rational animals can engage in 'thinking' properly speaking, and so in arguing and proving and inferring – in short, in 'ratiocinating' – still, rational beings could not do these things unless they were animals.

Further, we have seen that if, in that sense, human beings are, for Thomas, rational animals, they are also, in a certain sense, incarnate intellects: by which Thomas appears to mean at least two things, the first of which is that the characteristically 'discursive' nature of rational beings is the product of the dependence of human intellect on the five senses of the body; 'reason' *just is* intellect in the form it takes of that dependence. The second is that, definitive of rationality as that discursiveness is, such rationality would not be possible at all unless human beings were also capable of some activities which are purely 'intellectual', that is to say, unless human beings were capable of some cognitive activities which are not themselves the product of discursive rationality, but are, rather, presupposed to it. Such, then, is Thomas's concession to 'Augustinianism'.

If we combine these two propositions, first, that human beings could not be rational in the way that they are if they were not the sort of animals that they are, and second, that they could not be rational in the way that they are if they were not also intellectual, then we can conclude, for Thomas's part, with two consequences which follow from the conjunction. The first is that no human intellectual capacity is ever exercised except as the activity of an animal. The second consequence is that every activity in which a human being engages as an animal, being, as all such activities of humans are, activities of rational animals, in some way presupposes and engages with what I have described as the 'territory of intellect'. Now to say that transcendent ratiocination, proof of the existence of God, is a, or the, 'centrally' rational activity within this diversity and complexity of interrelationship between 'animality', 'rationality' and 'intellectuality', and that it is in that sense 'definitive' of the rational, is to say one thing very precisely, and is not to say a great number of other, imprecise, things at all.

In particular, it is to say nothing at all about where matters of logic and proof fall, by comparison with sex or music or poetry, on a scale of humanly affecting activities; nor is it absurdly to canvass any sort of role for a rational proof as an apologetic device likely to entice teenagers away from their clubbing and back to benediction and the holy rosary; still less is it to offer a reductivist account of every human activity as being 'rational' only in so far as it is reducible to some phenomenon of 'reasoning' (on which account, manifestly, music could not possibly be described as 'rational', as I have insisted it should: for manifestly, music does not involve anything reducible to 'ratiocination'; nor does poetry, or art, or making love). Nor yet does this centrality of rational proof entail that every exercise of 'reason' in any other form requires knowledge of reason's capacity to prove the existence of God. Indeed, it is manifestly possible to compose the most sublime poetry or music in the explicit denial of God's existence, and all the more possible in denial of the rational demonstrability of God's existence. Hence, the relationship of the 'peripheral' to the 'central' case of rationality is not that of the less to the more humanly appealing; nor that of the less to the more theologically persuasive; not at all that of the reducibility of the one to the other, and not even that the 'central' case be formally admitted as a possibility at all.

What does constitute the centrality of the demonstrability of the existence of God is simply that such demonstrability forms the point of convergence of an 'apophatic self-transcendence' which quite generally characterises every other form of rational activity in its widest sense. For it is true that every exercise of human reason in some way bears witness to a 'space' lying beyond its own powers to access and that every exercise of human reason is at least to that extent 'self-transcendent', that each may know in its own way that the conditions on which its own distinctive, particular, activities depend lie beyond its own scope. It is an everyday truth that music and poetry open up spaces beyond the power of music and poetry to gain entry; indeed, we can say of music that it 'carnalises' the inexpressible, it is the flesh made apophatic; but to the extent that such forms of human expression approximate to the condition of music as the limit case at one extreme, that space 'beyond' to which they point becomes increasingly indeterminate. For precisely because, as a form of human communication, music is most distanced from the formally linguistic, it is also the least determinate in the character of the 'otherness' it points to, or, as we might put it, is most free in its evocation of the transcendent. Nonetheless, the indeterminacy of human expression in regard to the otherness to which reason points is thus far quite general; for even verbal language as such cannot state all the conditions of its own possibility and so must, as Wittgenstein says, stay silent concerning that of which it cannot speak.[15] That being so, it follows that even if all human rationality, in whatever shape or form, knows there is something that it cannot know, those 'spaces' are thus far absolutely indeterminate as to their nature: there is nothing at all to guarantee that that which lies 'beyond' is anything but a vacuous, empty nothingness, an endless prolongation of postponements, as the post-modernists say. Hence, there are no guarantees in the nature of poetry, or music, or art, that the conditions of the possibility of any rational human activity are met at all – unless reason has some power to give a name to that 'otherness' which lies beyond it, a power, moreover, which it derives from its own relationship to its own created condition. In short, all that power of human creativity and expression to point beyond itself – which is the essential characteristic of 'rationality' – can be supposed to point beyond a nihilistic vacuousness, only if reason can justify the name of 'God' as that to which it points. In that sense alone does reason find its apotheosis in proof of God.

And here we close the loop upon a matter first addressed at the beginning of this essay, that of the relationship between a 'natural theology' and a 'negative theology'. If it is certainly wrong – in terms at least of the reading of Thomas – to set them in that opposition according to which a natural theology tells us about God those things – his existence and his nature – which a negative theology forbids us, nonetheless any account is equally flawed according to which a proof of God's existence leaves us with nothing at all but an unoccupied space of 'negativity' on the other side of creation. It is because they feared some such apophatically inspired absolutisation of the negative which would have to be indistinguishable from a nihilistic atheism (since it would allow no room for any criterion on which to distinguish them) that Milbank and Pickstock thought it necessary to attribute to Thomas some mode of experience, presupposed to reason's exercise, of the 'actuality' of perfection. But there is no need to appeal on Thomas's behalf to any such experience in order to insure against a purely nihilistic account of the unknowability of the rationally transcendent, or of the aesthetically sublime, as the case may be: and it is better not to do so, since, as I have said, there is absolutely no evidence that Thomas thought the human intellect was ever in possession of such

---

[15] Ludwig Wittgenstein, *Tractatus Logico-Philosophicus* 7, trans. C. K. Ogden, London, Routledge & Kegan Paul, 1962, p. 189.

an experience. For Thomas appeared to think that there are only two ways in which God can be known this side of death: either by reason's graft, or else by faith's gift. For Thomas there is no experience of God of any kind in this life.

Nor may a nihilistic account of the sublime be resisted on grounds of some such 'experientialist' appeal. For if I may here anticipate more of my subsequent argument than can as yet be presumed, just because a causal proof of the existence of God ends in an unknowable 'otherness', it is not the case that it leaves us with a merely empty space, for we know that whatever answers to reason's questioning must have the 'shape' of the question it answers to: and the question is a causal question. As we shall see, the reason we cannot know what God is is that we could not know how to describe that which accounts for there being anything rather than nothing otherwise than as a 'cause'; and we could not know what sort of cause it could possibly be which brings it about that there is anything created at all about which to ask that question. The 'shape' of this space is that of the unknowably causal, not the less unknowable for being described as 'causal', nor the less causal for being described as 'unknowable'.

But that 'shape', if causal, can also be said to be 'sacramental', in form. For if in its broadest sense music offers us a limit case of reason's shape as 'proto-sacramental', then that too is the shape which must be possessed by that very particular exercise of reason which consists in ratiocination, in inference, in argument and in proof. Reason is always bound to end up with God, so why not ratiocination too? For reason in that sense of 'reasoning' gives names to things; it names all that which music, through its very indeterminacy, its refusal of any 'constative' character, does not and cannot name, because 'naming' is precisely what music refuses to do. But if reason, in this form as reasoning, names – it has to, because that is just what *it* does – it does so also in the shadow of music's inarticulateness and indeterminacy, for if reason ever dares name the name 'God', it may do so only as that which utterly defeats its powers. Naming God is reason's supreme achievement, but only in so far as in doing so it knows that what it so names escapes from under the naming, dodging all the arrows of naming that reason can fire at it. And that, as Thomas says, is *quod omnes dicunt Deum*, naming stretched out to the end of its tether until its tether snaps. In God reason reaches the point of collapse, because over-weighted with significance.

As I have so often repeated, I have no intention of exegeting, still less of defending in point of formal validity, those famous and much derided 'five ways' of Thomas Aquinas – nor, incidentally, does the first Vatican Council hold any brief for them. But since we are at this point attending to the 'shape' of the reason deployed in such proofs, to what I have called the 'argument-strategy' by which they work, then we can at this point note that reason in this narrower sense of 'ratiocination' has, as music has, the shape of the sacramental, the form of the body's transparency to the mystery we call 'God'. When, in *Prima Pars* question 2 article 3 of the *Summa Theologiae*, Thomas tells us that we can, by these five ploys of inference, prove the existence of God, we have seen that he notes immediately afterwards that what proves God to exist also proves that in that case we have finally lost our grip on the meaning of 'exist', so that in proving God to exist we push reason beyond exhaustion. And so it is that by means of rational inference we do in a merely speculative way that of which the Eucharist draws us into the very life. Reason gets you to where unnameable mystery begins, but stands on this side of it, gesturing towards what it cannot know, and there it is 'kenotically' self-emptied, as we might say, stunned into silence at the shock of its final defeat – this reduction of talk to silence being what is otherwise called 'theology'. But by the Eucharist we are drawn into that same mystery as into our very *carnal* life, so that we live by the mystery, we eat it; though the mystery is no more knowable, as Thomas says, for being eaten than it is for being thought. For he tells us that we do not resolve the mystery by faith as if it were some conundrum of reason to which faith held the key, and that we do not know what God is even by the revelation of grace: by grace, he says, we are indeed truly made one with God, but as to him who is unknown to us, *quasi ei ignoto*.[16]

Therefore, to close the argument of this first part of my essay, we may say that this reason, in that sense and in that capacity which is exercised in its asking those questions which it knows to be unanswerable, is reason in the 'central' case, for the theological significance of all other forms of rational access to the transcendent is guaranteed by that supreme exercise of reason which, as we shall see, is its pursuit of questions to the point of exhaustion. For when reason has been pressed to the point at which its questions become demonstrably unanswerable, it does not thereby demonstrate a space which could not be occupied, some 'otherness' lacking every character and description except that of 'otherness'; but rather one which is demonstrably occupied by that which we could not comprehend, the Creator of all things, visible and invisible, and so their Lord; and being the origin of all things 'out of nothing', necessarily containing all the perfections of all the things created, and for that reason too, unknowable to us, because too comprehensively intelligible; but if unknowable because possessing every perfection, then also, and for that

---

[16] *ST* 1a q12 a13 ad1.

same reason, nameable by every name; and so to be praised by every form of creaturely praise.

Such, in a preliminary way, summarising ahead, as it were, of what follows, is the 'God of reason'; such is the 'reason' which knows God, the God who can be proved: in proving which, reason proves but the existence of a mystery, the mystery of creation. And in proving that, reason discovers itself to have been created by the mystery it shows to exist. *Et hoc omnes dicunt Deum.*

Part II

Univocity, 'difference' and 'onto-theology'

Does Scotus matter?

Having first given some account of the 'shape' of reason in its broadest sense, we must now make some progress directly with the nature of
reason in its narrower sense of 'ratiocination', and, more specifically, on
the matter of the logic of proof itself. And if we begin with Duns Scotus, this is because the primary issue is with the difficulty set against any
case for the possibility of proof of God, which is that any such proposal
must entail an 'onto-theological' consequence, and the charge of 'onto-
theology' is thought to stick on Duns Scotus most especially. Moreover,
some recent literatures have pressed the argument that the conception
of a natural theology itself has its origin, or at least its historically significant origin, in the early fourteenth century, in the thought of Duns
Scotus, and, as we have seen, there are those for whom natural theology is
inherently onto-theological. Scotus' historical significance has in this way
been reinserted into the record very recently by the followers of 'Radical
Orthodoxy', who seem united in their perception of certain conceptual
links within his thought which are definitive of this natural theology, and
in their hostility to it. In summary, the critique of Scotus seems to involve
four propositions: first, that a 'natural theology' maintains the existence
of God to be demonstrable without appeal to premises of faith; second,
that such a demonstration is logically possible only if 'existence' is predicable univocally of God and creatures; and third, that if existence is
to be predicable univocally of God and creatures, this can be so only
if we have available to us some concept of 'existence' which is neutral
as between any difference there can be between the Creator and the
created – the difference, namely, between 'infinite' and 'finite' being.
It is that third proposition which is said to be 'onto-theological'. Not
incidentally, moreover, a fourth proposition is presupposed to the third:
if there are any predicates predicable univocally of God and creatures,
a fortiori those same predicates must be predicable univocally, that is

to say neutrally, also as between any and all differences of creatures one from one another.

On this account, then, the systematic and explicit defence of those conceptual linkages is said to be found historically in the works of Duns Scotus in a form which contributed to a decisive turn within Western theological and philosophical traditions (though here, the Radical Orthodox thesis is less than precise as to the nature of this historical causation). Put in its most moderate and defensible form in a recent paper of Catherine Pickstock, this intellectual shift is not said to have been uniquely causal of subsequent developments in Western intellectual history, but only in the long run to have removed a conceptual barrier, set firmly in place by Thomas's doctrine of 'analogy', standing in the way of the development of a rationalist and secularist ideology,[1] of which Kant is the classical 'modern' inheritor. For Kant's 'speculative reason' is inherently secular, 'this-worldly' – indeed, one may say that Kant strategically secularises speculative reason precisely, as he puts it, 'so as to leave room for [practical] faith' – a conceptual move, as we have seen, which is governed by the argument that, were reason to be permitted theological ambitions, it could possess them only in competition with faith. And from this it would seem to follow that from any ground occupied by the one, the other must thereby be excluded. It is no purpose of this essay to engage in an argument with this historical aetiology, but only with the conceptual and logical linkages themselves which underlie it. Those linkages are, indeed, to be found in Duns Scotus, whose significance for this essay – the purposes of which are *entirely* conceptual – lies in the opportunity he provides for determining whether or not in truth they are unbreakable. In my view they are not: more particularly, I shall argue that the rational demonstrability of the existence of God is not logically dependent, in the way in which Scotus believes that it is, on the univocal predication of existence of God and creatures.

Scotus and univocity

I call a concept 'univocal' if it has that sameness of meaning which is required so that to affirm and deny it of the same subject amounts to a contradiction; also, if it has that sameness of meaning required such that it can function as a middle term in a syllogistic argument – thus that where two terms are united in a middle

---

[1] Catherine Pickstock, 'Modernity and Scholasticism: A Critique of Recent Invocations of Univocity', forthcoming in *Antonianum*. I am grateful to Dr Pickstock for allowing me sight of this paper in proof form.

term having this sameness of meaning, the inference does not fail by the fallacy of equivocation.[2]

So says Duns Scotus, as if with clarity: indeed, on one level what he says *is* clear, for at face value this definition of univocity is simply a restatement of the Aristotelian dictum latinised in much medieval discussion as *eadem est scientia oppositorum*[3] – you can know what it is to affirm something only if you know what would count as its negation; they are one and the same 'knowledge'. For if what you deny does not have the same meaning as what I affirm, then the denial does not contradict what is affirmed. As Anselm pointed out in his *Proslogion*, unless the fool, who says there is no God, agrees with the theist, who says God exists, about what to say 'God exists' means, then the atheist does not deny what the theist affirms, and may not be an atheist at all.[4] More simply, if I say that there is a cat on the mat and you say there is no cat on the mat, you contradict what I say if and only if we mean the same thing by there being a cat on the mat; otherwise you do not deny what I say. Hence, Scotus says, 'p' is univocally predicated so long as 'p' and '~p' are contradictories.

From this follows Scotus' second way of defining 'univocity'. Since a valid syllogistic inference justifies the relating of two terms to each other (the 'extremes') through their common relation to a third term (the 'middle term'), such validity can be secured only if the middle term has the same sense when related to the two extremes. Hence, the inference 'If every man is mortal, and if Socrates is a man, then Socrates is mortal' is valid only if 'man' has the same meaning in both antecedents; it would be an invalid inference if, for example, 'man' in the first antecedent had the gendered meaning in English of 'male' and had the generic meaning of 'human' in the second. For even if, as it happens, the consequent is true (Socrates being a male human), it would not follow as a conclusion from the antecedents, and the inference would be invalid.

That might seem clear enough, but in fact it is not in the least clear.[5] For what Scotus proposes as his second definition of univocity is, as far as this explanation goes, in fact but a condition of deductively inferential validity which depends upon, and is not itself a definition of, the univocal predication of terms. For of course we cannot know that a deductive inference is valid unless we know that the middle term is predicated univocally in both antecedents; hence we cannot know that the middle term

[2] Duns Scotus, *Ordinatio* 1 d3 1 q1–2, *Opera Omnia* III, p. 18, my translation.
[3] Aristotle, *Peri Hermeneias* 6, 17a 33–35.   [4] Anselm, *Proslogion* 1.
[5] An unusual occurrence in Scotus, who more frequently seems every bit as obscure as he is.

is univocally predicated from the fact that the inference is valid. To say, as Scotus does, that 'univocity' of meaning is that possessed by such middle terms as are required for deductive validity is to beg the question: the determination of validity presupposes criteria for the determination of univocity, not the other way round.[6]

It might seem, nonetheless, that all is not lost, since it would appear that even without this second criterion we can fall back on Scotus' first criterion for univocity: if a term is univocal then to affirm and deny it of the same subject amounts to a contradiction. As we shall see, however, this criterion too is contestable as a *definition* of univocity, stating conditions both necessary and sufficient. For Scotus' account gives only a necessary condition, and in any case *prima facie* there appear to be counter-examples: there are terms, predicated of the same subject, the affirmation and denial of which are genuine contradictories, even though the affirmation and denial are related only analogically. But much argument is required before that case can be made.

Ens is predicated univocally of God and creatures

Scotus says that 'being' (*ens*) is univocally predicated of God and of creatures. His argument for this proposition is based upon a general episte-mological principle familiar to those who know Descartes's *Meditations on First Philosophy*: if, of two properties potentially ascribable to a thing, one can be known with certainty to be ascribed to it, but the ascription of the other is open to doubt, then those two properties must be really distinct from one another. Alternatively the principle can take the form: if one can be certain of the existence of the one, but uncertain as to the existence of the other, then it follows that the one must be really distinct from the other, and must be capable of existing independently of it. In Descartes's *Meditations* this principle was drawn upon to show that the human soul can exist in separation from the body; for, Descartes maintained, since I can be certain that I exist (and I am my soul) while still entertaining grounds for doubting that I have a body, it follows that I, and so my soul, must be really distinct and can exist in separation from the body.[7]

---

[6] As Richard Cross rightly says (*Duns Scotus*, Oxford: Oxford University Press, 1999, p. 37), this account provides only necessary, but not sufficient, conditions of univocity. You could not have univocal terms which did not meet these inferential conditions. The problem with knowing what Scotus means by univocity is that he nowhere completes his account of it beyond the specification of these necessary conditions for it.

[7] Descartes, *Meditations* 6.

Scotus' employment of the same principle in arguing for being's univocal predication of God and of creatures may or may not be the source of Descartes's argument,[8] but it is certainly similar in form. It is possible, Scotus argues, to be certain that God exists while still uncertain whether God is finite or infinite, created or uncreated. In any case, it is intelligible to say that two people agree that God exists and at the same time disagree with one another as to whether God is finite and created, or infinite and uncreated. But they could not agree about the one and disagree about the other unless the extent of their agreement was to the same conception of existence as predicated of God; for their disagreement about the nature of God could be genuine – that is to say, a genuine opposition – if and only if it is in the same sense of 'exist' that they think God to exist, for *eadem est scientia oppositorum*. Consequently, it must be the case that existence is predicated univocally of what is finite and of what is infinite. Scotus puts it this way:

the intellect of a person in this life can be certain that God is a being [*quod Deus sit ens*] while doubting whether this being is finite or infinite, created or uncreated; therefore the concept of God as a being is other than this or that concept; and although included in each of these, it is none of them of itself, and therefore is univocal.[9]

The argument is extraordinarily simple. More, it is extraordinarily simplistic, thus far. It reduces – Scotus says – to this: that every philosopher is certain that God is a being of *some* sort; but they disagree about *what* sort of being God is, some thinking God to be fire, others that God is water; and at all events, philosophers have disagreed whether this being called 'God' is uncreated or created. But if you were to prove to a pagan idolater that God could not be, for example, fire, then, convinced sufficiently to change his mind on that score, he would have no need to change his mind on the score of his conviction that God exists, for 'that notion would survive in the particular conception proved about fire'.[10] It follows, Scotus thinks, that the same concept of existence, 'which of itself is neither of the doubtful ones, is preserved in both of them', and is therefore univocal.

---

[8] It is possibly the source, through the influence of 'Scotist' thinking on Descartes's Jesuit educators at his school in La Flèche.

[9] 'Sed intellectus viatoris potest esse certus de Deo quod sit ens, dubitando de ente finito vel infinito, creato vel increato; ergo conceptus entis de Deo est alius a conceptu isto et illo, et ita neuter ex se et in utroque illorum includitur; igitur univocus.' *Ordinatio* 1 d3 1, q1–2, *Opera Omnia* III, p. 18 (Frank and Wolter, *Duns Scotus*, p. 111).

[10] 'Non destrueretur ille conceptus primus sibi certus, quem habuit de ente, sed salveretur in illo conceptu particulari probato de igne.' *Ordinatio* 1 d3 1 q1–2, *Opera Omnia* III, p. 19 (Frank and Wolter, p. 112).

That, as it stands, the inference is invalid is easily shown. Suppose that you and I together espy an indeterminate moving blob on the horizon, and are both certain that 'there is something moving over there', while both being doubtful as to what it is that we are seeing, I thinking for the moment that possibly it is an ostrich, you thinking that it could very well be that I have some ostrich-shaped obstruction in my eye. How are we to analyse the existential quantifier, 'there is a...'? Do we have to say that whatever the moving object turns out in fact to be, neither of us will have to revise the meaning we had for 'there is a...' since there must have been agreement on the meaning of that expression in order to be able to disagree about what it was we had been thinking was there? Are we forced to say that there must be an indeterminate sense of the existential quantifier which is predicable univocally of the moving object over there and of the speck in my eye which moves as my eyeball swivels? That would be about as intelligible as saying that there is a univocal meaning for the demonstrative pronoun 'this', denoting some property of 'thisness' possessed in common by everything you can point to by means of the word; it would be as if someone were to say: 'This is an ostrich, this is a man; differ they may as much as an ostrich and a man do, but see how they share in both being "this"'!

It was on some such grounds that Henry of Ghent had argued against the univocity thesis.[11] It cannot be the case that what counts for the existence of something consists in some notion of what it is, neutrally, for anything to exist; for the concept of existence is determined as a function of what it is that is said to exist – the existence of a tree is an arboreal existence, the existence of a sheep an ovine existence. To which Scotus counters that such an argument would prove too much to be valid, since it would reduce the predication of existence to a pure equivocity. An argument constructed on the grounds that existence is determinate to that of which it is predicated, and purporting to show that therefore 'uncreated existence' and 'created existence' are two different concepts, would have the unacceptable consequence that all univocal predication is impossible. If we say that the meaning of any predication, and so of 'existence', is determinate to, and so variable with, the subject-terms of which it is predicated, then it would follow that, for instance, there is no concept of 'man' predicable of both Socrates and Plato, but rather that there are two different concepts, one of Socrates' being a man, another of Plato's being a man; and Scotus thinks this is absurd – as indeed it is. Besides, as Scotus points out, even if we say – as Henry of Ghent does – that the concept of 'man' is complex, and that we can distinguish within it between what is similar between Socrates and Plato and what

---

[11] See below, pp. 137–9, for a fuller discussion of Henry's position.

differs, just that which is thus distinguished as 'similar' would be the 'concept' of man predicable univocally of both.[12] Hence, even on Henry's account, if there is anything in the concept of 'man' similarly predicable of both Socrates and Plato, then that is the concept univocally predicable of both; and if there is not, then all predication collapses into meaningless equivocity. What holds, therefore, of Plato and Socrates holds equally of 'God' indeterminately between finite and infinite being: either 'being' is predicated univocally of God – finite or infinite as the case may be – or else there is no possibility of any talk about God, except by equivocation; and equivocal talk is not talk.

Scotus sets out his position on univocal predication of God and creatures compendiously as follows:

All metaphysical enquiry into God proceeds in this manner: you start from the formal notion of anything whatever and you remove from that formal notion the imperfection contained in its reference to creatures, holding on to the formal notion as such; then you ascribe to it the highest perfection and in that sense ascribe it to God. For example, consider the formal notion of 'wisdom' or 'intellect' or 'will'. Considered in itself and as such [any one of] these notions formally contains no reference to any imperfection and limitation, and therefore those imperfections which are contained in it in its reference to creatures are removed. In this formal sense, then, these notions of 'wisdom' and 'will' are attributed to God in their most perfect degree. Therefore, every enquiry into God supposes that the mind is in possession of the same univocal concept which it derives from creatures.[13]

Of course, Scotus is well aware that some creaturely predicates contain an *intrinsic* reference to creatures; for example, '. . . is fat', '. . . is exhausted', '. . . is green'. That is to say, some creaturely reference is contained in their very definition, in, as Scotus puts it, their 'formal notions', for each of these is intrinsically a property of something embodied. In consequence, it does not make sense to speak of 'considering' them minus their creaturely reference, except as metaphors, as, if we lived in a culture which thought of fatness as a sign of prestige and power, we might praise God by describing him as 'fat', or as, if in sentimental mood, we might describe God as exhausted forgiving sinners, so many are they, or that he is green with envy at the idolatrous worship of the rich and powerful. Other predicates, however, contain in their 'formal notions' no particular reference to anything created: there is no reason, deriving from the meaning of 'wise' or 'intellect' or 'will', why an uncreated being should

---

[12] Though directed against Henry of Ghent, Scotus appears to think his argument is effective against Thomas Aquinas' account of analogy, as does Richard Cross, who, like Scotus, claims that Aquinas' doctrine of analogy is reducible to Henry's: see his *Duns Scotus*, pp. 34–5: but see below, pp. 137–9.

[13] *Ordinatio* 1 d3 q1, arg. Iv, my translation.

not be so described, even if it is only from created beings that we know their meaning. All we need do is remove from these notions that reference to creatures which belongs to the creaturely contexts in which we have learned them, and then beef them up to their maximum degree of possibility. For in removing all creaturely reference we change nothing of the meaning of these notions considered in their 'formalities'. Therefore, Scotus concludes, they are predicated in the same sense, that is, 'univocally', of both God and creatures, albeit to different degrees. And what is true of 'wise' and 'intellect' and 'will' is true of 'being'. 'Being', therefore, is predicated univocally of God and creatures.

The problem of idolatry: Scotus and Thomas

If Anselm's 'fool', the atheist, is wrong in denying that there is a God, he must at least know what he denies; that is to say, 'God exists' must mean the same to him as it does to the theist. And if God does exist, then the atheist is 'wrong' in the plainest possible sense, in that what he says is straightforwardly false. That, as we have seen, is a straightforward application of the Aristotelian principle, *eadem est scientia oppositorum*. But what are we to say about Scotus' idolater, the person who worships as God some finite, created object: fire, water, or a tree? In what way, precisely, does the idolater get God wrong? Are we to say that the idolater is no better in practice than an atheist, since he worships as if it were God something which is not and could not be God, and so, though nominally a theist, that he fails to acknowledge the existence of the one true God, infinite, Creator of all things visible and invisible, omnipotent, omniscient – which no water, or fire or tree could be? Or, are we to say that he cannot mean by the word 'God' what the true believer means? That the idolater says 'God exists' is neither here nor there on this account, if the idolater does not mean what the true believer means. If that were the case, then it would follow that the true believer and the idolater use the word 'God' equivocally, that is to say, they do not truly disagree, for what the idolater affirms does not have the same meaning as that which the true believer denies. There can be no true *oppositio* because there is no *eadem scientia*.

In truth there is some measure of agreement between Scotus and Thomas on how to respond to these questions. Both reject the position that there is an equivocation between the true believer's and the idolater's use of the word 'God', though Thomas is inclined to take the case for saying that they are equivocating more seriously than Scotus does. As Thomas puts it, it could very well seem that the idolater simply does not understand the word 'God' at all if he thinks that a bit of bronze could be the one true God;[14] and after all, we might ask how you *could* think that an idol is the Creator of all things out of nothing. The idolater must be thinking of some other meaning of the word 'God' if his position is to be made intelligible.

But Scotus and Thomas are united in rejecting the understanding of idolatry according to which the idolater simply means something else than 'God' when saying that an idol is God. Moreover, they partially agree on the grounds for rejecting the position. First, Thomas points out, as we have seen Scotus to do, that equivocation does not derive from different subject-terms of predications, otherwise the predicate '. . . is a man' would be equivocal as predicated of Socrates and Plato; so, just because the Christian and the idolater predicate the name 'God' of diverse individuals, it does not follow that the name is being used equivocally[15] – equivocity derives from differences of meaning, not from differences of predication.[16] But secondly, there must be some relation of meaning between what the true believer and the idolater assert, because they contradict each other, which they could not do if they were using the word 'God' equivocally. As Thomas says: 'it is clear that the Christian who says that an idol is not God contradicts the pagan who says it is, because both use the name "God" to signify the true God'.[17] Beyond these points of agreement between them, however, Thomas and Scotus differ; for Scotus derives from them the conclusion that existence must be predicable not just non-equivocally – which is all Thomas believes the argument shows – but univocally of God and creatures, a conclusion which Thomas explicitly rejects. Let us therefore recall Scotus' argument.

Scotus says that both the true believer and the idolater are certain that God exists, but the idolater says that God is fire, while the true believer denies this, thus contradicting what the idolater says. But on the principle that the meaning of a predicate is univocal only if its affirmation and its negation of the same subject amount to a contradiction, it follows that it must be in the same sense of '. . . exists' that the idolater and the true believer say that God exists.[18] But since the true believer maintains that

---

[14] *ST* 1a q13 a10, *sed contra, praeterea.*

[15] 'nominum multiplicitas non attenditur secundum nominis praedicationem, sed significationem: hoc enim nomen *homo*, de quocumque praedicetur, sive vere, sive false, dicitur uno modo' – 'a multiplicity of names [equivocation] results not from the multiplicity of its predications, but from a multiplicity of meanings. For the word "man", whatever it is predicated of, whether truly or falsely, means just one thing.' *ST* 1a q13 a10 ad1.

[16] Ibid.   [17] Ibid.

[18] Note that if Cross is right that the contradictoriness condition for univocity is necessary but not sufficient, then this inference fails of validity. Indeed, unless the contradictoriness condition is both necessary and sufficient the whole case for the univocal predication of being as between God and creatures collapses.

God is an infinite being and the idolater that God is a finite being, it follows that there must be a univocal meaning to the predicate '. . . exists' predicable in common of finite and infinite being.

Thomas's rejection of this argument anticipates Scotus' defence of it by some thirty years. Indeed, if one did not know that Scotus was writing after Thomas, one might very well have supposed that Thomas's discussion of idolatry in the *Summa Theologiae* was written in explicit response to Scotus' argument in the *Ordinatio*, so precisely in 'Scotist' terms does Thomas identify the position he is rejecting. Thomas asks: 'Is the name "God" used in the same sense of God, of what shares in divinity and of what is merely supposed to be God?' The question seems odd, but simply means: when we – that is, believing Christians, who possess the truth about God – speak about God, we do so in a certain sense. But Christians also have reason to speak of things other than God as having a divine character; for example, a soul in the state of grace may legitimately be described as in some sense sharing in the divine, and pagans call their idols 'Gods', wrongly supposing them to be so. The question for Thomas, therefore, concerns what the relationship is between the meanings of the word 'God' in these two cases of 'sharing in the divinity' and 'idolatrous supposition' on the one hand, and the meaning the word bears as naming the one true God on the other. So Thomas first sets out the case for the 'Scotist' position that the word 'God' must be used univocally:

It seems that the name 'God' is univocally predicated of God in all cases, whether as of his [true] nature, whether as shared in, or whether in the suppositions [of the pagans]. For
1. where there is diversity of meanings there can be no contradiction between an affirmation and its denial; for where there is equivocation there can be no contradiction. But when the Christian says, 'an idol is not God', he contradicts the pagan who says 'an idol is God'. Therefore, 'God' is predicated in either case in the same sense [*univoce*].

Now while Thomas concedes to this position ('Scotist' *avant la lettre*) that the idolater and the true believer cannot be using the name 'God' equivocally, he will allow the argument no power to demonstrate that they are using the name univocally; the argument simply does not prove that conclusion. Thomas explains that if the idolater did not mean to affirm of fire or stone or a tree that it is 'the one true God, almighty and worthy to be venerated above all else',[19] then what the idolater says would in fact be true. For in the case that the idolater meant by 'God' something other and less than the one true God – for example, that the meaning of 'God' is 'finite being' – then it would be perfectly legitimate to say that fire is

---

[19] *ST* 1a q13 a10.

God; after all, the Bible, as Thomas points out, speaks of the 'gods' of the Gentiles, saying of them that they are in fact 'demons' (Ps. 95:51). Hence, if the idolater is to be said to be 'wrong about God' it must be because the idolater wrongly claims to be true of fire, or water, or a tree what the true believer claims to be true of the Creator of the universe, one God who is Father, Son and Holy Spirit. This, then, is why Thomas agrees thus far with Scotus; it cannot be the case that the true believer and the idolater have an entirely different meaning for the word 'God', or else there would be no contradiction between them. The disagreement between the idolater and the true believer concerns what the name 'God' could possibly be true of, the true believer maintaining that it could not be true of fire or water or of a tree that it is 'the one, true God'.

The difference between Thomas and Scotus, however, emerges from consideration of the answers Scotus and Thomas give to the question: if the idolater is in some way 'wrong' about God, in what way is he wrong? For Scotus, the idolater is 'wrong' because, knowing what the word God means, he misattributes it to something which could not in *any* way be God in the true sense; for there is no sense at all in which something other than God can be said to be 'divine'. For Scotus, then, the idolater is wrong in the way the atheist is wrong, in that what he says is simply false. For Thomas, however, there is a genuine, if only derived and secondary, sense in which what the idolater calls 'God' is truly divine. Therefore, Thomas says, as between what the idolater and the true believer affirm there is neither equivocity, nor univocity, but some analogy.

In later discussion[20] we shall attempt greater precision about what Thomas means by an 'analogical' predication, and in this article Thomas gives but a broad and general account: a word is used analogically, he says, when 'its meaning in one sense is explained by reference to its meaning in another sense', explaining that, for example, we understand a healthy diet by reference to health in the body, of which health a healthy diet is the cause.[21] Now since the idolater would not be making a mistake in supposing a bronze statue to be God if he did not do so in *some* sense related to that in which the true believer uses the word 'God', it follows that the idolater is, as it were, playing the same game as the true believer, for he abides by the same rules for the meaning of the word 'God'. Hence, if the idolater makes a theological mistake, he is still, we might say, 'doing theology' even if he is playing on the losing team – unlike the atheist, for whom there is no theology to do, and who will not play the game at all. If the idolater 'gets God wrong' he does so not in the way in which the plain atheist does, who, understanding exactly what the theist understands by

[20] See below, pp. 202–7.   [21] *ST* 1a q13 a10 *corp.*

'God', denies God's existence. Rather, Thomas says, the idolater's mistake is to suppose that that which does, genuinely, share in the divine nature – the bronze statue – is the divine being itself, and this mistake is like supposing that a diet is healthy in the same way in which a body is healthy – which, of course, it is not, for you cannot take a diet's blood pressure. Thus, the true believer knows *how* to say that the bronze statue is divine – by analogical extension from the true God – whereas the idolater does not.[22]

One further difference between Thomas and Scotus emerges from this, a difference which we shall have occasion to revisit later in this essay.[23] If Thomas believes that the true believer and the idolater contradict each other (as Scotus does), but unlike Scotus maintains that the senses in which they use the name 'God' are related analogically, not univocally, this is because Thomas does not accept Scotus' definition of univocity in the first place. For Scotus maintained that a term is predicated univocally only if its affirmation and negation of the same subject amount to a contradiction. But Thomas maintains that the affirmation and denial that a bronze statue is God amount to a contradiction between predicates which are predicated in an analogical relation with each other. This, as we shall see, Scotus does not allow. Moreover, we shall see that Thomas's opinion on this matter turns out to have important consequences for how he construes the legitimacy of arguments for the existence of God, his view on the logic of which being crucially different from that of Scotus. But it is to Scotus' views on that matter of logic that we must next turn.

Scotus, Thomas and Henry of Ghent on analogy

What motivates Scotus to insist that 'being' is predicated univocally of God and creatures (as distinct from his arguments in support of this conclusion) is his conviction that on no other account could the possibility of the natural knowledge of God be justified. In particular, he maintains that the view according to which predicates such as '. . . exists' and '. . . is good' are predicated analogically of God and creatures puts at risk this possibility. Now Scotus' arguments against this account of analogy are

---

[22] 'When the pagan says the idol is God he does not use the name as signifying a mere [false] supposition about God, for then what he says would be true; and even Christians use the word in this false sense, as when it is said in Psalm 95:51, "all their gods are devils." – 'Cum enim paganus dicit idolum esse Deum, non utitur hoc nomine secundum quod significant Deum opinabilem: sic enim verum dicaret, cum etiam catholici interdum in tali significatione hoc nomine utitur, ut cum dicitur (Ps. 95:51), *omnes dii gentium daemonia.*' *ST* 1a q13 a10, *corp.*
[23] See pp. 207–8 below.

sometimes read as if they were directed against Thomas Aquinas' version of it – or at least, as Richard Cross does, as being effective against
Thomas's version[24] – but they are, in fact, explicitly directed against a
quite different version of analogy found in the writings of Henry of Ghent,
and are effective, if at all, against it. At any rate, I shall argue against Cross
that Henry and Thomas differ quite fundamentally in their accounts of
analogy. Hence, there are two issues to be considered next: first, what is
it in Henry's account of analogy which, according to Scotus, puts at risk
the natural knowledge of God? Secondly, since Scotus is in agreement
with Thomas that the natural knowledge of God is possible, how far are
Scotus' arguments against Henry's account of analogy effective against
Thomas's?

For Henry, no predicates are predicated univocally of God and of
creatures. All are predicated 'analogically'. For any predicate predicated
analogically of God and of creatures, there are two, as he calls them, 'irreducible' concepts; that is to say, two concepts neither of which is capable
of further reduction to any simpler concept, one of which is predicated
of God, the other of creatures. The predicate '. . . is good', for example,
may seem to be a simple concept, but in fact is two diverse concepts, one
of which holds of God, the other of creatures. Since both are irreducibly
simple, these two concepts can have nothing in common with each other,
and yet, he says, they are 'like' each other, their likeness being founded in
the relationship of cause and effect. For God's goodness causes goodness
in creatures. Analogy for Henry is founded in the divine creative causality.

It is very difficult to know how to make any sense at all of this account of
analogy, and, in any sense one can make of it, it is open to very obvious
objections. What is most obviously hard to make sense of is on what
account of 'likeness' the two 'simple' concepts of 'good' are said to be
'alike'. Are they alike in sharing some common meaning? If not, then
how can they be alike at all? And if they are in no common respect 'alike',
how is analogy to be distinguished from equivocity? If they do share some
common meaning, in what sense of 'common'? Is the meaning they share
'common' in being univocally predicable of both? In that case, Scotus'
view wins the field, because, as we have seen, this is exactly the position
that he maintains about the predication of terms of God and of creatures,
namely that, once we have removed from the 'formality' of predicates such
as '. . . is good', '. . . is wise' and so forth that which is proper to creatures,
what we are left with is a common univocal meaning neutral as between its
predication of God and of creatures. But it is the point of Henry's case for
analogy that the 'likeness' between the concepts of uncreated and created

---

[24] Cross, *Duns Scotus*, p. 35.

goodness cannot consist in a univocally common meaning. Then, is the 'likeness' between the goodness of God and the goodness of creatures the likeness of analogy? That cannot be the answer, because it succeeds only in pushing the problem one step further on along a line of infinite regress. It is not surprising, therefore, that the nub of Scotus' criticism of Henry on analogy is that, on any account of what it could amount to, it reduces analogy, and so talk about God, either to equivocity or to univocity. Hence, it seems to Scotus that Henry's account of analogy, upon analysis, serves only to demonstrate his own conclusion, namely that either we cannot talk about God at all, or, if we can, some predicates must be predicable of God and of creatures univocally.

Of course, Scotus' argument does not finish off Henry's doctrine of analogy quite yet; for Henry had argued that what links the 'simple' concept of 'good' as predicated of God with the 'simple' concept of good as predicated of creatures is the divine causality, such that the divine goodness creates created goodness. That, he seems to think, is sufficient to establish a connection of meaning between the two simple concepts of goodness. But that response will not do either. For the word 'cause' as predicated of God will itself have to be predicated univocally of God and of creatures, or equivocally, or else analogically. But if 'cause' is predicated univocally of God and creatures, then again, Scotus' case wins. If 'cause' is predicated equivocally of God and of creatures, then the required link between God and creatures is not established. Hence, if 'cause' is not itself predicated either univocally or equivocally of God and of creatures, then it must be predicated analogically. But if so, then, on Henry's own account, there must be a simple concept of 'cause' predicated of God, and another simple concept of 'cause' predicated of creatures, neither reducible to the other, and linked through . . . *what*? Once again, the argument is set on the trail of an infinite regress.

Now as to the issue between Scotus and Thomas on analogy, this is extremely complex. Only on two conditions is the matter straightforward: first, if, as seems likely, Scotus does not distinguish between Henry's account of analogy and Thomas's, and second, if we further suppose, as Cross does, that Scotus is *right* thus to identify them. For Henry's account of analogy is plainly incoherent, so that if it is indeed also Thomas's account there is nothing for it but to abandon the Thomistic baby with the Ghentian bathwater. But in my view, Cross is wrong, as I shall argue in chapter nine:[25] Thomas's account of analogy is sharply to be distinguished from Henry's, in which case it becomes possible to read Scotus

---

[25] See pp. 179–83 below.

as offering *ad hominem* arguments against Henry which have no bearing at all on Thomas's version.

Especially if I am right and Cross is wrong about Thomas on analogy, however, the issues between Scotus and Thomas become more complex, since there is a number of propositions on which Thomas and Scotus can be construed as agreeing. On the one hand, there is no doubt that Thomas would have agreed with Scotus that, if Henry's account of analogy were right, then no natural knowledge of God would be possible, analogy having been reduced to equivocation – and both Thomas and Scotus wish to defend the possibility of the natural knowledge of God. On the other hand, there is less doubt still that Scotus, in arguing that some predicates are predicated univocally of God and creatures, knew that Thomas was opposed to this view. Hence, there is genuine disagreement between Scotus and Thomas about whether there are terms predicable univocally of God and of creatures, even if they are to a greater extent at cross-purposes over analogy than would allow for any clear-cut disagreement: in short, on the question of analogy, what Thomas defends is not what Scotus rejects.

The univocal predication of 'being'

Scotus is quite clear about one proposition central to his theological epistemology: 'being' (*ens*) is the proper object of the intellect and is predicated univocally of anything whatever. I say that Scotus is clear about this. But followers of Thomas Aquinas are likely to judge this proposition to be thoroughly confused when they read it in conjunction with another, equally unambiguous, statement of Scotus: *ens* is not a genus and the logic of *ens* is not that of a genus.[26] In saying this, Scotus is (among other things) denying that to say of *ens* that it is univocally predicated of everything whatever entails that *ens* is a sort of 'super-essence' standing logically to all the different kinds of thing which exist in the same relation that, for example, the restricted genus 'animal' stands to the different species of animal: for Scotus, *beings* are not species of *Being*.

Now for Thomas Aquinas, this conjunction of theses – of the univocity of *ens* plus the denial that *ens* is a genus – is simply incoherent. For Thomas, univocity is defined in reference to genus; as we shall see, for Thomas a term is predicated univocally if, whether truly or falsely, it is predicated in accordance with its definition, and a definition is the conjunction of the genus and a *differentia*. Thus a human being is generically an animal, differentiated from other animals by the *differentia* 'rational'.

---

[26] *Ordinatio* 1 d8 q1 a3, n. 108; *Opera Omnia* IV, pp. 202–3.

Therefore, its being false to say of a giraffe that it is a human being depends upon understanding '. . . is a human being' in the same sense as when we say with truth, 'Peter is human.' Of course, we could describe a particularly fetching giraffe as 'human' metaphorically, just as, if Peter is a particularly evil man, we could metaphorically describe him as a 'brute'. But we could know what is said in either case metaphorically only if we know in the first place what the primary, univocal, meanings of the predicates are.

Now since Thomas maintains that univocal meanings are determined by their definitions in terms of genera and *differentiae*, it would be impossible for him to know what Scotus means when he says both that *ens* is predicated univocally of everything whatever, and yet that it does not stand to the kinds of being of which it is predicated as genus does to species. Yet Scotus does say both, so at least to this extent agreeing with Thomas, that *ens* cannot be predicated of *entia* in the way in which the genus 'animal' is predicated of humans and brutes, or in the way in which the species 'rational animal' is predicated of Socrates and Plato. But if *ens* is not predicated of creatures in the way in which genus is predicated of its species, or in the way in which species is predicated of individuals, even less can it be the case that *ens* is predicated of the infinite and the finite as genus is to species. Yet, for Thomas Aquinas, such are the only ways in which it is possible to conceive of univocal predication. For Thomas, then, Scotus is simply confused.

It is therefore important to try to understand what Scotus is saying, not in the distorting mirror of his Thomist opponents, but in his own terms. And in his own terms, his position appears to be that the reason *ens* could not stand to *entia* univocally as a genus stands to its species is that a *differentia* which determines a genus to a species 'adds' something to the genus which it determines, and there is, *a fortiori*, nothing 'outside' *ens* which could be added to it. Whatever it is that differentiates *ens* into finite and infinite will therefore have to be intrinsic to it. Now we have seen that for Scotus, when we predicate terms such as 'wise' and 'good' of God, we do so from within the context in which we learn them; that is to say, as they are predicated of creatures. But in predicating them of God we 'remove' from them any creaturely reference which derives from the context in which we have learned them, and, he argues, we may do that because creaturely reference is not intrinsic to their 'formal notions' – there is nothing in the meaning of 'wise' or 'good' which determines their character to be *created* properties. With the concepts 'wise' and 'good' thus reduced to their character of neutrality as between creature and Creator, we can attribute them to God in their most perfect degree. But the distinction between their predication in *that* sense of God and in their imperfect degree of creatures is not such as to destroy their logical status as univocal. How so?

For the reason that the primary distinction between God and creatures is, for Scotus, the distinction between infinite and finite being, and the distinction between infinite and finite is not a difference in kind; it is a distinction of intensity, Scotus says, within a common, univocal, meaning, just as the distinction between 'red' and 'bright red' is not a distinction between colours, but a distinction of intensive degree of the same colour. The distinction between bright red and red is not, therefore, determined by a *differentia* which is added to 'red', thus creating, as it were, two species of redness, 'red' and 'bright red'. And yet, because the concept of 'redness' is 'indifferent to' its intensive degrees, it is univocally predicated of both. In just the same way, 'infinite' and 'finite' are not quasi-*differentiae* added to terms predicated of God and creatures – 'wise' or 'being' or 'good' – which would require their logic to be construed on the lines of genera in their relation to species; rather, since in their pure formalities such terms are 'indifferent to' their intensive degrees, they can be predicated univocally of both. Hence, it is in just such terms that the compatibility is made good between saying that these terms are at once predicated univocally of God and of creatures while not standing to them as a genus does to its species.

Univocity, inference and the 'difference' between God and creatures

So much for Scotus on the meaning of terms predicated in common of God and of creatures. Next we must consider what, for Scotus, are the implications of his theory of meaning for inference from creatures to God, and so for the possibility of natural knowledge of God. And immediately, one consequence is clear. Regarding as he does all accounts of analogical predication, whether Henry's or Thomas's, as reducing to equivocation, it follows that natural knowledge of God is possible only if some terms are predicable of creatures and of God univocally.

Scotus appears to take it as axiomatic that natural knowledge of God is possible; moreover, it would seem that what he means by 'natural knowledge' is both that it is rational knowledge (for reason is the means by which human beings 'naturally' know anything) and that it requires proof by inference (for if what is at stake is, properly speaking, knowledge; only such is, properly speaking, knowledge which is supported by a formal demonstration). In short, natural knowledge of any proposition is gained by inference from other propositions which are known to us by our natural powers; that is to say, either because they in turn are self-evidently true,

or because they are themselves capable, in turn, of rational demonstration. Now all valid demonstrative inference crosses some kind of 'logical
gap' between premises and conclusion; for if the conclusion were self-
evidently 'contained in' the premises – that is to say, if the conclusion
could be seen by simple inspection of them to be contained in the very
meaning of the premises – then no inference would be needed to extract
it from those premises, and there would be no 'gap' to be crossed by it.

How one construes this 'gap' between creatures and God, therefore,
determines how one construes the logic of inference between them. If
you supposed, as it seemed to most medieval interpreters that Anselm
did, that God's existence is self-evidently given in the very conception of
God, then strictly speaking no argument is needed to demonstrate God's
existence, and the conventional description of his *Proslogion* discussion as
the 'ontological argument' is a misnomer. And after all, it is perhaps better
to see Anselm's discussion as more in the nature of an exercise in that
conceptual ground-clearing which is needed so that the 'fool' can be got
to *see* how God's existence is undeniable, if only he will understand what
'God' means, than as an 'argument' properly speaking. But for Scotus,
the natural knowledge of God is gained by inference in a strict sense; and
for him, the gap which it is called upon to cross between creatures and
God is such that only if some terms are univocally predicable of both
could it be closed.

For if terms predicable of creatures and of God are predicated only
equivocally – that is to say, without any continuity of sense between
them – then no argument from the one to the other can possibly succeed.
But since, on Scotus' account of the matter, all accounts of analogical
predication reduce to equivocation, it follows that 'every enquiry about
God presupposes that the intellect has the same univocal concept that it
receives from creatures'.[27] For,

if you say that the formal notion is other as regards those things that pertain to
God [as Henry of Ghent said], a disconcerting consequence results, [namely] that
from the proper notion of anything found in creatures nothing can be inferred
about God, because the notion of what each has is entirely different; indeed,
there is no more reason to conclude that God is formally wise from the notion
of wisdom that we perceive in creatures than [there is to conclude] that God is
formally a stone.[28]

---

[27] 'Omnis inquisitio de Deo supponit intellectum habere conceptum eundem, univocum,
quem accepit ex creaturis.' *Ordinatio* 1 d3 39; *Opera Omnia* III, p. 26, my translation.

[28] 'Quod si dicas, alia est formalis ratio eorum quae conveniunt de Deo, – ex hoc sequitur
inconveniens, quod ex nulla ratione propria eorum prout sunt in creaturis, possunt con-
cludi de Deo, quia omnino alia et alia ratio illorum est et istorum; immo non magis con-
cludetur quod Deus est sapiens formaliter, ex ratione sapientiae quam apprehendimus
ex creaturis, quod Deus est formaliter lapis.' *Ordinatio* 1 d3 3a; *Opera Omnia* III, p. 27,
my translation.

Furthermore, the reason no theological inference is rationally possible without some univocity of terms has to do, simply, with the nature of inference itself; for equivocation is the natural enemy of validity. But here we run up against a problem with Scotus' argument, a problem disguised by the sheer complexity of his exposition. We have seen that Scotus defines univocity by reference to deductive validity: terms are used univocally only if their commonality of meaning is such as is required for a deductive inference to be validly drawn.[29] It follows that if we are to know on this criterion that a term is being used univocally, then we must know of a deductive inference in which it occurs that it is validly drawn by some means independently of our knowledge whether the terms in the premises are univocal. But now Scotus asks us to accept that univocity of meaning is itself a presupposition of inferential validity, so that it now appears that a test of an inference's validity is the univocity of its terms. The argument would seem, therefore, to involve a circularity, and it is reasonable to require Scotus to tell us either how inferences can be tested for validity by some means other than the requirement of univocity, or else how univocity can be tested by some means other than the requirement of inferential validity.

But the reason Scotus feels under no obligation to settle this matter one way or the other is that, as we have seen, his theory of meaning is constructed on the basis of a complete disjunction: either univocity or else equivocity. Since there is no other possibility, for the purposes of determining the logic of inference to God, univocity needs no further definition than is given in its contrast with equivocity; so long as terms are not being used equivocally, they are univocal. Since, moreover, everyone will agree that no inference is possible between terms whose meanings are equivocal, it follows that no inference is valid except on condition of the univocity of its terms. Therefore, Scotus says,

No real concept is caused naturally in the intellect in our present state except through those agents which naturally move our intellect. But the natural agents are the sense image – or the object revealed in the sense image – and the active intellect. Therefore, no simple concept naturally arises in our intellect unless it can come about by virtue of these causes. Now the active intellect and the sense image cannot give rise to a concept that, with respect to the object revealed in the sense image, is not univocal, but rather, in accordance with the analogical relationship, is altogether other and higher than the object. It follows that such an 'other', analogous, concept will never arise in our present state. Also it would thus follow that one could not naturally have any concept of God – which is false.[30]

---

[29] See pp. 126–8 above.
[30] *Ordinatio* 1 d3, 35, *Opera Omnia* III, p. 21, my translation.

That being so, we may now ask: if such are the conditions for valid inference from creatures to God, what, on Scotus' account, is the nature of
the 'gap' which inference thus closes? On this question we have already
made some headway. For Scotus, the ultimately determining difference
between God and creatures is that between 'infinite' and 'finite' being.
Furthermore, we know that if such is the ultimate 'ontological' distinction
between *ens* and its *entia*, then it is not one whose logical character is that
of genus to species: God is not a kind of being distinct from creatures of
other kinds, for the distinction between an attribute predicated of infinite
being and that same attribute predicated of finite being is that between
the maximal intensive degree of that attribute and some degree of limited
intensity of it, and differences of intensity are not differences in kind. For
this reason it appears to be mistaken, at least *prima facie*, to say, as some
do of Scotus' account of the difference between God and creatures, being
as it is defined within the univocal predication of terms, that it amounts
to no more than a 'quantitative' distinction, a 'distinction of degree' as
Cross puts it,[31] as if to say: God is what creatures are, only writ very large
indeed. It seems to be the nub of much criticism of Scotus' natural theology proceeding from Radical Orthodox quarters that if for Scotus God is
not different from creatures in kind, yet is rationally demonstrable from
univocal concepts in common, then two consequences follow. On the one
hand, the divine transcendence is thereby impugned, for the difference
between God and creatures is construed as a quasi-created difference,
being set on a common scale with creaturely differences – albeit at the
'infinitely maximised' end of it. On the other, by virtue of the divine existence being thus set on a common scale with creatures but in terms of
the contrast between infinite and finite, the implication is contained that
the difference between God and creatures is represented, paradoxically,
as a relationship of exclusion. For if God and creatures belong in any way
to a common scale, then whatever part of that scale each occupies, the
other must be excluded from that part of it.

But if that were how Scotus' account of the difference between God and
creatures had to be understood, it would turn out to the effect precisely
opposed to Scotus' manifest intention – which is, through the univocity
thesis, to place the existence of God in such degree of continuity with
creation that inference from the latter to the former is legitimised. But,
it will be argued, if the univocity thesis places God and creatures on the
same scale, and the account of their difference is explained as a matter of
quantitative degree, then it will follow that far from placing God and creatures in continuity with one another, they will be set disjunctively against

---

[31] Cross, *Duns Scotus*, p. 39.

one another; the finite and the infinite will be mutually exclusive terms. And from this there would follow one more conclusion of disturbingly damaging theological consequence, namely the logical impossibility that anything divine could be true of a creature, and equally the impossibility that anything true of a creature could be true of the divine. So much the worse, it would seem, for the incarnation.[32]

Thus, the judgement on Scotus of some recent critics. But the criticism is at least partly unjustified. It is true that, as Cross says, the 'basic model [of Scotus' infinity] is quantitative', for we proceed to disclose that intrinsic infinite degree of the divine attributes by abstracting 'the concept of infinity from that of spatial extension'.[33] But Scotus is not as naive as some of his critics suppose. In fact he uses a quantitative model only so as to demonstrate how the divine infinity altogether transcends our common notions of quantitative infinity.

For the quantitative infinity of, say, an infinite numerical series, is such that you can always add to it and, whatever finite number you subtract from it, there are always some numbers left. Moreover, he says, any quantitative infinity is 'composite', by which he means that it consists of parts each of which is finite. Therefore, no quantitative infinity can be perfect infinity; indeed, in principle any quantitative infinity is created, since it is nothing but the infinite (that is to say, endless) extension of what is finite. And it is precisely this notion of infinity as an infinitely extended version of created finitude which Scotus wants to differentiate from the qualitative, or intensively maximised, infinity of God.

By contrast with such quantitative infinities, therefore, 'qualitative' infinity consists in the maximal intensity of some property which can be possessed in less than maximal intensity. The infinite possession of such a property is its possession such that it has no parts, and so is utterly simple, and thus is such that nothing can be added to it. It follows from the fact that nothing can be added to the infinitely intensive degree of a property that the logic of the 'scale' on which greater or lesser degrees of intensity can be measured cannot be of the same kind as that of the 'scale' on which quantitative degrees are measured. By contrast with the way matters stand with quantitative infinities, 'bright red' is not a given level of redness plus a bit 'more' redness; 'perfectly red' is not 'red' plus endless further additions of redness.[34] For you do not get to the notion of a qualitative infinity, as you do in the case of quantitative, by way of

---

[32] For a discussion of this point, see below, pp. 217–18.
[33] Cross, *Duns Scotus*, p. 40.
[34] Not, of course, that 'redness' can change, be more or less. A *subject* can be more or less red, but not 'redness', as Scotus knows perfectly well.

endlessly adding *more* of the same to some finite possession of that property. It is hard to know how more explicitly than this Scotus could have rejected the Radical Orthodox criticism of his account of divine infinity, when he says:

While something actually infinite in quantity would not be missing any of its parts or lacking any part of quantity, still each of its parts would lie outside the other and consequently the whole would be made up of imperfect elements. A being infinite in entity ['intensively infinite'], however, would not have any being outside itself in this way. Neither would its totality depend on elements which are themselves imperfect in entity, for it exists in such a way that it has no extrinsic part; otherwise it would not be entirely whole. As for its being perfect, the situation is similar. Although something actually infinite in quantity would be perfect as to quantity, because as a whole it would lack no quantity, nevertheless each part of it would lack the quantity of the other parts. That is to say, an infinite of this sort would not be quantitatively perfect [as a whole] unless each of its parts were imperfect. An infinite being, however, is perfect in such a way that neither it nor any of its parts is missing anything.[35]

If, therefore, Cross is right to say that the 'basic model' of Scotus' notion of intensive infinity is quantitative, nonetheless it is so only as a starting point to be transcended. Scotus' critics appear to have been misled by the fact that inevitably – for us as much as for Scotus – we have no natural language in which to speak of intensive degrees of a quality except on the deficient metaphor of quantitative degrees – for the word 'degree' is itself a word of quantity. Thus, by way of example, for a medieval thinker such as Scotus, degrees of heat are intensive degrees of a quality, not, as for us, degrees on a numerical scale. But suppose you had confronted Scotus with the modern thermometer, a device which measures degrees of heat quantitatively as different lengths of a column of mercury in a glass tube read against a numerical scale. Then you could have shown him how to translate qualitative degrees of intensity into degrees on a quantitative scale, as a result of our common practice of which we have come to think of degrees of heat exclusively in quantitative terms; thus we read quantitatively what Scotus thought of qualitatively. Scotus' position with regard to intensive magnitudes is rather similar to this; for though we have no recourse but to think of qualitative degrees on a model of the quantitative, to conclude from that – especially in the face of Scotus' explicit denials – that he believes degrees of intensity *to be* additive quantities is grossly unfair, since it would be to mistake what is a

---

[35] *Quodlibet* q5 a7, quoted in Frank and Wolter, *Duns Scotus*, p. 153.

model of measurement for the reality of the thing measured.[36] And even if his critics do, Scotus himself had no intention of making that mistake.

That said, it is quite another matter whether all the main Scotist theses which we have examined are fully consistent with one another, which, in summary, are these: first, that a natural theology is possible, that is to say, formally valid inference from creatures to God is possible. Second, that no such possibility exists unless at least some terms are predicable univocally of creatures and of God, among them most particularly 'being'. Third, therefore, that no demonstration of the existence of God is possible on the basis of the analogical predication of terms alone, for in any case all analogy reduces either to equivocity, which yields no possibility of proof, or else to univocity, which does. Fourth, that the most fundamental distinction between God and creatures is that between 'infinite' and 'finite' being. Fifth, that though 'being' is predicated univocally of God and of creatures, 'being' does not stand to 'finite' and 'infinite' being as a genus stands to species; that is to say, God is not some kind of being standing in contrast to creaturely kinds. Sixth, it is possible to say that 'being' is fundamentally divided into 'infinite' and 'finite' consistently with saying that it is univocally predicated of both, because the distinction between 'infinite' and 'finite' is a distinction of intensive qualitative degree; and although we can at best represent that distinction in terms borrowed from extensive magnitudes, the logic of that distinction, and of the scale on which it lies, is quite other, in its nature and consequences, from that of a quantitative scale.

What, finally, are we to say of Scotus' way of determining the 'difference' between God and creatures? On the one hand, taken on its own, the univocity thesis would appear to place at risk the radical 'otherness' of God – and for sure, by comparison with Thomas Aquinas, there is a distinctly more optimistic 'cataphaticism' about Scotus' natural theology, for, as Cross says, 'the result of [this univocity thesis] is that the doctrine of divine ineffability, so strongly stressed by Aquinas . . . is greatly weakened in Scotus' account. He holds that we can know quite a lot about God "in a descriptive sort of way",[37] as he puts it.'[38] Moreover, on the same score, it is clear that Scotus believes the possibility of a natural theology – which he takes to be theologically axiomatic – depends upon

---

[36] Thomas agrees with Scotus here, noting that necessarily we think of intensive changes in a quality in terms of quantitative degrees of change. He also notes that we ought not to be misled by this necessity into reducing qualitative degrees to quantitative. See *Quaestio Disputata de Virtutibus in Communi*, a11 *corp.*

[37] 'In quadam descriptione' – *Ordinatio* 1 d3 q1 1–2; *Opera Omnia* III, p. 40), my translation.

[38] Cross, *Duns Scotus*, p. 39.

some reduction of what, on his account, he takes to be the excessive apophaticism of Thomas and of Henry of Ghent, which would seem to exaggerate the 'gap' between God and creatures to an extent such that, logically, no inference could possibly cross it. On the other hand, the potential risk implied by the univocity thesis to the transcendence of God is itself explicitly moderated in his account of the intensive infinity of the divine attributes, such that no one can say with fairness, as some have thought they can, that Scotus' God is nothing but a magnified, infinitely extended, creature. No doubt, then, Scotus wishes to have it both ways. But can he do so with consistency?

8   God, grammar and difference

'Difference' and 'the difference'

Whatever view one takes of Scotus' arguments that the possibility of a natural theology depends on the most general terms used of God and creatures being univocally predicable, at the very least they can be said to address a genuine problem about theological language in general. What *is* the difference between God and creatures? How are we to talk about that difference? Does such talk have a 'grammar'? And however we do talk about that difference – the 'gap', as it were, between God and creatures – is that gap so to be understood that any inference purporting to 'cross' it must, perforce, be invalid?

Today, and especially in some recent French philosophy and theology, the question of 'difference' as such has become much vexed both as a highly general question about language as such (in fact as a much too general question to be profitably disputed) and as a particular question about theological language. In this latter case, it arises as a question about 'the' difference between God and creation. But when it comes to that question, it is none too easy to know whether or not to say that 'the' difference between God and creatures is the 'ultimate' difference. Moreover, theologians are likely to be at a degree of loss to know what to say about that last question to the extent that they are in thrall to a 'deconstructionist' account of difference for which it would seem that, since difference itself is what is ultimate, there is not, and could not be, any one difference which is *the* ultimate difference. For to say that there is one ultimate difference, foundational of all the rest, would be, it is thought, 'ontotheological', and/or 'foundationalist' error, albeit dressed up in apophatic guise. Hence, the question arises: must our account of 'difference' be such that either theology is impossible, being dissolved into an endlessness of 'difference', or, if not impossible, then idolatrous and onto-theological, because settling down on a stably *divine* difference? The question taxes

Derrida,[1] and Caputo[2] and Marion,[3] in different ways, largely, it would seem, because Nietzsche much taxes all of them.[4] But all three are as much preoccupied with determining the relation of their own post-Nietzschean considerations about 'difference' to those of theologians in the high medieval, especially the high medieval apophatic, traditions. For this reason, and because their questioning of 'difference' raises some critical issues about how to read some authorities central to those medieval apophatic traditions, they form a convenient and contemporary point of entry into the question of 'difference' in so far as it is discussed within them.

Of course, the post-modern indebtedness to Nietzsche is as contentious in its reading of him as it is in its reading of the medieval traditions which it interprets in that Nietzschean light. But because it is with how in particular Jacques Derrida reads medieval apophaticism as a form of deconstruction, and because it is at least in part on account of his peculiarly 'French' reading of Nietzsche that he reads the medievals as he does, it is not my concern to debate with modern Nietzschean scholarship as to how far Derrida's interpretation of Nietzsche can be defended. For what matters to us is a question of our own: how far may Derrida's understanding of language and 'difference' throw light on the theological issue, addressed in its own terms in the Middle Ages, of *God's* difference, and of the capacity of language to identify and then cross it.

Nietzsche, Derrida, 'grammar' and God

In his *Twilight of the Idols*, Nietzsche tells us of his 'fear [that] we are not getting rid of God because we still believe in grammar',[5] thereby expressing, perhaps seminally for much French interpretation of Nietzsche, its logophobia, its fear of language. For all his supreme wordiness, Nietzsche fears language – it torments him with theological paradox. Language, constructed internally from the formal constituents of grammar, divides. Not that language fails merely as expression – because it divides into the artificial units of grammar what were, as if in some way prior

---

[1] Jacques Derrida, *On the Name*, ed. Thomas Dutoit, trans. David Wood, John P. Leavey and Ian McLeod, Stanford: Stanford University Press, 1995.

[2] John D. Caputo, 'Mysticism and Transgression: Derrida and Meister Eckhart', in Hugh J. Silverman, ed., *Derrida and Deconstruction*, London: Routledge, 1989, pp. 24–39.

[3] Jean-Luc Marion, *God without Being*, trans. Thomas A. Carlson, Chicago: Chicago University Press, 1991.

[4] In the construction of much of the argument of this chapter I am indebted to Mary-Jane Rubenstein for some important critical comments.

[5] Friedrich Nietzsche, *Twilight of the Idols* III.5, trans. Duncan Large, Oxford: Oxford University Press, 1998, p. 19.

to language, the natural and given unities of thought and experience – for language is there from the beginning as structure within thought and experience, which possess in consequence no prior unities for language then to betray.[6] Language taints in a manner which is original and originating, and the unities of experience which it fragments have no pre-existent 'presence', and are no more than those which language itself provides us with the possibility of envisaging. For that grammar which divides is also that alone which can generate a prospect of unity, a goal of experiential coherence which, nonetheless, can exist only as unachievable. Therefore, the coherences which language alone holds out as promise, language itself denies us. Hence, on the one hand, if language taints us with divisions, there are no unities prior to language which it taints. On the other hand, if the fragmentations of language are to be seen in some way as 'taint', then it is only on account of the expectation of a unity they frustrate that they are so to be seen.

Nor is this 'post-modern' paradox of language confined to its internal structure as, in the narrow sense, 'grammar'. For language holds out 'representational' promise too, the promise of determinable relationships with objects, relationships of truth and falsity with what it describes, only at the same time to deny us any finality in that determination. It is because of language that there are objects; it is within language alone that there can be a distinction between speaker and that which is spoken of. The prospect, therefore, of establishing objects for language to be about is at the same time given by language; hence, access to those objects is denied us by any route independent *of* language. The dualism of speaker and spoken of, of word and object, is therefore both constructed within language and deconstructed by it. Just that which promises is also that which disappoints. Language is, as it were, a Sisyphean striving, for it generates the very goal which it also frustrates.

'Grammar', therefore, is at once necessary and impossible in any absolute and final way. But it is the fear that language might be possible – might at some point resolve the paradox on the ground of some ultimate, redeeming 'reality', the fear that we are not in fact, and cannot ever be,

---

[6] Of course, as Mary-Jane Rubenstein has pointed out, there are accounts of an 'original condition' of pre-linguistic 'innocence', in which humans 'enjoyed a kind of pre-symbolic immediacy', a condition from which humans 'fell into language', and so into the world of 'binary opposition' – the 'subject-object' division – and so into 're-presentation'. Of such a kind is the account of Jean-Jacques Rousseau, for whom the transition from the 'state of nature' to that of civil society is precisely such a 'fall up' into language, and so, if from isolated individuality to society and from barbarism to civilisation, also from innocence to the possibility of evil. Nietzsche's account seems more drastically ironic in its consequences, less implicated in an essentially 'Romantic' dualism of 'innocence' and 'experience'.

'rid of grammar' – which, as God, haunts this Nietzschean mentality.[7] For language still holds out the promise of coherence and of fixed reference. And in so far as language can secure its hold on the meanings which it contains, and so be able to make finally 'present' the meanings which it seeks to disclose, to that extent speakers are trapped within their utterances, locked into an utterly deterministic world, a world determined by what can be said, since what can be said remains locked deterministically into its relations with its objects. Total loss of freedom is therefore the price to be paid for any grammar which could be shown to have resolved its own contradictions. And since the possibility of any such 'resolved' speech depends upon the existence of God, then the existence of God can be bought at the price only of a total loss of freedom. For, on Nietzsche's account, the possibility of speech's standing in fully determined relations with its objects requires a guarantee outside it, a 'foundation' of speech which is accessible within speech; and since such a foundation would have to take the form of an absolute presence, a self-confirming presence, itself requiring no further guarantees, that foundation would have to bear the name 'God'. Hence, if grammar then God, and consequent loss of freedom. But freedom, hence no resolved grammar, and no God.

Are we then to say that language has no foundations? Must we accept – because it seems to be entailed – that language could not have any describable foundations, since, were the foundations of language to lie within the range of the describable, they would therefore lie within the range of language itself? And how would that be other than to say that language is founded in itself, and so to say that it has no foundations? Or are we to say that language rests on indescribable foundations – to say which would appear to be but an oxymoron, since the word 'indescribable', for all its descriptive form, *a fortiori* describes nothing? Language can have no describable foundations, for to be founded upon something within itself is not to be founded; nor can it be founded on anything outside itself, since 'outside' language nothing is described as founding it.

If, therefore, we are to accept Nietzsche's proposition, we have got rid of God only in so far as we have got rid of grammar, and Nietzsche's rage against God is the rage of a beast mired in a marsh: language sticks to him and the more he rages against his entrapment the more he is mired. Of

---

[7] I am grateful to Hannah Pauly, an undergraduate student in the Faculty of Divinity in Cambridge, for reminding me of the significance of Nietzsche's 'fear': what troubles Nietzsche is not that we have 'got rid of God', but, on the contrary, that we have not, or, as Rubenstein puts it, that we have not got rid of God's 'shadow'. Zarathustra's proclamation of the death of God is a premature act of defiance. God, as it were, haunts the Nietzschean atheist still, for he fears that we have not 'got rid of grammar' (and perhaps cannot).

course, disconcerting and radical as this conclusion may appear to be – and it appeared so to Nietzsche – our culture in the late twentieth and early twenty-first centuries is largely unperturbed and has found it, as conclusions go, quite tolerable, even acceptably bourgeois.[8] It does not seem to follow, if language is foundationless, that we cannot speak, that because there is no finality to grammar there is no grammar at all, and that we human beings are therefore thrown as jetsam on some tossing sea of meaninglessness. As it turns out, the denial of God seems in our times unalarming; it seems only that we float without excessive anxiety on a surface, normally placid enough, on which the possibility of navigation is not removed for want of a determinate shore-line. For if there is no absolute positioning, we can at least establish relative position in reference to other boats. That there is no ultimate meaning does not entail that there is no meaning at all, since for the most part things can go on as if there were some ultimate meaning, our relative positions not being any different for not being absolute, just harder to calculate. All that follows from the absence of a shore-line – and all we need for the maintenance of a decent life – is to agree on a prescription: that if in one sense everything is arbitrary because nothing is absolute, then the only truly destructive arbitrariness is any claim to absoluteness made in the name of a particular, relative, position. Today, it is absolute claims which appear arbitrary and dangerous, intellectually, morally and politically. To acknowledge the arbitrariness of all positions seems the safer, more democratic, and more just, practical mentality, for which nothing is required except that nothing is required. For the rest, in any sense in which we need to know, we know where we are.

And so it is that in the late twentieth century, other ways were found in which to articulate these Nietzschean concatenations, which link the essential indeterminacies of language with human freedom, democracy, and the denial of God, and they draw the issues in more closely – indeed explicitly – with our own late antique and medieval sources. In much the same way as on Nietzsche's account, post-modernists link the determinacy of speech and the denial of freedom to God through the consequence that determinacy of grammar and reference would require that God is some absolute, self-confirming 'presence'; such a 'presence' would crush out and obliterate human freedom. And Jacques Derrida's philosophy of 'différance' is linked through a logophobia every bit as intense as Nietzsche's. As such, of course, Derrida's version of Nietzsche's concatenations is thus far also as theologically ambiguous as Nietzsche's are

---

[8] Such bourgeois complacency is exactly what Nietzsche feared would be the consequence derived by the 'moralistic' English, who would concede anything philosophically so long as they could keep their English morality intact. See Nietzsche, *Twilight* IX, 12, p. 49.

between an admirable scotching of idolatry, which attracts the theologians, and an outright denial of God, which of course worries them. Which way one reads it depends much on how one reads the complex and ever-modified story of his dialogue with 'negative theology'.[9]

And on the score of that dialogue, Derrida of course delights in a philosophy of ambiguity. Yet a philosophy of ambiguity is no excuse for an ambiguous philosophy. 'Tout autre est tout autre,'[10] he says, as if signifying some important truth: 'every other is totally other'. But it is hard to know what he could possibly mean, at any rate when construed as a general statement about the logic of 'otherness' as such.[11] And, surprisingly, too many critics and commentators have let him get away with it. 'Every other is wholly other' could perhaps mean that every case of otherness – of 'this' rather than 'that' – is a case of complete otherness, so that there are no differences within the logic of difference, no kinds of difference, and that all difference is univocal, whatever substantives one substitutes for the pronouns 'this' and 'that'. But that seems too obviously false. Or it could mean the opposite, namely that there *are* kinds of otherness, but that all othernesses are of completely different kinds from one another, and all difference is equivocal; which seems no more true, and for the same reason, namely that either way 'complete otherness' is an unintelligible notion. At any rate, so we shall see in due course. In the meantime, it would seem that if any sort of sense is to be attached to this oracular gesture, it is intended as a kind of 'deconstructionist' flag-waving: 'otherness' defeats all grammar, or, which is to say the same, there is no 'grammar' of 'difference' – indeterminacy rules. And, as we shall see, it is on account of this prioritisation of 'difference' that Derrida finds so much to fascinate him in the medieval traditions of negative theology.

Difference and hierarchy: the pseudo-Denys

At first blush, however, one would have supposed that classical forms of negative theology would hardly commend themselves to the 'democratic' temperament of post-modern philosophy, if only for the reason that

---

[9] See Jacques Derrida, 'How to Avoid Speaking: Denials', in Sanford Budick and Wolfgang Iser (eds.), *Language of the Unsayable: The Play of Negativity in Literature and Literary Theory*, New York: Columbia University Press, 1989, pp. 1–50.

[10] Derrida, *On the Name*, p. 76.

[11] Which you might say it is not, that it is intended ironically, as a *reductio ad absurdum* of any attempt to construct such a general logic of 'difference'. As we shall see, for Derrida, the statement 'Tout autre est tout autre' has a principally ethical force – see pp. 166–8 below. But no ethics, however rhetorically appealing, can provide excuses for bad logic; nor can appeals to 'irony'.

hierarchy is ineradicable from the earliest classical formulations of negative theology; they are born twins in their first incarnations. And if not
the first, then certainly the most influential of those incarnations in Western Christian thought must be that found in the pseudo-Denys' *Mystical
Theology*. For the pseudo-Denys a hierarchy is a differentiated structure
of differences. Thus, in the fourth and fifth chapters of that work he
describes a hierarchy of differentiated denials – denials, that is, of all the
names of God. Those names, to use a later, medieval, metaphor, form a
ladder, ascending from the lowest 'perceptual' names – 'God is a rock, is
immense, is light, is darkness . . .' – derived as metaphors from material
objects – to the very highest, 'proper' or 'conceptual' names of God: 'God
is wise and wisdom, good and goodness, beautiful and beauty, exists and
existence'. All these names the pseudo-Denys negates one by one as he
progresses up the scale of language until at the end of the work the last
word is that all words are left behind in the silence of the apophatic. This
ascending hierarchy of negations is, however, systematic, is governed by
a general theological principle and is regulated by a mechanism. It has a
grammar.

As to the general theological principle, the pseudo-Denys has already
said earlier in *Mystical Theology*[12] what he had emphasised in *Divine
Names*,[13] that all these descriptions denied are legitimate names of God,
and yield the possibilities of true and of false statements about God.
Hence, these fourth and fifth chapters of his *Mystical Theology* are, in the
first instance, expositions of an intrinsically hierarchical affirmative theology. Moreover, the foundation of this affirmativeness lies in God's being
the Creator of all things. It is God's being the cause of all which justifies
God's being described by the names of all the things he has caused, even
if what they mean as thus predicated of God must fall infinitely short of
what God is; nor is there any sign, anywhere in the *Corpus Dionysiacum*,
that Denys anticipates a problem of consistency between an epistemologically realist affirmative theology and a thoroughgoing apophaticism.

Indeed, it is probably one of the chief arguments of *Divine Names* that
if we are not to be misled in our theological language, we not only may
but must use as many different ways of describing God as possible:[14] as
he himself says, if we gain something in how we think of God by describing her as a 'king in majesty', then we ought to remember that she can
appear to behave towards us in a manner so irritable and arbitrary that
we may as appropriately describe her, in the manner of the Psalmist, as

---

[12] Pseudo-Denys, *Mystical Theology*, 1033B; *Complete Works*, p. 139.
[13] Pseudo-Denys, *Divine Names* 593C–D; *Complete Works*, p. 54.
[14] *Divine Names* 596A; *Complete Works*, p. 54.

behaving like a soldier maddened by an excess of wine.[15] Theological language, for the pseudo-Denys, consists not in a restraint, but in a clamour of metaphor and description, for negative theology is, essentially, a surplus, not a deficit, of description; you talk your way into silence by way of an *excessus* embarrassed at its increasing complexity of differentiation. Hence, if we must also deny all that we affirm, this does not, for the pseudo-Denys, imply any privileging of the negative description or metaphor over the affirmative. For those denials and negations are themselves forms of speech; hence, if the divine reality transcends all our speech, then, as he says in the concluding words of *Mystical Theology*, 'the cause of all . . . is' indeed, '. . . beyond every assertion'; but it is also, and by the same token, '*beyond every denial*'.[16] You can no more 'capture' God in denials than you can capture God in affirmations.

The point of the serial negations of the last two chapters of that work, therefore, is not to demonstrate that negative language is somehow superior to affirmative in the mind's ascent to God; rather it is to demonstrate that our language leads us to the reality of God when, by a process simultaneously of affirming and denying all things of God, by, as it were in one breath, both affirming what God is and denying, as he puts it, 'that there is any kind of thing that God is',[17] we step off the very boundary of language itself, beyond every assertion and every denial, into the 'negation of the negation' and the 'brilliant darkness'[18] of God. But even here we should note that this 'negation of the negation' entails neither that some ultimate affirmation gains grip, nor that some ultimate negation does so. The 'negation of the negation' is precisely the refusal of ultimacy to both the affirmative and the negative, to both similarity and difference. In this sense the theology of the pseudo-Denys is neither an 'apophaticism' nor a 'cataphaticism'. It is the entirely 'unclosed', 'unresolved', tension between both. It is within that tension that, for the pseudo-Denys, all theological language is situated; it is situated, in a certain sense, within indeterminacy.

So much for the theological principle of his apophaticism – which is necessarily at the same time the general principle of his cataphaticism. As for the mechanism which governs this stepwise ascent of affirmation and denial, we may observe how that mechanism is itself a paradoxical conjunction of opposites: the ascent is, as I have said, an ordered hierarchical progression from denials of the lower to denials of the higher names, and yet at every stage on this ascent we encounter the same phenomenon of language slipping and sliding unstably, as the signifying name first appears

[15] Ps. 78:65. See *Mystical Theology* 1048B; *Complete Works*, p. 141.
[16] *Mystical Theology* 1048B; *Complete Works*, p. 141.
[17] *Divine Names* 817D; *Complete Works*, p. 98.
[18] *Mystical Theology* 997B; *Complete Works*, p. 135.

to get a purchase, and then loses grip, on the signified it designates. We may say legitimately, because the Bible says it, that 'God is a rock' and as we say the words they appear to offer a stable hold on the signified, God: we have said, Denys supposes, something true of God, albeit by metaphor, and something of the divine reliability is thereby disclosed. But just as we have let some weight hang from the grip of this word 'rock' on the being of God, the grip slips: God is not, of course, 'lifeless', as rocks are, and we also have to say, since the Bible tells us we must, that God is love and must be possessed of intellect and will, and so enjoys the highest form of life of which we know. Hence, in order to retain its grip on the signified, the signifier has to shift a step up the ladder of ascent, there itself to be further destabilised. For God is not 'intelligence' or 'will' either, and the signified again wriggles away from the hook of the signifier and shifts and slides away, never to be impaled finally on any descriptive hook we can devise, even that of existence. For in affirming that 'God exists', what we say of God differs infinitely more from what we affirm when we say that 'Peter exists' than does 'Peter exists' from 'Peter does not exist'. For the difference between Peter's existing and Peter's not existing is a created difference, and so finite. Whereas the difference between God's existing and Peter's existing is between an uncreated and a created existence, and so is infinite.[19] Hence, any understanding we have of the distinction between existence and non-existence fails of God, which is why the pseudo-Denys can say that the Cause of all 'falls neither within the predicate of nonbeing nor of being'.[20] Mysteriously, the pseudo-Denys insists that we must deny of God that she is 'divinity';[21] more mysteriously still the signified eludes the hold even, as we have seen, of 'similarity and difference';[22] mysteriously, that is, until we are forced to discover just why God cannot be different from, nor therefore similar to, anything at all, at any rate in any of the ways in which we can conceive of similarity and difference; or else God would be just another, different, thing. Just so, for the pseudo-Denys: for 'there is no kind of thing', he says, 'which God is'.[23] Therefore, there is nothing we can say which fully circumscribes what God is, and, which is more to the point, there can be no language of similarity and difference left with which to describe God's difference. In short, for the pseudo-Denys, only the otherness of God could be 'totally' other, and that otherness of God is, perforce, indescribable – God's 'otherness' is to be *beyond* 'otherness'. Hence, as to 'this'

---

[19] See pp. 178–9 below for Thomas's discussion of this point.
[20] *Mystical Theology* 1048A; *Complete Works*, p. 141
[21] *Mystical Theology* 1048A; *Complete Works*, p. 141.
[22] *Mystical Theology* 1048A; *Complete Works*, p. 141.
[23] *Divine Names* 817D; *Complete Works*, p. 98.

difference between God and creatures, we cannot even describe it as *a* difference, *the* difference, of which we can give an account.

For the pseudo-Denys, then, we are justified in making true affirmative statements about God, because if God is the Creator of all things, all things must in some way reveal, in what they are, the nature of their origin. That is his concession, as we might put it, to 'foundationalism'. But creatures do not all reveal the same things about God, or in the same way, or to the same extent. For this reason, it is correct to say that, for the pseudo-Denys, there is a 'grammar' of talk about God, a grammar which governs equally its cataphatic and the apophatic 'phases'. For even if we do not have a proper 'concept' of God (there being no kind of thing which God is for there to be a concept of), we have a *use* for the name 'God', a use which is governed by determinable rules of correct and incorrect speech. In fact, it is clear that, for the pseudo-Denys, that grammar is complex and differentiated, governing, that is to say, different logics of grounding in truth, different logics of consistency, and above all, different logics of negation, negation being the foundation of all logic, and so of 'difference'. These 'logics' are determined by the order of creation in so far as creation is an order and scale of revelation, a hierarchy, for as some things are 'nearer' to God in their natures, and others 'further' from God, so their likeness to God is more or less 'similar'. Of course, all the names of God fall short of what God is: you can even say that God is equally 'other' than all these names, though they are not equally 'other' than God.[24] But because there is a hierarchy of affirmations, there is a corresponding hierarchy of denials.

For, in general, what you are doing in negating predicates of God depends on the logical standing of the predicates you are negating, and four logical types of negation – and so of 'difference' – seem to be theologically at play. First, at the level of metaphor, and so at the 'lowest' level of our discourse about God, we affirm and deny of God what is proper to material creation: 'God is a rock', 'God is a lion'. Obviously 'God is a lion' negates the force of 'God is a rock' to the extent that a rock is lifeless and a lion alive. Hence, one metaphor is negated by its *metaphorically* negative counterpart. But even metaphors which cancel each other in one respect are with consistency affirmed of one and the same thing in another, for there is no inconsistency in saying that God has the stability of a rock and the fierce energy of a lion. In any case, a negative metaphor, as 'no man is an island', negates an affirmative, such as 'some men are

---

[24] See *Divine Names* 680B; *Complete Works*, p. 68. This paradox is not entirely incoherent. All numbers fall short of infinity infinitely. Even so, 4 is larger than 2, and 5 than 4. Created differences are not eliminated by their all falling infinitely short of their uncreated cause.

islands', but is for all its negativity, still a metaphor. Consequently, the relations of affirmation to negation *within* the metaphorical differ from those between a metaphor, whether affirmative or negative, and its negation *as* a metaphor.

For, secondly, the negation of metaphor simply consists in a recognition of its literal falsehood: 'It is not the case that God is a rock', which is simply a way of acknowledging that 'God is a rock' *is* a metaphor. But then again, at a third level, a literal affirmation entails the negation of its literal contradictory, for *eadem est scientia oppositorum*.[25] Hence, you may legitimately say that 'God exists', which is in no way a metaphor, and is no more than to say the contrary of what the atheist says; and you may legitimately say that 'God is good', which entails the falsehood of 'God is evil'. In either case, the first, being true, excludes the truth of the second. And all these three relations of affirmation and negation are straightforwardly 'Aristotelian'; they are negations governed by the laws of classical logic.

But as to a fourth level of negation, that which the pseudo-Denys calls 'denial by transcendence', this is the 'negation of the negation', as when he says that the Cause of all 'falls neither within the predicate of nonbeing nor of being'. And it is clear that the pseudo-Denys' *apophatic* negations are of this last kind. For in the sense in which it is correctly said that 'God is not good', it is not now entailed that God is evil; in the sense in which God is said, correctly, not to be 'a being', 'not-being' *equally* fails of God. What is being negated, therefore, is that any creaturely understanding of the difference between good and evil, between being and non-being, finally holds its grip on God. The 'negation of the negation' is ultimately the negation of that hierarchy which structures the oppositions of affirmation and negation which lead up to it. For that hierarchy is a structure of differentiation, an articulation of a scale of negations; whereas the 'negation of the negation' places God beyond hierarchy itself, for to say that God is 'beyond both similarity and difference' is to say that God is not different by virtue of any of the differences on the scale, but that God is, ultimately, off the scale itself. But *how* do such denials – the double negation – achieve this?

It is sometimes said that they do so by 'going beyond' Aristotelian logic.[26] And this is in one way true, and in another way distinctly misleading. For in so far as what is meant by saying that the 'apophatic denials' reach out to some space 'beyond' the realm in which the principle of contradiction holds is that here, when talking about God, we

---

[25] Or rather, as Aquinas used to quote Aristotle's remark in *De interpretatione* 6 17a 31–33.

[26] For example, by Colm Luibheid; see *Pseudo-Dionysius: The Complete Works*, p. 136, note 6.

may happily say contradictory things without 'Aristotelian' scruple, this clearly misrepresents the pseudo-Denys's view. For it is, on the contrary, *because* two propositions which formally contradict each other *could not* both be true of God – in other words precisely because here, too, Aristotelian logic does hold – that we know our language to be failing of God. The 'negation of the negation' is not the abandonment of logic's hold on language. On the contrary, it is precisely because logic does retain its hold on language that the negation of the negation is the abandonment of language as such. Hence, for the pseudo-Denys there is no such thing as 'apophatic language'. If it is apophatic, then it is *beyond* language. If it is within language, then it is obedient to the laws of 'Aristotelian logic'. It is only 'beyond speech', therefore, that, for the pseudo-Denys, indeterminacy rules. In the meantime, and leading up to that point, there is a hierarchical differentiation and structure within negativity, and so within 'otherness', a hierarchy which is intrinsic to the statement of his apophaticism.

If we are to understand the theology of the pseudo-Denys we have to admit this hierarchy of negation and difference, and the consequent hierarchical ontology which underpins it. And such an admission will not be so readily conceded in some quarters today; for it is commonly supposed that if we are today to gain profit from the theology of the pseudo-Denys for our own theological purposes, it will have to be at the cost of his clearly 'pre-modern' hierarchicalism, for which (it is thought) any contemporary ontology can find no place. For no contemporary ontology concedes the pseudo-Denys's scale of being, descending, as I put it elsewhere,[27] like a laval flow from the pure fire of its origin down through the slopes of the volcano, hardening and cooling as it flows away from its source. Contemporary philosophies permit no conceptions which correspond with the pseudo-Denys's Platonic notion of 'degrees of reality' such that some things 'realise more' of what it is to exist than other things do, still less of the Christianised Platonic notion that the existence which creatures 'more or less' realise consists in their degree of participation in the divine existence. Hence, Christian theologies today, even those claiming much influence from the antique and medieval traditions of negative theology, may feel that they know what they can and what they cannot take from those sources: negative theology they will embrace, on condition of its detachment from a hierarchical Platonic ontology, and its corresponding epistemological hierarchy.[28]

---

[27] Turner, *Darkness of God*, p. 29.
[28] See ibid., pp. 26–33, for a fuller account of the role of hierarchy in the thought of the pseudo-Denys.

Perhaps theologians of that way of thinking will feel sustained in their hopes for such selectivity by the fact that the theology of the pseudo-Denys is governed by a double movement of thought, the one rooted in an antique hierarchical ontology, the other, corrective of the first, in the directly Christian teaching of the creation of all things 'out of nothing'. If, from the first point of view, a theological language of greater and lesser distance from God is legitimised, from the second point of view this hierarchicalism is radically qualified: all things are also in a certain sense equidistant from the God whose action sustains them equally in existence as opposed to the nothingness 'from which' they are created. For there is no such kind of thing as the kind of thing which exists; there is no kind of being, therefore, which, prior to or beyond its character as pure gift, has any claim on existence because of the kind of being that it is. Hence, even if, given its existence, an angel possesses an existence 'more necessary' than that of a worm, from this 'absolute' point of view of creation – that it exists at all – an angel has no better claim on existence than a worm has. The 'aristocratic' theological language of the angelic hierarchy cannot be justified except in its dialectical tension with, and ultimate subordination to, the 'democratic' ontology of creation *ex nihilo*. As 'the Cause of all' God stands in the same relation to the whole hierarchy as its Creator: he does not stand as top being *on* that hierarchy.

Nonetheless, those hopes are vain which are sustained by a prospect of a Dionysian apophaticism rooted in the democratic negativity of *creatio ex nihilo* but detached from a hierarchical affirmativity, not least because of the distortions thus visited upon the pseudo-Denys's theological project. For a theological apophasis whose denials are disengaged from the hierarchy of affirmations will have to abandon, along with the hierarchy of affirmations, also the pseudo-Denys's careful distinctions within the hierarchy of denials themselves – or, to put it in other terms, within the hierarchy of 'difference', and so within the differentiations intrinsic to our language about God.

Hence, it is not so easy as it might be thought to distil out, as a pure 'rhetoric', an apophatic theology from that hierarchical ontology which, in antique and medieval traditions, underpinned an affirmative theology. For it is once again necessary to emphasise that at work within the pseudo-Denys's articulation of theological language is the Aristotelian principle, *eadem est scientia oppositorum* – affirmations and their corresponding negations are one and the same knowledge. In general, therefore, 'otherness' and negation are inconceivable except in terms of 'sameness' and affirmation; hence, what it is to deny something – what kind of 'otherness' you thereby affirm – depends on what it is to affirm it. It further follows that if the logic of affirmation is hierarchically differentiated, then we have to say that the logic of negation and 'otherness' is differentiated. And it follows finally that if 'otherness' is differentiated, then the differences between one kind of otherness and others are themselves intelligible only against the background of sameness. The conception of an 'otherness' being '*tout* autre' is, therefore, strictly unintelligible. Just so, says the pseudo-Denys: to the 'tout autre' we would have to give the name 'God', for it is here alone that logic breaks down, and the principle *eadem est scientia oppositorum* itself fails, as it must, since God 'is beyond [not only] every assertion . . .[but also] beyond every denial'. As it were, to reverse Nietzsche's famous formulation: we can get God only at the point where we get rid of grammar, where we have pressed 'grammar' beyond its breaking point.

Hence to dislodge any one element in this complex structure of differentiated difference is to cause the whole edifice of theological language to collapse. What, of course, it collapses into if we remove from it that articulation of differentiated differences is precisely what we get in Derrida: a univocity of difference for which every difference is reduced to a generalised indeterminacy, an indeterminacy which is, moreover, logically impossible as of anything finite: 'total difference'. What the pseudo-Denys recognises is that no two anythings can be 'totally different', for that is why he concludes that God, being totally different from all creatures, could not be any kind of thing. As between God and creatures there is, of course, all the difference, but, being beyond description, it cannot be a difference of any kind; but the thought that that, precisely, is how God is different from creation – more 'other' in respect of any creature than any two creatures could be in respect of each other – is one which gets its full development in later Dionysian theologies, in particular those of Meister Eckhart and Thomas Aquinas, to the first of whom we must now turn, leaving the discussion of Thomas to the next chapter.

Difference and indistinction: Meister Eckhart

In the formulation of Meister Eckhart's theology, however, the Dionysian hierarchy – whether in the form of an ontology of degrees of being, or in that of the outflow of descending illuminations – notably plays little if any part. If 'difference' is central to that theology and spirituality, the carefully structured hierarchical gradings of the pseudo-Denys found in chapters 4 and 5 of his *Mystical Theology* in Eckhart are relatively underplayed, yielding central place within his theological scheme to one central distinction which entirely eclipses all others. This is the distinction, on the one hand, between those created distinctions which obtain between one creature and another – between each *hoc aliquid* ('this something') as an *unum distinctum* ('distinct individual') – and, on the other, that distinction which obtains between every *esse hoc et hoc* (this or that existent) and the *unum indistinctum* ('the-one-who-is-not-distinct') of the divine *esse*.

For Eckhart, a created individual is an instantiation of a kind, a *hoc et hoc*, a 'this, that or the other', enumerable on condition of falling under a description. I can count the number of people in this room if I know under what description something counts as a person, the number of desks if I know under what description something counts as a desk. But I cannot count the number of things in this room, because 'thing' is not a description definite enough that enumerable instances fall under it. Likewise, I can distinguish kinds from one another against the background of more general descriptions: I can tell horses from sheep because they differ as animals, or chalk from cheese because they differ in chemical composition or taste or texture. But there is here an apparent paradox, in logical form much the same as that of the pseudo-Denys: the less things differ, the easier it is to describe how they differ. It is easy to say how a cat and a mouse differ, because we can readily describe what they differ *as*; they belong, we might say, to a readily identifiable community of difference – that of animals. But how does this piece of Camembert cheese differ from 11.30 in the morning? Here, the community of difference is too diffuse, too indeterminate, for this difference, obviously bigger as it is than that of chalk and cheese, to be so easily described. In general, the bigger the difference, the harder, not easier, it is to describe the manner of its difference.

Of course, the logic of difference thus described does not require of us any deterministic account of types or species or 'categories', for this logic entails no particular ontological commitments as such. As it stands, however, this logic already has consequences for the question: how far can language cope with the difference between God and creation? It follows that it cannot cope at all; or, if we are to say anything about this distinction, it is the paradoxical sort of thing Eckhart says about it, namely that God is distinct from any creature in this alone, that if any creature is necessarily a distinct being, a *hoc aliquid*, God is not. A creature is, as he puts it, an *unum distinctum*, distinct from another by means of its difference in respect of some background sameness which they share, whereas God is an *unum indistinctum*, that is to say, is distinct from any creature whatsoever in this, that, unlike any creature, God is not distinct in kind from anything created at all – for there is no background against which a distinction of kind can be set. Therefore, God is distinct because God alone is not distinct. 'Indistinction', as he puts it, 'belongs to God, distinction to creatures.'[29]

Moreover, if God is not a describably distinct kind of anything, God cannot be an individual distinct from other individuals, and so cannot be counted at all. Suppose you were to count up all the things in the world on some lunatic system of enumeration – all the things that there are, have been and will be – and suppose they come to the number n. Then I say, 'Hold on; I am a theist and there is one being you haven't yet counted, and that is the being who created them all, God.' Would I be right to say that now the sum total of things is $n + 1$? Emphatically no. There is no need to paraphrase Eckhart here, for he says for himself in his *Commentary on Exodus*: 'God is one in all ways and according to every respect so that he cannot find any multiplicity in himself . . . Anyone who beholds the number two or who beholds distinction does not behold God, for God is one, outside and beyond number, and is not counted with anything.'[30] But, we may ask, how can God be one – *unum* – if not countable in any series, if not in any way another individual, so as not to be one more something, not a *hoc aliquid*; how an *unum*, if *indistinctum*? And if God is not an individual, is God therefore many? That neither, for the argument which shows that God is not one more individual must also show that God is not many more individuals. Neither one nor many: so neither an individual distinct from everything else, nor many, identical with everything else; hence 'one', but not an individual; 'distinct' from everything, but not *as* anything; hence, an *unum indistinctum*. And we should note that what holds for the divine oneness holds also for the Trinity itself. If there are in any sense 'three' in God, there is nothing of which there are three instantiations in God, any more than there is any 'one' instance of anything called 'God' in which there are 'three'. The same principle of apophaticism holds of the divine Trinity – not three instances of anything, as of the divine essence – there is nothing of which God is one instance. In God 'one' and 'three' are equally mysteries; and the Trinity is the 'negation of the negation' between them.

But if 'to know an affirmation is to know its negation', then God's being beyond difference entails God's being beyond sameness. If what Jacques Derrida means by saying that 'every other is completely other' is that there is no ultimate 'sameness' of such nature that it stands in no possible relation of 'otherness', then of course he is right, for of course every 'sameness' is determinable by reference to its differences from something

---

[29] Eckhart, *Commentary on Exodus* 20.104, in Bernard McGinn (ed) with Frank Tobin and Elvira Borgstadt, *Meister Eckhart, Teacher and Preacher*, New York: Paulist Press, 1986, p. 79.
[30] Ibid., 15.58, p. 63.

else. But then it follows also that there can be no ultimacy to any particular 'difference' either: it is 'différance' which is ultimate, not *a* difference. For 'sameness' and 'difference' have the same apophatic destination, as it were, in that they can only ultimately disappear into that same vortex of unknowing which is beyond both. Just as you could not have a sameness which establishes itself beyond all possible difference, so you could not have *a* difference which is, without qualification, altogether beyond all possible similarity.

With which Derrida may be construed as thus far agreeing: he affirms this hegemony of 'différance', he says, not in order to affirm some new ultimacy, only now a purely negative one, but in order to affirm only a *pen*ultimacy – which is not, we may add, to *insist* upon anything, but rather to *desist* from all possible forms of ultimacy, from every 'destination', even an ultimacy of the negative. To declare the ultimacy of 'différance' is precisely not to propose, but on the contrary to deny, some new ontology of difference, according to which *there is an ultimate difference*. But that is what he accuses the negative theologians of affirming when they insist upon their 'ontological distinction'. For it is precisely in that insistence of negative theology, in what appears to be a surreptitious, last-minute, retrieval of the existential quantifier 'there is a . . .' attached to their ultimate difference, that an onto-theological sleight of hand is forced out into the open, thus to regain for their apophaticisms a divine 'destination', their postponements and deferrals notwithstanding – a given, superessential presence of an absolute absence, generative of all lesser, postponable, essential difference. More to the point, it is precisely this dilemma which a natural theology, purporting to demonstrate that God exists, must face – since a natural theology would seem to say both that God's existence is unknowably 'other' and that it is demonstrable, in which case how could it be other than knowable? In any case, for Derrida, this *khora*, this 'place' of 'otherness', cannot possess the name of the God of the negative theologians because it cannot be, as God is, 'a giver of good gifts',[31] and could not therefore be the Creator. A 'place of indeterminacy' can *do* nothing.

Therefore, this tactic of the negative theologians contains, he thinks, an impossibility, a contradiction. For the theologians must choose one position or another, they must be required to resolve their ambiguities. On the one hand, they may mean that this 'there is a . . .' is itself cancelled as affirmative utterance by their negative theology of ultimate difference; and the tendency of their apophaticism would seem to force them down this line, for after all, the theologians do concede this 'erasure', for how

[31] Derrida, 'How to Avoid Speaking', pp. 106–8.

can they allow an ordinary, undeconstructed existential affirmation as a foundation for their apophaticism, and do they not insist that their God is 'being beyond being'[32] and 'within the predicate neither of nonbeing nor of being', as Denys says? On the other hand, if not thus apophatically cancelled, must not this 'there is a ...' remain in place as an existential quantifier, thereby onto-theologically and idolatrously cancelling the apophaticism? Hence, negative theology collapses either into the ceaseless penultimacy of an atheistic deconstruction or else into an idolatrous onto-theology. As a project, therefore, negative theology will resolve its ambiguities only to be caught on one horn or other of a dilemma.

To which, in turn, it may be provisionally replied: the negative theologies of the pseudo-Denys and of Eckhart do not affirm, as if at the last minute to hypostatise, some one difference as a sort of ultimate 'absence', any more than they affirm the ultimacy of some sameness and presence, of some given identity. For both recognise that *a* difference, *any* difference, is determinable. But what is 'beyond similarity and difference' is not in some measurable, calculable degree of difference from creation, even if different beings in the created order are in determinably different degrees of difference from God, because in determinably different degrees of difference from one another. God's 'difference' does not cancel created differences. Nor is 'the ontological distinction' between God and creatures in any *knowable* sense or degree 'beyond' anything knowable; for our language of 'difference', that is to say, our language as such, falls short of God to a degree which is itself absolutely beyond description; it therefore could not be the case that we could say *how* different God is. This ontological distinction is 'beyond' precisely by reason of its unknowability and indetermination, so that it inhabits some place neither of absolute presence nor of absolute absence; hence, we might just as well say, as Nicholas of Cusa in fact does say, that God is *ly non-Aliud* ('the one and only not-other') as say that he is in any way *'ly Aliud'* ('the absolutely other')[33] – which, after all, is the same logic as Meister Eckhart's '[God is] distinct by virtue of indistinction'.

In the meantime, Derrida's collapsing of all 'otherness', whether created or uncreated, into a uniformly 'total' otherness, is logically incoherent nonsense, yet it is a nonsense which appears to be forced upon him

---

[32] Eckhart, Sermon 83, *Renovamini Spiritu*, in *Meister Eckhart: The Essential Sermons, Commentaries, Treatises and Defense*, ed. Edmund Colledge and Bernard McGinn, London: SPCK, 1981, p. 206.

[33] Nicholas of Cusa, *De ly non-Aliud*, the text and translation of which are in *Nicholas of Cusa on God as Not-other*, ed. and trans. Jasper Hopkins, Minneapolis: University of Minneapolis Press, 1979.

out of grounds in a hardly more than rhetorical, and hyperbolic, moralising about the 'otherness' of the 'other *person*'. Derrida's generalised apophaticism of 'otherness' as such seems to have its roots in a view of the 'otherness' of persons which takes to a point of absurdity their irreducible inaccessibility to my subjectivity, to my *ego*, so that he can insist that

God, as the wholly other, is to be found everywhere there is something of the wholly other. And since each of us, everyone else, each other is infinitely other in its absolute singularity, inaccessible, solitary, transcendent, nonmanifest, originally nonpresent to my ego ... then what can be said about Abraham's relation to God can be said about my relation without relation to *every other (one) as every (bit) other [tout autre comme tout autre]*, in particular my relation to my neighbor or my loved ones who are as inaccessible to me, as secret and transcendent as Jahweh.[34]

It is true that it is such things which you have to say if you are to speak intelligibly of an 'otherness' which is 'totally other'. But if no such otherness could be a finitely knowable, determinable, otherness, then it could not be true of any finite relation, which is why Derrida's principle, 'every other is completely other', is not only a straightforward logical absurdity, it is also an ethically offensive one, for all its apparently benign origins in Levinas's less radically stated ethics of 'alterity'. For the 'otherness' of another person is not and cannot be an absolute heterogeneity; an incorrigible and incommunicable 'thisness' which is not a this *something or other*; it cannot be an absolutely inaccessible 'singularity', not unless some ethic is to be founded upon the otherness of the other as some blank, anonymous reference point of a semantically empty demonstrative pronoun. For I love my 'loved ones' certainly as 'other', perhaps as 'irreducibly other', but certainly not as '*wholly* other', for that is to love them into a vacuous non-entity, and if I love you as making 'all the difference', it is as making all the difference to a shared whatness, that is, to what we humans are. It is God whom we cannot love on terms of any antecedently given common ground, which is why Eckhart can say that 'you should love God as he is nonGod, a nonspirit, a nonperson, a nonimage'.[35] But if that is so, it is also why, as Eckhart says, we cannot know or love God as any sort of individual, for there is no sense to the notion of an individuality, but of no sort, which is why my 'singularity' cannot be total: it is only God who is totally singular, not being any sort

---

[34] Jacques Derrida, *The Gift of Death*, Chicago: Chicago University Press, 1996, p. 78 (emphasis added).
[35] Eckhart, Sermon 83; *Essential Sermons*, p. 208.

of thing,[36] and so, paradoxically, is not in any created sense an individual at all.

In consequence, Derrida can have no God precisely because either he collapses all the differentiations of difference into a monolithic, logically and ethically vacuous univocity of absolute difference, or else he reduces it to a multifarious equivocity, depending on which way we (and he) read it. But neither Eckhart nor Thomas Aquinas thought either of these things: either, that is to say, that there is no end to difference, or that there is *a* difference at the end. That being said, however, Derrida's question remains a fair one, requiring an answer: how consistently with this emphatic negativity, and on what grounds, can the theologians say, 'God exists'? What is the logic of this 'existence' of God?

---

[36] It will, of course, be said that there being common ground between God and human beings is precisely what the incarnation brings us news of, such that we can love God and be loved by God on that common ground – without it we could not love God at all. Just so. The gift of that common ground is what Eckhart, following Thomas, means by grace. But rather than Eckhart's apophaticism standing in the way of such a gift's being given and received, it is precisely Derrida's which does so, for it is as excluding the possibility of an 'economy of gifts' that his conception of 'otherness' is stated in terms of incommunicability. Eckhart's, as we have seen, is an 'otherness' which is *beyond* both 'otherness' and 'sameness', as is that of the pseudo-Denys.

9 Existence and God

The logic of existence

It is not impossible to reconstruct a response from Thomas to the dilemma posed at the end of the last chapter, and it is obviously important that we should find some way of doing so, because the dilemma strikes at the heart of my argument in this essay. For if logic required a choice between the rational demonstrability of the existence of God, but at the price of abandoning a theological apophaticism, and holding on to the apophaticism, but at the price of abandoning the rational demonstrability of God – then it would seem that my argument would fail just as its critics say it must: the existence of God is rationally demonstrable on pain of onto-theological error – in short, of idolatry. But I shall argue in this chapter that the case for maintaining both propositions does not yet have to be abandoned, and that Thomas is not without resources to repel the 'Derridean' counter-argument. And we may begin by noting that Thomas himself entertains an objection similar in form to Derrida's, albeit to a different, if closely related issue.

The objection arises in connection with Thomas's doctrine of the divine simplicity, and more particularly with the proposition that definitive of that simplicity is the identity of God's *esse* and *essentia*. It would seem, Thomas says, that since we can know *whether* God exists (*an Deus sit*) but not *what* God is (*quid sit Deus*) *esse* and *essentia* can no more be identical in God than they are in anything else. The objection is doubly significant in its bearing on our discussion, for, in the first place, in posing this objection Thomas is explicitly screwing up the tension between his theological apophaticism and his case for the rational demonstrability of God's existence. For if by demonstration we can know God to exist, then how can it be the case also that we do not know the divine *esse*? Put in the starkest possible terms, Thomas's position seems to be straightforwardly self-contradictory in that it seems to amount to saying that we can know God's existence, but also that we cannot. He cannot have it both ways. If God's existence is unknown to us in principle, then no proof can make it known to us. And if a proof can make God's existence known to us, then God's existence is not unknown to us.

But this objection is significant for a second reason, which brings us back to our earlier discussion of Scotus. For the principle underlying it is just that which Scotus employed in his argument that *esse* is predicated univocally of God and of creatures. For if, Scotus argued, we can know that *p* while not knowing whether or not that *q*, then *p* and *q* must be really distinct. Hence, if we can know *that* God is 'being' (*ens*), but be so ignorant as not yet to know whether God is infinite or finite being, then *esse* must be predicable in some one sense independently of the distinction between infinite and finite, and so univocally of both God and creatures. Consequently, as Cross comments,[1] what gives way in Scotus' case is the apophaticism, which yields inevitably to his principal concern, which is for the rational demonstrability of God's existence. As we shall see, Thomas feels uncompelled by the force of this dilemma to abandon either the apophaticism or the rational demonstrability of God, and his reply to the objection is to make a distinction and to note how

Esse can be understood in two ways. In the first sense it means 'the act of existing' (*actus essendi*); in the second it refers to the formation of [an affirmative] proposition which the mind constructs by means of a predicative form. Hence, in the first sense of *esse*, we cannot know the *esse* of God any more than we can know his essence, but only in the second sense. For we know that the proposition which we construct about God when we say 'God exists' is true. And we know this from his effects, as we showed in q2 a2.[2]

Let us say, for the purposes of exposition, that the first manner of understanding *esse* is as expressed in judgements of 'actuality', and the second is as expressed in affirmative predicative propositions, and note, as a first step of explanation, that we cannot get at the distinction in the logical form Thomas here has in mind by means of any purely grammatical devices. For the one statement '*x* exists' can be a proposition of either logical form, regardless of what value we substitute for the variable '*x*'. Moreover, we ought not to allow this terminology, descriptive of the second sort of proposition as 'predicative', to mislead us into supposing that, for Thomas, *esse* in this sense is logically a predicate, for it is not. As we shall see, what Thomas appears to mean by the ascription of *esse* in

---

[1] Cross, *Duns Scotus*, p. 39.

[2] '*Esse* dupliciter dicitur: uno modo, significat actum essendi; alio modo, significat compositionem propositionis, quam anima adinvenit coniungens praedicatum subiecto. Primo igitur modo accipiendo *esse*, non possumus scire *esse* Dei, sicut nec eius essentiam: sed solum secundo modo. Scimus enim quod haec propositio quam formamus de Deo, cum dicimus *Deus est*, vera est. Et hoc scimus ex eius effectibus, ut supra [q2 a2] dictum est.' *ST* 1a q3 a4 ad2.

this second sense is not that *esse* is predicable of the variable '*x*', but that any such statement of existence – 'God exists', or for that matter, 'cows exist' – may be replaced by some affirmative statement in which 'God' and 'cow' form predicates of something or other: 'something or other is God'; 'something or other is a cow'. To put it in the terms of modern logic, the 'exists' in predications of this kind is analysable in terms of the 'existential quantifier'.

Esse as true affirmative predication: the 'existential quantifier'

Geach explains why in this second sense it cannot be existence which functions as predicate:[3] if, in that sense of '*x* exists' in which it figures as an answer to a question whether there are any such things as *x*s, you treat the grammatical predicate '. . . exists' as a logical predicate, as if ascribing some *attribute* of existence to what '*x*' refers to, then you will find yourself in all sorts of muddles, familiar to readers of Plato, about how to handle negative statements of existence. To take, in the first instance, existential statements about individuals, we can see why, in '*N* does not exist', you cannot treat '. . . exists' as a predicate denied of the person '*N*' stands for, since clearly in such expressions *N* cannot stand for anything at all. Supposing a child, having seen the play *Hamlet*, were to ask where Hamlet's grave is, you could in reply say, 'It's not like that – unlike Ian McKellen, Hamlet does not (really) exist.' Now, leaving aside complex further questions which arise concerning judgements of existence and non-existence in fictional contexts,[4] it is quite clear that in 'Hamlet does not exist' we cannot treat 'Hamlet' as functioning logically as a proper name, and '. . . does not exist' as a predicate attributing non-existence to him. For if we do, then we are forced into the analysis that 'Hamlet' stands for a person, as names do, which person, on the other hand, lacks the attribute of existence; as if to say, absurdly, 'There is some person, Hamlet, who does not exist.' And that is clearly nonsense, as implying first that 'Hamlet' 'stood for something and then in effect denying that it does so'.[5] But if the negative form cannot be analysed logically in subject – predicate terms, neither can the affirmative, since what holds for affirmations must hold also for their corresponding negations. Hence,

---

[3] Peter T. Geach, 'Form and Existence', in *God and the Soul*, London: Routledge & Kegan Paul, 1969, pp. 42–64. Much of the argument of this chapter is indebted to Geach's seminal paper.

[4] For example, we can quite legitimately say that, at the end of the play, Hamlet, who was once alive, no longer exists and is presumably buried somewhere in Elsinore.

[5] Geach, 'Form and Existence', p. 54.

it cannot be the case that in 'Ian McKellen exists', '. . . exists' is a predicate either. As Geach says, the difference asserted between 'Hamlet' and 'Ian McKellen' in 'Hamlet does not exist and Ian McKellen does' is not that between two persons, Hamlet and Ian McKellen, but between two uses of the grammatically proper names 'Hamlet' and 'Ian McKellen'. To say that Ian McKellen does exist is to say that the proper name 'Ian McKellen' has reference, whereas 'Hamlet' in 'Hamlet does not exist' does not. It makes no sort of sense to treat both as having reference, the one possessing the attribute of existence, the other not possessing it.

But a second sort of case is more immediately relevant to Thomas's distinction. Where what are in question are propositions which answer to the query whether there are any, but whose grammatical subject is an unquantified general term, the same holds true – that existence is not a predicate – though in other respects their logic is different from those whose subject-terms are proper names. No more is some reference made to dragons in the case of 'Dragons do not exist', of which the attribute of 'existence' is then denied, than in 'Hamlet does not exist' is reference made to a person, Hamlet, who lacks 'existence'. In just the same way, in affirmative existential statements of this sort, such as 'cows exist', it is not the case that reference is made to cows as being in possession of the attribute of existence, though in this sort of case we do not say, as we do in the other, that 'cows' is in use as a proper name, whereas 'dragons' is not. In fact, in 'Dragons do not exist' we are not predicating anything at all *of* dragons, for 'dragons' is itself a predicative expression and 'Dragons do not exist' takes analysis in terms of, as the logicians say, the 'existential quantifier', so as to read, 'Nothing at all is a dragon'; just as in the case of the affirmative 'Cows exist', we do not predicate existence of cows, for it takes the analysis 'Some things or other are cows.' Now it is clear that when Thomas distinguishes between a statement of God's *esse* as a statement of God's *actuality* (*actus essendi*) and a statement of God's *esse* as a *predicative* statement, he is treating 'God exists' in this second sense (as when answering the question 'Is there a God?') as having the same logical form as 'Cows exist' (as when answering the question, 'Are there any cows?'). Hence, just as 'Cows exist' bears the analysis, 'Some things or other are cows', so 'God exists' bears the analysis, 'Something or other is God.' That is to say, in 'God exists' in this sense we are not predicating existence of God, but rather we are predicating 'God' of something or other.

Of course, this analysis of 'God exists' is defensible only if 'God' is treated as functioning in 'God exists' not as a proper name, such as 'Daisy', but as a descriptive, predicable expression, such as 'cow' – what Thomas calls a *nomen naturae*. For proper names cannot function as predicates, whereas 'cow' can, for it is used to predicate of some animal or other the sort of thing that it is, its 'nature'. But Thomas is emphatic that 'God' is not, logically, the proper name of God, which is why, he says, though undoubtedly mistaken, polytheism is not incoherent; you would be making a mistake of fact, not of logic, were you to think that there are many Gods, whereas to think that Peter can be many (as distinct from thinking that there can be many called 'Peter') is to fail to understand how to use the name 'Peter'.[6] To say 'God exists', therefore, as answering to the question 'Is there a God?', is to say that something or other answers to the description 'God', in the same way as to say 'Cows exist' in answer to the question 'Are there any cows?' is to say that some things or other are cows. And, Thomas says, 'God exists' in that sense is what his proofs prove to be true: they prove that something or other answers to the descriptive term 'God'.

But it is just at this point that the objection first raised in the passage cited earlier raises its head again. It may be objected now, as then, that to maintain that 'God' is a descriptive predicable expression, a *nomen naturae*, and that 'God exists' is analysable as 'something or other is God', must be inconsistent with Thomas's also saying that we do not know *what* God is. For, the reformulated objection now goes, if 'God exists' is analysable into the existential quantifier as 'Something or other is God', where this means 'Something or other answers to the description "God"', then, to know that the proposition is true we must be in possession of a description of God, and so we must know what God is. But the objection contains a confusion. What we need to know is the *logic* of the word 'God' and to know how to use the word. And, as Thomas says, we do not need to know what God *is* in order to know how to use the word 'God' as having the logical character of a *nomen naturae*, any more than we do in many another parallel case. To adapt an example of McCabe's:[7] I do not know, in any technical sense, what a computer is. But I know very well the effects computers have, for example, in editing a text for publication, and through my knowledge of the effects on my writing – for example, of my being able to cut and paste with ease – I know how to use the word 'computer'. Of course, just because I know how to use the word 'computer' from its effects on my writing it does not follow that 'computer' means 'machine for cutting and pasting text'.[8] Nor ought I

---

[6] *ST* 1a q11 a3 *corp.*

[7] Herbert McCabe OP, 'Aquinas on the Trinity', in *God Still Matters*, London and New York: Continuum, 2002, pp. 37–8.

[8] For, in general, as Thomas says, that on account of which we use a word to describe something or other is not always the same as what the word means: 'aliud est quandoque id a quo imponitur nomen ad significandum, et id ad quod significandum nomen imponitur'. *ST* 1a q13 a2 ad2.

to suppose that I *do* know what computers are, or how they do what they do, just because I know how to use them to cut and paste text. In just the same way, Thomas says, though we do not know what 'God' means, we do know from God's effects how to use the word 'God', and by what logic the word is governed; nor, by virtue of that ought I to conclude that what God is, and what 'God' means, is confined to our knowledge of those effects.[9] So there is no obstacle to the word's being understood as a *nomen naturae*, logically functioning in the same manner as 'cow', in the fact that we do not know the 'nature' which it denotes.

Esse as 'actuality'

But, Thomas says, distinct from such predicative forms of existential judgement are judgements of *actuality* (*actus essendi*), and these cannot be analysed out in the same way, and in this he is on common ground with a number of contemporary logicians in resisting the claims of existential quantification in the analysis of all existential judgements.[10] For here we must note the difference between 'Hamlet does not exist' and 'Lawrence Olivier does not exist'. Whereas 'Hamlet does not exist' is true in that 'Hamlet' never named a person, 'Lawrence Olivier' in 'Lawrence Olivier does not exist' does name a person: a person who no longer exists, for Lawrence Olivier is dead. We should say with Geach that in 'Hamlet does not exist' no person is named who ever possessed or did not possess *actuality* – because 'Hamlet' is said thereby not to name – but that in 'Lawrence Olivier does not exist' a person is named who once possessed actuality and now does not. There is not and cannot be any logical obstacle to our saying that the person named 'Lawrence Olivier' no longer possesses actuality; on the contrary. If we had to say that 'Lawrence Olivier' no longer names the person who was once actual, then we could not say that it was that same person who now does not exist; we should then have no way of saying that *Lawrence Olivier* is dead. Indeed, logic would leave us with no room for saying that anything at all ceases to exist if we had to say that what once named an existing thing no longer names the thing which has ceased to exist; the confusion arises, as Wittgenstein says, from failing to see that when *N* dies it is the *bearer* of the name who dies, not its *reference*.[11] It is therefore for the sort of reason that we do want to say, 'There is a person, *N*, who no longer exists', that Thomas sees the need

[9] *ST* 1a q13 a2 *corp.*
[10] For example, J. L. Mackie, *The Miracle of Theism: Arguments for and against the Existence of God*, Oxford: Clarendon Press, 1982, p. 47.
[11] Ludwig Wittgenstein, *Philosophical Investigations*, 1. 40, trans. G. E. M. Anscombe, Oxford: Blackwell, 1958, p. 20.

to distinguish between the '. . . exists' of existential quantification, and the '. . . exists' of actuality.

Now this in turn explains something of what is meant by speaking of *esse* as 'actuality', or, as Thomas says, the *actus essendi*. If proper names retain their references in both affirmative and negative judgements of actuality, then, as Geach says, there can be no difficulty in saying of the existence thus attributed that it is a logical 'predicate'. For if 'Lawrence Olivier existed but no longer exists' refers to Lawrence Olivier, then his being once actual and then non-actual can safely be said to be predicated of him. What, then, are you predicating of Lawrence Olivier when you predicate *esse* of him? Thomas's answer to this is radical; though it may also appear, infuriatingly, either extreme in boldness or else innocuously vacuous, or in turns both. At any rate, he appears to want to say two sorts of thing which are at the least not easy to reconcile with each other.

'Esse' is not predicated univocally

On the one hand he can sometimes appear to reduce the predication of *esse* as 'actuality' to near vacuousness – specifically in denying that there is any 'concept' of *esse*, for in the sense in which there is a 'concept' of man, or of cheese, there can be no 'concept' of existence. Concepts are expressed in descriptions which tell you what something is, whereas to say that something 'exists' is not to say anything further about what it is. And this is, of course, right. For the difference between chalk and cheese, or between any two kinds of thing, is not at all the same kind of difference as that between either of them existing and their not existing. The sort of difference involved in 'This isn't cheese (it's chalk)' is quite different in logical kind from that involved in 'There *was* some cheese, but there isn't any cheese left.' The first is a difference of kind, and is what we refer to when we say that there is a difference of 'concept'. The second is not some difference in kind and cannot fall under any concept at all.

It is therefore no use looking for some same attribute *additional* to what all things are by way of tracking down what they have in common as existing, as you do when, knowing that some things are animals, you look *in addition* for whatever will tell you whether they are humans or brutes – that is, by looking for the presence or absence of signs of rationality. Nor do you see a thing's *esse* by observing whether there is the sort of difference between its existence and its non-existence which there might be between two things which differ in colour, or weight, or size. Knowing what or how a thing is, you do not get at a thing's *esse* by staring at it a bit harder so as to glimpse something else about it that it possesses in common with everything else actual, and which you might have so far missed. To put it in Thomas's terms, a thing's *esse* is neither its substantial nor its accidental *form*, nor is a thing modified by existence's being predicated of it in any of the ways in which a thing is modified by form, for *esse* is the *actuality*, he says, of all things 'and even of forms themselves'.[12] And in this, too, Thomas must be right. For again, were a thing's *esse* to make any formal difference to it, then it could not cease to exist, for what first existed and then no longer does would not be the same thing. Hence, there cannot be a difference *in form* between an existing and a non-existing *x*.[13] *Esse*, therefore – not being the object of any concept – cannot be predicated univocally, for were it predicable univocally that could be in terms only of some same formal characteristic predicated of all things said to exist. That, essentially, is the mistake of Duns Scotus.

Moreover, Thomas presses the point so hard, and with such a degree of firmness, as would appear to place at risk another doctrine central to his account of *esse*, namely that in any created thing there is a real distinction between its *esse* and its essence. Even if *esse*, he says, is not a formal attribute of what exists, *esse* is predicable only as a *function of some form*.[14] A sheep's existence is an ovine existence, a cow's a bovine, a man's a human existence, or, as Thomas says more generally, 'for a living thing to exist *is* for it to be alive'.[15] And it follows from this that, when you speak of the existence of anything, you speak of much more than the existence of just it: when you say that *x* exists you are saying that there exist (are 'actual') all those conditions which must obtain – the sort of 'world' – such that that kind of thing can exist in it. A sheep cannot exist without an ovine world – requiring (at any rate until recently) there to have been at least two other pre-existing adult sheep, one male and one female, and requiring a whole range of other conditions, atmospheric, chemical, biological, environmental, and so forth, such as permit the possibility of the kind of thing a sheep is to exist at all. To give such an account is to engage in the forms of scientific knowledge which explain what it is like that there should be sheep – or, as Thomas puts it, it is to know the answer to the question *quid est?*, the answer to which yields knowledge of its 'essence'. But you do not get at a thing's actuality by any other means than by knowing in such ways the essence which it

---

[12] *ST* 1a q4 a1 ad3.

[13] It was such considerations which led Kant to say that 'existence is not a predicate'. But, as we have seen, there is no need to deny that existence, as actuality, is predicated of what exists to avoid the absurd conclusion in question.

[14] '*Esse* . . . per se convenit formae quae est actus.' *ST* 1a q75 a6 *corp*.

[15] 'Vivere viventibus est esse'. *ST* 1a q18 a2 *sed contra*. Thomas refers to Aristotle, *De Anima* II.4, 415 b13.

actualises. To put it in other terms, what you predicate when you predicate *esse* of a thing is the value of the variable '*x*' in '*x* exists'. It is for this reason – that existence is predicable only as a function of some form – that there can be no univocal predication of *esse* as between different kinds of thing.

'*Esse*' is not predicated equivocally

On the other hand, to deny that *esse* as 'actuality' falls under any *concept* additional to a thing's essence, and that it is predicable only as the function of some form it actualises, is not to reduce the predication of *esse* to equivocal vacuousness, as if to say that there is *no* distinction between a thing's *esse* and the essence it actualises, or as if predications of existence are entirely redundant. For in saying that a thing's *esse* is not distinct from it by virtue of being some additional form, it is not entailed that a thing's *esse* and its essence are identical, and so must be equivocally predicated of everything of which it is true. This, as Thomas explains, does not follow, and in any case could not be true. There must be a real distinction between *what it is* that exists and *that by virtue of which* it exists. For any two individuals which belong to a common genus share something of a common form, as a man and a horse do, both being animals. Likewise, any two individuals of the same species share in that the same form is predicable of them both, as two human beings do. But no two individuals can share a common *esse* in the sense of actuality: a horse's *esse* is distinct from a man's, as Socrates' *esse* is distinct from Plato's, or else when Socrates dies Plato dies too. Hence, in whatever belongs to a genus there is necessarily a real distinction between that which it is (*quod quid est*) and the (substantial) form by which it is what it is on the one hand, and its being actual – that by which it *is*, on the other.[16] It does not follow, therefore, from the fact that *esse* is not a 'form' distinct from a thing's essence that it is identical with the essence it actualises, and therefore is predicated equivocally of all the things which exist. *Esse*, to repeat what Thomas says, is the actualisation *of* form: it is not itself a formal actualisation.

Created *esse*

If, then, *esse* is not something *additional* to a thing's essence in the way in which a form determines what it is, nor is it *identical* with the essence it

---

[16] *ST* 1a q3 a5 *corp.*

actualises, we are faced with two questions about Thomas's doctrine of *esse*. First, *what* is predicated of a thing when we say that it 'exists'? That is, what do we predicate when we predicate 'actuality'? Second, if not predicated univocally, or equivocally, *how* is *esse* predicated? In addressing the first question we should note that the 'real distinction' between *esse* and *essentia* holds for Thomas only as of *created esse*. And the expression 'created *esse*' is not a neoplasm. This is important. For, contrary to what some have maintained, no doubt with a mind to distinguishing his position from that of Duns Scotus, Thomas holds that it is no part of the meaning of *esse* that it is created. He says clearly enough – thus far in agreement with Scotus: 'to be caused is not part of what "being" means absolutely speaking, for which reason you can come to know of an uncaused being'.[17] If, then, there can be no doubt at all that Thomas thinks that *esse* is predicable of both God and creatures, equally Thomas unhesitatingly rejects any 'Scotist' proposition about *esse* being predicable in 'onto-theological' univocity of God and of creatures, as in due course we shall see. In the meantime, then, what you predicate when you predicate *esse* of a creature and strictly *as created* is that it stands against – that is to say, in contradictory opposition to – there being nothing at all; for that is what it is for a creature to be created: it is for it 'to be' in that sense which contrasts with there being nothing whatsoever. As Herbert McCabe says, when speaking of God as 'the source of *esse*', we are speaking of 'the being of the thing not just overagainst a world-without-it, but overagainst *nothing*, not even "logical space"'.[18] And this accords well enough with what Thomas says about the divine action of creating, which is the cause of things not merely as to *how* they are in this or that respect ('secundum quod sunt *talia*'), or even merely as to *what* they are ('secundum quod sunt *haec* per formas substantiales'), but as to their existence as such in every respect;[19] and their 'existence as such' can contrast only with nothing. But to say this much already has the oxymoronic shape of the apophatic, because, as we shall see,[20] there are bound to be problems with the logical standing of that 'overagainst' which, definitive of created *esse*, stands in contrast with 'nothing', for nothing is not *something* of such kind that something else can stand in ordinary logical relations of contrast with it. This is what McCabe means when he says that there is no 'logical space' within which that contrast, which yields Thomas's notion of created *esse*, can be construed. That is how we have to speak, when speaking

---

[17] 'Quia esse causatum non est de ratione entis simpliciter, propter hoc invenitur aliquod ens non causatum.' *ST* 1a q44 a1 ad1.
[18] McCabe, *God Matters*, p. 59.   [19] *ST* 1a q44 a2 *corp.*
[20] See chapter 11 below.

of *esse*. The force of the word 'actual' by which *esse* is said to 'actualise' is that which stands in contrast to there being nothing whatsoever.

This can be put in other terms. You can imagine, and describe, the difference between a world in which this sheep 'Dolly' exists and a world in which Dolly does not exist. You can imagine, and describe, the difference between a world in which there are sheep and a world in which there are not and have never been any. The difference between Dolly's existing and her not existing is just a difference in the ovine world, and you do not get at the created *esse* of Dolly by contemplating that difference. Likewise, the difference between there being any sheep at all, and there being no sheep at all, is just a difference within the animal world, and you do not get at the created *esse* which sheep possess by contemplating that difference either. You get at Dolly's *esse* in its character as created by contemplating the difference between there being Dolly and there being nothing whatever. And if that, as Thomas says, is to grasp the sheep's *esse*, this is because to grasp a created thing's *esse* is to grasp its character as created. And this is to say, *esse creaturae est creari* – the *esse* of a creature *is* its being created, and the logical form of the predicate '. . . is created' is exactly the same as the logical form of '. . . exists' as predicated of a creature.[21] So much for *what* is predicated by the predication, '*x* exists', except to say – in anticipation of the argument of chapter eleven – that it follows from this that we do not grasp fully the *esse* of a creature until we have shown that it is created. That is to say, what reveals the nature of created *esse* is precisely the same as what shows God to exist *as* the Creator of *esse*.

Esse and analogy

In turning, then, to the question of *how* existence, in the sense of 'actuality', is predicated, we are brought to Thomas's famous teaching that existence is predicated 'analogically'. Famous it is, and famously misunderstood. To say that existence is predicated 'analogically' is in the first instance to say no more than that it is predicated neither equivocally nor univocally. On this matter, it is fair to comment that too much has sometimes been made of Thomas's so-called 'doctrine of analogy' – metaphysics of baroque complexity were once constructed on the back of a late medieval version of it. In fact the texts in which he introduces the term are remarkably off-hand and casual, as if he were throwing in a mere

---

[21] This is not to say that '. . . exists' and '. . . is created' mean the same, even when predicated of creatures. The square of 1 is 1, and the square root of 1 is 1, but 'square of' and 'square root of' do not mean the same.

term of art to do a job which logic requires to be done: that is, to stand for whatever those forms of predication are which could not be read as either logically univocal or logically equivocal. At all events, Thomas is much clearer about how existence is not predicated than about how it is.

We have seen that the content of the expression 'x exists' is the value of the variable 'x' – to that extent, Henry of Ghent follows Thomas precisely.[22] What it is for a sheep to exist is simply what it is to be a sheep. What it is for there to be sheep, the species, is given in the description of the kind of animal world which includes ovines. Hence, what it is for a thing to be created is whatever it is for that thing to be brought to exist 'out of nothing' – that there should be such a world rather than nothing at all. For that reason, what it is to be brought to be out of nothing differs for every kind of thing in the sense that every meaning for the expression 'x exists' is determinate to a substitution for x, descriptive of a kind; in this sense there is nothing 'in common' between different values for the expression, just as there is 'nothing in common' between 4 as the square of 2 and 9 as the square of 3 – '... exists' cannot be predicated univocally. But in the sense in which both values are derived by the same function of 'squaring', operating upon different variables, we cannot say that 'square of...' is an equivocal term. And, in sum, it seems that Thomas meant little more than this when he says that *esse* is predicated 'analogically' – just *not* equivocally, *not* univocally.

Nonetheless, a little further clarification seems desirable. For to understand how existence is predicated of creatures, it is helpful to set its logic in contrast with other, non-existential, predications. Some predicates are predicated univocally and can only be predicated in a univocal sense – except, of course, when they are predicated metaphorically. In the predicate form 'x is blue', the predicate '... is blue' has the same meaning for all values of the variable x, since no matter what x stands for we know what will count as its being blue. Let us say, then, that predicates of the same kind as 'x is blue' are 'non-relative-to-subject' and that in this they differ from 'relative-to-subject' predicates such as 'x is large'. For what counts for a large x depends upon the sort of thing x stands for; manifestly there is no such single size, regardless of what sort of thing the adjective qualifies, as that denoted by the word 'large', for if there were, then a large mouse would turn out to be larger than a small elephant. It was, of course, Plato's notorious mistake to suppose that all large things must 'participate in' a 'form of largeness',[23] a mistake he later came to acknowledge as incorrigible within his 'theory of forms', at least for relational predicates. Hence, his later doubts about that theory.

---

[22] See pp. 130–1 above.   [23] See *Phaedo* 100e ff.

That said, for any given kind of thing which can be 'large' or 'small', there are some dimensions which make for a large one, some, necessarily less than the first, which make for a small one. And relative-to-subject predications share this much with non-relative-to-subject predicates, in that they are restricted in domain of reference – indeed, in the cases in question, to the same domain of reference. For nothing can be large or small except something which has mass; nothing can be blue which does not have a surface, and nothing which has a surface can be without mass. Both relative-to-subject and non-relative-to-subject predicates of these kinds are, we might say, 'topic-specific', in that they can be literally true only of a restricted range of values substituted for the variable x. And this, in turn, determines a meaning for the word 'metaphorical'. For a metaphorical predication predicates a term of a subject which falls outside of the domain to which that predicate is topic-specific, as when we substitute 'mood' for x in the expression 'a blue x', or 'mind' for x in the expression 'a capacious x'. Such metaphorical expressions are, therefore, all literal falsehoods.

What, then, of predications of the kind 'x is good'? Clearly, on the one hand, such predications share this much with subject-relative predications in that there is no single set of descriptions which have to hold true of all values for x in 'x is good'. For, of course, an undergraduate essay is a good one on account of certain descriptions being true of it, none of which are possessed of whatever counts for a good father, or apple, or time of the day for having a party. Clearly, we have to know what kind of thing x stands for if we are to know what will count as a good one of that kind, for it is in virtue of knowing what kind of thing is being said to be 'good' that we know what characteristics of the thing make for its being a good one of that kind.

On the other hand, 'x is good' differs from 'x is large' in that, whereas the latter predication is restricted to a determinate range of subject-terms, the former is not, for there is no restriction of any kind at all on what value can be substituted for the variable x in 'x is good'; of anything at all that exists there can be a good one of its kind. From which it follows that if '. . . is good' can be stretched across every kind of thing, it is nonetheless never stretched across kinds of thing in that manner in which terms are predicated metaphorically. For the predicate '. . . is good' has no *primary* sense restricted to some particular domain of good things, such that its predication of objects in other domains is non-literal – in the way in which '. . . is large' is predicated in its primary, and literal, sense of dimensive objects and therefore necessarily in metaphor, and in a secondary, derived, sense of anything lacking in dimensions, as moods and minds do. There are therefore no 'secondary' senses of the word 'good' either, no matter what it is predicated of: a good apple is good as apples go, a good time for celebrating is good as times for celebrating go, and so across the range, unrestrictedly, of anything at all. Hence, if '...is good' is not a univocal predicate, then neither is it ever, nor can it possibly be, a metaphor.

How, then, is the logical behaviour of predicates of the form '...is good' to be understood? As we have seen, one way of explaining the logic of 'a good x' is that it is similar in form to that of mathematical functions, such as 'the square of x'. The value of the whole expression varies with the value of x, for if x is 2 then the value of the whole expression is 4; if x is 3, then 9. But in either case there is a common definition of the function 'the square of...', for in either case the same *function* is performed on x. In this sense alone is there, for Thomas, a common definition of 'good', and it is not such as to attach a univocal meaning across all its predications, nor yet does it leave those manifold predications in a condition of meaningless equivocity. For though on the one hand the conditions on account of which a good x is said to be good will vary across all the different kinds of things so described, in every such case the description of a thing's goodness will have been obtained by the same kind of judgement. For the thing's possession of those characteristics make it to be a good one *on account of the relation in which they stand* to the kind of thing that it is: roughly, for Thomas, a thing is a good one of its kind if it possesses the characteristics which make it to be a fully realised version of the sort of thing that it is.[24] In that sense, and in that alone, is there a 'concept' of goodness, in which one knows how to give a meaning to the expression 'a good x' when one knows the value for x. The predication of '...is good' is rule-governed. And the rule which thus governs it Thomas calls 'analogy'.

What holds logically for 'a good x' holds logically for 'x exists'. From the fact that the *esse* of any created thing consists in its 'standing overagainst there being nothing at all', therefore, it does not follow that every kind of thing stands in the same relation of contrast with nothingness. Even if, as Thomas puts it, there is a real distinction between a thing's *esse* and its form, still God cannot bring it about that something exists rather than nothing without bringing it about that this kind of thing exists rather than that kind of thing. For just as the notion of a thing which is of such a kind as to exist is simply incoherent, so also is the notion that existence is predicable without reference to, and so as if univocally of, the kinds of thing of which it is predicated, as Scotus thought. Anything at all which

---

[24] Or, as Thomas puts it, a thing's good is what fully realises it, makes it most 'actual': and that is its 'perfection', its most desirable condition – *ST* 1a q5 a1 *corp.*

is created is a created *something* or other. For it to exist is for it to be created; and for it to be created is for it to stand over against nothing. But *how* it stands over against nothing is determined by the kind of thing that it is. Hence, what you know about the meaning of '... exists' in '*x* exists' is that it is the actualisation of some nature, but you do not know what it is to actualise in this case until you know what nature it is that in this case it actualises. *Esse* is relative to the form it actualises – it is not univocally predicated – even if in every case it is that by which form is actualised, that is to say, stands opposed to there being nothing, so that it is not equivocally predicated either.

But for Thomas, it is God who brings it about that there is anything at all rather than nothing, and it is God's being the cause of *esse* as such – of the actuality of all things actual – which justifies our predicating *esse* of God. To repeat what Thomas says: 'Esse causatum non est de ratione entis simpliciter, propter hoc invenitur aliquod ens non causatum.' It would seem, then, that both those who criticise Thomas for maintaining the proposition that there is a 'common conception of being', and those who deny that he maintains it, will need to explain more than they usually do about what it is they are respectively affirming and denying that Thomas maintains. For of course Thomas denies that existence is predicated univocally, even of creatures – *a fortiori*, not of creatures and of God. Conversely, in the sense just explained, he does of course deny that 'existence' is predicated equivocally. Of course, Thomas would never have said that there is some 'common conception' of existence predicable whether of all creatures or of creatures and God; but this is for the reason that on his account 'existence' is never grasped in any concept anyway: to repeat, for Thomas a 'concept' is our grasp of what a thing is, not of its 'actuality'. All the same, Thomas does maintain that *esse* is predicable non-equivocally not only of every creature that exists, but also of God and of creatures – and if we allow that he says this, we might just as well allow him to say (for it is at the very least misleading to deny it) that *esse* is 'predicable in common' of both God and creatures: of creatures as created *esse*; of God as *esse*'s Creator. And say it he does. Is this 'onto-theology'?

Ipsum esse subsistens

It is at this point that we move back from the question of the logic of the predication of *esse* to what it is that is predicated of a thing when we say of it that it exists. If for a created thing to exist is for it to be created, then 'to be created' gives us the fundamental meaning of *esse* as 'act', 'actualisation' – as also, conversely, the fundamental meaning of 'act' as *esse*. Of course, for Thomas, 'act' has many other meanings – or at least uses – than that of 'act of existence', for Thomas happily speaks by extension from this primitive meaning, of how a person's running is an act, in the sense that it is the 'actualisation' of a person's potentiality to run when that person might have been sitting;[25] or of the way in which a material object's being red is the actualisation of one of the colours it could be, and not of others; of the way in which my thinking about the square of minus one, is the actualisation of the intellect's capacity to think indifferently about anything at all. But all these uses of the word 'act' are parasitical upon a basic use and meaning, which is that according to which *esse* is the most fundamental actualisation of anything at all. Why?

Because in every other, parasitical, use of 'act', what is actualised is some already existing potentiality. If Frieda runs, then Frieda existed in such and such a nature which can run; if the lintel is red, then the lintel existed in bare pine to be painted one colour or another; if I think of the square of minus one, then I have a mind which could think of that, or of something else. But if what actualises is a thing's *esse*, and if the existence which *esse* denotes is that it exists rather than that nothing at all exists, then it cannot be the case that in the same sense there exists some potentiality which *esse* actualises. For the potentiality which *esse* actualises is brought about by its actualisation: the potentiality exists only *as actualised*, and cannot exist prior to it, as it were 'awaiting' actualisation.

It does not follow from this that what exists cannot not have existed, nor that it cannot cease to exist. It is crucial to Thomas's understanding of *esse* and *essentia* that they are 'really distinct' in any creature, for anything at all which exists as an actualised potentiality has been caused to exist and can be caused to cease to exist, even were it the case, as he thinks it coherent counter-factually to say, that it has endlessly existed and will endlessly exist.[26] The contingency of a created thing lies in its createdness, not in any finite parameter of endurance. That said – the real distinction notwithstanding – a thing's *esse* is that by which the potentiality exists which it actualises. It makes no sense to say of what *esse* makes to be that it in any way 'exists' in potency 'to be'.[27]

---

[25] See Aquinas, *Expositio Libri Boetii de Hebdomadibus*, lect. 2, introd., Latin text and trans. by Janice S. Schultz and Edward Synan, Washington: Catholic University of America Press, 2001, pp. 16–17.

[26] Aquinas, *De aeternitate mundi contra murmurantes*, in Baldner and Carroll, *Aquinas on Creation*, pp. 114–22.

[27] This does not mean that created causes cannot cause something to be which did not previously exist. Of course, parents can cause children to be. What Thomas means in saying that *esse* is the act of existence by contrast with nothing is that the fact that there

But if that is so, if *esse* is therefore to be understood in relation to the potentiality it actualises, how can we in any way speak of God as *ipsum esse subsistens*, and so as 'pure act' – as Thomas does? It is clear to Thomas why we must say that God is '*pure* act'. On the one hand there cannot be anything in God which his existence 'actualises', no potentiality of any sort, for God cannot be brought into existence or be caused to cease to exist, else God would be, simply, a creature. On the other hand it seems hard to know what sense it makes to say that God is 'pure *act*' but that there is nothing of which that act is the *actualisation*, as if we were to say that Frieda is running, but that her running is not the exercise of any capacity to do so. For, as we have seen, *esse* is intelligible only as the function of some form. But God is not some kind of thing; he possesses no 'form' which his *esse* actualises. So what sort of sense can we make of saying that God is *just* his actualisation, *esse*, but nothing actualised?

It might seem that Thomas's own argument has, by his own devising, manoeuvred him into the jaws of the Derridean trap. If we are to be permitted to say that God exists at all, the predicate '. . . exists' will have to retain some connections of meaning with our ordinary senses for the term as we know how to use it of creatures. But that 'ordinary sense' in which we use it of creatures is, it would seem, intrinsically tied in with their creatureliness as the actualisation of a potency. But if it cannot be in that sense that God may be said to exist, what sense can there be left to the term 'act' when, as Thomas says we must, we describe God as 'pure act'? Is this an *aporia*, an impossible dilemma?

It would seem not. It is clear from Thomas's latest writings – from the *Summa Theologiae* in particular – that far from seeing this problem as an intractable dilemma or theological blind alley, the 'pincer move-ment' which leads to it has been a carefully designed theological strategy, designed to manoeuvre the theologian into exactly that position where she ought to find herself – just in that place where, constrained by our ordinary discourse to be, we discover that that ordinary discourse is inca-pable of capturing the meaning it must nonetheless point to. Of course, we could not know what it means to say that God is 'pure act', *ipsum esse subsistens* – as we have seen Thomas to say, 'we cannot know the *esse* of God any more than we can know his essence'. In fact the incomprehensibility of the statement 'God is *ipsum esse subsistens*' is not an *aporia* reductive of Thomas's theological metaphysics to absurdity. It is, on the contrary, a

---

is anything at all, rather than nothing, is, and can be, brought about only by God. No more than any created cause can parents bring anything about *ex nihilo*. But that created causality which truly causes something to be is itself caused to exist, as everything at all is caused to exist, and so is caused *ex nihilo* by God alone.

precise theological statement, intended to mark out with maximum clarity and precision the *locus* of the divine incomprehensibility, the *ratio Dei*, the most fundamental of the 'formal features' of God, to use Burrell's terminology.[28] Since it is far from being the case that describing God as 'pure act' gives us some firm purchase on the divine nature, one may go so far as to say that talking about God thus is already a kind of failed speech, a 'babble'; for to pretend that we remain in full command of the meaning of such words through any self-evidently meaningful extension of their ordinary senses is idolatrously reductive of theological language. It is only just *in*appropriate to call such theological speech 'babble' in so far as, unlike mere babble, to call God by the name 'pure act', or *ipsum esse subsistens*, retains that degree of connection with the logic of our ordinary discourse which licenses us to derive, with consistency and coherence, what follows from saying it, and what does not. This is not absurdly to attempt to eat one's cake and have it. We know that, in so far as a creature is 'in act' it is, Thomas says, to that degree 'perfect' and so 'good' in some respect, *secundum quid*. From this we know that if God is 'pure act' then God is wholly perfect and good in every respect, *simpliciter*. We know this because we know what *esse* as 'act' means of a creature: it means the actualisation of a potentiality. Hence, whatever 'pure act' means, we know better than to attribute to God, in his character as pure act, anything which follows from a thing's having potentiality. But if we do not know what 'pure act' means anyway, in the sense that we possess some concept of it, then it follows that we know no better what 'wholly perfect' or 'good *simpliciter*' means than we know what 'pure act' means, except that they must be true of God, which is enough to know that their contradictories are false.[29] We can, in short, know enough about what God is to know what God is not; and so we know in saying anything we are entitled to say affirmatively about God – 'God exists' – what we are denying in so saying. To that extent, theological talk has a grammar. It is a language. But that said, it is the grammar of a mystery, of language which breaks down according to determinable rules of breakdown. Theological speech is subject to a sort of *programmed* obsolescence.

---

[28] See chapter 2, pp. 41–2 above.

[29] Of course, it does not follow from this that all language about God is logically negative – this conclusion is what Thomas denies in what he understands (correctly or otherwise) to be the position of Moses Maimonides. To repeat a position so frequently stated in this essay: to suppose that all statements about God are logically negations is to reduce 'apophaticism' to the standing of literal falsehood. Any sense in which it is said 'apophatically' that God is not good would thereby be reduced to the statement that God is evil.

Thomas and 'onto-theology'

And so we return to the question whether to say that *esse* is predicable of both God and creatures is 'onto-theological'. Thomas, of course, knows no such nomenclature; but he knows the question and entertains it for himself. If God's simplicity gets its root meaning in the identity of God's *essentia* and *esse*,[30] this poses the further objection that if God's *esse* and God's *essentia* were identical, if God were to be described as *ipsum esse subsistens*, it would seem to follow that God's existence (*esse*) was an existence of no particular kind – 'unspecific existence'. From that it would seem further to follow that the name 'God' would simply name 'existence in general', that is, unspecifically any kind of existence, whether created or uncreated – and this would appear fatally to break the firm rule of the logic of *esse* on which we have seen Thomas so to insist: *esse per se convenit formae*, it makes no sense to speak of *esse* but of no particular kind. Now this would seem to be a telling objection, particularly as posed for so enthusiastic a follower of the pseudo-Denys as Thomas, for the pseudo-Denys's famous saying, 'There is no kind of thing that God is', could easily be interpreted as entailing the consequence, 'God exists, but his existence is of no kind; hence, God is, unspecifically, "existence as such".' In turn, that could be interpreted in one of two ways: either as meaning that 'God' names the overarching category of 'being' of which all beings other than God are instances, from which the pantheistic consequence would follow that all created beings are 'instances' of God; or else as meaning that both God and creatures are instances falling under the general category of 'being'. Both would be forms, one supposes, of onto-theological error, since either way the difference between God and creatures would be reduced to that which could obtain between 'beings' belonging to the same, albeit most general possible, category.

The objection provides Thomas with an opportunity to clarify what could possibly be meant by the pseudo-Denys's *dictum*. In agreeing that God is not 'any kind of thing', or that God is *ipsum esse subsistens*, Thomas is not consenting to some notion – as one might be tempted to suppose – that the name 'God' names an utterly empty category. That we cannot form any 'concept' of God is due not to the divine vacuousness, but, on the contrary, to the excessiveness of the divine plenitude. That excessiveness eludes our language because we could not comprehend it except in a surplus of description which utterly defeats our powers of unification under *any* conception, an excessiveness which is exactly captured in the

---

[30] *ST* 1a q3 a4 *corp.*

full text of the Dionysian formula, 'There is no kind of thing which God is, *and there is no kind of thing which God is not.*' If ever there were a compendious statement of the relationship between the apophatic and the cataphatic in the pseudo-Denys's writing, this is it: for it says that God is beyond our comprehension not because we cannot say anything about God, but because we are compelled to say too much. In short, for the pseudo-Denys, and for Thomas following him, the 'apophatic' consists in the *excessus* of the 'cataphatic'.[31]

And so Thomas makes a distinction between two logically different kinds of 'unspecificness', or, as we might put it, two kinds of 'undifferentiation', or, as we might put it in a third set of terms, between two ways of being 'beyond both similarity and difference'.[32] In the first kind of case, he explains, further specification is *excluded*, as 'reason is excluded by definition from irrational animals'. In that case, he adds, the exclusion of the specification 'rational' adds content to the concept 'animal', since, by virtue of the exclusion of the *differentia* 'rational', we know that what is referred to is, specifically, non-human animals – brutes. By contrast, in the second kind of case, 'unspecificness' is achieved by *indifference to either inclusion or exclusion*, as when we speak of the *genus* 'animal in general' indifferently as between 'rational' and 'non-rational', between humans and brutes.

When we say, therefore, that God is *ipsum esse subsistens* – hence, that there is no kind of thing that God is – we could mean that God's existence is 'unspecific' in either sense. To mean it in the second sense would turn out to mean that God's existence is such as to be indifferent to any kind of specification – and that, for sure, would be 'onto-theological' error, since it would certainly entail that the name 'God' named the entirely empty category of '*ens commune*', as if God were some most general 'concept' of which beings are 'instances' – or, on the contrary, that God is just another 'instance' of 'beings' falling under that general concept.

And, of course, Thomas denies that the identity of *essentia* and *esse* in God entails that second kind of 'unspecificness'. For God's simplicity consists, on the contrary, in this alone, that in God all specification of this and that *is excluded* – 'there is no kind of being that God is', or, as we might put it, if 'specificness' is excluded from God, then 'exclusion' is excluded from God. The paradox is, therefore, that this kind of 'unspecificness' of the divine *esse*, this 'otherness', this being 'beyond similarity and difference', is such as to be totally *inclusive*, which is the opposite of what one might have supposed. For note that the specific difference 'rational'

---

[31] For a fuller discussion of this point, see my *Eros and Allegory*, pp. 53–6.
[32] *ST* 1a q3 a4 ad1.

divides the genus 'animal' into exclusive species ('rational' and 'non-rational'), such that, if the one then not the other: if any animal exists, then it is either a rational animal or a non-rational animal. Both belong to the same genus, but, of course, there cannot exist an animal which is, just, generically an animal, being neither rational nor non-rational. But if, *per impossibile*, a generic animal could exist, it could not be *neither* rational *nor* non-rational, for then it would have none of the character of either; it would have to be *both rational and non-rational* in some way which excluded both specifications, in order to exclude the disjunction between them, and thus contain the notions of both in some non-exclusive way: by, to use an expression of Eckhart's (though not of Thomas') 'negating the negation' between them.

No doubt, such a supposition of an actually existent genus is absurd, for a genus as such cannot exist. But the hypothesised absurdity brings out a central paradox of language about God of which, at this point in his argument, Thomas is acutely observant. For it is by virtue of the divine nature's excluding every possible specification – that is to say, by virtue of excluding every *differentia* whatever – that God's nature is such as to exclude all exclusion; hence, God stands in no relation of any kind of *exclusion* with anything whatever. God, as Eckhart says, is distinct in this exactly, that God alone is 'indistinct' – not, as Thomas observes, by virtue of an 'indistinctness' which is an excess of indeterminacy taken to the point of absolute generalised vacuousness, but by an excess of determinacy, taken to the point of absolutely total plenitude: 'There is no kind of thing', the pseudo-Denys says, 'which God is not', or, as Thomas himself put it, God is 'virtually' everything that there is, containing, as it were, every *differentia* as the cause of them all, but such that 'what are diverse and exclusive in themselves pre-exist in God as one, without detriment to his simplicity'.[33] That is why we cannot comprehend God: the 'darkness' of God is the simple excess of light. God is not too indeterminate to be known; God is unknowable because too comprehensively determinate, too *actual*. It is in that excess of actuality that the divine unknowability consists.

If there are therefore no grounds in logic for disallowing Thomas to say, as he does with some essential clarifications and precisions of terms, that *esse* is predicable 'in common' of God and creatures, what can justify our predicating *esse* of God? The full answer to this cannot be obtained until the penultimate chapter of this essay, but what we can say in the meantime is that, whatever are the grounds on which we are enabled to

---

[33] 'Quae sunt diversa et opposita in seipsis, in Deo praeexistunt ut unum, absque detrimento simplicitatis ipsius.' *ST* 1a q4 a2 ad1.

understand created *esse* as that which stands against there being nothing at all, just the same are the grounds on which we are able to say that the *esse* of a creature is to be created. But in knowing that for anything to exist is for it to be created is thus far to understand the name 'God' as the pure, undifferentiated, wholly inclusive 'act' from which all exclusion is excluded. We know God, in short, in so far as we know the *esse* of creatures, as Creator of all things, 'visible and invisible', and as the exemplar and cause of all that is, so that whatever is true of a creature is in some way true of God. From a proof of God we shall know that something or other answers to all that. But what it is, the divine *esse*, that is and must be utterly beyond all thought. Thus does Thomas escape through the horns of the Derridean dilemma.

Part III

Inference and the existence of God

10   Analogy and inference

Milbank on Thomas and proof

In chapter 2 I considered Gunton's reasons for denying the consistency of Thomas's natural theology with Christian faith, and then set out, very briefly and without comment, Milbank's different, indeed opposed, argument to the same general effect. Milbank's case needs to be revisited, because, unlike Gunton, who maintains that Thomas does offer what may be called an 'onto-theological' natural theology, Milbank denies that Thomas offers any such thing, though on grounds similar to Gunton's, namely that any proposal for a natural theology would be at least potentially onto-theological. Hence, since Thomas clearly resists all onto-theological forms of metaphysics, Milbank concludes that Thomas, at any rate in his last and most mature work, the *Summa Theologiae*, did not offer, and logically could not have offered, any sort of 'stand-alone' natural theology, and that he eschews any formal, strictly probative arguments for the existence of God.

In that second chapter I made the case for saying that, at least in the most general terms, Thomas's conception of natural theology has, in virtue of its articulation of the interplay between the apophatic and the cataphatic, the same shape as that of formally revealed theology, for, as I argued in chapter 3, those dialectics of natural reason respond exactly to what the formulation of a Christian theology of the incarnation and of the Eucharist demand of it. Hence, in chapter 4, but especially in chapters 5 and 6, I was able to argue the case more specifically that, for Thomas, reason in principle has the 'shape' of the sacramental, that it embodies a certain 'proto-sacramentality', as I put it. In so far as it takes us beyond the issues canvassed in those first six chapters, my argument thus far has been confined principally to resisting objections to the main theses of this essay, a case, as I have put it, of the truth of these matters consisting in whatever survives the *elenchus*.

To this end, then, in chapter 7 I set out, as fairly as I was able, Scotus' view that a natural theology is possible only if in principle some terms, above all 'existence', are predicable univocally of God and of creatures, a position which has been seen in recent literatures to be haunted by the ghosts of 'onto-theology'. This is because in general and in principle whatever account you give of the logic of inference from creatures to God will have to be such that it can cross the gap of 'difference' between God and creatures, and so in Scotus' case it would seem that he buys the possibility of crossing the gap only at the implicitly onto-theological price of closing it down to a difference within a community of univocity between them. But if, in chapter 8, I set out in emphatic terms the radical nature of 'the' difference between God and creatures, and in chapter 9 offered an account of the predication of *esse* of God in Thomas which is resistant to the virus of onto-theology, it may seem now that I have thereby set an insuperable obstacle in the way of the next step of my argument. For if the 'gap' is as radical as I claim it to be for a pseudo-Denys, an Eckhart and a Thomas, then, to put the matter as plainly as possible, the issue is forced whether that gap between God and creatures is not now so great as to be beyond the power of any possible inference to cross it. That, then, is the problem which we must now face in this and the next two chapters.

The logic of proof

In this chapter, therefore, we are first brought to the question of the logic of proof. In a recent article, Milbank writes of how there is in Thomas's *Summa Theologiae* 'a much more integral relation between sacred theology and metaphysics'[1] than there is in his earlier *Summa contra Gentiles*. In the earlier *Summa*, the overall structure and balance indicate just how much room Thomas was at that stage of the development of his theology prepared to allow for natural reason within the articulation of his theology, for three out of four parts of this vast work could be said to rely upon philosophical arguments principally or alone, and only in the final part is any explicit reliance on the authority of faith appealed to. This is so, the fact notwithstanding that in the first three 'philosophical' parts of his work, scriptural and other Christian authorities are frequently invoked; for such appeals appear but to serve a purpose of reassurance for Thomas's Christian readers that his philosophical arguments in no way lead him astray from central Christian teachings and theological traditions. Moreover, there appears to be an apologetic purpose of the *Summa contra Gentiles* – thought by Milbank to account for the prominence given to metaphysics which Thomas did not elsewhere accord to it. But the fact of an apologetic purpose, if such it be, cuts both ways. For it

---

[1] John Milbank, 'Intensities', *Modern Theology* 15.4, October 1999, pp. 445–97.

would be no compliment to Thomas's good theological faith to suppose that he would have adopted the theological strategies of the *Summa contra Gentiles* as an apologetic tactic had he thought that to do so would be in any fundamental way inappropriate and distorting of good theological method. It seems that Thomas was prepared to employ a wide variety of expository methods, adapted to different purposes – as is shown by his having adopted a third, quite different expository scheme in his last, and again incomplete, work, the *Compendium Theologiae*.[2] Thomas, at least, appears to have attached little systematic significance to different strategies and 'mixes' of metaphysics and revealed theology, preferring, it seems, to fit horses to courses.

Milbank, however, sees the structural differences between the heavily metaphysical *Summa contra Gentiles* and the much lighter philosophical emphases of the *Summa Theologiae* as indicating a significant conversion to a maturer theological strategy. In the later *Summa*, he says, 'the "preliminary" role of metaphysics on its own as establishing God as first cause is now barely gestured towards, and instead the focus is upon the need of *sacra doctrina* itself to deploy philosophical arguments' ('Intensities', p. 454) within and for strictly theological purposes and not on account of any claim for an 'autonomous reason'. Thus far this is more or less exactly what I argued in chapter 2 about the structure of the first twenty-six questions of the *Summa Theologiae*. Moreover, in agreement not only with Thomas, but also (as it happens) with the propositions of the first Vatican Council, Milbank adds that the recourse of *sacra doctrina* to philosophical arguments is not necessitated by any '*innate* deficiency' on the part of *sacra doctrina* in comparison with what it 'borrows' from philosophy – as if the transition from rational argument to theological faith were a transition from philosophically guaranteed certainties to a faith 'clinging to uncertainties' (ibid.). For on the contrary, the reconceived relation between philosophical argument and *sacra doctrina* found in the *Summa Theologiae* now ensures that 'one passes imperceptibly from the relatively discursive to the relatively intuitive as one more nearly approaches the pure divine insight' (ibid.). Therefore, rather than being necessitated on account of theology's deficiency, Milbank argues,

[*sacra doctrina*'s recourse to discursive reason] is necessary on account of the innate deficiency of human reason, which cannot, short of the final vision of glory, grasp what is in itself most intelligible, but must explicate this in terms of reasons clearer to humanity, but in themselves less clear, which is to say, *less rational*. (Ibid., emphasis original)

---

[2] The structure of the *Compendium* is organised around the three 'theological' virtues of faith, hope and charity. The work is left incomplete in mid-course of the discussion of hope.

It is, Milbank thinks, at the heart of this reconceived relation between philosophy and *sacra doctrina* that Thomas moves away from a more 'Aristotelian' and pagan-rationalist formula to a more openly Augustinian position; within the *Summa Theologiae* '*a posteriori* demonstration from creatures plays a weak role ... and there is in fact much more Augustinian *a priori* (so to speak) argument – in terms of "what must" belong to perfection – than is usually allowed' (ibid., p. 455).[3] And it is in this connection that the dominating Augustinian – and ultimately Platonic – principle governing Milbank's reading of Thomas becomes most explicitly acknowledged. If we are to know the most perfect good 'to be', there must exist, prior to any theological expansion of the radical unknowableness of God into an account of the divine attributes, 'a certain preontological insistence of the ideal', so that we can respond to it; respond, that is, to 'an as it were *a priori* vision of the good' (ibid.). But since Thomas explicitly prohibits any *a priori* philosophical theology which, in the manner of Anselm's *Proslogion* argument, would purport to prove the necessary existence of the highest perfection from that perfection's being the highest, there is no argument which by itself can get you to that *a priori* vision – indeed, it could not have the character of the *a priori* if it was argument from creatures which got you there – and so 'the only thing that authenticates perfection must be *some* sort of experience of its actuality' (ibid., p. 456). Moreover, such an experience of 'highest perfection' must be presupposed even to Thomas's *a posteriori* proofs of the existence of God (ibid., pp. 459–60). Why so?

For these reasons, Aquinas' argument for a first mover (the 'first way') has validity, Milbank thinks, only because the starting point, or premise, motion, 'is understood from the outset as being undergone with a purpose, or for a reason, and on account of a goal in accord with nature' (ibid.); hence, all motions, being 'aims towards perfections', are knowable in that ontological dependence on their first cause in which demonstration of God would consist, only in so far as the perfections aimed at are already known in their participations 'of the supreme end, the supreme good'. Hence, 'the first mover is really radically presupposed' to the premise from which the arguments proceed (ibid.). Fergus Kerr argues to a similar end as regards the logic of proof when he notes that if Thomas's arguments for God proceed, as Thomas says they do, from the divine *effects* to God as their cause,[4] then one has to doubt whether he can be regarding them as formally valid proofs at all: for one is constrained to ask, 'Why should

---

[3] Milbank, 'Intensities', p. 455. Milbank does not explain on what standards of strength and weakness the 'strength' of the role of *a posteriori* arguments in the second question of the *Summa* is here being assessed.

[4] Thomas Aquinas, *Summa contra Gentiles* 1, 12, *Opera Omnia* 14, Leonine: Rome, 1926.

we regard features of the world as "effects"? Is that not what argument for the existence of God is supposed to achieve – to demonstrate, philosophically, that things are "caused" in such a way that they may be called "effects", thus of some "cause"?'[5] Hence, an argument which works up to God by inference from 'effects' must presuppose the existence of God in the very characterisation of its premises *as* 'effects'. Of course, as we saw earlier, it would follow from either account that, considered as formal demonstrations, the five ways would be simply invalid, since they would fail by the fallacy of *petitio principii*. For while they would appear to be proving a conclusion, they would in fact presuppose that conclusion at least implicitly as a premise.[6] For which reason Milbank and Kerr (one imagines supposing Thomas to be incapable of such elementary failures of logic) charitably read them as not being intended as formally valid proofs of the existence of God.

The case against Milbank

It is possible to contest this construction on Thomas's strategy in the 'five ways' on a number of counts, however, two in particular deserving comment. The first is the importation into Thomas's thinking, at just the wrong point, of the 'Augustinian' principle that you cannot know relative degrees of imperfection in creatures without first knowing, in some way, whether by 'intuition', or as the object of some 'experience', supreme perfection to exist. Thomas certainly maintains that there could *be* the degrees of goodness which we perceive only if there were an absolute good in which created goods participated; indeed, for Thomas, 'a participating *x*' and 'a created *x*' are extensionally, and possibly also intentionally, equivalent. But whether or not it means the same to say that a thing 'participates in another' as to say that it 'is created', what is certainly true is that anything which participates in another *is* created. Moreover, what shows that the goods we perceive *are* participating, and so created, goods, is whatever shows the supreme good to be, and to be their Creator. Hence, so far as concerns what is at stake here, Milbank is right: there are but two possible ways of reading Thomas's strategy. The first is that there is a logically valid proof, which starts from the degrees of created goodness which we perceive and concludes to the existence of the supreme good which is their creating cause – in which case, general standards of validity of proof preclude there being, presupposed to our perception of these

---

[5] Fergus Kerr, *After Aquinas: Visions of Thomism*, Oxford: Blackwell, 2002, p. 59. But see note 24 below.

[6] In fact any such presupposition would have to be no more than implicit, since there is absolutely no indication that Thomas admits to making it in *ST* 1a q2 a3.

created goods and required as a premise, some *prior* knowledge of the supreme good's existence. The second is that presupposed to the five ways there is some such prior 'intuition' or 'experience' of the supreme good, such as would be required to perceive the created goods from which the 'arguments' proceed as participating and as created – in which case an argument from motion could not be, and probably could not have been intended to be, a logically valid proof. And of course Milbank settles for the latter to the exclusion of the former.

But why settle for that second option? In particular, why settle for it in view of the fact that lying before us in the text of *Summa Theologiae* 1a q2 a3 *corp.* is just the evidence we need that Thomas chose the first option and that he thought the existence of a supreme good can be proved – the so-called 'fourth way'? For here Thomas does not say: we know that there are degrees of goodness in things only because we know *a priori* that there is a supreme good, there being no proof of anything in that, and Thomas is explicit about his argument-strategy here: it is meant as proof, for this, he says, is the fourth of the ways in which *Deum esse probari potest.*[7] Besides, there is no evidence whatever that Thomas thinks the general proposition to be true – as Anselm, Bonaventure, Descartes, and above all Augustine certainly did – that we can perceive relative degrees of a quality only if we have prior knowledge of what would count as the maximal degree of it. In fact Thomas says the inverse of what Milbank claims for him: he argues that we know there must be a supreme good because there are degrees of goodness in things. As he puts it, we 'meet with'[8] greater and lesser degrees of goodness and truth in things anyway, and the argument then goes on to show how it follows that there must be some maximal degree of such qualities, not that we could not know of such degrees of goodness and truth unless we already had some 'glimpse' of them in their maximal degree. And whatever one thinks of the validity of such an inference, or of the further, insufficiently explained, inference that whatever accounts for our capacity to judge degrees of goodness must be the cause of them, the argument is clearly presented *as* an inference, moreover to a *cause*, 'which we call God'. Hence, even if, as Milbank believes, the force of the argument from motion (the 'first way') depends upon the presupposition that there is a supreme good which is the end of all motions, the proposition that there is a supreme good is itself capable of

---

[7] Thomas's choice of words rules out Milbank's suggestion that the five ways are intended as *demonstrationes* in some weaker sense than 'strict proof': *potest probari* is as strong as you can get in point of apodeicticity.

[8] 'Invenitur enim in rebus aliquid magis et minus bonum, et verum, et nobile; et sic de aliis huiusmodi.' *ST* 1a q2 a3 *corp.*

being demonstrated (*potest probari*) by an independent proof (the 'fourth way').

Which brings us to the second, and more critical, misreading. It seems crucial to Milbank's case – though of course it is not the whole of it – that Thomas could not consistently have intended the five ways to be logically valid proofs of the existence of God, for it is Milbank's view that logically valid proofs of the existence of God are impossible, short of engagement in a form of 'Scotist onto-theology' – which Thomas, by anticipation, rejected. Here, we are brought back in turn to that persistent tendency within Milbank's work to play Thomas off against Scotus, a tendency which does so on the one hand to Scotus' disadvantage, as we have already had cause to observe, and on the other hand on terms and rules of contest which, remarkably, owe far more to *Scotus* than they do to Thomas, as we shall now see.

It is, in the first place, Scotus, not Thomas, who anywhere says that demonstration of the existence of God depends logically upon 'being' being predicated univocally of God and of creatures, such that analogical predication would rule out scientific demonstration:

The active intellect and the sense image cannot give rise to a concept that, with respect to the object revealed in the sense image, is not univocal but rather, in accordance with an analogical relationship, is altogether other and higher than the object. It follows that such an 'other', analogous, concept will never arise in the intellect in our present state. Also it would thus follow that one could not naturally have any concept of God – which is false.[9]

Thomas nowhere says any such thing – in fact, as we shall see, he explicitly anticipates Scotus' objection, and rejects it. Moreover, it is Milbank, not Thomas, who repeats this Scotist *nostrum* as a crucial step in his account of why Thomas cannot be offering proofs from the natural light of reason: 'one can point out', he says,

that in the realm of metaphysics even the relative certainty profered by reason is very weak. For scientific demonstration proper depends, for Aquinas after Aristotle, on a univocity of terms answering to a univocity between causes and effects. For Aquinas, this contention disallowed a transgeneric 'science' in the strictest sense . . . Aquinas . . . by identifying God with non-generic *esse*, and by specifically excluding God from *genus* and from substance in the sense either of distinct

---

[9] 'Sed conceptus qui non esset univocus obiecto relucenti in phantasmate, sed omnino alius, prior, ad quem ille habeat analogiam, non potest fieri virtute intellectus agentis et phantasmatis; ergo talis conceptus alius, analogus qui ponitur, naturaliter in intellectu viatoris numquam erit, – et ita non poterit haberi naturaliter aliquis conceptus de Deo, quod est falsum.' Duns Scotus, *Ordinatio* 1 d3 n. 36; Frank and Wolter, *Duns Scotus*, pp. 112–13.

essence or self-standing individual . . . also ensures that there can be only an analogical or not strictly scientific approach to the divine. Hence . . . his 'demonstrations' of God's existence can only be meant to offer weakly probable modes of argument and very attenuated 'showings'. ('Intensities', pp. 454–5)

Twice in this passage Milbank stakes a claim on Thomas's behalf for the impossibility of a strictly scientific demonstration which depends on inference between terms predicated analogically. But to conclude from this that no scientific demonstration of the existence of God is possible – on the grounds, of course, that any sense to a term predicated of God can be only 'analogically' related to the sense that term has of creatures – is to misunderstand equally what is required of valid inference, of the structure of the arguments for the existence of God in Aquinas, and of the logic of analogy. We shall see later in this chapter that, on the score of univocity, what is required of any valid inference is no more than that any term occurring more than once in the *premises* of a valid inference (the so-called 'middle term') is used in the same sense (univocally) on every occasion of its occurrence. It is *not* required that there be a univocity of terms in premises and conclusion. It is true that, as Milbank says, Aristotle goes further and maintains that no conclusion may follow in a valid demonstration whose terms are not predicated according to a sense univocally the same as those same terms occurring in the premises. In the *Posterior Analytics* Aristotle makes this clear:

It is impossible to prove a fact by transition from another genus, e.g. a geometrical fact by arithmetic . . . every proof has its own subject-genus. Therefore the genus must be either the same, or the same in some respect, if proof is to be transferable; otherwise it is impossible; for the extremes and the middle term must be drawn from the same genus, since if they are not connected *per se*, they are accidental to one another . . . nor can one science prove the propositions of another, unless the subjects of the one fall under those of the other, as is the case with optics and geometry, or with harmonics and arithmetic . . .[10]

and no doubt Milbank takes comfort from the exception which Aristotle makes to this general rule of syllogistic inference. For, on his account, a philosophical proof of the existence of God would have validity only as 'falling under' the principles of revealed theology in the same way as the subject-matter of optics 'falls under' that of geometry. Milbank's way of putting it is that the arguments for the existence of God gain what little power of proof they possess from their equivalent 'subalternation' to an already given, revealed, and so faith-based premise – the given experience of divine perfection. But, according to Milbank, otherwise than within that theological subalternation the five ways have no probative power of

---

[10] Aristotle, *Posterior Analytics* 1.7, 75a38–b18.

any kind. That, however, as I have argued, makes no sense at all of what 'proof' is. For that subalternation guarantees nothing even 'weakly' or 'probabilistically' to Thomas's arguments by way of proof. Since, on the contrary, that 'subalternation' reduces them to straightforwardly invalid arguments, committing the fallacy of *petitio principii*, we are once again brought back to a choice of readings of Thomas's 'five ways'. Either Thomas means what he says – and he *says* the 'five ways' are proofs – in which case he at least cannot suppose them to beg the question; or else Milbank is right, and Thomas's conclusion ('God exists') follows only from a conjunction of premises which include an explicitly theological presupposition – in which case neither he nor Milbank have any business describing them as 'proofs' of any sort, 'weak' or 'strong'.

Be that as it may, Milbank's objection in principle to strict proof of God's existence appears to rest on the supposition that if transgeneric demonstration is invalid, then an inference which purported to transgress the boundary between any created genus and God, who is beyond every genus, must by at least the same token be invalid.[11] But this is a significant *non sequitur*, the full and disastrous theological consequences of which I shall examine later in this chapter. At this point let us confine ourselves to saying, first, that it *is* a *non sequitur*. To suppose without more ado that because an inference is invalid by the fallacy of equivocation if it crosses from one genus to another it must be at least as invalid if it crosses from generic being to God, who is beyond every genus, is to suppose, without more ado, that the gap to be crossed between one genus and another and the gap to be crossed between generic being and God are logically the same kinds of gap, only – one supposes – 'bigger' in the latter case. And, secondly, it is a significant *non sequitur* because that, once again, is exactly the supposition which Scotus makes. For though Scotus, like Milbank and Thomas, denies that God belongs to any genus, and though Scotus, unlike Milbank and Thomas, so construes the 'gap' between God and creatures as to be logically of the same kind as that between one genus and another, Milbank, like Scotus and unlike Thomas, holds that inference could cross the gap between creatures and God only if that gap fell univocally within a common genus. It is beside the point at this stage that, unlike Scotus, Milbank thinks it to follow that inference cannot cross it, since it is impossible that terms could be predicable univocally of God and of creatures. For Milbank's assumption about inference and univocity is Scotist, not Thomist. If this must have the consequence that Scotus is simply confused about how God and creatures differ, it equally means that Milbank has, conversely, conflated what holds of the logic of inference

[11] Milbank and Pickstock, *Truth in Aquinas*, p. 28.

between genera with what holds of the logic of inference between generic being and God. And this, in turn, entails a Scotist confusion on Milbank's part concerning the logic of analogical predication.

'Transgeneric' inference

For there are, according to Thomas, two kinds of predication of terms across genera. The first is that of the most general transcendental predicates of 'existence', 'goodness' 'oneness' and the like, which are predicated analogically. The second is that of metaphor. It is of course obvious why no formal demonstration is possible from premises whose terms are literally predicated to conclusions which are metaphorical extensions of them: nothing in the physics of colour could ever strictly entail conclusions about the blueness of a mood, or in the physics of heat about the fieriness of a temperament.[12] Nor thus far is the case much different with transcendental terms when predicated by that sort of analogy which we may call 'proportional',[13] as existence and goodness can be, and here Aristotle is of course in a limited connection right: what characteristics you describe as making for a good apple provide no grounds for determining what makes for a good time of the day for having a celebration, for the evidence for the one can serve no purpose of evidence for the other. After all, a good time for celebrating is under no requirement to be sweet, juicy and firm, as a good apple presumably must be. Moreover, just so far as concerns the logic of this *proportional* analogy, Milbank is right too; no possible argument from creatures to God could be generated on the basis of 'analogy' so understood.

Not that all inferences between one genus and another by analogy of proportion are logically impossible, Aristotle notwithstanding. Under certain conditions inference between terms analogically related is of course possible, precisely through their analogically proportional connections of meaning. For even if it is the case that, taken by itself, the description of what makes for a good time for celebrating cannot be derived from what makes for the goodness of an apple, it does not follow that the

---

[12] Though of course we do gain in knowledge from metaphors; we say something true of a temperament when we say it is 'fiery', something else when we say that it is 'volatile'. There are all sorts of ways in which we gain knowledge by transgeneric transfer, and poetry exploits many of them, music others.

[13] It is disputed whether Thomas in fact offers any account of what later came to be called 'analogy of proportion', or whether not only the name but also the conception is a later development of late medieval 'Thomist' commentators. In fact it does not matter much whether analogy of this sort is to be found in Thomas. Clearly there is an analogy of this kind, and it is certainly consistent with Thomas's account of the logic of 'transcendental' terms.

meaning of the predicate '. . . is good' as predicated of a time for celebrating bears no connection with the meaning of '. . . is good' as predicated
of apples. As we have seen, the predicate '. . . is good' is not, and cannot
be, predicated either metaphorically or equivocally. There is always some
relation, in fact some 'proportion', determining the meaning common to
all such predications.

And as to analogical predication of this kind, the word 'proportion'
is used in a sense derived from arithmetical proportions, denoting the
equation, $a:b::c:d$. No variable on either side of the equation is found on
the other, yet, given the values of the variables a, b, and c, we can, on
certain conditions, derive the value of d. Thus, if $a = 2$, $b = 4$, and $a = 6$,
we may derive the value of d as being 12. But we can thus derive the value
of d if and only if we know in what relation of proportion a stands to b. For
in deriving 12 as the value for d I had simply assumed that the proportion
which obtained between a and b was that of multiplication by 2; but of
course, if the proportion between a and b were that of the square of, then
even though the values of a, b and c remain the same, the value derived
for d will be 36, not 12. Given, then, the values for three of the variables
and a definition of the proportions in which they stand one to another,
we can derive, by analogical argument, the value of the fourth.

It is, therefore, in that same sense in which a's relationship to b is
'proportionally the same' as c's relationship to d that we can say that
there is a sameness in which '. . . is good' is predicated of times of the day
and of apples, even though there is nothing in common between them
by way of descriptive characteristics. For those descriptive characteristics
stand in the same relation as each other to what it is for anything to be
good, and to know that is to know the definition of 'good' – roughly,
for Thomas, the desirability of a thing's realising the potentialities of
its nature, the potentialities of the kind of thing that it is. It is because
one set of characteristics has to do with an apple's being a desirable one
of its kind, and another, wholly different, set of characteristics has to
do with a desirable time for celebrating, that, wholly different as they
are, these characteristics determine senses of the predicate '. . . is good'
which are neither univocally nor yet equivocally related. They are related
'proportionally'.

It is clear, moreover, that the *logic* of this kind of 'proportional analogy' by which transcendental terms are predicated across genera can
hold between created goods without reference to the divine goodness on
which, *ontologically*, they depend. Of course, for Thomas (as Milbank and
Pickstock are right to say), the 'full realisation' of a thing is to be found
in the divine conception of it – and, in general, anything good is, he says,
truly said to be good 'by the divine goodness' itself, as Thomas reports the

Platonici as maintaining:[14] that is to say, *that* any creature is good depends on its participation in the divine goodness. But it does not follow from this, he insists, that, as Milbank and Pickstock infer,[15] we can only know the goodness of creatures in so far as we have some already given awareness of their perfect realisation in the divine mind, or that in some way the logic of the predication of goodness of creatures requires some reference to the divine perfection itself. For if it is true that a creature is said to be 'good' by virtue of a likeness to the divine goodness (*similitudine divinae bonitatis*), nonetheless Thomas is emphatic: that goodness of a creature belongs to the creature itself, and is formally its own goodness, denoting it as such (*sibi inhaerente, quae est formaliter sua bonitas denominans ipsum*).[16] You can know what makes for a good apple without knowing anything of the divine mind, or even that there is a divine mind at all.

To summarise: so far as concerns the meaning of transcendental predicates, it is clear that some 'proportional' analogy holds between all their predications, such that those predicates are never predicated either univocally or equivocally across genera. They are not predicated univocally across genera, because, as we have seen, no two different kinds of thing called 'good' need possess in common any of the characteristics in virtue of which they are thus described. Nor yet are they predicated equivocally across genera, because it is not in any case the simple possession of those characteristics which determines their goodness, but the relation in which those characteristics stand to the full realisation of the sort of thing that it is. Hence, as Thomas says, in the analogical predication of such transcendentals, there is always something in common, and something in which they differ.[17]

Secondly, so far as concerns *inference* by proportional analogy across genera, this *is* possible in so far as two conditions are met: first, that we know the meaning of such predicates, and secondly, that we know the values of three of the variables, from which it is possible to derive the value of the fourth. It is, of course, this second condition which is of significance for theological argument. For since this condition cannot in principle be met in the case of arguments for God, it follows that no knowledge of God can be derived by an inference of 'proportional analogy' from our knowledge of creatures, short of our already knowing that God exists.

For while from our knowledge of goodness in one genus of creatures we may be able to learn what goodness is in another – it is common sense that we do thus learn how to use words such as 'good' 'by analogy'

---

[14] *ST* 1a q6 a4 *corp.*
[15] Milbank and Pickstock, *Truth in Aquinas*, pp. 28–30.
[16] *ST* 1a q6 a4 ad1.   [17] *ST* 1a q13 a5 *corp.*

(indeed, how else could we do so?) – this is possible because we know what sort of things both are, and so can come to learn what will count as a good instance of the one from what counts as a good instance of the other. But it is precisely this which is not the case with God, for we do not know what sort of thing God is. Consequently, we cannot construct a valid inference to the existence of a divine goodness by proportional analogy from what goodness is in any creature; all we can know is that the divine goodness must stand in some similarly proportional way to the divine self-realisation, or, as Thomas calls it, the divine 'perfection' – that perfection itself being, of course, equally beyond our comprehension. By this proportional analogy we can know only that *if* God exists, then to say 'God is good' retains some connection with our ordinary meanings of creaturely goodness; but we cannot argue to the *existence* of the divine goodness – but only dimly to the 'how' of the divine goodness – by any such analogy with what goodness is in creatures.

Nor does Thomas suppose that we can. It is abundantly clear that Thomas offers no argument to the existence of God by way of analogy, however conceived. Therefore, we ought to examine whether, as it might seem, the case is different with Thomas's own example of those terms whose analogical predication is most directly comparable with the common predications of God and of creatures, namely the predication by what has been called the 'analogy of attribution' – the kind of analogy by which the predicate '. . . is healthy' is predicated in common of a symptom and of its cause.[18]

Once again, it is clear that Milbank is wrong in attributing to Thomas the view that inference from one term to another related by analogy is in general impossible. For had Thomas thought so, he would have had to suppose that medicine cannot in principle have the character of a science. It is precisely because health in an organism is the cause of healthy urine that '. . . is healthy' is predicated analogically of urine; and it is precisely because of that causal connection that the diagnosis of health in the organism from its symptoms in the urine can be scientific. So far from it being the case, as Milbank puts it, that 'scientific demonstration proper depends, for Aquinas after Aristotle, on a univocity of terms answering to a univocity between causes and effects', it is the argument from effect to cause which underpins the validity of the analogical predication 'urine is healthy' – knowing how and why, and under what causal conditions, you can describe urine as 'healthy' *just is* that in which medical science consists.[19] There is nothing in Aquinas' account of the logic of inference and of analogical predication which prohibits, on the Aristotelian ground,

---

[18] *ST* 1a q13 a5 *corp.*   [19] Aquinas *In* IV *Metaphysicorum*, lect. 1, 534, 544.

the inference from health as effect to health as cause, and so from 'health' in the sense of effect, to health in the sense of cause analogically related to it.

Yet it does not follow from this that an argument from creatures to the existence of God is any more possible by means of this kind of analogy than by means of the other; indeed, inference from creatures to God by analogy of attribution is as demonstrably impossible as it is in the case of proportional analogy. For in the case of analogy of attribution, both the meaning of 'healthy urine' in its analogical connectedness with 'healthy organism', and the possibility of inferring the health of the organism from the health of the urine, depend upon our knowledge of the causal mechanisms which underlie that connection. But this is precisely what we do *not* know about God, in the absence of any already given proof. For even were we to possess some argument which does demonstrate the existence of a cause of the universe – and we should need to know at least that much already if any talk of a theological analogy of attribution is to be justified in the first place – we should thereby know that we have no comprehension of what that causal mechanism is by which God creates the universe. For this reason a causal proof is presupposed to a predication of terms of God by analogy of attribution, not the other way round. And even then, by such analogy we should know no more than that, since God is the cause of the universe, and since there is no knowable causal mechanism by which he causes, it follows that even if we are justified in our predications of God by analogy of attribution, we could not know the meaning of what we are justified in attributing to him. Such a causality being incomprehensible to us, it follows that we cannot know, in advance of a demonstration of God's existence, but only on the strength of one, that any sort of analogy holds between God and creatures.

From this there appears to follow a consequent ordering of logical dependencies. Names predicated of God by proportional analogy are justified through their dependence on predications by analogy of attribution. For it is only if there is some causal link between God and creatures, such as to justify the claim to equivalent proportionality between them, that inference by proportional analogy is possible from what we know about creatures to what we can come to know about such names of God. But if a justification of inference by proportional analogy thus depends upon analogy of attribution, analogy of attribution can, in turn, derive its justification only from such knowledge as we can obtain as to there being a causal link between God and creatures. In short, the justification for analogy of *either* kind depends on our knowing already that God is the Creator of all things, visible and invisible.

Thus far, then, Milbank is right. None of our human rational procedures for inferring knowledge of God's attributes – and they are all analogical of one sort or another – can stand on their own as inferences demonstrating that there is a God to be thus talking about. You cannot argue *to* God's existence *by* analogy. Hence, we are able to conclude that no proof of the existence or nature of God can depend upon our knowing in advance that some analogy between creatures and God could hold.[20] To put it in another way, if an argument for the existence of God is to succeed, it cannot depend upon analogy: it must demonstrate analogy; it will be an argument to, not from, analogy. But that, in turn, brings us back to Milbank's strictures against the possibility of such proof as contains terms in the premises connected to terms in the conclusion only by an 'analogy' which stretches across the infinite 'gap' between creatures and God. For even were he to concede that transgeneric inference is possible, it would not, it appears, have to follow that an inference could stretch without breaking across the gap between creatures and God. Nor, Milbank thinks, does Thomas allow it. But on both counts he seems to be wrong.

Thomas on inference from creatures to God

Before considering whether there is a case for the possibility of a causal argument, let us first consider what Thomas's view of the matter is in principle. There are at least two important texts in which Thomas explicitly raises the question of whether the transcendence of God – which entails God's being spoken of 'analogically' – rules out the possibility of inference being valid to God from creatures, and in both his answer is in an unambiguous negative: such inference is *not* thereby ruled out. The first of these we have already considered:[21] on the one hand, Thomas, we saw, maintains that the Christian, who believes in the one true God, and the idolater, who worships some creaturely object as if it were God, contradict each other, which they could not do unless there were something in common between the ways in which they think of God. For unless the idolater was affirming of the idol that it is 'God' in some sense related to that in which the Christian denies that it is God, it could not be the case that the affirmation and the denial were contradictories. Consequently, the Christian's 'God' and the idolater's 'God' cannot be equivocal terms.

---

[20] It goes without saying that no argument for the existence of God could depend upon our knowledge in advance that such analogies do hold, for that would be simply to beg the question.

[21] See pp. 132–6.

On the other hand, when the idolater says that this idol is God and the true believer denies it, the word 'God' cannot be used univocally in both cases, for the one is saying of the Creator of all things visible and invisible that it is God, the other that a creaturely idol is God. And the word 'God' cannot be predicated univocally of God and of the creature. Hence, when the pagan and the Christian disagree whether an idol is God, the name 'God' is used, Thomas says, analogically (*analogice dicitur*).[22]

It follows then that, for Thomas, there can be formal contradiction between two analogically related propositions. And it follows from that that there can be no objection to there being a formally valid inference between premises and a conclusion analogically related to them across the 'gap' between creatures and God. Why? For the reason which Scotus gives: for if, on his account, an inference is valid only on condition that the terms related to each other by it are such that 'to affirm and to deny [them] of the same subject amounts to a contradiction', then, on Thomas's account, that condition is met by terms which are related to each other analogically. Hence an inference will not, for Thomas, be invalidated by the fact that it connects terms logically related to each other by analogy if, as in the case in question of 'God', to affirm and deny of a bronze statue that it is God amounts to a contradiction. As far as Thomas is concerned, all that is required for the validity of such inferences is that there should be no equivocation between premises and conclusion. That premises and conclusion are related analogically can therefore place no obstacle in the way of the inference between them being logically valid.

If this argument may seem to relate with comparative indirectness to the issue of inference to an analogical conclusion, a second text, found in the *Summa contra Gentiles*, could not meet the point more squarely. There Thomas considers 'the opinion of those who say that God's existence cannot be demonstrated but can be held by faith alone', and in the course of doing so entertains Milbank's Aristotelian objection to his own view that God's existence is demonstrable: 'if the principles of demonstration have their origin in knowledge of sense, as is shown in the *Posterior Analytics*, what wholly exceeds every sense and sensible thing seems to be indemonstrable. But the existence of God is such. Therefore it is indemonstrable.'[23]

But Thomas rejects this counter-argument. If it were valid, he comments, it would prove too much. For on that account – 'if there were no substance knowable beyond sensible substance' – then nothing beyond natural science would be knowable, which even Aristotle denies. He adds that it can be no further objection to the validity of such proof that we

---

[22] *ST* 1a q13 a5 *corp.*   [23] Aquinas, *Summa contra Gentiles* 1.12.

cannot know the 'essence' of God, and so cannot construct any non-equivocal sequence of premises entailing God's existence, since in proofs of the kind in question it is the divine effects[24] which function as premises, not the divine nature.[25] For we cannot construct an argument for God's existence out of premises definitive of the divine nature, as Anselm famously supposed, that nature being unknown to us – we are in possession of no definition of God in the first place.[26] But if the arguments for the existence of God are constructed from premises descriptive of the effects of God in creation, and not from any definition of God, then of course the conclusion of such an argument will have to contain terms not univocally related to those of the premises; it could not be an argument for the existence of *God* if that were not so, but only for 'just another, creaturely, being'. Hence, the only tests of such an argument's validity could be those of logic; you could not rule out the argument's validity on the grounds alone that the conclusion contained terms not univocally related to the terms of the premises. That, in any case, is pure Scotism.

The same point needs to be made to those who would rule out such a possibility on the rather similar grounds of formal logic. It is often said that from premises employing sense-bound intra-mundane notions of cause (with whatever consistent univocity of sense) you could not in principle conclude to a non-sense-bound extra-mundane cause. For to be non-sense-bound and extra-mundane – and so God – the conclusion would have to contain terms so transcending in meaning that of the terms of the premises as to render the inference invalid. And there seems to be a general principle at stake here: surely, it will be said, the conclusion of a valid inference must be in some way 'contained' in the premises if the conclusion is to be validly 'extracted' from them. But how could God be in any way 'contained' in premises derived from creatures, derived as cause from effect, without God's thereby being conceived of as a cause within, and not *of*, creation? And how, if not 'contained' in the premises, could an inference from creation to God be justified? So it may well be said.

Of course, since Kant, nearly every philosopher, and as many theologians, have taken this objection to proofs of the existence of God to

---

[24] This is an ellipsis. Kerr is, of course, right (see pp. 196–7 above) that you cannot *prove* the existence of God from what you *know* are the divine effects, because that is simply to beg the question. To prove the existence of God *is* to prove that creatures are 'effects' of a divine creating causality. Nor is Kerr entirely right when he comments that, in saying that the 'five ways' argue from 'effects' to 'cause', Thomas is evidently making creation *ex nihilo a presupposition* of their validity (Kerr, *After Aquinas*, p. 59). As I argue at pp. 239–42 below, for Thomas, the five ways do need to be taken in conjunction with the account of *creatio ex nihilo* in that what shows God to exist is just what shows the world to be created *ex nihilo*, and so that the world is a divine 'effect'.

[25] *ST* 1a q2 a2 ad2.   [26] *ST* 1a q2 a1 *corp.*

be unanswerable. But perhaps one of the reasons it has been taken to be unanswerable is the very great degree of unclarity with which this so-called principle of deductive logic is promoted. The only completely transparent sense in which a conclusion can be said to be 'contained' in the premises of an inference is, once again, that of the *petitio principii*. Of course, 'if all the apostles are Jews and if Peter is an apostle, then Peter is a Jew' is a case of an argument in which the consequent is 'contained' in the antecedents. But since you would have to know that Peter is an apostle in order to know that the antecedent is true – that *all* the apostles are Jews – it is hardly the case that the consequent is thus derived from the antecedents. If anything, the major premise is (partially) derived from the conclusion already known. Otherwise than in a tautological case of this kind, there seems to be no very clear way of settling the question of how what is 'contained' in the premises of an inference is to be determined so as to rule out 'something else' appearing in the conclusion, otherwise than to say: a conclusion is 'contained' in a set of premises if and only if it follows from them by means of a logically valid inference employing non-equivocal terms. It might seem as if this is just to turn the tables on the opponent by begging the question. But it is hard to see why one may not do so, at least until some other sense is provided of the expression 'contained in the premises' which can be given a coherent meaning.

That being so, all we need is a logically valid proof of the existence of God meeting the following conditions: first, that no equivocation occur in the premises; secondly, that the conclusion contain terms which are *not* univocally the same as those contained in the premises, for otherwise the argument could not be said to conclude to God; nor alternatively may terms in the conclusion be equivocally related to the premises, for then the inference could not be logically valid. This, again, appears to be Thomas's view of the matter. For in further response to the 'Aristotelian' objection he simply says that its 'falsity is also shown by the effort of the philosophers who have tried to prove that God exists'[27] – if a proof proves, then you will have to abandon any such *a priori* presuppositions as would entail its impossibility.

Such an argument, as I have said, would not be an argument *by* analogy from creatures to God, for, God's existence not being presupposed, no such analogy could, short of circularity, be presupposed in the premises, but only entailed in the conclusion. It would, therefore, be an argument *to* analogy, demonstrating a two-part conclusion. First, in demonstrating the existence of God it would demonstrate that God cannot be named by names univocally predicated of him and of creatures; and second, by

[27] *Summa contra Gentiles* 1.12.

the fact of the argument's validity, it would follow that names of God lay in a degree of continuity with our names for creatures which ruled out their being equivocally predicated – for the validity of the argument would itself rule out equivocity. Our saying that such names are predicated 'analogically' would therefore get its sense from this double conditioning: we know that we are *justified* in predicating existence of God from the success of the argument; we should know that the proposition 'God exists' has some meaning from what showed it to be true. But just that same argument's success would also demonstrate that, as predicated of God, we do not otherwise have any grip on what 'exists' in that case means. In short, such an argument would demonstrate simultaneously the need for, and the inseparably mutual logics of, both affirmative and negative theologies. It would thereby demonstrate the possibility and necessity of analogical predication of God, as it would also provide a sense for the expression 'the analogical predication of terms of God'. A term is predicated analogically of creatures and of God when we know from creatures that it must be true of God too, but also know that *how* it is true of God must be beyond our comprehension.

'Validity is as validity does'

But is such an argument to be had? In advance of some substantive account of how such an argument might be validly conducted – and this will be a matter for the next two chapters – it is here necessary to clear away some objections in principle. In effect, the answer to all objections in principle has to be: validity is as validity does – or as the scholastic logicians used to say, *ab esse ad posse valet illatio*. There cannot be a *general* case against arguments from premises to conclusions not univocally continuous with them, for we can easily construct counter-instances. Geach quotes one from Quine: from the relational term, 'smaller than' and the general term, 'visible', both belonging to the universe of things which we can directly observe, we can form the compound term 'smaller than any visible thing', which is in perfectly sound logical order, yet could not, *a fortiori*, have application within that same universe of directly observable objects. As Quine points out, the compound gets us out of the universe within which the uncompounded terms both have application, 'without a sense of having fallen into gibberish'. He adds, 'The mechanism is of course analogy, and more specifically extrapolation.'[28] Now what holds for this simple compounding will hold for any argument whose premises

---

[28] Willard Van Orman Quine, *Word and Object*, Cambridge, Mass.: MIT Press, 1960, p. 109, and Peter T. Geach, 'Causality and Creation', in *God and the Soul*, pp. 80–1.

contain the simple uncompounded terms and the conclusion the terms thus compounded: what holds is that such an argument will not fail of the fallacy of equivocation. Conversely, those premises will, on condition of the formal validity of the argument, entail a conclusion whose terms are not univocally related to the premises: the 'worlds' of 'the visible' and 'the invisible' are heterogeneous, generically distinct.

There seems to be no good reason for denying that what holds for Quine's case holds equally for one of Geach's on the score of inferential validity; on the one hand, an argument, if it could be constructed, whose premises contained the uncompounded terms 'cause of' and 'every mutable thing', both having univocal application within the domain of our human, natural, rational experience, all other conditions of inferential validity being met, would not fail of the fallacy of equivocation just because the conclusion entailed was the existence of the 'cause of every mutable thing'. On the other hand, since it would be clear that the relational term 'cause of' in the conclusion could not be understood in the same sense as it is understood in the premises – for the cause of every mutable thing could not be a cause in the same sense as that of any mutable cause – the argument would trade in no theologically offensive univocity, thereby reducing God to 'just another cause'. For the argument would have demonstrated the necessity of an analogical extrapolation which could not have been presupposed to it.

To some, however, there will seem to be good reason for objecting to Geach's case, if not to Quine's, for it will be said that the two cases are crucially different: for is not God *infinitely* different from any creature? Even were it conceded that Quine is right and that transgeneric inference is possible – and Milbank does not concede even this much – the objection remains that what may hold for inferences from one genus of creatures to another cannot be supposed to hold between any creatures and God, for the 'othernesses' in question are not comparable, the one being finite, the other infinite, and in the latter case the gap to be crossed by inference must be infinitely too big to be bridgeable, and no rational argument could possibly get you across it. But can this objection be sustained, intuitively obvious as it must sound to most?

In answer, let us return to the matter of God's 'difference'. God, the pseudo-Denys says, is 'beyond both similarity and difference'. Now though, as I have argued elsewhere,[29] the pseudo-Denys appears, in a manner characteristic of Platonists, to treat relational predicates of 'similarity' and 'difference' as attributes of God in the way that substantive predicates such as 'existence' and 'goodness' may be treated, it is fairly

---

[29] Turner, *Darkness of God*, pp. 41–2.

clear that in fact the pseudo-Denys regards 'similarity' and 'difference' as second-order predicates qualifying the predication of the substantive divine attributes – they are, as Burrell argues, 'formal features'.[30] The assertion that the 'cause of all' is 'beyond similarity and difference' entails that the predication of God's attributes is not governed by the same logic as governs their predication of anything other than God. Hence, there can be *no* calculation, whether in terms either of sameness or of distinction, of the 'gap' between God and creatures. But that in turn is to say that the question of 'sameness' and 'distinction' can arise only as between creatures. If this is so, then clearly there can be no good sense, but only a misleading one, in any, even casual and metaphorical, calculation of the greater and lesser degrees of 'distance' which lie between Creator and creatures as contrasted with that between one creature and another; for it is not on some common scale of difference that these differences differ. Indeed, that is precisely what is meant by saying that nothing can be predicated univocally of both God and creatures.

Therefore, when it is said: that 'God's difference from creatures is incomparable with any creaturely difference', one has to agree. But tempting as it no doubt is to think of God's difference from creatures as being 'greater' than that between any two creatures, we should note that God's difference cannot be said to be both 'incomparable' and '*greater*', as if to say: it is of this kind or that, only infinitely so. You cannot say, 'The difference between chalk and cheese is of *this* kind, and the difference between God and cheese is of *that* kind – see how incomparably bigger the one difference is from the other!', for 'bigger' *is* a term of comparison, and presupposes a common scale. If we can agree with the pseudo-Denys – and I argued in chapter 8 that we have every reason to do so – that God 'is not any kind of being', then it follows that there should be no issue over *how* God is different from every created being which *is* of some kind, belonging, as one says, to some genus or other. For if God is not any kind of being, then his difference from creatures is not a difference of any kind, hence is not a difference of any size, hence is not incomparably greater, but, on the contrary, is, simply, incommensurable. 'Greater' and 'lesser' cannot come into it, logically speaking.

Besides, while it is possible to sympathise with Christian theologians who think that, in their proper concern to defend the divine 'transcendence', they should go in for maximising gaps between God and creatures to an infinite degree of difference, it is less than helpful to put it this way, and if they insist, they should be asked to consider how, consistently with such a strategy, they will accommodate Augustine's fine words: 'But you,

---

[30] See pp. 41–2 above.

O Lord, were more *intimate* to me than I am to myself' – *tu autem eras interior intimo meo*;[31] for Augustine's sense of the divine 'otherness' is such as to place it, in point of transcendence, *closer* to my creaturehood than it is possible for any creatures to be to each other. For creatures are more distinct from each other than God can possibly be from any of them: as Eckhart said, 'distinction belongs to creatures, indistinction to God'. The logic of transcendence is not best embodied in metaphors of 'gaps', even infinitely 'big' ones, and if we must speak in such metaphors, we should at least acknowledge that, since we are in possession of no account of the gap to be crossed between God and creatures, there is no warrant on that account for the objection that rational inference could not cross it.

Here, then, we are brought back to the argument of chapters 8 and 9, and to the question of how to speak of the divine 'difference'. The upshot of that discussion may now be seen to be that the 'logic of transcendence' and the 'logic of immanence' are 'dialectical', by which I mean that though, through the constraints of language, we have to see these terms as opposed to each other – or at least as being drawn towards different poles of meaning – nonetheless their 'logics' are mutually interdependent. You cannot understand immanence except as a form of transcendence, or transcendence except as a form of immanence. The only way we have of giving expression equally to this twin polarisation on the one hand, and to their dialectical mutuality on the other, is oxymoronic – the openly delivered and unresolved statement of the negation of the negations between them. It is this unresolved and unresolvable tension between the immanence and the transcendence of God which gives rise to the overstressed rebarbativeness of those theologies which seek to give expression to these tensions, and explains the 'brilliant darkness' of the pseudo-Denys, the God who is 'distinct by reason of indistinctness' of Meister Eckhart, and Nicholas of Cusa's description of God as the 'not-Other'.

It is these 'negations of the negation' – necessarily failing in any attempt at resolved affirmativity – between immanence and transcendence, because between similarity and difference – which determine the sense in which we can, and the sense in which we cannot, speak of 'the difference' between God and creation. It is not, I said, *a* difference; it is such as to be 'incommensurable' – that is to say, it is such that this difference cannot be set in *any* form of contrast with any sameness. For that reason, I have argued further, the difference between God and creatures cannot stand on the same logical ground that differences between creatures stand on. Therefore, no *a fortiori* case seems warranted that, since

---

[31] Augustine, *Confessions* 3.6.7

there are objections to arguments across genera, even if successful, they must apply all the more so to supposititious arguments for God. Hence, it is a logically open question whether an argument can get you 'across' the gap. You have just to find the right argument to do it. *Ab esse ad posse valet illatio*: if the thing is done then it is not impossible.

A riposte from Loughton

This response to objections cannot, however, be regarded as yet fully convincing, for it may appear that the case for the incommensurability of the gap between God and creatures must work against the case for saying that it can be crossed by any rational inference. Kevin Loughton[32] has argued that a dilemma of this kind, at least apparent, remains to be resolved. He restates the objection as follows: if God's difference from creatures is such that it cannot be understood in contrast with any sameness with creatures, then the converse must hold true too. For if there is no 'sameness' between God and creatures to be set in contrast with 'difference', then there cannot possibly be any inference from creatures to God. For inferences require a gap to be crossed, and then cross it. Hence, either an inference is possible between God and creatures, in which case there is a gap between them and the inference crosses it – in which case the difference is not 'incommensurable' and you are straight back into Scotus' univocity. Or else there is no gap to be crossed – the difference is 'incommensurable' – in which case no inference is necessary, or even possible, which is Milbank's position.

The dilemma, so posed, at the very least demands of my case some further clarification. And in support of the view that the case for the 'incommensurability' of the gap between God and creatures cannot be made consistently with that for inference across it, let us return yet again to the notion of 'difference'. I argued in chapter eight that 'difference' is 'intra-generic', for generic language is language descriptive of the kinds of ways in which things can differ from one another. Consider, then, the cases of Peter, a police officer, who is 5′ 3″ tall, and of Susan, a social worker, who is 5′ 8″ tall. There is an 'intra-generic' difference between being a police officer and being a social worker, and there is an 'intra-generic' difference between being 5′ 3″ tall and being 5′ 8″ tall; the first of professions, the second of heights. In each case the differences are on a common scale. We can therefore sensibly answer the question 'What is the difference between Peter and Susan?' either by saying that they practise

---

[32] PhD student in the Faculty of Divinity at the University of Cambridge in detailed correspondence about the argument of this chapter. Much more in this chapter than I have explicitly acknowledged has been revised in the light of Loughton's critical comments.

different professions or by saying that Susan is taller than Peter. But we cannot sensibly answer the question about their difference by saying that Peter is a police officer and Susan is 5' 8" tall. For there would appear to be no common 'trans-generic' standard either of comparison or of contrast between heights and professions. And so the descriptions in question offer information neither about their similarity nor about their difference.

Nonetheless, there obviously is a difference – because it is 'trans-generic', Thomas calls it a *diversitas*[33] – between practising a profession and being of a certain height. Why, then, should we not say of all such 'diversities', even within creation, that they are 'beyond similarity and difference'? Simply because they are not. There is no problem at all constructing a context against the background of which we can re-establish these diversities upon common logical ground, and so establish their relations of similarity and difference, and consequently inference between them. For example, all we need to know is that Peter's height falls well below the required minimum for a male police officer and that Susan's height well exceeds that for a female police officer,[34] and we can conclude that there is this difference between Peter and Susan derivable from the profession of the one and the height of the other, namely that whereas Peter must have been granted a special dispensation from the height requirement, Susan, had she applied to be a police officer, would have needed no such concession. Hence, there are constructible 'differences' between 'diversities' such as to validate the possibility of inferences between them; they are not, in the sense in which the difference between God and creatures is, incommensurably different.

But no such case can be made for the difference between God and creatures, for this must be, on my argument, an absolutely incommensurable difference, and it would seem that inference from the one to the other must be ruled out on the very account of that difference which I have supplied by way of grounding its incommensurability. For that difference is 'beyond similarity and difference' in just that sense that no possible common logical ground can be found between God and creatures. Hence, no possible inference can be constructed between them.

A Christological response

To which I reply that the premises are true – God is incommensurably different from creatures and there is no common logical ground between God and creatures – but the conclusion that therefore no inferences can

---

[33] *ST* 1a q3 a8 ad3.
[34] There are of course no longer, as there once were, minimum height requirements to join the police force in the UK.

be constructed between them is invalidly drawn. And there is a theological reason for rebutting Loughton's objection. For were we to concede to the objection's force as an absolute prohibition of inference from creatures to God, a more drastic consequence would seem to follow. If we had to say that incommensurability precludes inference, then all prospect of defending the coherence of a Chalcedonian Christology would have to be abandoned. Thomas, at any rate, who knows no way at all of making complete sense of Chalcedonian Christology – it is an incomprehensible mystery – is convinced that he can rebut arguments purporting to show that it cannot make sense at all, and that it is contradictory nonsense. And such sense as we can make of that Christology manifestly can and must allow for the possibility of inference from what is true of Jesus the man to what is true of the God Jesus. Hence, at least in this case inferences from what is true of a creature to what is true of God may legitimately be drawn; indeed, the legitimacy of their being drawn would be required by Christological faith. Thomas, therefore, could not have accepted any argument from which it followed that inferences, logically of the same kind as those constructible between Peter's height and Susan's profession, *could not* obtain; that is, that they involve a contradiction, between the human and divine natures in Christ, even though the divine and human natures are in themselves absolutely incommensurable, there being no 'third' term, common to both, on the ground of which inferences between them may be constructed.

In the first place, then, Thomas's Christology requires no diminution of his emphasis on the absolute incommensurability of God and creatures. On the contrary, the incommensurability between the divine and human natures in Christ is, for Thomas, quite fundamental to his Christology. For Thomas's Christology is faithfully 'Chalcedonian', and he sees that this incommensurability is crucial to the doctrinal formula of Chalcedon which proclaims Jesus Christ to be one person who was fully human and fully God. It is only because of the incommensurability between Creator and creature that the predicates '. . . is human' and '. . . is God', do not, and cannot, refer to natures standing in relations of mutual exclusion. For it is just on account of their incommensurability – on account, that is to say, of their not occupying common logical ground – that exclusion cannot come into it. For one thing to exclude another there must be some 'space' from which they exclude each other. As McCabe puts it:

Being human and being, say, a sheep occupy mutually exclusive territories in the common logical world of animals. It is part of the meaning of being human that one is not a sheep . . . But just what or where is the common logical world that is occupied in mutual exclusion by God and man? . . . a man and a sheep make two animals: God and man make two what? It may be part of the meaning of man that he is not any other creature; it cannot be part of the *meaning* of man that he is not God. God is not one of the items in some universe which have to be excluded if it is just man that you are talking about. God could not be an item in any universe.[35]

And, as he goes on to point out, it is for want of understanding how fundamentally the Chalcedonian formulation relies upon this 'apophatic' doctrine of God (as Thomas puts it, the *ratio Dei*) that a critic such as John Hick can read the Chalcedonian decree as enmeshed in self-contradictoriness. For, Hick argues, just as of one and the same shape it is contradictory nonsense to say that it is both a square and a circle, so it is also 'as devoid of meaning' to say 'without explanation, that the historical Jesus of Nazareth was also God'.[36] The teaching concerning Christ that he is one person who is both truly divine and truly human is, of course, wildly implausible. It is perfectly reasonable to think it false to say this of any historical person. But contradictory it is not, except on some quite idolatrous account of God, which, again, we have already in chapter 9 established reasons for seeing off: God cannot be exclusive of anything at all. For if, as Christians wish commonly to say, the immanence of God is shown most visibly, and dramatically, in the hypostatic union of human and divine natures in the one person of Jesus Christ, that very assertion of immanence resists that devoidness of meaning in which formal contradictoriness consists precisely because it is understood in terms of the absolute incommensurability of the human and divine natures.

Conversely, just because, as McCabe puts it, it cannot be part of the *meaning* of God that being God excludes being man, so it cannot be part of the meaning of God – and therefore of the God Jesus – that he *is* man. As Thomas points out, what you say of Jesus in so far as he is man cannot be said of Jesus in so far as he is God:[37] 'Jesus is God' is true, 'Jesus was born of Mary' is true, 'Jesus died on the cross' is true; but it is not in so far as Jesus is God that Jesus was born of Mary or that Jesus died on the cross, for it is on account of his being a man that these things could be true of Jesus. Clearly, to say of Jesus that he is God is not to say the same thing as to say of Jesus that he is man, nor does the former entail the latter, even if both the former and the latter are true. It is just that, as McCabe says, 'what it is to be God' cannot stand in relations of exclusion with 'what it is to be man'.

Likewise, just because it cannot be part of the *meaning* of man that being human excludes being God, so it cannot be part of the *meaning* of

---

[35] McCabe, *God Matters*, pp. 57–8 (emphasis original).

[36] John Hick, in idem, ed., *The Myth of God Incarnate*, London: SCM Press, 1977, p. 178.

[37] *ST* 3a q16 a5 *corp.* and a11 *corp.*

man that man *is* God: 'Jesus is God' is true and 'Jesus is man' is true, but it is not in so far as Jesus is God that Jesus is man. For 'Jesus is the Son of God' is true; 'Jesus is co-eternal with the Father' is true. But it is not on account of Jesus' being man that Jesus is the Son of God or co-eternal with the Father, but on account of Jesus' being God. To say, 'Jesus is truly man', is not to say the same thing as to say, 'Jesus is truly God', and again, even if both are true, the truth of neither entails the truth of the other. It is just that, as McCabe says, 'what it is to be man' cannot be logically exclusive of 'what it is to be God'.

To explicate these logical relations is simply to re-explicate the logic of 'incommensurability' already explained: the 'difference' between Jesus' being human and Jesus' being divine is thus far to be explained in those same terms in which, in general, the 'difference' between God and any creature is to be explained – Thomas's Christology is fully dependent upon his doctrine of God. The which to summarise: that difference is not of that kind which falls within any 'common logical world' such that, first, by virtue of the one nature occupying some part of it, the other nature is excluded from that part; or, secondly, that, by virtue of this 'incommensurability', the distinction collapses into identity. For here in Thomas's Chalcedonian Christology, as in general in his philosophical theology, the pseudo-Denys's formula applies: 'the Cause of all is beyond similarity and difference'; as does Meister Eckhart's formula: 'God is distinct by virtue of *in*distinction'; as does also McCabe's: 'God could not be an item in any universe.' This, for Thomas, is what it is to do your Christology *sub ratione Dei*.

But, that being said, does it not follow that doubts about the possibility of inference between *incommensurabilia* are thus far reinforced? Will it not follow, now more clearly than ever – since 'what it is to be God' and 'what it is to be man' are shown to occupy *no* 'common logical world' – that inference between creatures and God is ruled out? For what could 'inference' from creatures to God mean except that they do occupy some 'common logical world', for inference is nothing but that occupation? For Thomas, at any rate, there is not and cannot be any dilemma here; on the contrary, it is precisely on account of the logic of incommensurability which obtains between them that inferences from the human to the divine *are* possible in the person of Jesus Christ. From the fact that what is true of God in virtue of being 'God' is not, in virtue of the meaning of man, true of man, it does not follow that you cannot say of the man Jesus what you can say of God, or that you cannot say of the God Jesus what you can say of the human person. For if it is false to say that '*qua God*, Jesus died on the cross', still, because Jesus is God, it *does follow*, if Jesus died on the cross, that 'God died on the cross' is true. And if it is false to say that '*qua man* Jesus is the Son of God', still, because the second person of the Trinity became man, it *does follow* that 'the man, Jesus, is the Son of God'. If it is false to say that '*qua God*, Jesus was born of Mary', still, because the baby born is God, it is true and it follows that, as Nicaea says, Mary is *theotokos*, the 'mother of God'.

Further objections and answers

These things are simply a matter of the 'logic' of the incarnation, at any rate of a Chalcedonian Christology. It is, of course, possible for Christian theologians to abandon the logic, and some do explicitly, as we have seen Hick does; though it is more common for Christian theologians thoughtlessly to dismiss the Chalcedonian Christology, unaware that in doing so they run the risk of abandoning the subtle and complex logic of transcendence on which it relies. As McCabe says, it is one thing to wish to construct a modern Christology in terms other than those of Chalcedon – and there is every reason for doing so, in view of the archaically esoteric character of the technical language of *ousia*, *hypostasis* and *prosopon* in which it is couched, the historical senses of which are so difficult to retrieve. But it is quite another thing to construct a modern Christology in such terms as entail the falsehood of Chalcedonian Christology.[38] For quite apart from considerations of historical continuity of doctrinal tradition which such an abandonment would put at risk, there is the consequence that, in rejecting Chalcedonian formulas on the score of their falsehood, the doctrine of God on which they rely, and, together with it, the logic of the *ratio Dei*, will be thrown out as baby with the bathwater. And that, in Thomas's view, would place at risk the whole theological project as such.

Now what is clear from Thomas's reconstruction of this 'incarnational logic' is that, although constructed in a manner in key respects different from Bonaventure's (canvassed in chapter 3), it has much the same outcome: it is that that logic is central not only to his Christology, but to the whole theological enterprise as such, for the simple reason that his Christology is central to the whole theological enterprise as such. What counts for the *ratio Dei* Christologically must count for the *ratio Dei* for theology in principle. Not only is Christ at the centre in terms of what theology is substantively about – in terms, that is to say of its material object; Christ is also at the centre of theological method, regulatively normative of its formal object, and so of how it knows its own object. What

---

[38] McCabe, *God Matters*, p. 55.

we must say about God as adequate to the central Christian doctrine of the incarnation, must be said about God *simpliciter*.

As we have seen, what 'must be said about God' – how this *ratio Dei* is to be understood – is governed by the double nature of the 'logic of transcendence', and this logic places upon the theologian an obligation to construct theologically within the complex tensions – constraints which are also opportunities – of the apophatic and the cataphatic, of the absolute transcendence of God, a transcendence intelligible only in so far as it cannot, as transcendence, be set in any relations of disjunction with the divine immanence. And these are tensions which require us to say that the 'difference' between God and creation is neither *a* difference, on all fours with other, created, differences, nor, that being said, is it a difference which simply collapses into identity – God is different, therefore, 'by indifference'. These constraints of 'logic' are not, however, imposed as regulative upon theological method, as if imported from some alien territory of the philosophical, even if it is very hard to see how they could ever have been formulated with any degree of precision without the resources of metaphysics and logic derived from philosophical traditions far more ancient than Christianity itself. In themselves, however, these constraints are imposed upon the theologian as *necessities of thought* imposed by the articulation of Christianity's own central doctrines, and especially of Christological faith.

But what appears to emerge from Thomas's account of that logic of transcendence, that *ratio Dei*, as required in the construction of his Christology, is that the 'incommensurability' of the difference between God and creatures is not such as to entail the impossibility of inference from creatures to God. For that is precisely what, on his view, the doctrine of Christ does allow us to see is permitted: in Christ, what is true of the man who is God is true of the God who is man. This is not to say, to repeat, that what is true of man *qua* man is true of God *qua* God, for the nature of man, as a creature, is incommensurable with the nature of God, who is the Creator. But it is true to say that anything predicable of the man Christ is predicable of the God Christ and *e converso*. Hence, from the fact that Christ the man died on the cross, it follows that God died on the cross; from the fact that Christ was born of Mary, preached, was thirsty, became exhausted, suffered torment in his passion and died, it follows that God was born of Mary, preached, was thirsty, became exhausted, suffered torment in his passion and died. Hence, in Christ, inferences from what is true of a creature to what is true of God *are* possible, notwithstanding the fact that, even in Christ, there is no possible 'common logical ground' which the divine and human natures occupy; as Chalcedon puts it, the divine and the human natures remain 'unconfused'.

Loughton, however, who is happy to accept that such inferences from creatures to God are logically warranted within the articulation of a Christology, further objects that Christ is a 'unique' case, known to us by revelation alone, and so what we know to be possible on that ground of faith bestows no general licence for a purely *rational* inference from creatures to God which could be established independently of that Christological faith. And this much must be conceded to the objection, that of course the incarnation of the second person of the Trinity in the person of Jesus is a contingent, and therefore historically particular, event; and that the vicissitudes of Jesus' life – his being born of this woman, Mary, in that stable in Bethlehem, that he lived for some thirty years or so, met with those particular followers, preached to those particular crowds, met with opposition from those particular factions, suffered in those particular ways and was executed by that particular method – are equally contingent. We could not know of the validity of just those inferences from the contingent events of Jesus' life to their being true of God on any grounds other than faith: we could not know them by reason alone, or as being true of any human person other than Christ. But it is not by virtue of just those historically contingent inferences that anything follows by way of licence more generally to predicate, on grounds of reason alone, anything true of creatures also of God. For that is not the point, as we shall see.

Secondly, it must be conceded that of course it is only by faith that we know that what can be said about the man Jesus can be said about God – for it is only by faith that we know that Jesus is God. If anything at all follows from the 'logic of incarnation' about the theological potential of a purely natural reason, then *ex hypothesi* it is on grounds of faith that we know it. But, as the reader will no doubt be aware by now, the proposition which it is the purpose of this essay to demonstrate is precisely that: namely, that *on grounds of faith* we know that inference from creatures to God is possible, or, more precisely, that to rule that possibility out on grounds of faith is in some fundamental way to misconstrue the nature of faith.

Even so, it is in only one sense that Christ is a 'unique' case, and in another not. For of course the individual person Jesus Christ is, as is any other person, unrepeatable; there cannot be two Jesus Christs, just as you are unrepeatable, and so am I: there cannot be two Denys Turners. *Qua* person, therefore, Jesus Christ is 'unique' as *any* person is 'unique'. This is simply a matter of the logic of individuation, having no theological consequences beyond what ordinarily follows from the unrepeatability of persons. But *qua* incarnation of the second person of the Trinity, Christ is not logically unique, for as Thomas says, we know from faith that there is and will be only one such incarnation, for just one incarnation is sufficient unto the divine salvific purposes. But there is nothing in the logic of incarnation to prohibit there being, or having been, more than one such incarnation,[39] and since what is at stake here is a matter of the logic of incarnation and of what that logic entails for our knowledge of God, the objection cast in terms of the 'uniqueness' of Jesus Christ would seem to lack force relevant to my argument, either way, for or against it.

How near are we at this stage to demonstrating the proposition that a Christology *demands* in general, and not merely permits in the particular case, the possibility of rational inference from creatures to God? I said that it is true but beside the point that nothing concerning reason's theological potential is in general derivable from the historically contingent truths of the life of Jesus, and from the consequence that, if true of the man Jesus, they are therefore true of God. But what *is* derivable is that if *any inference at all* from something true about a creature to something true about God is theologically justified, then it must be inconsistent with Christian faith in Christ to maintain that, on grounds of logic alone, such an inference is in principle impossible. For nothing logically impossible is credible. Conversely, anything to be believed must be logically possible. For Christians to accept this impossibility would be for Christians to know that their faith in Christ is thereby destroyed. Since, therefore, as the first Vatican Council proclaims, 'created reason is completely subject to uncreated truth', Christians know, on grounds of faith, that it cannot be the case that such inferences are impossible. For if the thing is done, it is possible, *ab esse ad posse valet illatio*. The thing is done, Christologically. Therefore it is possible *simpliciter*.

Moreover, from the fact that it is by faith that we know that the impossibility of such inference must be ruled out, it does not follow that the possibility of such inferences cannot be known by natural reason. On the contrary, it cannot matter on what grounds we know that natural reason is capable of constructing inferences from creatures to God; if we know that it is possible for natural reason to construct such inferences, then we know that it is possible for natural reason to know of the possibility of doing so. For as I argued in chapter 1, it is easy here to confuse two propositions and vital not to do so: the first, which I maintain, is that we know on grounds of faith that inference from creatures to God is possible; therefore, inference from creatures to God is possible, whether or not within faith. For faith comes into it as illuminating a rational non-impossibility. But this proposition is not to be confused with a second, which Loughton maintains, that inference from creatures to God is possible only within the ground of faith, that is to say, that such inference is not otherwise

---

[39] *ST* 3a q3 a7 *corp.*

possible than *within* faith, where faith functions as a premise of an inference. If the first is true, then, of course, reason could in principle know, on its own ground, that it is capable of inference from creatures to God, a matter which it is for natural reason to demonstrate; and I emphasise again, nothing at all in what either Thomas Aquinas or Vatican I says about faith endorses any particular arguments of reason to that effect. Of the success or otherwise of such arguments it is for reason alone to judge. Indeed, one can go further than this: since all that faith entails about the natural capacity of reason is that that capacity cannot be denied access to knowledge of God, and since it is entirely a matter for reason to discover what arguments there are which succeed, it is neither here nor there from the point of view of faith whether any actual arguments have been discovered which do succeed. And it is equally irrelevant, from the point of view of faith, whether any valid arguments to God are ever discovered. What matters from the point of view of faith is that the possibility of such an argument's being valid is not ruled out in principle. We know that, in a sense more than usually concrete, in Christ.

But to say this is to take a step into territory of theology beyond the scope of this essay, though that step was first adumbrated in chapter 6. For what links the argument here from the *logic* of the incarnation with the account I gave earlier of what I called the 'sacramental shape' of reason in the wider sense of the word is the proposition that creation itself has a quasi-sacramental character. To say this is to return, once again, to the language and thought of pre-modern theologies. That creation in its own character as creation has a quasi-sacramental form is there in Hugh of St Victor, who concedes a certain general sense in which the words of Scripture, but also all creation, being in both cases 'signs of something sacred', may be called 'sacraments'.[40] It is there in Bonaventure, for whom Christ's human nature, being the résumé of all creation, and so a *minor mundus* incorporating all the meaning and reality of the *maior mundus*, is the explicit 'sacrament' of the world's implicit created sacramentality.[41] But it is there in a form most significant for the purposes of my argument in Thomas, who argues that anything at all in the sensible world is a sign of something sacred, and so in a general sense is a 'sacrament' even if, other than in the cases of the seven sacraments of the Christian dispensation, they lack the character of a sacrament in the strict sense, for only those seven are 'causes' of our sanctification. And, significantly, it is just that text in Romans (1:19–20) to which Thomas appeals in support of his view that rational proof of God is possible that

[40] Hugh of St Victor, *De sacramentis* I.ix.ii; Migne, *Patrologia Latina*, 176:317D.
[41] Bonaventure, *Itinerarium Mentis in Deum* 1.12.

Thomas here appeals to in support of his saying that 'the created things which we can sense are signs of the sacred'.[42] The connection of thoughts between creation's power to disclose God and its possessing in a general sense the form of the sacramental is in Thomas incontestable.[43]

Now the sense in which creation as such may be said to have that character of the sacramental is a matter which the next chapter will go some way towards exploring in purely philosophical terms. Of course those 'philosophical terms' do not include within their vocabulary the term, or the conception of, 'sacramentality' as such, for we can know the 'shape' of creation, and so of reason, to *be* 'sacramental' in form only from within what is revealed to us in Christ. But it is, precisely, 'in Christ' that that 'shape' is disclosed for what it is. On account of which, it seems to me that at the theological core of the case for saying that there is some imperative of *faith* which requires the possibility of a rational knowledge of God is a Christological consideration, a consideration which Christology as such demands precisely because of the need to read a doctrine of creation and a doctrine of Christ in terms of mutual dependence, and certainly not, as in chapter 1 we noted some to suppose, as if threatening each other in terms of mutual exclusion. It is not, therefore, some 'uniqueness' of Christ which prevents this theological entailment of reason's power to know God, but, on the contrary, the universal significance of Christ which requires it. Such is the territory of theology on to which this essay cannot, as I say, beyond this point venture.

In fact, of course, the position of natural reason is not limited to a merely abstract philosophical *possibility* conceded to it by faith, although all I have attempted to show by way of philosophical argument in this chapter is the negative case that there are good reasons in logic for resisting the philosophical case against the possibility of such inference. Conversely, any philosophical case more positively claiming to *justify* such inference from creatures to God beyond the bare possibility of it in principle, rests, as I have conceded, on the success of an actual demonstration of the existence of God. This is for the reason that any technical devices of logic available to us within our human language for the construction of language about God – the forms of analogical predication – depend for their validity upon a causal nexus being established between God and creation – that is to say upon a proof that the world is created, and so that there is a Creator. It is therefore to the task of showing what the general shape of such a strategy of proof must be that we must finally turn.

---

[42] *ST* 1a q2 a2 ad1.   [43] *ST* 3a q60 a2 ad1.

11 Why anything?

The conditions of proof

If in any way the preceding arguments have succeeded in removing reasons for doubting – whether of philosophical or theological provenance – that a rational proof of the existence of God is in principle possible, where do those arguments leave us as to the 'shape' of such a proof, as to its 'argument-strategy'? From what has been established, so far, as to Thomas's mind on this question, we know something of the conditions which any such proof must meet. First, of course, any such argument must meet the ordinary, secular, conditions for inferential validity, and at least that it trades in no equivocation of terms. Second, such a proof will need to demonstrate that there is something which answers to the description 'God', the minimum for which description being, as we shall shortly see, that something answers to 'Creator of all things out of nothing'. Thirdly, the description 'Creator of all things' must be shown to be *quod omnes dicunt Deum*. This third condition requires that even if what is shown to exist does not, as proved, bear the names of the God of faith, the names of him whom Christians worship and pray to, love and submit their wills to, nonetheless, the God thus shown must also demonstrably be none other than that of Christian faith and practice and prayer. The God of proof must be 'extensionally equivalent' to the God of faith.

But if that third condition is to be met, then the God thus demonstrated to exist must be unknowably beyond the descriptions shown to be true of her, a condition which yields the paradox that, if a proof proves God to exist, it also proves that the meaning of existence, as predicated of God, has passed beyond our understanding in a very simple sense: we do not know what we have proved the existence of, for we do not know what God is otherwise than in terms, inevitably falling short of God, drawn from what we describe creatures to be. Thereby it follows, negatively, that there can be no univocity of terms predicated of God and of creatures and that no proof of the existence of God can rely upon any such univocity obtaining. Hence, if general conditions of inferential validity are to be met by a proof of God's existence, this will be because the argument-strategy of such a proof succeeds in 'crossing the gap' (which is not a gap) from creatures to a God who is unknowably incommensurable with any creaturely existence, a God who is thus at once 'wholly other' (as Derrida would say) and 'not-other' (as Nicholas of Cusa would say), or (as the pseudo-Denys says) is 'beyond both similarity and difference'. And from this paradoxical conjunction of conditions follows another; that a rational proof of the existence of God is constrained by the constraints which, quite generally, govern the 'grammar' of all theological language, namely of a complex interplay and dialectic of the affirmative and negative, the 'cataphatic' and the 'apophatic' – constraints of which Christian believers know simply from within their attempts to articulate their own central doctrines; above all, the doctrinal formulations of their Christology. In short, the 'shape' of a proof of God's existence must be the 'shape' of faith itself; shorter still, it must have the 'shape' of Christ. A rational proof of the existence of God is thus incarnational in both source and form. Between them, such would appear to be the formal, that is strictly logical, and the substantive theological conditions which any proof of God's existence must meet.

Parasitical atheisms

However, in addition to such logical and theological conditions, there are broader epistemological, psychological and cultural conditions to be met, if not so as to conform to formal criteria for validity, then at least as providing reasons for believing that it matters that proof of the existence of God is possible. If we begin from the proposition that there are no grounds in faith for supposing a rational proof of God's existence to be impossible, and if, as I argued in the last chapter, there are reasons of faith – centrally, of a Christological sort – for supposing that objections to rational proof must be removed, a proof, just in so far as it is proof, will prove by rational means alone, and will not rely in any form of dependence as an inference on any premises of, or on any other kind of assumptions about, the truth of faith's claims. If that is the case, moreover, it could reasonably be expected of a rational proof that whatever claims it makes on the human mind, it will make them with at least some theoretical power to convince the mind of the atheist, or that at the least it should raise a question for atheists, in as much as they too are committed to rational argument, about the rational adequacy of their position. That being so, having considered in some detail in the preceding discussion why Christian theologians in the majority are far from convinced that rational proof of God's existence is in principle possible, and even that it is desirable, it is worthwhile giving some thought to the question why non-Christians are equally unconvinced by, and even less interested in, any such possibility.

It is said that no one ever came to believe in the Christian God by way of a philosophical proof of the existence of God. It is not clear to me how one can be so sure of that,[1] even if it is obvious that no one would live a life for a 'rational' God, still less die for one. But if it were true it would hardly be a surprising fact, given the hostility to proof among Christians themselves. More than that, even among those who, in our cultures and societies of the West, no longer profess any Christian belief, or even any theistic position at all, and who hardly know any longer what it is that they no longer profess, there are many for whom the question whether there is or is not a God seems not to matter, for on their account nothing hangs on whether there is or is not a God, nothing follows either way. It seems to be true that for very large sectors of the populations of Western countries, life is lived broadly in a mental and emotional condition of indifference to the question. And it is also true that, even among some intellectual elites, for many of whom it is fashionable to permit theism as an option within a generalised and vaguely post-modern relativism of thought (for which there can be no grounds for ruling out any fundamental beliefs anyway), the licence granted to theism can seem to amount to no more than a higher, if more theoretically relativist, form of this more generalised and popular indifference. But such mentalities represent a different kind of challenge to the theologian than that posed by the orthodox and plain atheist, who can seem today to be as much an anachronism as an orthodox and plain theist. But at the least the good old-fashioned militant atheists flatter the theologian to the extent of wishing to argue about the matter, seeing in the question of God a battleground of last resort, a final contest about the world, and about all that is in it, and about us.

Theologians, after all, are as easily seduced by the flattery of 'relevance' as are any other academics, and there are some of the theological company who yearn for the good old days – perhaps they survived until the late nineteenth century, perhaps until Nietzsche – when it was still agreed that everything depended on whether or not there is a God, when it was still relatively clear what it was to think the existence of God, hence, what was to count as atheism was to the same extent unproblematical.

---

[1] Of course it will not be relevant if no one finds it attractive to have the truth of theism imposed upon them by argument. On the contrary, their dislike would be some sort of testimony to the argument's force. Being convincing is not a psychological matter of winning enthusiastic consent, but rather of bringing a person to acknowledge a truth whether she likes it or not.

In those good old days atheists knew what they were denying. For, once again, the Aristotelian principle holds: *eadem est scientia oppositorum* – affirmations and their corresponding negations are one and the same knowledge; hence, in the days when there was some clarity about the affirmations, it was possible to enter the atheistical lists on behalf of clear-minded denials. In the mid-nineteenth century Ludwig Feuerbach was one such atheist: everything, he thought, that the theologian says about God is true; his atheism took the form that none of what the theologians say is a truth about *God* – all are truths about the human 'species-being', as he put it, and so in their theological form they are alienated truths, truths projected from the human on to the divine. You have therefore only to reverse subject and predicate – turn God, the subject for theology, into the 'divine' as predicate of the human – and the alienated truths of theology become truths repossessed in humanism; thus, paradoxically, do you realise all the truth of theology in its abolition as atheism: atheism for Feuerbach is Christian theology done *sub ratione hominis*.[2]

That, of course, is true flattery to the theologian, for in Feuerbach everything depends on the logically complete, and overtly theological, disjunction: either God or the human, but not both. Hence, it matters as much to Feuerbach as to the theologian which is affirmed. Indeed, so craven did he think Feuerbach's flattery of the theological to be that Karl Marx wished a plague to be visited on the disjunction itself, that is to say on the houses both of the theologian's God and of Feuerbach's humanist atheism, equally complicit did he think them to be in a 'theological' view of the world. Feuerbach, Marx said, can no more get his humanism going without the negation of God than the theologian can get his theism going without the negation of man. For the socialist, however,

the question of an *alien* being, a being above nature and man . . . has become impossible in practice. *Atheism*, which is the denial of this unreality, no longer has any meaning, for atheism is a *negation of God*, through which negation it asserts the *existence of man*. But socialism as such no longer needs such mediation.[3]

Karl Barth went even further than Marx in the exact specification of Feuerbach's theological parasiticalness, taking (it might be thought) unseemly pleasure in the recognition of Feuerbach as his own atheist familiar, for he belongs, Barth says, 'as legitimately as anyone, to the profession of modern Protestant theology':[4] in truth, *eadem est scientia oppositorum*. Feuerbach is a distinctly *Protestant* atheist.

[2] Feuerbach, *The Essence of Christianity*, 1.2, pp. 12 ff.
[3] See Karl Marx, *Early Writings*, trans. Rodney Livingstone and Gregor Benton, London: Penguin Books, 1975, p. 358 (emphasis original).
[4] Karl Barth, 'An Introductory Essay' to Feuerbach, *Essence of Christianity*, p. xi.

For this reason it is possible to sympathise with those theologians who long for a vigorous form of denial to grapple with, for it would reassure them in their hopes for a territory of contestation which has some sort of intellectual ultimacy about it; for theologians' interests of 'relevance' are served not alone on condition that God exists, but as much on the less exacting condition that there is thought on both sides to be some genuine argument to be settled as to *whether* God exists. Alas, for such today those good old times are long gone, and good-quality atheist opposition is hard to find. And if that is so it is perhaps because Christian theists have themselves abandoned the business of argument: if Christian theists themselves suppose that no argument is relevant to the business of religious belief, it can hardly be surprising if most atheists share their view of the matter, and pass theists by untroubled by theological challenge to their complacent agnostic indifference.

The converse is as evident, however: that what militant atheists there are today – a Richard Dawkins, or an A.C. Grayling – are unlikely to rouse many theists to the limits of their powers of contestation, and one suspects that Marx might be right after all, that the complicity between a certain kind of theist and the counterpart atheist, their common interest in the territory contested, is just too comfortable, too mutually parasitical, too like the staged contest of a modern wrestling match. There might be some little entertainment in the antics, but there is no real edge to the competition because little that matters hangs on its outcome.

And by way of illustrating this suspicion, a certain kind of generalisation suggests itself, derivable from the particular relation of Barthian theism with Feuerbachian atheism, whose character consists in that which obtains between an object and its image in a mirror: all the connections of thought are identical, but their relations are, as it were, horizontally reversed. The generalisation is that historically, many a philosophical, principled, not merely casual, atheism is the mirror-image of a theism; that they are recognisable from each other, because such atheisms fall roughly into the same categories as the limited theisms they reject; that they are about as interesting as each other; and that, since narrowly liberal or fundamentalist or conservative atheisms are no more absorbing than narrowly liberal, fundamentalist or conservative theisms, neither offers much by way of intellectual stimulus to the theologian.

And one reason for this atheistical failure of interest to the theologian is its failure of theological radicalness. Such atheists are but 'negative' theologians *manqué*: in a sense which I shall shortly clarify, they give shorter measure than good theologians do in the extent of what they deny. It is indeed extraordinary how theologically stuck in their ways some atheists are, and one might even speculate that atheists of this species have an interest in resisting such explorations of Christian faith and practice as would require the renewal of their rejection of it. One supposes that it must be upsetting for atheists when the target of their rejection moves; for in so far as a moving Christian target does upset the atheist, it reveals, depressingly, the parasitical character of the rejection. An intellectually static atheism can have no wish for an intellectually mobile theism.

Of course, the contrary proposition is equally plausible. There have always been Christian theisms which are parasitical upon forms of atheism, for they formulate a doctrine of God primarily in response to a certain kind of grounds for atheistic denial. In our time, the ill-named 'creationists' seem to offer but a craven reactionariness, trapped as they are into having to deny the very possibility of an evolutionary world, simply because they mistakenly suppose an evolutionary world could be territory left vacant for occupation only by atheists. Naturally, to think that a 'place' has to be found for God somewhere in the universe entails expelling a usurping occupant somewhere from it; and since the parasitical theist and atheist agree that evolutionary biology, or historical evidence, or cosmology, occupies the space where, were there a God, God ought to be instead, they are playing the same game, though – alas for the theist – on rules of the atheists' devising. Hence, the theists play it on the undemanding condition that they play on the losing team.

That sort of argument between theist and atheist is entirely profitless to either side, and it would seem to be of some serious cultural value, in a society which no longer seems to know how to argue about anything which might matter very fundamentally, if atheists could be encouraged to engage in some more adequate level of denying, for thus far they lag well behind even the *theologically* necessary levels of negation, which is why their atheisms are generally lacking in theological interest. One could go so far as to say that such atheists are, as it were, but theologians in an arrested condition of denial; in the sense in which atheists of this sort say God 'does not exist', the atheist has merely arrived at the theological starting point. As we have seen, theologians of the classical traditions, a pseudo-Denys, a Thomas Aquinas or a Meister Eckhart, simply agree about the disposing of idolatries, and then proceed with the proper business of doing theology and of engaging with its more radical denials . And that is why it has seemed to me to be theologically necessary to demand, of theists and atheists alike – for *eadem est scientia oppositorum* – that they re-learn what it might be to deny the existence of God, and that they learn to distinguish what they deny from an authentically 'classical' theism, for which the existence of God is in any case understood only on the other side of *every* denial.

'Kenotic' reason

But if such theisms and their counterpart negations in atheism seem equally to fail of intellectual radicalness, this will be so at least for the reason that their failure as answers can be traced back to the questions to which they purport to be the answers. For a 'scientific' answer which purports to displace the possibility of a genuinely theological question is bound to be as inappropriate as will be a spuriously theological answer to what is a genuinely scientific question. Fundamentalism of either sort, whether theistic or atheistic, will equally, and for the same reason, fail of radicalness, because neither can acknowledge the sort of question to which 'God exists' is the answer; and here we return to the argument of chapter six and to the case for saying that what is definitive of reason – as identifying the 'central' case of it – is its insistence upon a certain kind of question. I use the word 'insistence' here in a literal sense: there are questions which insist themselves upon the rational mind with the inevitability of the 'natural', so that if, without good grounds in logic, the legitimacy of such questions is denied, or the questions are arbitrarily side-stepped, something of our human nature is denied or evaded. And it is questions of that sort which determine the form, the 'argument-strategy', of rational proof of God.

At this point, then, it becomes clear that the failure of radicalness which unites the 'parasitical' atheist and the counterpart Christian believer in a common bond of intellectual complacency consists in a failure of nerve in respect of reason – a failure to concede to reason either its rootedness in our animal nature or its power of self-transcendence, or both. And it will also be clear by now that at the heart of my argument in this book is a proposition about the nature of reason which I have extracted from the thought of Thomas Aquinas. And that proposition is that we are animals who know God and that reason is *how* animals know God. To recap: I argued that for Thomas humans are 'essentially animals', and that our animality is essentially rational. We are not animals *plus* rationality. Rationality is the form of our animality, we are the sort of animals whose bodies are the bearers of significance. Bodiliness is the stuff of our intellectual being, as intellect is the form of our bodily stuff, and the conjunction is our 'rationality'. And so, as our rationality from one side is rooted in our bodily animality, so, on the other, reason has in its nature the capacity to surpass itself, for, as I have put it, reason exhausts itself as reason in its fulfilment as intellect. And I said further that reason thus 'abolishes itself in its self-realisation' in its entertaining a certain kind of question, for reason reaches its limit not in some final question-stopping answer but rather in a final answer-stopping question.

Proof comes into it on the one hand as the characteristically and centrally rational activity of demonstrating the necessity of that question, and on the other as the demonstration of the impossibility of taking full rational possession of what must count as its answer. For the answer could not have the form of a knowable 'something'. And so I said that on this account of it, reason is 'kenotic', for as it were from 'below' it completes itself in its self-emptying, apophatic, depletion in that which is 'above' it. We humans are rational precisely in so far as our animality thus opens up to that which unutterably exceeds its grasp – as it does in poetry and music in one way, but in our rationality narrowly conceived in the way of 'naming' that to which it opens up. For naming too is what animals do, but what they thus name is a mystery always beyond the power of the naming to capture. Reason ends where the mystery of creation begins; and they meet in the radicalness of the limit question it perforce must entertain.

A limit question

And that 'limit' question is: 'Why is there anything at all rather than nothing?' It is, Thomas thinks, a question the rational mind opens up to naturally, yielding to the pressure of its own native energies as reason, which is to wonder about causes.[5] This is the question with which 'reason' reaches its limits, for it is a question the answer to which must in the nature of things defeat our powers of comprehension, so that in its encounter with the necessity of asking that question, 'reason' achieves its apotheosis as 'intellect'. But now we must in turn interrogate the question itself, since in our times it is much doubted that it is a genuine question at all. For at the prospect of a question whose answer must be incomprehensible to us the mind might boggle, and we are constrained to ask: how unintelligible can a question be allowed to get? At any rate, degree and kind of 'unanswerability' would seem to be one test of intelligibility. As Wittgenstein says, 'doubt can exist only where there is a question: and a question only where there is an answer';[6] and how could an answer beyond our power of understanding be an answer? Moreover, in general it is thought – and in general it is true – that questions also, and not just answers, should be tested for sense, for, as Richard Dawkins rightly says, 'the mere fact that it is possible to frame a question does not make it legitimate or sensible to do so',[7] and being unanswerable might seem to

---

5 Aquinas, *In I Metaphysicorum*, lect. 3, 55.
6 Wittgenstein, quoted in Derek Parfit, 'Why anything, why this?', in *London Review of Books* 22.2, 22 January 1998, p. 24.
7 Richard Dawkins, *River Out of Eden*, London: Phoenix, 2001, p. 113.

be as clear-cut a way as any of a question's failing the test of legitimacy, however generously that test may be conceived. Smart, however, also an atheist, disagrees: 'I do think that there is something ultimately mysterious', he says, 'in the fact that the universe exists at all, and that there is something wrong with us if we do not feel this mystery',[8] even though, as he adds, it is a question 'which has no possibility of an answer'.[9] Hence, even if the question must be interrogated for sense, so must the test of unanswerability itself be interrogated, for it is neither self-evident *a priori* what kind of 'unanswerability' rules out a question's bearing sense and what does not, or that, on the contrary, every question you can seem to answer one way or the other does make sense.

On the one hand, then, just because you can answer a question it does not follow that the question is well asked, for crooked questions will yield deceiving answers. Fergus Kerr appropriately notes how the question 'Can a machine think?' may have all the appearance of innocence, but is in fact question-begging. The question makes sense only on the supposition that it is possible to conceive of an activity called 'thinking' independently of what body that activity occurs in, and that is already to suppose a challengeably 'Cartesian' and 'dualist' conception of 'thinking'.[10] The question could make no sense to Aristotle, for whom it is inconceivable that what humans do by way of thinking could be done otherwise than by animals with a certain kind of body, so that for him to answer 'yes' *or* 'no' would be equally misconceived,[11] just as to be forced to answer either way the counsel's question 'Have you stopped beating your wife yet?' is manifestly unfair. The question 'Can a machine think?' itself needs to be challenged rather than answered.

On the other hand, if it is to be said that the question 'Why anything?' is 'unanswerable' except in terms which defeat our powers of comprehension, we need to clarify in what way this is so. After all, an atheist who has persevered through all the preceding argument of this essay, and has so far been persuaded by the 'apophatic' emphases of that argument to

---

[8] Smart and Haldane, *Atheism and Theism*, p. 36.   [9] Ibid., p. 35.

[10] Fergus Kerr OP, *Theology after Wittgenstein*, Oxford: Blackwell, 1986, pp. 185–6.

[11] My guess is that an 'Aristotelian' answer to this 'Cartesian' question would in fact be: 'In a sense, yes; that is, in so far as, and to the extent that, a machine is a true replica of a human body, we can speak intelligibly of a machine replicating some aspects of "thinking"; and in a sense, no, because a machine is only ever a replica of a human body, so the machine's thinking is a more or less passable imitation of "thinking".' But you can get a sensible answer to the Cartesian question only by starting from a notion of 'thinking' which is intrinsically tied in with its relation to real human bodies, not by starting from a notion of thinking severed from any relation with either a human body or a machine. For on that account it is as sensible to ask, 'Can a human person compute?' as it is to ask, 'Can a machine think?' And that is plainly silly.

abandon a merely 'parasitical' anti-fundamentalism, may well be experiencing some degree of exasperation at what he will perceive to be the theist's evasiveness as to what it is that he is now expected to deny. In that exasperation he may very well be tempted to protest: 'It is all very well your embarking upon a project of re-educating me in what I am supposed to deny, but if you, the theist, won't affirm anything comprehensible at all, and you appear to resist doing so, then why do I, the atheist, need to do any denying in the first place, since you theologians have already done all the denying there is to be done? Does not your so-called "negative theology" amount to little more than a strategy of evasion which kills God off by a death of a thousand qualifications? You say that your question "How is it that anything exists?" yields the answer "God"; and you then say, "God exists", but only to add: "in no knowable sense of existence"; is "one", but you qualify: "not as countable in a series"; is "good", but not, you say, "on any scale", not even on the top of one. Might not your negative theologian just as well be an atheist as affirm so incomprehensible a God? Only give me something affirmed and I shall at last have something to deny. All you are doing is endlessly postponing God; so all I have to do is tag along while you get on with the denials I thought it was my job to deal in and wait until you actually affirm something, which, by the sound of your pseudo-Denys and Thomas and Eckhart, you are never going to get round to doing. What sense can there be to the question when on your own account there is so little sense or content to the answer?'

It has to be admitted that the objection has some force. The theist cannot be allowed to retreat to a position of theological post-modernism, a position of endless deferral, according to which there is only postponement, only *pen*ultimacy, an endlessly contingent 'otherness', no rest in any ultimate signifier which could stabilise the whole business of signification upon a foundational rock of fixed and determinate reference. But even if the theists resist so self-destructively defensive a ploy, are they not then forced back, as once before, on to the Derridean dilemma which we encountered in chapters 8 and 9: might not they now be differently accused – precisely because they do not want to go so far down the postmodern road of an intellectual nihilism – of a form of intellectual cheating, of attempting to eat their cakes and have them, as if, on the one hand, to say with Eckhartian negativity that God is a 'being transcending being and a transcending nothingness', and on the other still to insist, with unblushing affirmativeness, that *there is* one such? It is all very well, it might be said, to dramatise rhetorically high-sounding metaphors of 'abysses' and 'nothings' and 'being beyond being', but must not the theist insist upon a residual affirmation, slyly inserted and left lurking there, unexcised by all this negativity? Is there not an irreducible anomaly in saying that '*there is* something outside language'? For either the 'there is' is itself inside language and we can make sense of it but with the consequence that the 'something' must be inside language too, and so not God; or else the 'there is' is outside language, and *ex hypothesi* we can make no more sense of it than we can of the 'something'. The theist has got to have it one way or the other. But one way is the way of 'onto-theology'; the other leaves us with no language of existence in theological use. In short, either way the Nietzschean dilemma will eventually catch up with the negative theologian – if you want God, you have got to have grammar; or if not Nietzsche's, then Derrida's – you cannot both fully deconstruct grammar, that is, deny any ultimate signifier, and keep God. But this negative theology appears to be constrained both to say that 'God exists' is an ultimately undeconstructible existential affirmation, and to deconstruct, deny of possibility, any ultimate true existential statement, lest the divine existence should be left vulnerable to an idolatrous reduction to an onto-theological 'thinghood'.

As an atheist response to the theist, this line of attack, though promising, is not yet quite fair. There is something which the theist affirms – asking the question 'Why anything?' just is its affirmation – but it is something affirmed about the world, namely that the world is created. That, as we have observed Thomas to think, is our starting point for talking about God, and so long as we remain resolutely anchored in the implication of that starting point – that in speaking thus about the world the theist is always speaking of the ultimately ungraspable, that we do not know what God is – the theist can feel justified in all manner of talk about God, and can safely and consistently allow that everything true of creation, everything about being human, is in some sort grounds for a truth about God. For in saying that what the theist affirms is something 'about the world' we are not denying that the theist is talking about God: saying that the world is created is, on the contrary, how to talk about God. The negative theologian still has plenty to say about God, more than enough for the atheists to get their denying teeth into.[12] Negative theology does not mean that we are short of things to say about God; it means just that everything we say of God falls short of him.

A digression on Thomas's theological 'method'

But now we must entertain another sort of objection to the proposition that the argument-strategy of Thomas's proofs is shaped by the force of

---

[12] In short, there is a genuine argument to be had, for example, with those who reject theism on the grounds of its incompatibility with the existence and quantity of evil in the world.

the 'Why anything?' question. The objection here is less the systematic objection to the legitimacy of the question in principle, than exegetical, concerning its relevance in the context of Thomas's arguments. It will be contested that the question 'Why anything?' is Leibnizian in origin[13] and that it does not occur *in situ* where Thomas's arguments for the existence of God are formulated. And so it will be asked on what account of Thomas's actual text can my case for the strategically determining character of that question be made good. In answer to which objection it is necessary to take up two issues concerning the general character of Thomas's argument-strategy for a proof of God. The first issue is that if the question is not raised by Thomas in that form, on what grounds may one read his arguments for the existence of God in terms of it? And the second issue follows from the first: if you do read Thomas's argument-strategy in terms of the Leibnizian question, how is Thomas's procedure for proof of God to be distinguished from Leibniz's, superficially similar in general structure as they are? For both appear to argue for the existence of a 'necessary being' by inference from the contrasting contingency of the world – its existence rather than nothing – a contingency which appears to be what forces upon our minds the question, '*Why* is there anything at all?' in the first place.

It is convenient to take up the second issue first, and Mackie's discussion of Leibniz's argument-strategy helps to clarify the distinction between his and Thomas's: the distinction would appear to lie in the distinct conceptions of contingency which underlie them. For Leibniz, Mackie says, a thing's existence is contingent if it depends upon how things are, such that, had things been otherwise, that thing would not have existed. Hence, by contrast, an existence is necessary if it is not dependent upon how things are, for it would exist whatever states of affairs obtained. Now Mackie argues that Leibniz's argument for the existence of God relies upon the premise that the world as a whole is contingent in this sense, but that this premise

is not available: though we have some grounds for thinking that each part, or each finite temporal stretch, of the world is contingent in this sense upon something else, we have . . . no ground for thinking that the world as a whole would not have existed if something else had been otherwise; inference from the contingency of every part to the contingency of the whole is invalid.[14]

Be that conclusion as it may, the second account of contingency maintains that a thing's existence is contingent if and only if it might not have existed,

[13] See 'On the Ultimate Origination of Things', in *G. W. Leibniz: Philosophical Writings*, London: Dent, 1934, pp. 32–41.
[14] Mackie, *Miracle of Theism*, p. 84.

and a thing's existence is necessary if and only if it is not the case that it might not have existed, and this account of contingency and necessity appears to be Thomas's – as employed for example in his 'third way'. But, as Mackie says, to argue on this account of the contingency of the world as a whole to the existence of a necessary being requires showing that there *has to be* a necessary being, a proposition with which Thomas undoubtedly agrees. Of course, of such a being, *if* it exists, it has to be the case that its existence is necessary. But, Mackie argues – and here again Thomas agrees with him – it does not follow from the meaning of 'necessary being' that the proposition 'A necessary being exists' is a necessary truth. A thing's character of being 'necessary' is not, and cannot be, any part of an argument that it *does* exist, and, as Thomas says, Anselm's so-called 'ontological' argument, which appears to rely on this fallacious inference, must for that reason be invalid.[15]

It was Kant's contention that all forms of cosmological argument for the existence of God, including Leibniz's, must fail in virtue of their reliance on this fallacious inference underlying 'ontological' arguments.[16] But Kant's argument that *all* cosmological proofs must presuppose the invalid inference from a thing's character of being a necessary existent to the necessity of its existence would need to be investigated further, in view of Thomas's explicit disavowal of Anselm's fallacy in the article of the *Summa* which immediately precedes that in which the 'five ways' are expounded.[17] At any rate it is clear that for Thomas 'God exists' is a contingent truth, for its denial, though false, is not a contradiction; for, as we have seen, a thing's *actuality* (*esse*) is never derivable from any characterisation of its kind.[18] Indeed, it is precisely for this reason that God's existence cannot be demonstrated from any account of what God is and that any demonstration of God's existence would have to argue 'from the world' and not by the 'ontological' strategy. Such a demonstration will show that 'God exists' *is* true; and, he thinks, God's necessary existence can itself then be *further* demonstrated. Likewise, that there can be only one God can, he thinks, be demonstrated, even if (as we have seen) it would not be contradictory to think, as Hume surmised,[19] that there

---

[15] *ST* 1a q2 a2 *corp.*

[16] See Kant, *Critique of Pure Reason*, B 635–6.   [17] *ST* 1a q2 a2 *corp.*

[18] Incidentally, this suggests a further difference between Thomas and Kant, for Kant rejected the ontological argument on the grounds that 'existence is not a predicate'. As we have seen, Thomas maintains that existence in the sense of 'actuality' is a predicate, and, in that sense of actuality, is not reducible to that sense of 'exist' as the existential quantifier ('there is an *x*') which, of course, Kant and Thomas agree is not a predicate (as also Mackie, see *Miracle of Theism*, p. 83).

[19] David Hume, *Dialogues Concerning Natural Religion* V, ed. and introd. Norman Kemp Smith, Oxford: Clarendon Press, 1935, pp. 207ff.

might be many gods answering to a causal question about the world's existence – for, as we have seen Thomas to say, logically 'God' is not a proper name, but a *nomen naturae*, and so possesses a logically proper plural.[20] Thomas, for sure, thinks it false to say there are many gods; and he thinks that it *further* follows (easily enough) from a proof of God's existence that there could only be one God, since neither any one of a team of gods taken severally, nor any team of gods taken collectively, could stand as a good answer to the question, 'Why is there anything at all?' In any case, it is clear that, in so far as Kant is right that cosmological arguments such as Leibniz's depend upon the invalid inference of the ontological argument, Thomas's proofs are to be differentiated from that of the eighteenth-century rationalist philosopher. Thomas's, at least, do not so depend. Thomas's 'Why anything?' question arises from a sense of the world's contingency quite different from Leibniz's.

Which brings us to the second issue, now long postponed, concerning how to place Thomas's arguments for the existence of God within the structure of the exposition of the *Summa Theologiae*, such that there would appear to be good grounds for reading the five ways in terms of the 'why anything?' question. Milbank suggested that one of the reasons for doubting that the 'five ways' presented in *Summa Theologiae* 1a q2 a3 could have been intended to be full-blown apodeictic proofs is their manifestly cursory character. Moreover, if it mattered to Thomas as much as I claim it did that rational proof is possible, it is said[21] again that he could reasonably have been expected to provide us with more than the compressed, elliptical and, on his own standards of argument, clearly insufficiently articulated, *schemata* for argument that we find at the outset of his *Summa*. And it is true that, as set out in that work, the 'five ways' look more like an *aide-memoire* for proofs than the adequately complex and full-blooded exposition which would be required to be convincing as 'stand-alone' arguments. Nonetheless, there may well be a practical reason for this which has to do with the pedagogical purposes of the *Summa Theologiae* and one not bearing the weight of theological significance which Milbank attaches to Thomas's brevity. This vast *Summa* is often represented as a beginner's manual, intended for students setting out on the process of theological learning, and so it is – as Thomas says in the general Prologue to the work, he intends it *ad eruditionem incipientium*. But if this is its general purpose it is perhaps better to see it as a manual for the *teachers* of beginners than as a textbook for the use of beginners themselves, for

---

[20] See above, pp. 172–3.
[21] For example, by my colleague in the Cambridge Faculty of Divinity, Dr Anna Williams, in private correspondence.

that general Prologue makes clear that the revisionary purpose his work is meant to serve is principally curricular in character,[22] that of setting out the ordering of the questions in a manner which is more coherently teachable than is done in the standard teaching texts available at the time; presumably Thomas has in mind the unhelpfully haphazard structure of Peter Lombard's *Sentences*. But if that is its purpose, then it is perfectly understandable that Thomas should be more concerned with argument structures than with the detailed exposition of the arguments themselves, for he could expect teachers to fill in those details which would be beyond the knowledge and experience of beginners. Hence, even if, taken on their own, the expositions of the 'five ways' are unconvincingly abbreviated, it is perhaps fairer to read them more as amounting to heads of argument, outlines for a five-fold argument-strategy, than as arguments proper in which would be set out in full exposure the connective tissue of inference, suppressed as it is in the text as it stands.

Secondly, it might further be conceded that in any case Thomas does not see the validity of the particular proofs he sets out in *Summa Theologiae* 1a q2 a3 as having any crucial role to play within the theological and methodological architectonic which is the *Summa* as a whole. This is not to say, however, that the arguments thus elliptically set out are not valid proofs, or at least proof-structures, or that Thomas did not consider them so; only that the question whether they are valid or not does not matter, as it were, from the point of view of the *Summa*'s 'architecture'. But that, in turn, raises the question what the 'architectonic' considerations are within which the 'five ways', and their relatively cursory character, fit.

We derive one kind of answer to this question if we suppose, as I have supposed throughout this essay, that what matters to Thomas from the point of view of faith, and of its theological articulation, is not that any particular proofs of the existence of God are known to be valid, but that the possibility of such proof is not denied on grounds of faith. If that is so, then it might very well be thought sufficient to the purpose for a theologian merely to sketch the outlines of the sort of argument which

---

[22] 'We have come to the conclusion that beginners in this learning are in multiple ways handicapped . . . in part because of the multiplication of pointless questions, articles and arguments; in part also because what such [students] need for the purpose of acquiring knowledge are not transmitted in accordance with the discipline's [own proper] ordering, but as required by [the ordering of] books commented on, or as the opportunities for disputation dictate; and partly because of the frequent repetition, the tedium and confusion which [those books] generate in the minds of their hearers.' – 'Consideravimus namque huius doctrinae novitios . . . plurimum impediri: partim quidem propter multiplicationem inutilium quaestionum, articulorum et argumentorum; partim etiam quia ea quae sunt necessaria talibus ad sciendum, non traduntur secundum ordinem disciplinae, sed secundum quod requirebat librorum expositio, vel secundum quod se praebebat occasio disputandi; partim quidem quia eorundem frequens repetitio et fastidium et confusionem generabat in animis auditorum.' *ST Prologus.*

could be considered to do the theological job required, and what would not: Anselm's 'proof' will not do,[23] and no good theological purpose is served by supposing that it will. But the arguments presented as the 'five ways' illustrate how and where human reason unaided by grace serves a theological purpose, exercising its powers, as reason characteristically does, in formal demonstration of God from creatures. But there is another kind of answer, more positively supportive of the reading of the 'five ways' as intended to be formally valid demonstrations, and that answer involves conceding that their probative value was never intended to be read off from the abbreviated text of *Summa Theologiae* 1a q2 a3 taken on its own.

For there is much to be said for the view that the article containing the 'five ways' is intended merely as the point of entry into a circle of highly complex argumentation which is completed only with the discussion of God as Creator, some forty-three questions further on in the *Prima Pars*, and that the reader is not expected to read the 'five ways' as having any validity as proofs except within that complex circle of argument taken as a whole. On one score at least this is clear. As I said in chapter 1, the demotic optimism of the five times repeated refrain, *et hoc omnes dicunt Deum*, cannot be conceded with any degree of plausibility at least until it has been shown, to any reader at all, Christian or otherwise, that what the 'five ways' have shown to exist is also extensionally equivalent to what 'all people' believe God to be, namely the Creator: and we get no argument to this effect until question 44. Moreover, even that argument will be insufficient to convince the Christian believer until it is shown that, whether as 'first cause' or even as 'Creator', the God thus demonstrated to exist is extensionally equivalent to the trinitarian God of Christian faith; and the demonstration of that is not begun until question 27. In short, if Thomas does think, as I believe he does, that a principal methodological purpose of the 'five ways' is to articulate a primitive meaning for the *ratio Dei*, constituting, as I argued in chapter 2, the formal object of *sacra doctrina* itself, then, from that point of view alone, the arguments presented in question 2 article 3 could not be fairly conceived as intended to 'stand on their own' for any good theological purpose whatever. They serve the purpose that rational proof may serve only within that wider philosophical and theological context.

Contingency

But, from the point of view of the thesis of this essay, there is the more important consideration that unless they are taken in conjunction with the much later discussion of creation, Thomas did not mean the 'five ways'

---

[23] As Thomas argues in *ST* 1a q2 a1 *corp.*

to be taken as valid proofs at all. Haldane comments: 'The core issues in these proofs are those of existential and causal dependence. Such themes place them firmly within the tradition of cosmological speculation as to why there is anything rather than nothing and what the source of the universe might be.'[24] And it is just here that we return to the question 'Why is there anything rather than nothing?' as being fundamental both to the argument-strategy of the 'five ways' as proofs and to Thomas's conception of God as Creator. For it is a question which gets us to the point of seeing the world as created; that is to say, as standing in that relation of absolute contingency to there being nothing at all which constitutes the 'act of existence', *esse*. It is for this reason that the question leads us to the point at which we know that we should have to say of what answers to it, that it itself is *esse* without qualification – *ipsum esse subsistens*, as Thomas says. And, as we have seen, as far as Thomas is concerned, this 'primitive' understanding of God as *ipsum esse subsistens* is the understanding of the God of Exodus, the 'I am', now reconceived in explicit terms as the Creator of all things 'out of nothing'. It is that God whose existence is shown by the 'five ways', the sense and purpose of which proofs are incomplete except in that connection; and, crucial to that understanding of creation, and so of the strategy of the five ways, is how we are to construe the contingency of the world in its character of createdness.

If that is so, then we may return to the question asked earlier: what is the minimum the atheist has to deny if his denials are to be worth the theologian's bother entertaining? And the answer is going to have to be that the atheist's minimum denial is of the validity of the question itself, 'Why is there anything at all?' Once you admit that question you are already a theist. For since any question which is not merely idle must have an answer, you have conceded, in conceding that the question is intelligible, that there is an answer: the world is created out of nothing. For if it is a valid question – that is to say, if nothing in the nature of the question itself places it beyond the bounds of sense – then human reason by the very fact of asking it has already been placed outside the universe of what there is, *whatever* there is: reason is, as it were, displaced, forced out of its natural, intra-mundane situatedness, forced by this question to confront the mystery that there is anything at all.

What the question's legitimacy expresses, therefore, is a sense of the world's radical contingency – there might have been nothing at all, so its existence must have been brought about. But to get at the precise form of that contingency which forces us to conclude that the world has been brought about, we should note that our everyday notions of contingency

---

[24] Smart and Haldane, *Atheism and Theism*, p. 133.

cannot capture the sense of the *world's* contingency as such, for they are, as Mackie notes, intra-mundane; they concern the contingency of things and events *in* the world. And even in that intra-mundane connection contingency is a pluriform concept. For how things 'might have been otherwise' can come in kinds and degrees. For example, Denys's height is contingent: he happens to be 5′8½″ tall. But it is easy to imagine his being 5′9″ tall, though he is not and never will be; or his being 5′8″ tall, which he is not but about forty-five years ago was. So he is 5′8½″ tall, but he might not have been. His being the height he is is a 'contingent' fact about Denys.

Denys's height, we may say, is very contingent in that it is only very loosely connected with his identity as a person. It would not be hard to think of Denys being 5′8″, because there would be little difficulty in accepting that Denys would still be the same person if he were half an inch shorter than he is. But is Denys contingently English? Suppose you thought he was Irish and then I tell you he is English. This might be a surprise; and you might change your view of Denys a bit more than if you thought he was 5′8″ and he turns out to be half an inch taller, because his nationality is somehow less 'contingently', more 'necessarily', tied up with his being him than his height is. Then again, Denys is heterosexual. But is he contingently heterosexual? Perhaps there is a version, recognisably still of Denys, which is gay, but it is harder to think that Denys is so contingently heterosexual as he is 5′8½″ tall or English, for it would at least be less than clear that Denys could be otherwise in sexual orientation in quite the same casual way in which he could be otherwise in height or nationality.

Next, Denys is male. But is he contingently male? A human being is contingently male or female. But is this human being, Denys, who is male, contingently male? Children, at least, give thought to this question and puzzle, not just about the answer, but also about the question itself: 'What if I had been born female or male?' (whichever is the counter-factual). The question puzzles because though, perhaps, we think we can think of ourselves as being otherwise in gender, we can feel uneasy about thinking thus: would I really be the same person were I female? Then again, how are we to think about the question 'Suppose I were my sister?' To be sure, as questions go, that has got all the way to the incoherent end of the scale of oddity, for we can only most idly wonder how the I which I now am could possibly be the same I which my sister is. Were I my sister, I would be my sister, not I. And so on, for we can easily think of other problematically odd cases: 'Suppose I were an angel?' For my part I do not think I am at all contingently human; I could not be an angel, for there is no angelic 'I' which could be continuous with the 'I' I now am. Therefore, Denys is not at all contingently human; necessarily not his sister; he is perhaps contingently male; certainly contingently heterosexual; even more loosely attached to his nationality, and it is only with the very slackest of threads that Denys is attached to his height. There are degrees of contingency and necessity.

All these degrees of contingency and necessity betoken degrees to which my selfhood and identity, given that I exist, are tied in with different features of the world – sometimes crucially, sometimes more or less incidentally. The 'scale' of contingency and necessity could be said, therefore, to be 'essential' – rather than, as I shall shortly explain, properly 'existential' – because the degree of contingency and necessity in question has to do with how far something true of who or what I am is tied in with my being just this, or just this kind of, being. In short, all these kinds of contingency are of Mackie's 'Leibnizian' sort, since in every case their contingency consists in some things in, or features of, the world being the way they are in so far as other things are the way they are. But how far do we move on to a different scale of contingency with the question 'What if *I* did not exist?' Children find this question endlessly puzzling, but being somewhat less egotistic in adulthood than children customarily are, adults can easily imagine a world without them in it, and one comes to admit that it would hardly be different at all from the one I am in, as with age one is increasingly caused to contemplate approaching expiry. And when that happens, despiriting as the thought is to one's sense of self-importance, it should not take long before the world closes up on the gap left behind by my demise. Were I not to have existed, there would have been very little missing (and no doubt even less for many to regret). I conclude that I, my existence, is very contingent indeed, the degree of contingency being measured by what would be missing if I ceased to exist. But that there would be *something* missing, if not very much, means that the contingency of my existence is still of the 'Leibnizian' kind. Even if, antecedently to my existing, there was no necessity for me at all (thus: Denys would not be missing from anything had I never existed) still, given that I exist, certain necessities do obtain: things other than me could not have existed if I had not: for example, my children. And things now true could not have been true had I not existed: for example, my mother could not have been Denys's mother.

An 'existential' question

It follows that even the question, 'What if I did not exist?' is still a question concerning the nature of what there is, for all its apparently existential character. For the explanation of my existence is still tied in with features of the world as it is; it is still an existence to be explained against the background of what other beings there are, and what kind of beings they are. I am, as it were, part, if only an insignificant one, of the world's actual story, and so even this question remains on the scale of 'essential' contingency and necessity – for my having existed is still a state of affairs, and my ceasing to exist is another state of affairs. But finally, what are we to say about that ultimately odd question: 'What if *nothing at all* existed?' – or, in other words: 'Is the world as such contingent?' The answer to this question has to be that the world – everything that exists – is absolutely, in every possible respect, and awesomely contingent; but that it is contingent in a purely 'existential' way in that it is from this contingency that we derive our primitive notion of 'existence' itself, what Thomas calls *esse*. And we can see the nature of this radical contingency from the fact that the answer to the question 'Why anything?' could not be provided by anything counting as, in any ordinary sense, an 'explanation'. There simply cannot be an 'account' – in the ordinary sense, an 'explanation' by reference to antecedent states of affairs – by way of answer to the question 'What if nothing at all existed?' because the 'What if . . . ?' part of it means, 'What state of affairs would have obtained had nothing at all existed?', and obviously no state of affairs of any kind would have obtained if nothing at all had existed. If not very much would be missing if I did not exist, nothing at all would be missing if nothing at all existed; because, to be missed, there has to be something that what is missing is missing *from*. So the question itself seems to spin off the world entirely, as having no purchase on anything at all *in* it.

It seems that at any rate this is what Thomas thinks, and that it is precisely in its 'spinning off the world' that the question acquires both the character of the properly theological and of the properly existential. It is the properly 'existential' question because, as we saw in chapter nine, we get at the notion of existence, *esse*, in its proper sense, precisely as that which stands against there being nothing at all, occupying a territory divided by no 'logical space' from 'nothing'. It is, therefore, the centrality of this *esse* to Thomas's metaphysics which places the 'Why anything?' question at the centre of his arguments for the existence of God. For it is this *esse*'s standing in absolute, unmediated, contrast with nothing at all which gets to the contingent heart of creation, and to the heart of the sense in which creation is contingent.

And it is the properly theological question because Thomas took the view that the very first thought which leads to God is the most primitive thought of all, one which is ultimately amazing: the thought that though there might have been nothing, and though there can be no possible *reason* supplied why there should be anything, nonetheless, something exists. And this is the 'first' theological thought in two senses: it is 'first', in that it arises out of the most primitive and, as one might say, childish of questions, the sort of question which, by education and other kinds of training, we can be got to be too sophisticated to entertain, or else, by means of a very common form of miseducation, we can be got to confuse with ordinary requests for an explanation concerning what there is. And it is 'first' also because it lies at the root of all human perception of God. And the drift of theological education, as Thomas envisages it in his *Summa Theologiae*, is not towards learning and adult wisdom, to scientific explanation, but back as far as we can go towards conscious childhood, there to recover that all too elementary and awesome thought: there might have been nothing at all. So *why* is there anything?

Which is why it is also the most radical causal question you can ask. But now it is important to attend to just how extreme is the oddity of this question in respect of what could count as its answer, for there may be some imprudently optimistic Christian apologists who unwisely suppose that, on the contrary, it is just another perfectly reasonable and ordinary request for an explanation in terms of causes. If we can sensibly ask, 'How has this kitten come about?' and sensibly answer, 'Because of the unruly things its parents got up to a couple of months ago'; and if we can sensibly ask: 'How is it that there are such things as cats at all?' and give a sensibly evolutionary answer explaining the emergence of the species 'cat' from whatever cats emerged from; and if we can sensibly ask how it is that we have the sort of world in which evolutionary processes occur and answer in terms of very general geophysical characteristics of the universe; if we can answer all these questions about how it is that there is this or that bit of the universe; and if we can ask how it is that we have the sort of universe that we have rather than any other, and explain that in terms of its initial conditions, why must it not make sense to ask the same of *all* of it, 'How is it that there is anything rather than nothing?', and name the answer the 'cause of the universe'? If we can do physics, why can we not do theology?

A legitimate question

And in response to the imprudently optimistic Christian apologist it becomes important to distinguish two argument-strategies for contesting the existence of God, which consist in two ways of contesting the theist's way of posing the question 'Why anything?' These are two ways of being an atheist along the lines which I noted earlier when I distinguished between its 'parasitical' and the 'non-parasitical' forms. The first, represented by Dawkins and, as we shall see, Russell, simply refuses to allow the question itself any sort of legitimacy. The second, represented (as we have seen) by Smart, allows the question but cannot see how any structure of valid argument could possibly get you to the answer 'God'. The first says the question does not make sense. The second admits that the question makes sense but denies that God is the answer to it. Now I shall not in this essay address this second form of atheism at all, for, as I have repeatedly insisted, the question with which this essay is concerned is whether there are grounds for ruling out in principle the possibility of rational proof, whether that ruling out is on the authority of reason or of faith. It is no concern of this essay to consider the validity of any *particular* arguments for the existence of God, Thomas's or anyone else's – hence, the very specific case mounted against such proofs in Thomas by Kenny,[25] or the more general arguments pressed against all forms of proof by the likes of Mackie and Smart, form no part of my agenda. It is with those atheists who contest the legitimacy of the question that we must be concerned.

[25] Anthony Kenny, *The Five Ways*, London: Routledge & Kegan Paul, 1969.

12   Refusing the question

We must therefore now ask, is the question 'Why anything?' legitimate? Is it, as some say, less a legitimate question than a question-begging question, a philosophically disguised version of the 'wife-beating' question? For it would seem that those who wish to deny the legitimacy of the question do so because they too assume, as I do, that *if* you may legitimately ask it, then it has to have an answer. *If* it has an answer, then the name of the answer would have to be 'God', for the answer would bear the name of the 'Creator' of all things, visible and invisible, 'out of nothing'. Of course, I should say that *if* 'God' is the name of the answer, then, though the question is intelligible to us, the answer could not be – but the atheistic opponent would say that it is just because the answer could not be intelligible to us that the question lacks sense. To which I would respond: if the question makes sense then the sense it makes *requires* that the answer must lie beyond our comprehension. But that does not settle the matter, for the atheist will still demand to know why it is a question which I am compelled to ask, and so am constrained thus to answer. Even more, why should I be required to concede that the question makes sense at all?

And, of course, among those for whom the question does not make sense is Bertrand Russell, who maintained on a famous occasion in discussion with Frederick Copleston on the BBC Third Programme that all you can say about the world, however it has come about, is that it is 'just there, that's all'.[1] There cannot be a question 'How come there is *anything* there?' because you could not give any account of the answer, the business of accounting for things belonging within the world; there is no question which can have a purchase on anything which might count as the cause of it. Clearly, that is something to be argued about as theist does with atheist. For Thomas it is an intelligible question, one the answer to which would bear the name 'God'.

But Russell's resistance to this argument-strategy seems to this extent justified. All these questions about items in the universe either have their

---

[1] In *The Existence of God*, ed. John Hick, London: Macmillan, 1964, p. 175.

answers in terms of other parts of the universe, or else explain why we have the sort of universe we have rather than all the other possible universes:[2] that is what it means to say that they have to do with the explanation of *what* there is, and so answers to the different question, 'Why is there *this* universe?' One bit explains another and we could grasp all the explanations required if we had enough information about all the parts of it. But Russell says that we cannot explain there being anything at all rather than nothing at all in that sort of way; at any rate we cannot explain the absolutely contingent fact of there being anything at all in terms of how so far we have used the word 'cause', because it is not possible to get the notion of 'cause', of which we know the meaning only from our experience *in* the world, to do any work, to carry any meaning when used *of* the universe itself. The statement '*x* causes there to be something rather than nothing' collapses, Russell says, into nonsense: for neither the variable '*x*', nor the verb 'caused there to be' can possibly bear any meaningful substitution when used of everything there is. Hence, it would seem that the question 'Why anything?' is question-begging in the wife-beating manner. For to suppose that there is such a question to be asked about everything is already to suppose that it would make sense to speak of a 'cause' of everything; and it is Russell's view that 'cause' cannot bear any such sense. In this conclusion, of course, Russell shares common ground with Kant, for whom 'so employed, the principle of causality, which is only valid within the field of experience, and outside this field has no application, nay, is completely meaningless, would be altogether diverted from its proper use'.[3]

It may seem surprising to some theists that Thomas was rather more in sympathy with Russell's view of this than with the imprudently optimistic Christian apologist. At any rate he would have agreed with Russell to this extent, that the question 'What accounts for this cat?' is of a wholly different kind from 'What accounts for there being anything?' And he would have agreed with Russell's reasons: for if our ordinary causal questions about particular bits of the universe are answerable in terms of other bits of it, the trouble with the question 'Why is there anything at all?' is that it is in the nature of the question that you have run out of bits of the universe in terms of which to give an answer. And that is just another way of saying what I said earlier, namely that if nothing existed nothing would be missing, for there would be nothing for it to be missing from. Hence, in the same sense in which we can understand questions in the

---

[2] Of course, one possible answer to that last question might very well be that all the possible universes actually exist. But even if that is true, there could still be an explanation of why that is so.

[3] Kant, *Critique of Pure Reason*, B664, p. 528.

form 'Why is there *this* rather than *that?*', we cannot understand what would count as an answer to the question 'Why is there *anything* rather than *nothing?*'

Moreover, it is clear that for Thomas the question at the very least lies at the limits of logical oddity, and just how odd can be best understood from its eccentric syntax, from the curious logic of the 'rather than' or – and here we return for the last time to the question – of 'difference'. As we have seen, we can get such relational expressions going when we can supply symmetrical values for the variables p and q in the expression 'p rather than q': for example, 'red rather than green'. The 'rather than' has the force of an intelligible contrast because red and green are both colours, and so we know what they differ *as*. But what is to be made of the 'p rather than q' if 'red' is substituted for p and 'Thursday' for q? – for it would seem odd to consider what 'red' and 'Thursday' differ *as*. All the same, as I suggested in chapter ten, no created difference between two things, properties or descriptions, however diverse, is beyond all possible containment within some context which could make sense of how they differ, and since I happen to think of days of the week as having colours, in that context it makes perfectly good sense to contemplate the disjunction 'red rather than Thursday', though admittedly it is the rather special one in which Thursdays are blue. But eccentric as the 'rather than' has become in this case, an ultimate oddity is inflicted upon the 'rather than' if you substitute 'anything whatever' as a value for p and 'nothing' as a value for q. Has the 'rather than' any meaning left? Is it still intelligible? In a way, yes, it is intelligible, it has the force of a very radical sort of 'might have been', of an existential contingency pushed to the very limit. A thing which is red, like a letter-box in the UK, might have been green, as letter-boxes are in Ireland, but there are no doubt good reasons why they are red in the UK and green in Ireland, some prior states of affairs – which account for the colours they are – providing a kind of 'causal narrative'. But if we could imagine that rather than there being anything at all there might have been nothing at all, we have, indeed, some force of contrast going for this 'might have been' but not one to be accounted for in terms of antecedent states of affairs, no possible background context to make sense of it, no explanatory causal narrative, for *a fortiori* there is nothing left to account for the fact that there is something rather than nothing, no bit of the world there functioning to explain the existence of things, but only 'nothing'. And 'nothing', as we have seen Thomas to say, is not a peculiar sort of causally explanatory 'something'; it is not an antecedent condition; it is certainly not the cosmologist's 'random fluctuations in a vacuum'; neither, alternatively, is there some specialised theological sense which might give force to that sort of 'out of' which is 'out of nothing'; the '*ex*' of '*ex nihilo*' means, Thomas says, just the contrary: the negation negates the 'out of' itself, as if to say, 'We have a making here, but no "out of",[4] no antecedent conditions, so no process, no event; an "after", but no "before".' It is just for this reason that the notion of a 'cause of everything' strains at the lines of continuity with our ordinary, intra-mundane, explanatory employments of cause with a force such that, for Russell, it has there broken free of its moorings altogether. And if Thomas would resist taking the conclusion to that extreme, at least his sympathies, one would guess, are nearer to Russell than to the imprudently optimistic Christian apologist.

That said, for Thomas, Russell's conclusion is one step ahead of the case which supports it. For Russell's saying that 'that the world is is just a fact' is itself questionable as to its epistemological standing. When by way of answer to the question 'How is it that anything at all exists?' you say, as Russell does, 'It's just a fact', your answer is not itself an empirically 'factual' answer to a question concerning what the facts are, because you are not asking any sort of empirical, factual question. As Wittgenstein makes clear in the *Tractatus*, there is no possible sense of 'fact' in which 'that there is anything at all' can be a fact, Russellian 'brute' or otherwise. It is clear enough, even, or perhaps especially, on Russell's account, that 'that the world is' cannot be a 'fact'. For it is on his account that a 'fact' is, and can only be, what some true statement states concerning something *in* the world, for 'facts' need contexts to be facts *in*, and 'nothing' is not a context. Moreover, if not a 'fact', neither is 'It just is' an explanation, as if, accepting the reasonableness of the question 'What accounts for there being anything?', it offers the answer 'Nothing' by way of rival to the theistic answer 'God'. On the contrary, as we have seen, it is a refusal of legitimacy to the question itself; it is to say that there is nothing to the question, there is no question to answer. The question does not arise.

But the question does arise, at any rate in the sense that it is a question which gets asked; for human beings ask questions, they 'wonder at causes', as Thomas says,[5] and ought not be stopped doing so prematurely. They ask 'Why anything?' with seeming intelligibility, so that if you are to rule the question out, that is to say, proscribe it, it would seem reasonable to ask on what grounds it should be refused legitimacy: you cannot without some grounds for doing so declare an end to discussion by ruling it out just by *fiat*, for that is to reduce the refusal to no more than saying, 'It's just a fact, and *that* it's just a fact is just a fact', which is to lapse into the merely assertoric. And for the matter of that, *quod gratis asseritur gratis negatur*. For which reason, if the world's existence is not *just*

---

[4] *ST* 1a q45 a1 ad3.   [5] Aquinas, *In I Metaphysicorum*, I, lect.1, 35.

a fact – because not a 'fact' at all – then neither is the question whether its existence does or does not need an explanation a matter of free evaluation, as if anything at all which is not a question of 'fact' is a question of how you choose to view things. The question arises as a causally explanatory question – it has grammatically the same shape that demands for an explanation of events in the world have – and to that extent the question retains its lines of continuity with all the causally explanatory questions which lead to it. But its logical oddity lies in its self-cancelling character: for we know this much at least about what must count as its answer, that the bringing about of anything 'out of nothing' cannot be any kind of causal *process* such that any kind of causal law governs it, for it is not in any sense a 'process'. Hence, if, being a causal question, the answer to it must have the character of a cause, we have, in thus answering the question, lost control over the understanding of the causality involved.

It is, moreover, important to understand correctly what it is that we could not understand about the nature of the divine causality: our 'loss of control' is such as to make it irrelevant what *kind* of causal explanation is in question. It may very well be true that, as Swinburne says,[6] the divine causality is best understood on the model of human, intentional, 'agent' causality, rather than on the model of efficient, natural, causality; and it may very well be true that, as Kerr says,[7] Thomas's model of efficient causality is in any case nearer to our contemporary conceptions of 'agent causality' than to that of a post-Humean efficient causality. But either way we would have to enter the same apophatic reserve in ascribing causality to God – and here Mackie appears to agree with Thomas. As he says, it is only 'by ignoring such key features [of human intentional activities as their embodiment, as their being fulfilled by way of bodily changes and movements which are causally related to the intended result, and so as having a causal history] that we get an analogue of the supposed divine action'.[8] By the time you have performed the necessary apophatic surgery on this 'agent causation' as predicated of God, there is no more left to it than in the case of any other causality in need of surgical reduction as predicated of God. Indeed, the same is left, whatever one's causal model, namely whatever it is that answers to the causal question, 'Why anything?' Whatever our model of causality, we know that we do not know in what way God is a 'cause'. We know this not because we do understand what kind of cause God is, and so know that God is not a cause in any ordinary sense. On the contrary, it is because we know only what kinds

---

[6] Richard Swinburne, *The Existence of God*, Oxford: Oxford University Press, 1979, pp. 130ff.
[7] Kerr, *After Aquinas*, pp. 46–8.   [8] Mackie, *Miracle of Theism*, p. 100.

of cause there are in creation that we have to concede the mind's defeat in respect of the divine causality. Whatever 'grip' theological language has on anything at all it has on the world, and on a question which arises about its existence, a question which is the expression of a kind of ultimate astonishment: it might not have been at all, and that it is has been brought about. That is not, and could not be, just a 'fact' *in* the world; nor is it just a fact *about* it. But if, as I have said, an atheist is to offer anything more to the debate than to brush the question 'Why anything?' aside with a merely rhetorical gesture of refusal, we should need to hear of a reason for denying its legitimacy.

And the main reason for doing so is, as we have seen, that the question is said to involve the circularity of the wife-beating question: that it presupposes an answer to what it purports to ask about. The question, I have said, is 'causal' in shape. And it is true that if you can sensibly *ask* a causal question about the world then you have presupposed that a causal *answer* concerning the world makes sense, and you have got God in one move; or at least you have got to a point where, given a number of subsequent moves, what is recognisably the God of Christian belief can be shown to exist. But, the argument goes, at least since Kant we have known that there is reason to doubt – if no more than that – that a causal answer concerning the world could make sense. You cannot, therefore, without circularity press the case for saying that a causal answer about the world *does* make sense on the strength of an assumption that the question 'Why anything?' is legitimate. In argument what is merely assumed has no strength at all.

The case for denying the question's legitimacy would therefore seem to rest on a general epistemological ground, namely that causal language does not, because it could not, have any application to the world's existence as such. And such a ground is clearly contestable in principle. After all, if it involves a circularity to rest a case for saying that causal language does have application to existence as such on the grounds that the question 'Why anything?' is legitimate, it is but to traverse the same vicious circle in the opposite direction to rest the case for causal language's *not* having application on the grounds that the question is not legitimate. Furthermore, if any presumption is to be made on either side, it is that the case against the question's legitimacy has to be made out in such general and essentially contestable terms as Kant's critical rationalism, given the *prima facie* reason for supposing its legitimacy. For *prima facie* – that is to say, other things being equal – there is nothing to be said for ruling out a question, unless there is an overwhelming reason in principle for doing so, if, as in this case, that question lies so obviously in continuity with the sort of intra-mundane causal questions human beings naturally persist in asking about the world. And this antecedent probability that the *question* is legitimate survives, notwithstanding the fact that the *answer* is known in advance to break the links of continuity with those less radical causal questions, placing the answer beyond the reach of our powers of comprehension. What is at stake here – in one way or another it is the central issue of this essay – is the conflict between two forms of theological 'agnosticism', that of Kant and that of Thomas Aquinas.

Apophaticism or agnosticism?

It is a conflict in which the opposing sides occupy some common ground. Thomas and Kant contest the common territory of the unknowability of God. For both, God could not be the cause of all that is in the sense in which anything in the world is a cause. For both, then, what a cause in the world explains could not in the same sense of 'explanation' be what God's existence explains – neither Thomas nor Kant has any greater need for God as an explanatory *hypothesis* than did Laplace. For both, what reason knows is all the world needs by way of explanation as to *how* it is, and God is not something known in any of the ways in which the world needs to be known; except that, for Thomas, the mystery *that* it is at all compels upon reason an acknowledgement that its deficiency is already theological: but not for Kant.

Even in thus differing, however, Thomas and Kant still occupy some apparent common ground, though it is now narrowing down. For what their agreement thus far amounts to is a shared denial that God is a possible object of knowledge in any of the ways in which created things are. For Kant, speculative reason's falling short of God consists in the impossibility that the transcendental conditions of human knowledge and agency – the conditions of the possibility of our knowing the world and of acting as free agents within it – could themselves be an object of our knowledge and agency in the world. Hence, they cannot be an object of knowledge at all; not one arrived at, therefore, even by inference, whether from the nature of things, or from the fact of the existence of things rather than of nothing. And it is just here that Thomas's theological apophaticism parts company with Kant's rationalist agnosticism. For whereas Kant's agnosticism is the proposition that God is unknowable to reason in the sense that no speculative inference from the world could get you to God, Thomas's apophaticism begins with the proposition that God can be demonstrated to exist, but that what such inference to God succeeds in showing is precisely the unknowability of the God thus shown. The difference would thus appear to be this: that for Thomas, what the proofs prove is that God's existence could not be an object of thought; whereas for Kant, *because* God could not be an object of thought, there can be no showing that God exists.

For which reason Kant must rule out the legitimacy in principle of the question 'Why is there anything at all?', and Thomas has no need to rule it out in order to meet Kant's agnostic condition that God could not be 'an object of thought', and the difference between them now turns out to be a difference concerning the nature of the divine unknowability, of the possibilities of inference, and, in general, of reason as such. What for Thomas is an 'apophaticism' of reason, allowing the extension of its inferential reach beyond its own bounds into the unknowability of God, is, in Kant, a simple agnostic curtailment of reason: rightly Kant must refuse God a place *within* the bounds of reason so curtailed. But why conceive of reason so? Of course, to repeat, you *could* just leave the matter there and say that Thomas's arguments could not succeed if Kant is right that the legitimacy of the 'Why anything?' question is ruled out in principle. But to do so is now beginning to seem as arbitrary a decision as its contrary. Do we have to conclude, then, that there is no argument to be had between those for whom the question 'Why anything?' is legitimate and those for whom it is not, as if to say that not being a matter of fact it is simply a matter of how you choose to view the matter? It certainly will not do merely to assert either case; nor do I say that the question is incapable of being settled, there being no reasons which could ultimately settle a question about reason and its scope. In any case, it certainly *is* true that if Kant is right about the limits of reason then Thomas is wrong about them, and vice versa, so that the issue between them is of that sort which *needs* to be settled by some means of argument. And so we have finally to ask: how is the question to be settled, and what is at stake, one way or the other? In particular, what else is lost by the refusal to allow this question, other than the legitimacy of an argument-strategy for proving God, whether the grounds for the refusal are philosophical or theological?

Refusing the question

First, let us draw together some of the lines of argument which have run through the course of this essay. In particular, first, we can now revisit for the last time the post-modern crux, the 'Derridean dilemma', which has dogged so many steps on the way of my argument for proof of an unknowable God. For again and again it has seemed that proof and unknowability work against each other: that proof might be had at the price of an 'onto-theological', and so idolatrous, theism, or else that resistance might be made to 'onto-theology', but only at the price of abandoning the possibility of proof. Or, as I put it otherwise in chapter eleven, the dilemma is whether to say that the 'there is' in 'there is a God' lies 'within' language, or 'outside' it, either answer having unacceptable consequences. For if the 'there is' lies within language, and so retains its connective tissue unbroken with our ordinary senses of 'there is', then this would appear to buy into a 'Scotist' and onto-theological univocity; whereas if we seek to evade this horn of the dilemma by saying that the 'there is' lies on the other side of language, then we become impaled on the dilemma's other horn. For in breaking the tissue of connection with our ordinary meanings of 'there is', the existence of God is placed beyond the reach of any possible proof precisely because it is placed beyond the reach of language.

It is because this post-modern crux – 'post-modern' it is even if it is still fundamentally 'Kantian' – must be taken seriously that I have devoted so much of this essay to elucidating the argument-*strategy* of Thomas's 'five ways', and so little to the arguments themselves. And from my account of that argument-strategy it can now be seen that the means of escape from the 'Derridean dilemma' is *through* its horns, as the classical logicians used to say. For if that argument-strategy consists in the justification principally of a *question* – the question 'Why anything?' – then we can say that it is the question which lies on the 'inside' of language, and so of reason, and so of logic, and it is the answer which must lie on the other side of all three. Hence, while the question retains its lines of continuity with our ordinary causal questions, the answer does not and could not do so. In short, the existence of God is in the nature of a demonstrated unknowability. *Et hoc omnes dicunt Deum.*

But if such are the lineaments of an answer to the most basic problem of reason and proof, they also contain, secondly, the principal elements of a response to Christian theological scruples about admitting the possibility of a rational proof of God. That response too begins from the nature of reason – its 'shape'. It is a shape which is determined by an interplay between the cataphatic and the apophatic, between word and silence, which also determines the shape of faith. The question 'cataphatically' asks, and 'God' is given to the question as its 'apophatic' answer. More specifically, the shape of reason is 'incarnational', and it is so precisely in that exercise of reason in which, at the end of its tether, it reaches that question it can ask, though it cannot take hold of the mystery which answers to it. That question 'Why anything?' confronts reason as a question about the *esse* of creatures, about that which is most fundamental to them as their 'actuality', their standing over against there being nothing at all. And it is there, in their deepest reality, that creatures reveal the Creator who has brought them to be, *ex nihilo*, so that as the questioning gets closer and closer to God, it gets deeper and deeper into, not further distanced from, the creature. In Thomas's proofs the intimacy (the inwardness of God to all things) and the transcendence of God (his total otherness) have the same source in the divine creative activity, and so for Thomas the more profoundly the creature is known the more clearly is it known to be intelligible only as mystery – the *mysterion*, or *sacramentum*, which is creation. Thus is the argument-strategy of the five ways not only not set in some way against the mystery of faith; in a certain manner its shape – in the character of its determining question – anticipates, but in no way displaces, that shape and that 'interrogation' (as Barth would put it) of faith.

But we are able to grasp this 'proto-sacramentality' of reason only if we fully grasp what is different about this question 'Why anything?', a difference which neither the parasitical atheist nor the theistic counterpart seems able to grasp. It is that, whereas all the other questions were what I have called 'essential' questions, having to do with what there is, this question, the form of our puzzlement that there is anything at all, is the one truly existential question. Nothing is asked or answered about the kind of world we have, and what answers to the question 'Why anything?' cannot make any difference to how the world is. As I have argued, however, too often theologians I have described as 'parasitical' appear to think that they can create a role for themselves of a pseudo-scientific character by means of a quite mistaken and idolatrous account of how theology can tell us of a difference God makes to the way things are, hoping to find for themselves a purchase on something to say that others cannot, a particular difference that their theism makes to our ordinary routine ways of explaining things. They will derive no comfort in such hopes from Thomas Aquinas. For him, to say that the world is created adds nothing at all to our information about the kind of world we have got. As Thomas said, who thought the world is created – it amounts to his reply to Aristotle, who thought that it is not – the difference between a created and an uncreated world is no difference at all so far as concerns how you describe it; any more, as later Kant said, the difference between an existent and a non-existent 100 Thaler bill can make a difference to how a 100 Thaler bill is described.[9] As we have seen, for Thomas, the logic of '. . . is created' is the same as the logic of '. . . exists': an uncreated x and a created x cannot differ in respect of what an x is, and so to say that the world is created makes not the least difference to how you do your science, or your history, or read your literatures; it does not make that

---

[9] Kant, *Critique of Pure Reason*, B627, p. 505.

kind of particular difference to anything. The only difference it makes is all the difference to everything.

And what kind of difference is that? What you mark by way of difference in saying that the world is created out of nothing is that it stands before us not in some brute, unmeaningful, Russellian 'just thereness', in that sense as something just 'given' in which further questions are gratuitously ruled out, and that just at the point where the questions are beginning to reveal something wholly unexpected about reason: that at its limit it reaches a question which strikes it quite dumb with awe. For, in saying that the world is created out of nothing, you are beginning to say that the world comes to us, existence as such comes to us, from an unknowable 'other'; that is to say, you are claiming that existence comes to us as pure gift, that for the world to exist just is for it to be created. As for why it exists, goodness only knows what the reason is. Of course, it might be the case that the world exists for a reason which only an omnipotent goodness knows, as a sort of act of love. But that would be another story which we could not tell for ourselves, but only if we were told it first, as being about the giving of a sort of second, superadded, gift which we call 'faith'.

What, then, is at stake between the theist and the atheist as Thomas conceives of the issues? Why does it matter whether the existence of God can be rationally proved? What is at stake is an issue which is, after all, central to all human intellectual preoccupations as such. It is an issue about the nature of reason, and so of intellect, and about how to take responsibility for all that intellect is capable of, about how to respond to the demands which, of its nature, it makes on us to persist with rational enquiry to the end of its tether. What, then, does the atheist have to deny? What the atheist has to deny is the legitimacy of a certain kind of question, to deny which requires setting *a priori* limits to a capacity which is, as Aristotle says, potentially infinite; which being so, Thomas Aquinas adds, it is not going to be satisfied by – that is to say, enjoy any question-stopping complacency in – even an infinite object. For what, on this account, marks the limit of reason, is not its resting in a full stop of 'just thereness', but its insistence upon asking a question, a question the answer to which it knows to lie beyond its scope. By means of that question the closed, determinate, circle of reason is cracked open into an indeterminacy, the 'grammar' of 'otherness' collapsing into the 'unsayability' of the '*tout autre*', but into an 'otherness' which is so absolute as to be not only not inconsistent with its intimacy to our created world and to ourselves, but also more than that: that 'otherness' is the foundation of the very possibility of that intimacy. For God's intimacy to the world as Creator is the foundation of that ultimate intimacy of God to creation which is the incarnation. Deny that possibility and with it the right to ask that question, and you do, for certain, deny God; and you have got your atheism in one move. But in denying the legitimacy of the question you also deny intellect its nature, or, which is to say the same, you deny to our nature its character of intellect. And that, as I have argued, is done just as easily by means of bad theology as by means of a myopic scientism, for *eadem est scientia oppositorum*. If all the atheists wish to deny is an idolatrously bad theology, well and good. But if what they deny to reason is the possibility of an enquiry which takes us beyond anything the best science asks about, then they betray their own scientific calling, and something fundamental to being human, that is to say, to what is 'rational', is denied in the process. On what account of 'faith' could it be worthwhile for the Christian to join unholy forces with the atheist in ruling out that possibility?

13 The God of reason and the God of Christ

The starting point of my argument was the standpoint of faith, and the negative, 'defensive', proposition that the exclusion on grounds of faith of any possibility in principle of a rational demonstration of the existence of God is to get something wrong about the nature of faith. The conclusion arrived at by the end of the last chapter was that to exclude that same possibility on rational grounds is to get something importantly wrong about the nature of reason. What linked these two propositions together was a complex argument, which was intended to show that the 'God of reason' – the God whose existence is rationally demonstrable – is, in the opinion of Thomas Aquinas at least, none other than the God of the Hebrew scriptures, the God of 'Abraham, Isaac, and Jacob'. *Ipsum esse subsistens* is none other than the 'I am who I am' of Exodus, whom 'all people know as God'. And perhaps I should emphasise for the last time: such an equivalence does *not* depend upon any tendentiously un-Hebraic (because 'metaphysical') exegesis of Exodus; it is not an exegesis of Exodus of *any* kind.

I argued, further, that Thomas's God of the 'five ways' is the Creator of all things out of nothing, and that the logic of those five proofs withstands critical examination – and is meant to – only in its dependence on the doctrine of *creatio ex nihilo*. But if that is so, and the Creator God may with justification be identified with the God of the Hebrew scriptures, then it is in the light of their revelation of just that God that the truths of Christian faith – of the Trinity, of the incarnation, of the Holy Spirit in the church – are to be accepted in the Christian's *act* of faith, by which Christians are made to be sharers in the divine life itself. In short, Thomas's God, known in faith but shown also by reason to be our Creator, is the *ratio Dei* in the light of which is constituted equally the act of faith itself and the 'formal object' of Christian theology. Therefore, Thomas's *ipsum esse subsistens* is not only the 'object' of Christian theology, as that whose inner life is thereby explored, but also the light in which that exploration is conducted, the *ratio* of his theological enquiry. Thomas's God of the proofs is the God of Christian theology.

But then if it is true that this God of reason is demonstrably the God of the Hebrew scriptures, revealed to the people of Israel through their history and traditions and writings, then it can be said not only that this God is the God of Christian theology but also, and *a fortiori*, that this God is the God of Jesus' *own* faith. For the God whom Jesus knew as his Father, and ours, and whose Spirit constituted his own very life, was none other than the 'I am who I am' of Exodus. It seems to me that all these connections of thought are obvious to any Christian whatever, except for the one proposition which, on the grounds of all the others, is so frequently excluded nowadays as incompatible with them: Thomas's demonstrable God of reason.

And here, apart from seeking to demonstrate that there is no such inconsistency with faith as is so commonly supposed, I have offered a Christological reason of a positive kind in support of the decree of the first Vatican Council which declares it to be, on the contrary, a matter of faith that the existence of God can be known by reason. As I have put it in the course of my argument, the 'shape' of Thomas's *proof* is 'proto-sacramental' and so has the shape of *Christ*; and the shape of Christ is the shape of Christian *belief* and so of Christian *theology*. Reason, as we might put it, is governed by an incarnational logic: it has that 'kenotic shape' because, rooted though it is in our animality, reason opens up, in its own kind, into the mystery which lies unutterably beyond it, for it can, out of fidelity to its own native impulse, ask the question which it knows it could not answer, the asking being within its powers, the answering being in principle beyond them. Of such a kind, I say, are Thomas's proofs. And so it is that 'reason' is a point of entry into the 'darkness of God' in its way, just as, in its own distinct way, the human nature of Christ is, as Bonaventure tells us, a *transitus* into the *Deus absconditus* of Christian faith.

Dominus illuminatio mea . . . quem timebo? Why, I ask, in conclusion, this theologically motivated resistance to proof of God, this *fear* of the light of human reason, this faith-induced loss of intellectual nerve? There are all too many explanations of political, economic, social and cultural kinds for a nihilistic post-modern irrationalism: for, contemplating the vicissitudes of the last appalling century, strewn as our inheritance of it is with the debris of officially declared military violence, of systematic economic exploitation, of racism, genocide, and of the consequent near to manic explosions of terrorism, who should be surprised if our age should look into the mirror of such a history, and declare itself to be 'post-modern', since all its values appear to have been dissolved in the corrosive acid of 'alterity'? Yet it can seem to be an intellectual and moral betrayal of their God-given task that the theologians too should with such casualness and with careless inattention to their own traditions, and on their own ground of faith, find reasons to collude in this *trahison des clercs*, and should abandon so lightly their responsibilities to engage our atheological age on terms of argument. Whenever responsibilities to reason have been shirked, either on the side of belief in God or in its mirror-image of atheism, then space is left free for its occupation by the exercise of mere, irrational, power. There is, I have claimed, an argument to be had with disbelief; and if, as it would seem, there is a prior argument to be had about the nature of argument itself, about what by way of truth can and what cannot be won by means of rational discourse, there are at least moral reasons of their own, as well as intellectual, why theologians should be among the first to see the importance of staking a claim for reason. For rational is what we are by nature, and it is that nature which the Christian God assumed so as to save; it has that form which the Christian God took on so as to transform.

I do not imagine that in this essay I have done more than to have offered some case for a greater theological trust in reason than is customary today, and to have cleared away a little of the clutter of misconception, philosophical and theological, which has for several centuries stood in the way of a more theologically positive understanding of reason. It is no case of mine that rational argument, even in that expanded and deepened sense for which I have argued in this essay, has much apologetic power to dissuade the atheist of his convictions; but the believer who, of set theological purpose, refuses to stand on the ground of the atheists' denials and to challenge them on shared rules of contest concedes the territory of reason, and so of the human, at a price which in the end will be paid in the quality of faith itself.

List of works cited

PRIMARY SOURCES (LATIN TEXTS AND TRANSLATIONS OTHER THAN MY OWN)

Anselm of Canterbury, St, *Proslogion*, in *Anselm's Proslogion*, trans. and introd. M. J. Charlesworth, Oxford: Clarendon Press, 1965.

Aristotle, *De interpretatione*, ed. and trans. E. M. Edghill, Oxford: Clarendon Press, 1926.

Aristotle, *Metaphysica*, trans. W. D. Ross, Oxford: Clarendon Press, 1908.

Aristotle, *Posterior Analytics*, trans. and commentary by Jonathan Barnes, 2nd edn, Oxford: Clarendon Press, 1994.

Augustine, *Confessionum Libri Tredecim*, ed. L. Verheijen, Corpus Christianorum Series Latina XXVII, Turnout: Brepols, 1981. Translation and Latin text in 3 vols. with introduction and commentary by James J. O'Donnell, in *Confessions: Introduction and Text*, Oxford: Clarendon Press, 1992.

Augustine, *De Trinitate*, in Corpus Christianorum Series Latina L–LAA, Turnhout, 1968. Translation with introduction and commentary by Edmund Hill OP, in *The Trinity*, New York: New City Press, 1994.

Augustine, *Enarrationes in Psalmis*, Migne, *Patrologia Latina* XXXVII.

Augustine, *De civitate Dei*, Migne, *Patrologia Latina* XLI. Translation, *Concerning the City of God against the Pagans*, trans. and ed. Henry Bettenson, Harmondsworth: Penguin Books, 1972.

Bonaventure, *Itinerarium Mentis in Deum* (Latin text and trans.), in *The Works of St Bonaventure* II, ed. Philotheus Boehner OFM, and Sr M. Frances Laughlin SMIC, New York: The Franciscan Institute, 1990.

Denys the Carthusian, *Difficultatum Praecipuarum Absolutiones* (Appendix attached to his *Commentary on the Mystical Theology* of the Pseudo-Dionysius), in *Doctoris Ecstatici D. Dionysii Cartusiani Opera Omnia*, XVI, Tournai: Typis Cartusiae S. M. de Pratis, 1902.

Denys the Carthusian, *De contemplatione*, *Opera Omnia* XVI.

Duns Scotus, *Ordinatio* (*Opus Oxoniense*), in *Doctoris Subtilis et Mariani: Joannis Duns Scoti Ordinis Fratrum Minorum Opera Omnia*, Civitas Vaticana: Typis Polyglottis Vaticanis, 1950–. Except where noted as being mine, the translations are taken from William A. Frank and Allan B. Wolter, *Duns Scotus: Metaphysician*, Indiana: Purdue University Press, 1995.

Eckhart, Meister, *Meister Eckhart, The Essential Sermons, Commentaries, Treatises and Defense*, trans. and ed. Edmund Colledge and Bernard McGinn, London: SPCK, 1981.

Eckhart, Meister, *Meister Eckhart: Teacher and Preacher*, ed. Bernard McGinn, with Frank Tobin and Elvira Borgstadt, New York: Paulist Press, 1986.

Gallus, Thomas (Vercellensis), *Super Canticum Canticorum Hierarchice Exposita*, in *Thomas Gualterius, Abbas Vercellensis, Commentaires du Cantique des Cantiques*, ed. Jeanne Barbet, Textes Philosophiques du Moyen Age 14, Paris: de Vrin, 1967. For a partial translation of this text see Denys Turner, *Eros and Allegory: Medieval Exegesis of the Song of Songs*, Kalamazoo: Cistercian Publications, 1995.

Gerson, Jean, *De mystica theologia: Tractatus Speculativus*, in *Jean Gerson, Oeuvres Complètes*, ed. Palémon Glorieux, Paris: Desclée et Cie., 1960–73.

Gregory the Great, *Homelia in Evangelia*, Migne, *Patrologia Latina* LXXII.

Hugh of Balma, *Viae Sion Lugent*, ed. Francis Ruello, in *Sources Chrétiennes*, Paris: Editions du Cerf, 1995.

Hugh of St Victor, *De sacramentis*, Migne, *Patrologia Latina* CLXXIV.

Jerome, *Homelia in Hezechielem*, Migne, *Patrologia Latina* XXV.

Nicholas of Cusa, *De ly non-Aliud*, in *Nicholas of Cusa on God as Not-other*, ed. and trans. Jasper Hopkins, Minneapolis: University of Minneapolis Press, 1979.

Pseudo-Denys, *Mystical Theology* and *Divine Names*, in *The Pseudo-Dionysius: The Complete Works*, trans. Colm Luibheid and Paul Rorem, New Jersey: Paulist Press, 1987.

Thomas Aquinas, *De aeternitate mundi contra murmurantes*, *Opera Omnia*, *Opuscula* I, Rome, 1882. Partial translation in Baldner and Carroll, *Aquinas on Creation* (see Thomas Aquinas, *Super Libros Sententiarum* . . . , below).

Thomas Aquinas, *De unitate intellectus contra Averroistas*, in *Aquinas against the Averroists*, ed. and trans. Ralph McInerney, West Lafayette: Purdue University Press, 1993.

Thomas Aquinas, *Expositio in Octos Libros Physicorum Aristotelis*, ed. P. M. Maggiolo, Turin: Marietti, 1965. Translation, R. J. Blackwell, R. J. Spath and W. E. Thirlkel, *Commentary on Aristotle's Physics*, Notre Dame: Dumb Ox Books, 1999.

Thomas Aquinas, *Expositio Libri Boetii de Hebdomadibus*, introd., Latin text and trans. by Janice S. Schultz and Edward Synan, Washington: Catholic University of America Press, 2001.

Thomas Aquinas, *In XII Libros Metaphysicorum Aristotelis Expositio*, ed. M. R. Cathala and Raimondo M. Spiazzi, Turin: Marietti, 1950. Translation in Aquinas, *Commentary on Aristotle's Metaphysics*, introd. and trans. John P. Rowan, Notre Dame: Dumb Ox Books, rev. edn, 1995.

Thomas Aquinas, *Quaestio Disputata de Virtutibus in Communi*, Parma edn, reprinted New York, 1948–50. Translation in *On the Virtues in General*, trans. J. P. Reid, Providence: The Providence College Press, 1951.

Thomas Aquinas, *Quaestiones Disputatae de Potentia*, Turin: Marietti, 1953. Partial translation in McDermott, *Thomas Aquinas* (see next entry).

Thomas Aquinas, *Summa contra Gentiles*, *Opera Omnia* XIV, Leonine edn, Rome, 1926. Partial translation, Timothy McDermott, *Thomas Aquinas: Selected Philosophical Writings*, Oxford: Oxford University Press, 1993. Complete translation, *Saint Thomas Aquinas: On the Truth of the Catholic Faith*, trans. A. C. Pegis, J. F. Anderson, V. J. Bourke and C. J. O'Neill, 5 vols., Indiana: University of Notre Dame Press, 1975.

Thomas Aquinas, *Summa Theologiae*, ed. T. Gilby and T. C. O'Brien, *Opera Omnia* VI–XI, Leonine edn, translated in 60 vols., London: Eyre & Spottiswoode, 1964–73.

Thomas Aquinas, *Super Libros Sententiarum Petri Lombardi Scriptum*, ed. P. Mandonnet and M. F. Voos, Paris: Lethielleux, 1929–47. Partial translation by Steven E. Baldner and William E. Carroll, in *Aquinas on Creation*, Toronto: Pontifical Institute of Mediaeval Studies, 1997.

William of St Thierry: *Meditations*, in *The Works of William of St Thierry: On Contemplating God, Prayer, Meditations*, trans. Sr Penelope CSMV, Kalamazoo: Cistercian Publications, 1977.

SECONDARY SOURCES

Austin, J. L., *How to Do Things with Words*, Oxford: Oxford University Press, 1962.

Barth, Karl, *Dogmatics in Outline*, trans. G. T. Thomson, London: SCM Press, 1949.

Burrell, David, 'Distinguishing God from the World', in Brian Davies OP, ed., *Language, Meaning and God: Essays in Honour of Herbert McCabe OP*, London: Geoffrey Chapman, 1987.

Caputo, John D., 'Mysticism and Transgression: Derrida and Meister Eckhart', in Hugh J. Silverman, ed., *Derrida and Deconstruction*, London: Routledge, 1989.

Cross, Richard, *Duns Scotus*, Oxford: Oxford University Press, 1999.

Davies, Oliver, *Meister Eckhart: Mystical Theologian*, London: SPCK, 1991.

Davies, Oliver, 'Revelation and the Politics of Culture', in Laurence Paul Hemming, ed., *Radical Orthodoxy? A Catholic Enquiry*, Aldershot: Ashgate, 2000.

Dawkins, Richard, *River Out of Eden*, London: Phoenix, 2001.

Derrida, Jacques, 'How to Avoid Speaking: Denials', in Sanford Budick and Wolfgang Iser (eds), *Languages of the Unsayable: The Play of Negativity in Literature and Literary Theory*, New York: Columbia University Press, 1989.

Derrida, Jacques, *The Gift of Death*, Chicago: Chicago University Press, 1996.

Derrida, Jacques, *On the Name*, ed. Thomas Dutoit, trans. David Wood, John P. Leavey and Ian McLeod, Stanford: Stanford University Press, 1995.

Descartes, René, *Meditations*, in *The Philosophical Writings of Descartes*, trans. John Cottingham, Robert Stoothoff and Dugal Murdoch, vol. II, Cambridge: Cambridge University Press, 1984.

Dubarle, André-Marie, 'La signification du nom de Yahweh', in *Revue des sciences philosophiques et théologiques* 34, 1951, pp. 3–21.

Feuerbach, Ludwig, *The Essence of Christianity*, trans. George Eliot, New York: Harper Torchbooks, 1957.

Geach, Peter T., 'Form and Existence', in *God and the Soul*, London: Routledge & Kegan Paul, 1969.

Geach, Peter T., 'Causality and Creation', in *God and the Soul*, London: Routledge & Kegan Paul, 1969.

Gilson, Etienne, *L'Esprit de la philosophie mediéval*, Paris: de Vrin, 1944.

Graham, Gordon, *The Philosophy of the Arts: An Introduction to Aesthetics*, 2nd edn, London: Routledge, 2002.

Gunton, Colin, *The Triune Creator: A Historical and Systematic Study*, Edinburgh: Edinburgh University Press, 1998.

Heidegger, Martin, 'The way back into the ground of metaphysics', in Walter Kaufmann, ed., *Existentialism: From Dostoevsky to Sartre*, New York: Meridian Books, 1969.

Hick, John, ed., *The Existence of God*, London: Macmillan, 1964.

Hick, John, ed., *The Myth of God Incarnate*, London: SCM Press, 1977.

Kant, Immanuel, *Critique of Practical Reason*, trans. and introd. Lewis W. Beck, New York: Liberal Arts Press, 1956.

Kant, Immanuel, *Critique of Pure Reason*, B599–642, trans. Norman Kemp Smith, London: Macmillan, 1965.

Kenny, Anthony, *The Five Ways*, London: Routledge & Kegan Paul, 1969.

Kerr, Fergus, OP, *After Aquinas: Versions of Thomism*, Oxford: Blackwell, 2002.

Kerr, Fergus, OP, *Theology after Wittgenstein*, Oxford: Blackwell, 1986.

Lash, Nicholas, *A Matter of Hope: A Theologian's Reflections on the Thought of Karl Marx*, London: Darton, Longman and Todd, 1981.

Leibniz, Gottfried W., *G. W. Leibniz: Philosophical Writings*, London: Dent, 1934.

Lubac, Henri de, SJ, *The Mystery of the Supernatural*, London: Geoffrey Chapman, 1967.

Lubac, Henri de, SJ, *Surnaturel: Etudes historiques*, Paris: Aubier, 1946; 2nd edn, Paris: Desclée de Brouwer, 1991. There is no English translation.

McCabe, Herbert, OP, 'The Eucharist as Language', in *Modern Theology* 15.2, April 1999, pp. 131–41.

McCabe, Herbert, OP, *God Matters*, London: Geoffrey Chapman, 1987.

McCabe, Herbert, OP, *God Still Matters*, London and New York: Continuum, 2002.

Mackie, J. L. *The Miracle of Theism: Arguments for and against the Existence of God*, Oxford: Clarendon Press, 1982.

Marion, Jean-Luc, *God without Being*, trans. Thomas A. Carlson, Chicago: Chicago University Press, 1991.

Marx, Karl, *Early Writings*, trans. Rodney Livingstone and Gregor Benton, London: Penguin Books, 1975.

Milbank, John, 'Intensities', in *Modern Theology* 15.4, October 1999, pp. 445–97.

Milbank, John, and Pickstock, Catherine, *Truth in Aquinas*, London: Routledge, 2001.

Milbank, John, Catherine Pickstock and Graham Ward, eds., *Radical Orthodoxy: a New Theology*, London: Routledge, 1998.

Montemaggi, Vittorio, ' "La rosa in che il verbo divino carne se fece": Human Bodies and Truth in the Poetic Narrative of the *Commedia*', forthcoming in *Dante and the Human Body*, Dublin: University College Dublin Foundation for Italian Studies, 2004.

Nietzsche, Friedrich, *The Birth of Tragedy*, ed. Raymond Geuss and Ronald Speirs, trans. Ronald Speirs, Cambridge: Cambridge University Press, 2000.

Nietzsche, Friedrich, *Twilight of the Idols*, trans. Duncan Large, Oxford: Oxford University Press, 1998.

Nygren, Anders, *Agape and Eros: A Study of the Christian Idea of Love*, Part I, trans. A. G. Herbert, London: SPCK, 1932.

Parfit, Derek, 'Why Anything, Why This?', in *London Review of Books* 22.2, 22 January 1998, pp. 24–7.

Pascal, Blaise, *Pensées*, ed. H. F. Stewart, London: Routledge & Kegan Paul, 1950.

Pickstock, Catherine, *After Writing: On the Liturgical Consummation of Philosophy*, Oxford: Blackwell, 1998.

Pickstock, C., 'Modernity and Scholasticism: A Critique of Recent Invocations of Univocity', forthcoming in *Antonianum*.

(See also, with Milbank, above).

Plantinga, Alvin, 'Reason and Belief in God', in Alvin Plantinga and Nicholas Wolterstorff, eds., *Faith and Rationality: Reason and Belief in God*, Notre Dame: University of Notre Dame Press, 1983.

Quine, Willard Van Orman, *Word and Object*, Cambridge, Mass.: MIT Press, 1960.

Rubenstein, Mary-Jane, 'Unknow Thyself: Apophaticism, Deconstruction and Theology after Ontotheology', in *Modern Theology* 19.3, July 2003, pp. 387–417.

Schopenhauer, Artur, *The World as Will and Representation*, trans. E. F. J. Payne, New York: Dover Publications, 1969.

Sells, Michael A., *Mystical Languages of Unsaying*, Chicago: University of Chicago Press, 1994.

Smart, J. J. C., and John J. Haldane, *Atheism and Theism*, Oxford: Blackwell, 1996.

Swinburne, Richard, *The Existence of God*, Oxford: Oxford University Press, 1979.

Turner, Denys, *The Darkness of God: Negativity in Christian Mysticism*, Cambridge: Cambridge University Press, 1995.

Turner, Denys, *Eros and Allegory: Medieval Exegesis of the Song of Songs*, Kalamazoo: Cistercian Publications, 1995.

Wittgenstein, Ludwig, *Philosophical Investigations*, trans. G. E. M. Anscombe, Oxford: Blackwell, 1958.

Wittgenstein, Ludwig, *Tractatus Logico-Philosophicus*, trans. C. K. Ogden, London: Routledge & Kegan Paul, 1962.

Vatican Council I, *Dogmatic Constitution on the Catholic Faith*, in Norman P. Tanner, *Decrees of the Ecumenical Councils*, II, *Trent to Vatican II*, London: Sheed & Ward.

Zwingli, Ulrich, *On the Lord's Supper*, in *Zwingli and Bullinger*, ed. and trans. G. W. Bromiley, Library of Christian Classics XXIV, London: SCM Press, 1953.

Index

Affectivism, 76–7, 79

Anselm, 127, 132, 142, 196, 198, 209, 241

Apophaticism, 23, 48–56, 63; Bonaventure on, 52–3, 62; exaggerated forms of, xiv, 12, 234–6; and faith, 75, 76; and self-transcendence, 118–19. *See also* Thomas Aquinas: God: unknowability of

Aristotle, 15, 27, 30, 93, 101, 150, 159–60, 200, 202, 208, 210, 229, 234, 257

Athanasius, 29

Atheism, xii; Feuerbach's, 227–31; militant, 228–31; and negative theology, 230–1; Nietzsche's, 150–4; parasitical, 227–31, 246–7, 257; Thomas Aquinas and, 258–9

Augustine, xii, 33, 198, 213; and Bonaventure, xii; and drama, 112; influence on Thomas Aquinas, xiv; as Platonist, xiv

Augustinianism, xi, xii, 117, 196, 197; intellectualism, 77, 84; radical, 90

Austin, J. L., 68–71; on 'performative' utterances, 68–71, 72

Averroists, 90

Barth, Karl, xii, 16, 28, 44, 230; creation, 9, 10, 12; election, 9, 10; faith, 9, 10; on Feuerbach, 229; reason, 10

Barthians, x, xi, xii, xviii, 8–14, 15, 16, 20

Basil the Great, 29

Bernard of Clairvaux, xiii, 54

Blond, Philip, 26, 27

Body: as language, 73, 92–4; and reason, 83, 89–92; resurrection of Jesus, 68–71, 72

Bonaventure: apophaticism, 51, 52, 58, 261; being, 26, 27; cataphaticism, 52–3; Christocentrism, 52–62, 224; coincidence of opposites, 57–60; creation, 52, 56; divine *esse*, 56–8; hierarchy, 52, 53, 56, 60–1; hypostatic

union, 58–60; as mystical theologian, xiv, xviii, 51, 198, 220; oneness of God, 57; passion of Christ, 52, 60–1; Trinity, 58–60

Burrell, David, 41–2, 213

Caputo, John, 150, 162

Chalcedon, Council of, 59, 217–19, 220

Christ: Barth on, 9, 13; light of, 48, 50; passion of, 52, 53, 60–1; resurrection of, 21, 68–71, 72

Christology, 25, 51; Bonaventure, 51; Thomas Aquinas, 215–21, 224. *See also* McCabe, Herbert, OP

Cloud of Unknowing, 55–6

Copleston, F., 248

Creation, xiv, 3; causality, 225, 248–51; contingency, 242–5; *ex nihilo*, 9, 12; freedom, 32–3; proof of God, 241–2; Peter Lombard, 30–2; Pseudo-Denys, 161; sacramental character of, 224–5; Trinity, 11. *See also* Thomas Aquinas: Creation

Cross, Richard, 128, 133, 137, 138–9, 144, 145, 146, 170

Dante Alighieri, xviii, 98, 104, 108–16

Davies, Oliver, xix, 100, 105, 108

Dawkins, Richard, xii, 230, 233, 246

De Lubac, Henri, 14

Denys the Carthusian, 54, 77, 81–2

Denys, Pseudo-, *See* Pseudo-Denys

Derrida, Jacques, 103, 150, 154, 159–60, 161–2, 164–8, 227, 236, 255–6

Descartes, René, 128, 198

Difference, 161–2, 163–4; and God, 149–50, 163, 212–16, 219–20, 250–1; hierarchy, 160–2; Meister Eckhart, 162–6; Pseudo-Denys, 149, 157–8

Dubarle, André-Marie, 44

Duns Scotus, John: analogy, 136–9; being not a genus, 141–8; criticism of Henry